CAMBRIDGE TEXTS IN THE
HISTORY OF POLITICAL THOUGHT

AUGUSTINE: POLITICAL WRITINGS

This collection brings together thirty-five letters and sermons of Augustine, bishop of Hippo from AD 396 to 430, that deal with political matters. The letters and sermons are both practical and principled and treat many essential themes in Augustine's thought, including the responsibilities of citizenship, the relationship between the church and secular authority, religious coercion, and war and peace. These texts complement Augustine's classic *The City of God against the Pagans* (also available in the Cambridge Texts series), and give students direct insight into the political and social world of late antiquity with which Augustine was immediately involved. The slave trade, tax collection, clerical harassment, and murder are amongst the topics with which he deals. The volume contains clear, accurate modern translations, together with a concise introduction and informative notes designed to aid the student encountering Augustine's life and thought for the first time.

E. M. ATKINS is Lecturer in Theology at Trinity and All Saints College, Leeds. She co-edited (with M. T. Griffin) and translated *Cicero, On Duties* for the Cambridge Texts in the History of Political Thought (1991).

R. J. DODARO is Professor of Patristic Theology and Vice-President at the Patristic Institute, the Augustinianum, Rome. He is the co-editor of *Augustine and his Critics* (with G. Lawless, 2000).

CAMBRIDGE TEXTS IN THE
HISTORY OF POLITICAL THOUGHT

Series editors

RAYMOND GEUSS, *Lecturer in Philosophy, University of Cambridge*
QUENTIN SKINNER, *Regius Professor of Modern History in the
University of Cambridge*

Cambridge Texts in the History of Political Thought is now firmly established as the major student textbook series in political theory. It aims to make available to students all the most important texts in the history of western political thought, from ancient Greece to the early twentieth century. All the familiar classic texts will be included, but the series seeks at the same time to enlarge the conventional canon by incorporating an extensive range of less well-known works, many of them never before available in a modern English edition. Wherever possible, texts are published in complete and unabridged form, and translations are specially commissioned for the series. Each volume contains a critical introduction together with chronologies, biographical sketches, a guide to further reading and any necessary glossaries and textual apparatus. When completed the series will aim to offer an outline of the entire evolution of western political thought.

For a list of titles published in the series, please see end of book

AUGUSTINE
POLITICAL WRITINGS

EDITED BY

E. M. ATKINS

Trinity and All Saints College, Leeds

AND

R. J. DODARO

Institutum Patristicum Augustinianum, Rome

CAMBRIDGE
UNIVERSITY PRESS

PUBLISHED BY THE PRESS SYNDICATE OF THE UNIVERSITY OF CAMBRIDGE
The Pitt Building, Trumpington Street, Cambridge, United Kingdom

CAMBRIDGE UNIVERSITY PRESS
The Edinburgh Building, Cambridge CB2 2RU, UK   www.cup.cam.ac.uk
40 West 20th Street, New York, NY 10011-4211, USA   www.cup.org
10 Stamford Road, Oakleigh, Melbourne 3166, Australia
Ruiz de Alarcón 13, 28014 Madrid, Spain

First published 2001

Printed in the United Kingdom at the University Press, Cambridge

Typeface Ehrhardt MT 9.5/12pt   *System* QuarkXPress® [SE]

A catalogue record for this book is available from the British Library

Library of Congress Cataloguing in Publication data

ISBN 0 521 44172 2 hardback
ISBN 0 521 44697 x paperback

Contents

Contents

Editors' note

There has been consultation and collaboration between us on every aspect and at every stage. The primary division of responsibility, however, is as follows. The Introduction was the joint responsibility of Robert Dodaro and Margaret Atkins. Robert Dodaro furnished the list of Principal dates, the Bibliography, the Biographical notes, and most of the annotations on the text. The translation was the work of Margaret Atkins, who also prepared the Translator's notes and the map. She also contributed to the annotations.

Three scholars deserve our particular thanks: Peter Garnsey read the whole manuscript and gave invaluable advice at each stage; George Lawless also commented helpfully on the entire manuscript; Peter Glare read a draft of the translation and suggested numerous improvements. In addition, we are grateful to Caroline Humfress for advice on Roman law, Claire Sotinel for help with the Biographical notes, and Aldo Bazan and Allan Fitzgerald for technical assistance and advice.

This volume is dedicated with gratitude to our respective parents.

Introduction

Why letters and sermons?

'I beg you as a Christian to a judge and I warn you as a bishop to a Christian', wrote Augustine in a letter to Apringius, proconsul of Africa. In the *City of God* Augustine lays out on a vast canvas the themes of Christianity and paganism, providence and power, empire and church, and divine and human justice, writing as a learned Christian apologist, an intellectual addressing his peers. It is easy to forget that he was also, and before all else, a Christian pastor. As a bishop, he struggled with the daily reality of political life in a society in which 'church' and 'state' had never been, and could not conceivably be, disentangled. In this context, 'justice' referred not to the rise and fall of empires, but to the decision whether to punish or to pardon a Donatist thug who had beaten up one of his priests. 'War' was not merely a theological construct: an instrument of divine wrath or divine education. It was happening in the next province, where one of Augustine's old acquaintances was responsible for warding off the barbarian raiders. 'Civic power' may have been embodied symbolically in the emperor in distant Rome, but here in north Africa it was men like Augustine's correspondent Apringius who made the decisions that mattered.

The exigencies of daily life raised large political questions: how can punishment be justified at all? Is the gentleness of Christ compatible with responsible government? Ought the force of law to be used to deter those tempted by heresy? Augustine wrote about such matters, but not in the *City of God*. To discover the everyday political thinking that constituted both the background to and the outworking of the large-scale ideas of his *magnum opus*, we need to turn to the occasional writings of the busy bishop. In other words, we need to read his letters and his sermons. Here we find Augustine reflecting on practical issues as they arise, as he answers a request, intercedes with an authority, debates with an opponent, or advises a friend. We also hear him encouraging, teaching and chastising his congregation from the pulpit in reaction to current events. The bishop is thinking on his feet, and his answers are often *ad hoc* and *ad hominem*. He does not articulate grand theory in these documents. Yet to read through them is to become aware of the way in which fundamental ideas about God and humanity, filtered through Augustine's pastoral experience, shaped a distinctive and challenging intellectual response to the problems of his society.

Between the two cities

The consequences of the conversion in 312 of the emperor Constantine upon relations between Christians and the secular powers were complex, and took time to develop. First, the laws, which had always favoured the official religion, now protected the property of Christian churches and privileged Christian priests; by the late fourth century they also forbade pagan practices and rendered heresy illegal. Secondly, as public careers were opened to Christians, the successful were faced with the problem of how to exercise civic power in a manner compatible with their faith. Thirdly, the bishops who led the Christian congregations, which came to constitute a majority in many towns of the empire, wielded great influence, individually and collectively, both as moral guides and as public figures. Fourthly, it had begun to matter how the mass of ordinary people lived their lives, and not only for reasons of public order. For the virtues of the ordinary man and woman were both a sign and an integral element of their faith; moreover, both bishops and emperor believed themselves responsible for the souls of their people. Bishops, therefore, had no choice but to involve themselves in political matters, as intercessors, advocates, advisers, teachers, preachers and leaders. Fortunately, Augustine's early life had prepared him well for the more worldly aspects of his eventual career as a bishop.

Augustine was born in 354 in Thagaste, then in the Roman province of Numidia, today the town of Souk Ahras in Algeria. His father, a modest landowner and town councillor, was ambitious for his clever son, and his ambition fuelled Augustine's own. The boy was clearly gifted with words, and one route to social and economic advance was the art of public speaking; for oratory in Augustine's world was a means to impress the powerful, to persuade the masses and to exert influence on legal and political decisions. Augustine's parents encouraged his further schooling, and sent him at the age of seventeen to the city of Carthage to study rhetoric. By 376 he was himself teaching rhetoric in Carthage, and soon he wrote the first of his many books, on this very subject.

At the age of twenty-eight, dissatisfied with the students in Carthage, and eager to further his career, he crossed the sea to Rome. Before long he had caught the eye of Symmachus, the prefect of the city, and when Symmachus was asked to find a professor of rhetoric for the city of Milan, where the Western emperor had his court, he recommended Augustine for the job. The political and religious tensions in the imperial city at the time would have given Augustine a taste of the complexities of power in the Christianised empire. The young emperor, Valentinian II, was under the sway of his mother, a so-called Arian rather than orthodox Christian, while further west in the empire the usurper Magnus Maximus, who presented himself as a staunch Catholic, had taken control. Augustine also witnessed direct conflict in Milan when Arian imperial troops attempted to seize a Catholic basilica, with Ambrose, the Catholic bishop, inside.

Augustine's new position enabled him to make influential friends. His duties included delivering panegyrics on ceremonial occasions in honour of important citizens, and he made at least one speech in praise of the emperor and another for his commander-in-chief. The lad from the provinces was rising to fame, and his hope that one day he would secure a provincial governorship was not unreasonable. Yet his success did not satisfy him. He became increasingly disenchanted with the intrigues and infighting inseparable from public life, and he found the orator's need to compromise the truth through flattery increasingly burdensome.

Augustine's restless intelligence had always been seeking more than worldly success. He had looked to philosophy, and to the Manichaean religion, to satisfy his spiritual longing, and neither had proved adequate. At last, in Milan itself, he found what he was looking for, in the sermons of Ambrose, which finally eased his way back to Christianity, the religion of his mother and of his childhood. Two years after arriving in Milan he decided to resign his post, seek baptism and abandon Italy for a religious and philosophical retirement with a group of like-minded friends in Thagaste.

Augustine, as he himself later put it, had left the service of the emperor for the service of God. He thought that in doing so he had exchanged the anxieties of political ambition for philosophical calm. However, the church was as eager as the empire to exploit the talents of its citizens, and few men possessed Augustine's combination of intellectual penetration, political acumen and skill to persuade. The church needed him, though, as a pastor: within a decade of his conversion, he reluctantly accepted the positions of first priest, and then bishop of the port of Hippo, near to his birthplace. His new responsibilities, contrasting so sharply with those he would have had either as a public servant or as a private philosopher, were to dominate his thinking and writing for the rest of his life.

Scripture was the basis of the Christian's life and thought; as a new priest Augustine had requested time from his bishop to study the Bible in order to equip himself to meet his congregation's needs. Now, as a bishop, one of his main functions was to mediate to his people his understanding of the word of God. Many of his extant sermons and numerous commentaries on scripture reflect this role.

Augustine also became involved in combating both paganism and heretical or sectarian movements within the church, in particular Donatism, which was local to north Africa, where it commanded strong support (for the origins of this movement see pp. 127–8). Again, Augustine's extant writings include a number of pieces of polemic directed against such non-Catholic groups. His role in tackling such problems extended beyond his own diocese: the bishops of north Africa met in annual councils which decided matters of ecclesiastical discipline, which included promoting common strategies for dealing with groups like the Donatists. On occasion, the councils petitioned the emperor himself for legislation to assist in this work.

International affairs also impinged upon life in Hippo. In 410 an army led by Alaric the Visigoth sacked the city of Rome, an event which was in fact more of a symbolic than a material blow to the Romans. However, Roman refugees fleeing the barbarian forces poured into Hippo, and exaggerated reports of the attack frightened the Africans. Augustine's *Sermon on the sacking of the city of Rome*, included in this volume, provides a formal theological explanation of God's decision to allow such events to take place. Thus, it foreshadows one of the major themes of the *City of God*. The consistent pressure from the movement of barbarian tribes through Europe and north Africa meant that warfare was never far from Augustine's mind; indeed, as he lay dying in 430 Hippo itself was under siege from the Vandals.

Augustine transferred his allegiance when he converted, but he did not abandon his weapons. He employed his oratory in the pulpit, his legal knowledge in judging disputes and opposing heretics, his political experience and contacts in negotiating with statesmen and winning their support. He added to these skills regular meditation upon scripture, which constantly shaped his use of them. Moreover, as a Christian he returned to his African roots. He never rejected the imperial machine with which he had worked so closely, but as a provincial on the margins of the empire he could view it with a degree of detachment. Milan, like any other human authority, was there to serve the purposes of God.

Humanity and Christ

A couple of years before Augustine began to write the *City of God*, he exchanged letters with a pagan called Nectarius, who was pleading with him to intercede on behalf of the population of his native town, Calama, not far from Hippo. Nectarius tried to flatter Augustine by comparing him with the Roman statesman and political thinker Cicero. Augustine, however, saw clearly that Christianity required the transformation of the classical Roman understanding of civic virtues. Nectarius' earthly patriotism was certainly commendable, but unless he came also to accept that his true homeland was 'the heavenly city', it would remain misdirected and fruitless, for he could not help his fellow citizens to flourish in the fullest way while still encouraging them in false religious belief (Letters 90, 91, 103 and 104).

In particular, the fundamental role played by Christ sets Augustine's political thought apart from the classical tradition. Augustine believed with orthodox Christianity that Christ was fully human; therefore he was able to exemplify a just human life, which consisted in love of God and neighbour. Yet the incarnation meant that Christ was also the unique instrument of grace by which God assisted human beings in living justly. They needed such grace because they had inherited the effects of the sin of Adam, and, consequently, left to themselves were unable to know completely, or to want whole-heartedly, what justice required. Christ, though, was free from original sin, and thus able to offer to the rest of humanity the cure, a life in full communion with God, which was established through baptism. However, baptism did not entirely eradicate the effects of original sin before death; even the saints had continually to struggle against these effects during their lives.

Only in the life, death and resurrection of Christ, therefore, can civic virtues such as piety and courage be seen perfectly fulfilled. Consequently, it is natural for Christians to use Christ as a model to imitate, as Augustine suggests when he repeatedly commends gentleness by referring to the story of the woman caught in adultery (Jn 8; cf. Commentary on the gospel of John, 33, Sermon 13 and Letter 153).

On the other hand, because Christ in Augustine's view was both divine and sinlessly human, we cannot simply imitate him. In the first place, we can never possess the virtues as fully as he does. Secondly, we can do so at all only by a process of conversion and continuous acknowledgement of our failures and dependence upon his justifying grace. Augustine, therefore, uses the apostles and martyrs as role-models for the Christian. In this, they function as the Christian equivalent of the ancient Roman civic heroes, whose acts of selfless courage inspired other citizens. Yet they are not, and no human except Christ could be, flawless heroes. So, for example, where the Romans represented a man like Regulus as perfectly brave, Augustine argued that the Christian martyrs could not completely overcome their fear of death. Even the great saints, then, must confess their weaknesses; thus Augustine proclaimed Daniel, for example, as virtuous precisely because despite his heroism he was prepared to do just that (*Sermon on the sacking of the city of Rome*).

The theme of the Christian's need to confess both his own sin and his dependence on grace appears regularly in Augustine's correspondence with those in authority. For example, he writes to Macedonius, the current vicar of Africa, responsible for the legal administration of the region, to whom he has just sent the first three books of the *City of God*. An important theme of the letter is the contrast between Christian teaching on grace and the pagan philosopher's belief in the self-sufficiency of the wise man (Letter 155).

This letter also sets the traditional Roman virtues in the context of the 'heavenly commonwealth', the communion of the angels and saints who live in blessedness with God. Faithful Christians on earth are journeying towards this commonwealth, moved by a desire to share its happiness. In this eschatological perspective, the civic virtues are transformed into aspects of the love of God and neighbour. Furthermore, in heaven they will no longer be needed, or, rather, they will dissolve into the simple act of loving and enjoying the presence of God.

At the same time, Augustine does not deny the value of civic virtues for purely earthly purposes: Christian and pagans alike benefit from just, peaceful and orderly societies. Indeed, he both defends Christianity against its detractors and criticises paganism by arguing that only true religion can in fact protect even the narrowly civic functions of the virtues. Similarly, he argues to Nectarius that the paganism of his protégés encourages vices which damage the very town that Nectarius claims to love. Civic virtues are as necessary for well-being as Cicero himself thought; they are best secured, however, in Augustine's view, by the Christian churches, in which public exhortations to peace can regularly be heard (Letters 91 and 104; cf. Letter 138).

The responsibilities of power

Augustine's belief in the fallenness of human nature was not based purely on abstract theology; the evidence for it could be seen all around him. In many modern societies the violence that underpins social harmony is implicit or unacknowledged: it hides in inaccessible military bases, in prisons and law-courts, in slums and in streets that we avoid. Our long-distance wars are mediated to us through the softening lens of television. Augustine, however, could not afford to neglect the question of violence, in practice or in theory. For him, it constituted the most urgent and the most basic problem of politics.

Violence was a problem for two reasons. First, it destroyed the fragile 'earthly peace' which was the condition for the flourishing of any society, religious or secular; the need for physical security, sustenance and freedom to cooperate was recognised by everyone. Secondly, to engage in violent behaviour was to disobey the Christian summons to live in gentleness, to return good for evil, and to forgive. It harmed the perpetrators as much as the victims, or, rather, it harmed them more, for it drew them away from the path to eternal life.

The Christian, however, seemed caught in a dilemma. Those who disturbed the peace could be restrained only by the use of force. Was it possible for officials committed to mercy to protect their society either from enemies without or from criminals within? In particular, therefore, Augustine was forced to ponder the justification for and the role of the two types of violence normally seen as legitimate: warfare and institutional punishment.

Augustine's response to the dilemma was to distinguish sharply between authorised and unauthorised use of force. He appealed to the well-known thirteenth chapter of St Paul's letter to the Romans, where

Paul argued that 'higher authority' is ordained by God, and urged the Romans to respect it. From this Augustine deduced that those who had specific responsibilities – as governors, judges, soldiers – were justified in employing or authorising the use of force for the purposes of their office. It was important for others, therefore, to respect their right to do this: Christians should obey the laws. However, the point of distinguishing the legitimate use of force was not to encourage rulers to employ harsh measures without fear of acting unjustly. The function of law was to restrain violence and secure peace: its use should be impersonal and never vengeful, and limited to the minimum necessary. Augustine interprets Romans 13 in the context of Psalm 2.10, 'Be instructed, all you who judge the earth', which he took as a warning to earthly judges against corruption (Sermon 13). Moreover, it was the legitimisation of specific uses of force that made it possible for Augustine to insist firmly that unauthorised violence could have no justification.

When Augustine reminds rulers of their own obligation to justice, he is not mouthing empty pieties. For he believed that on the day of judgement, each of us would be called to render an account of our lives. Those in positions of responsibility over others, whether governors or bishops or fathers, would have to account for any injustices they committed in exercising them. Moreover, they were accountable to God for the wellbeing of those in their care. Consequently, Augustine took the responsibilities of power with enormous seriousness. For the same reason, he also argued that those subject to specific authorities should not try to usurp their role: each will have to render his own account to God.

At this point, it is important to recognise the practical context of Augustine's comments about law. In his society, laws were not proposed and passed by a centralised government, then automatically applied and enforced by an impersonal police force and separate judiciary. First, while there also existed a body of inherited law, much of the law was made by the emperor in response to appeals from the provinces, from officials, or from influential groups or individuals. Secondly, the extent to which a law was promulgated and followed was partly up to the local governor and partly up to the initiative of local communities. Moreover, the same officials who were responsible for governing provinces presided over legal trials. Finally, although much of the late Roman penal system seems by our standards grimly barbaric, there was no requirement on judges to impose a set minimum penalty: they were free to respond to appeals for leniency.

There was, then, room for discretion and for initiative. This flexibility increased the seriousness of the burden (as Augustine termed it) of responsibility: one would be judged not by the simple criteria of obedience or efficiency, but on one's judgement in employing or applying law fairly and mercifully, with consideration for the well-being of all those involved, both individuals and groups.

What, however, counted as 'well-being'? For Augustine, of course, this included not only basic physical welfare and communal peace, but also moral and religious flourishing. All of these should be taken into account. Augustine does not, in principle, exclude any of these considerations from the responsibilities of any particular office, by, for example, limiting the churchman's concern to religious issues, or the statesman's to social. The emperor makes the laws, and that includes laws relating to religion; the bishop may seek to enforce or mitigate the laws, and that includes laws relating to secular peace.

However, each office had its own specific duties and its own emphases. What, then, was the primary responsibility of a Christian who held secular office? He must, of course, protect the peace and requite injustice by means of the established laws. He could, and should, use force where authorised and where necessary. He should do so to protect his community both materially and also religiously. In all of this, Augustine shares the general assumptions of his society, even if the clarity of his rejection of unauthorised force is unusual. What is distinctive, however, is his repeated reminder to the powerful of their own flawed nature. Those who judge will themselves be judged, and they should recognise with fear and trembling their own injustice. Without self-examination, confession and repentance, no earthly judge can hope for the God-given wisdom to make sound decisions (see e.g. Sermon 13). Such repentance, however, will encourage the judge to exercise his office with a justice that is properly imbued with humility and mercy.

In all this, Augustine speaks as a Christian to Christians. In the letter to Apringius, he is interceding for a criminal to ask for a merciful verdict. He makes it clear that he would have interceded also with a non-Christian official, but that his arguments would have been different. The Christian ruler is under the obligation to exercise mercy, and also, although Augustine presses the point only gently, under an obligation to listen to the bishop's advice (Letter 134).

The primary responsibility of the bishop himself, was, of course, religious. Yet at least two of his pastoral duties had clear political implications. The first was education in the virtues, exercised on his congregation through preaching: Augustine describes the churches memorably as 'sacred lecture-halls for the peoples of the world' (Letter 91). He also counselled individual Christians in political matters; moreover, as he suggested to Apringius, the bishop could give orders as well as advice even to a Christian proconsul.

A second important role was that of intercession, a traditional duty of a priest (indeed, even the pagan Nectarius invoked this fact (Letter 90)). It was the bishop's role to intercede both for individuals, for example to seek to mitigate a sentence (Letters 134 and 153), and also on behalf of the community, for example to protest about an oppressive official (Sermon 302). Relatedly, the bishop assumed a right and a duty to try to influence the application of law in the cause of effective justice. A striking example comes in Letter 10*, where Augustine asks his fellow-bishop Alypius to appeal to the emperors to authorise punishments of slave-traders which would be less cruel than those applicable in theory under present law, and therefore at the same time far more practicable and efficacious.

The bishop was naturally more likely to get involved in cases which had a religious dimension, for example, where members of the rival Christian group, the Donatists, had physically attacked Catholic Christian priests (Letters 133 and 134), or where there was a dispute between rival groups about the ownership of church property. However, as the cases discussed in Sermon 302 and Letter 10* show, there was no theoretical limitation on the bishop's area of concern.

In another area, custom inherited from the pre-Christian world gave the bishop unsought political responsibilities. Christian churches, like pagan shrines before them, were respected as places of asylum, and protected as such by both civil and religious law. On one occasion Augustine was asked to intervene in a dispute between a citizen who was alleged to have breached the right of asylum and the bishop who had disciplined him. We include here the two letters Augustine wrote, one to each man; these show him mustering all the moral pressure he can to make peace between them (Letters 250 and 1*). Asylum provides a clear example of a more general truth about Augustine's political thinking. For the most part, he assumes rather than argues for the rights and duties of a bishop. Civic responsibility was not something that he and his fellow-bishops actively sought. It came with the job, and with social expectations of the job. It was up to them to respond, making use of the law and the authorities as best they could.

What of the ordinary citizens? It will be clear by now that Augustine emphasised their duty both to obey the established authorities and to refrain from taking the law into their own hands by indulging in unauthorised violence. There were, however, critics of Christianity who saw Christian gentleness as hopelessly idealistic: how could a society defend itself if its members turned the other cheek to their enemies, and only returned good for evil (Letter 136)? In reply, Augustine pointed out the political benefits of a society in which citizens did in fact return good for evil. Peace was the basis of the existence of a city, as Cicero himself had believed. Truly benevolent citizens would both maintain peace, and also seek the genuine well-being of fellow-citizens who had harmed them. Augustine exploits Cicero and Sallust to argue that the great pagan Romans had themselves acknowledged the civic value of the gentler virtues (Letters 91 and 138).

The Christian citizen also had positive ethical duties with their own political implications, such as almsgiving. In the documents included here, Augustine suggests these indirectly, by recalling the example of the martyr Laurence, whose dedication to the poor contributed to his condemnation (Sermon 302), and by satirising those who prefer temporary earthly wealth to the lasting treasures of heaven (Sermon 335C). Finally, ordinary citizens (or at least those who were fathers) had their own burden of responsibility. It was their job to educate the members of their households to be peaceable citizens themselves; where they had not yet succeeded in educating them, they ought to control them. Augustine rebukes his congregation sharply after a local mob has lynched an unpopular imperial officer: if every member of a Christian family had been restrained from violence, the outrage would not have occurred (Sermon 302).

The ambiguities of punishment and war

The Christian is permitted to resort to violence only in the exercise of specific, publicly authorised, roles. Yet authorisation does not remove the tension between the grim necessity of war and punishment and the persistent Christian longing for peace and pardon. Augustine refuses to resolve the tension by giving simple precedence to either justice or mercy; once more, the complexity of his ideas reflects the complexity of his actual experience.

Judgement was one of the responsibilities of both secular and ecclesiastical rulers, and Augustine repeatedly returns to this theme.

Furthermore, the secular authorities must punish the guilty, which might seem to conflict both with their own exercise of Christian gentleness, and with the bishops' practice of interceding on behalf of the condemned. Augustine's most extended reflection on punishment is in reply to Macedonius, who raises a series of questions about the compatibility of judgement and forgiveness (Letters 152 and 153; see also Letter 95). Augustine emphasises the impersonal nature of political punishment: the judge must never be tempted to think of himself as effecting revenge. He recognises two legitimate purposes of punishment, to deter future wrongdoers and to stir the convicted person to repentance. Deterrence requires strict judgements; repentance, however, may best be secured by leniency. In particular, capital punishment conflicts with the purpose of securing repentance (cf. Sermon 13). To advocate forgiveness is not to condone the crime: the judge is to hate the sin, but love the sinner as a fellow human being. Moreover, the judge will be more inclined to responding mercifully to intercession the more that he remembers that he too is a sinner, equally dependent upon the forgiveness of God. Augustine uses the parable of the woman caught in adultery to powerful effect in reminding judges of this (Commentary on the gospel of John, 33, Sermon 13 and Letter 155).

Augustine is reluctant to accept not only the death penalty, but also punishments that threaten the bodily health or basic needs of the wrong-doer. In his reply to Nectarius, he argues that he wants the pagan rioters to be fined, but not reduced to poverty, let alone punished physically. They may be deprived of 'the means to live badly', but not of the means to live (Letter 104). When he writes to Apringius and Marcellinus to beg them to spare the Donatist thugs who had savagely attacked his own priests, he appeals both to the aim of persuading the criminals to repent, and to the principle of refraining from bloodshed (Letters 133 and 134). His request to the emperor to modify the harsh penalty for illegal slave-trading, while primarily pragmatic, is also in keeping with this second principle (Letter 10*; cf. also Letter 100).

The primary justification for punishment was for Augustine the repentance and conversion of the transgressor. Furthermore, neither he nor his society distinguished sharply between secular and religious responsibilities. There was, then, in principle no difficulty with using the law to suppress paganism, or even to persuade heretical or sectarian Christians to join the church of the Catholics: for this would be in their own true interests. It is worth noting here that Augustine has little time for the view – which many today would take for granted – that our freedom even to harm ourselves should be respected. He argues against this explicitly with a Donatist who is being prevented from burning himself to death (Letter 173), and in another context he endorses Cicero's praise of the ruler who 'pays attention to his people's interests rather than their wishes' (Letter 104).

Is it, then, justifiable to see Augustine as the first Christian apologist for religious coercion? Christian bishops in both East and West had readily accepted the occasional use of imperial power to enforce various forms of religious conformity at least since the council of Nicea in 325, and several important theologians before Augustine reflect this. Augustine's African predecessor Optatus of Milevis, albeit somewhat inconsistently, had defended on scriptural grounds a much fiercer use of secular force than he himself would ever approve. However, Augustine treats the subject more extensively and reflectively than any other early Christian writer.

At the same time, it is a mistake to interpret Augustine's attitude to coercion as a fixed theory. It developed as a series of *ad hoc* responses to specific situations, and, as so often with his thought, was marked by his awareness of the tension between different aims and ideals. Centuries later, quotations from Augustine would be used to justify religious persecution by institutions and in circumstances unimaginable in his day. The later medieval and post-Reformation writers who were eager to exploit his authority were less attentive to the nuances and the context of his arguments. His rejection of the death penalty, of course, was also often ignored.

It took time for Augustine to accept the need to compel the Donatists in particular to return to the fold. He was persuaded to do so by his fellow-bishops primarily on pragmatic grounds. In the early letters included here he prefers to oppose the Donatists only with argument (Letters 51 and 66), for, as he later explained, he did not want people pretending to be Catholics through fear of the law. Two things above all changed his mind: one was the persistent violence of certain groups of extreme Donatists, which, it seemed, could not be kept under control while the Donatist church continued to flourish. The second was that experience showed him that individuals who became Catholics through fear of the law often grew into a deep and genuine faith (Letter 185). Coercive laws, therefore, could be used for the proper purpose of bringing about true repentance, to the benefit of the former sectarian. Law, however, is a blunt instrument, and Augustine's defence of its use did not allow him to distinguish the lukewarm Donatists who might well become sincere Catholics from peaceable but deeply convinced opponents. The latter would be forced either to compromise their principles or to suffer for them, and would in either case lose their freedom to worship as Donatists.

One final point: it is worth noting also that the Donatists were on weak historical grounds when they attacked the Catholics' use of imperial laws, for they themselves, as Augustine repeatedly pointed out, had been the first to appeal to the emperor when the dispute originally arose (see further pp. 127–8).

The question of war was no simpler than that of punishment. Here too, Augustine is often seen as an innovator and described as 'the first Christian just war theorist'. In this case, the label is certainly misleading, for at least two reasons. First, no major Christian theologian since the time of Constantine had been a pacifist, and Christians had for a long time taken it for granted that war was permissible. In such a context, of course, to insist on the need for justice in war is to limit, rather than encourage, violence. Secondly, Augustine had no systematic theory of what would count as a just war, or a just way of waging wars. The nearest he comes to this is when he is defending the authority of the Old Testament by arguing that the leaders of Israel were justified in fighting wars at God's command; here, he assumes as common ground with his opponents the idea that properly authorised human wars, fought with the aim of securing peace, are acceptable. On the other hand, he was indeed clear that there were unjust ways of fighting, and that Christians should no more act unjustly in war than in other areas of life.

The choice between accepting and rejecting the legitimacy of war was not a choice between biblical idealism and empirical pragmatism. Both scripture and experience provided evidence on either side of the debate. On the one hand, sayings of Jesus such as 'turn the other cheek' suggested that Christian gentleness should exclude all violence whatsoever. On the other hand, Augustine points out, practising soldiers are accepted as faithful believers in both the Old Testament and the New (Letter 189). On the one hand, in a sinful and violent world it was possible to protect society only by military force, as was all too clear in an age marked by barbarian invasions in both Europe and north Africa. On the other hand, the direct experience of warfare brought home its horror: both the brutality of the fighting itself and the suffering of its refugees. War might be a necessity, but it could not, in Augustine's world, be idealised.

Three letters to soldiers included in this volume illustrate Augustine's approach to the question (Letters 189, 220 and 229). He keeps clearly in mind that the goal of any war should be peace, and moreover that where possible peaceful methods of securing peace should be preferred to fighting. Yet at the same time he recognises the genuine courage of soldiers, and the value of the security they offer to both church and society. The Christian should accept the hardships of war as a temporary necessity, and not be over-impatient for the perfectly just society of heaven.

In 427 Boniface, a Roman commander in north Africa whom Augustine had known for many years, rebelled against the imperial authorities. Augustine writes to him urging him to renew his loyalty to Rome: he is neglecting his duty to protect the province against barbarians, he is allowing his soldiers to indulge in plunder, and he is breaking his oath as soldier. In the conduct of war, no less than in the rest of life, irresponsibility, theft and breaches of promise are wrong. (Cicero, after all, had argued, using the notable example of Regulus, that one should keep promises even to an enemy.) Augustine's recognition of the ambiguity of war does not allow him to relax the moral demands upon the Christian soldier, or forget that the individual is called to sanctity.

Scripture and experience

Augustine reads his experience through the lens of scripture, and scripture, in turn, through the lens of experience: each enlarges, limits and guides possible interpretations of the other. Consequently, his political ideas are not static, rigid or idealistic, but instead flexibly pragmatic. The interpretation of scripture, he is well aware, is a task both subtle and provisional. Moreover, human society as it actually exists contrasts so sharply with what it would be in a fully redeemed and Christ-centred world that it is not possible to draw political answers from the Bible in any simple way.

The interpretation of scripture is complex simply on account of the quantity and variety of texts, quite apart from the obscurity of individual passages. Augustine consistently refuses either to simplify the meaning of specific texts or to gloss over the tension between those that appear to conflict. For example, when discussing the injunction 'turn the other cheek' (Mt 5.39), he explains why this cannot be taken literally. For when Christ himself was struck (Jn 18.23), he did not in fact turn the other cheek, but instead rebuked his assailant (Letter 138). In the first place, then, the phrase is to be understood metaphorically. Secondly, it cannot be understood without taking into account a range of other relevant texts, some of them clearly incompatible with pacifism; moreover, this range of texts is, in principle, open-ended. On the other hand, the command must not be brushed aside: 'turn the other cheek' both licenses the church to preach non-violence in certain situations and, more fundamentally, constitutes a constant reminder of the Christian's obligation to 'train the heart' to peaceful purposes. Augustine's method never allows him to reduce the message of the New Testament to easy or straightforward slogans. It also prevents him from treating his conclusions as closed to the possibility of revision in the light of changing experience or further scriptural reflection.

Again, the Bible should not be used as a blueprint for the perfect society. For Augustine, politics is indeed the art of the possible, and his political thinking is neither utopian nor revolutionary. He is firmly convinced that the lives of individuals may be transformed by holiness, but he does not expect the Christianisation of the empire to produce whole communities of saints. Therefore, one must work within the limitations of the existing systems: so, for example, although it never occurs to Augustine that slavery might be abolished (or even voluntarily renounced by individual Christians), he attempts to influence legislation so that it can effectively combat the cruel, and illegitimate, slave-trading in Africa (Letter 10*). In a different age, he might well have seen the practicability of abolishing the slave trade, and supported it whole-heartedly; his actual political efforts, however, were directed to goals that were limited and achievable. In other words, he did not see scripture as defining a fixed political ideal. Rather, it offered broad guidelines for thinking through decisions, and a constant reminder to use and influence existing institutions in as peaceable and loving a direction as possible.

Conclusion

Sermons and biblical commentaries are perhaps unexpected sources for political thought. Many of the documents translated here are not exclusively, nor even primarily, on political topics. Yet it is important to study whole texts rather than short extracts, so that Augustine's ideas are not abstracted from the context in which they are embedded. We need the theological context in order to understand how the model of Christ and biblical exegesis shape Augustine's views; we need also the practical context in order to grasp clearly both the precise issues at stake and the range of responses available to him. Augustine's pastoral writings do not include clear-cut and systematic political theory, but they are underpinned by a consistent and coherent view of humanity and society. On the basis of this he tackles fundamental questions of political authority in the form of concrete practical problems. Sometimes, this leads him to articulate uncompromising principles; more often, he allows Christian ideals such as mercy to put whatever pressure they can on the social structures of a fallen world. That pressure, in turn, will only be maintained if Christian leaders are faithful to their call to constant conversion. Augustine is never tempted simply to reduce politics to ethics. On the other hand, without an ethics grounded in faith and humility, political society, in his view, has little hope to offer.

Translator's notes

Traduttore, traditore, say the Italians: 'the translator is a traitor'. I hope that the following notes will alert the reader to some of the ways in which the vast differences between Augustine's world of thought and our own are reflected in the language that he uses.

Courtesy titles

The etiquette of late antique letters was elaborate. A large number of honorific titles was used which conveyed, more or less specifically, a range of social nuances which we cannot now recover in all their subtlety (for a comprehensive survey, see O'Brien, *Titles*). Some of these terms were technical: *illustris* ('illustrious'), *spectabilis* ('admirable') and *clarissimus* ('renowned') referred to three levels of rank in the late imperial élite, *illustris* being the most senior title, then *spectabilis*, then *clarissimus*. Certain epithets, such as 'holy' and 'blessed', were normally reserved for Christian ecclesiastics; others such as 'beloved' were also specifically Christian in usage.

Such language should not, of course, be taken at face value (we ourselves rarely feel affection for those we address as 'Dear Sir'). Abstract nouns were also used honorifically; I have translated such phrases as, for example, 'your holy self' rather than 'your holiness'.

Commonwealth, government, empire, public life

Res publica means literally 'public thing'. In Letter 138.10 Augustine refers to Cicero's well-known definition, which may be literally translated: 'the "public thing" is a thing of (belonging to) the people'. Concretely the phrase can refer to public affairs or to the organs that administer public affairs (roughly what we would call 'the state'), or to a political society as a whole. Sometimes, therefore, it has been natural to translate as 'public life', sometimes as 'government' or 'empire'. In Letter 138 in particular, where Augustine plays upon Cicero's definition, the word 'common-wealth' has proved to be the most convenient translation.

Hand over, handers over

The Donatist controversy arose when certain bishops were accused of handing over the scriptures to the authorities under persecution. They were described as *traditores*, from the verb *tradere*, to hand over. *Tradere*, significantly, can also mean 'betray'; *traditores* were both 'handers over' and traitors. (Judas' act of handing Christ over to the authorities was the supreme act of betrayal; the Latin New Testament uses *tradere* for this.)

Just, justice; unjust, injustice

The virtue is a complex one. Augustine inherited Cicero's analysis of justice as the supremely social virtue: the just man puts the good of society first. As a trained lawyer, he was conscious too of the narrower sense of *iustus*: just according to the code of human or of divine law. In Christian texts the word is also deeply influenced by biblical usage: the just man is righteous and honest. St Paul in particular infused the word with a further nuance: the just man is the one justified by the grace of God. Augustine allows the terms 'just' and 'justice' to convey all these nuances simultaneously. He tends to use *iniquus* and *iniquitas* as the contraries of *iustus* and *iustitia*.

Love

Augustine uses interchangeably several words for love: *caritas; amor, amare; dilectio, diligere*. He himself agreed that these words were not used with distinct senses in scripture (*civ.* 14.7). In general, therefore, I have freely used 'love' to cover all these, occasionally preferring 'charity' for *caritas* (which is rarely used in non-religious contexts). In Sermon 335C.2ff., however, Augustine self-consciously defines his terms to distinguish desire for what is good from desire for what is bad (see note *ad loc.*).

Piety, pious, devoted; impiety, impious

Pius can mean 'loyal, devoted' and Augustine sometimes uses it in this way, especially of familial affection; where I have translated, for example, 'devoted father', the association with piety should be kept in mind. However, he normally uses *pius* and *pietas* to refer to loyalty to the church. To be 'pious' is to embrace the life and orthodox faith of the Catholic church. Not only people, but also beliefs, practices and laws may be pious; they are 'impious' when they are either directed against (orthodox) Christianity or used to promote a false sect or false gods. Sometimes, therefore, *impius* means roughly 'heretic' or 'unbeliever'. The reference need not be narrowly religious: in Letter 10*.3, slave-trading is described as *impietas*, in Letter 153.3 it is a mode of *pietas* to love a sinner *qua* human being.

Pursue, pursue action against, harass; pursuit, legal action, harassment

The root meaning of the Latin *persequor* (noun, *persecutio*) is 'follow through' or 'follow persistently'. In a legal context, *persequor* is neutral in tone, meaning simply, 'to pursue action against', without the implications of malicious or sectarian attack that the English 'persecute' conveys. (The Donatists protested that the Catholics' pursuit of legal action against them was unjust, but they were prepared to resort to legal action in their own interest.) The words can also be used in a non-legal context to mean pursue, or harass (whether justifiably or not). Sometimes they connote hostile or illegal actions (cf. Letter 88.1). Letter 185.6–11 in particular exploits the range of senses of *persequor* and *persecutio*.

Security

Salus means security, health and well-being. In Christian Latin the term also covers what we describe as 'salvation': the ultimate security and well-being of eternal life with God. Because Augustine likes to compare heavenly and earthly *salus*, I have used an English word that can cover both types. (In many cases 'salvation' would have been a possible, and perhaps more natural, translation.) A third use of *salus* was to address the recipient of a letter. Here I have used the translation 'greets' or 'sends greeting'. However, Christian writers were sensitive to the triple sense (see the greeting of Letter 220, below, p. 218).

Temporary

Augustine frequently contrasts what is eternal and everlasting with what is *temporalis*. The usual English translation is 'temporal', but 'temporary' better catches the sense of unease that Augustine conveys. The problem with things that are in time is, precisely, that they change and disappear.

I have translated Augustine's own text of the Bible, rather than use a modern version, because the precise wording is often important to his argument. Where the Latin text, or the Septuagint (LXX) which lies behind it, differ from the Hebrew, I have noted this in the reference.

Principal dates

AD	Ecclesiastical and political events	Augustine
354		Birth at Thagaste.
361–3	Reign of the emperor Julian. Imperial rescript grants Donatists official toleration. Return of Donatist bishops from exile.	
370	Rogatist schism within Donatist church.	
371		Goes to Carthage to study rhetoric.
373	The emperor Valentinian I issues an edict to Julianus, proconsul of Africa, banning rebaptism (*C. Th.* 16.6.1) (20 February).	
375	Gratian and Valentinian II succeed the emperor Valentinian I in the West.	Returns to Thagaste to teach grammar.
376–7	Virius Nicomachus Flavianus vicar of Africa at Carthage.	Returns to Carthage to teach rhetoric.
380	The emperor Theodosius I issues an edict making Catholic Christianity the religion of the empire (*C. Th.* 16.1.2).	Writes *De pulchro et apto*.
383	Rebellion of Magnus Maximus.	Goes to Rome to teach rhetoric.

AD	Ecclesiastical and political events	Augustine
384	Quintus Aurelius Symmachus appointed urban prefect of Rome.	Appointed by Symmachus as orator of the city of Milan. Leaves Rome for Milan. Delivers panegyric in honour of the emperor Valentinian II.
385		Delivers panegyric in honour of Flavius Bauto, *magister militum* or military commander-in-chief to the emperor Valentinian II.
386	Imperial troops surround a Catholic basilica at Milan in a foiled effort to seize it for the use of Arians.	Conversion to Catholic Christianity. Resigns post as orator of the city of Milan.
387	Magnus Maximus invades Italy.	Baptism at Milan by Ambrose, the city's bishop (24/25 April).
391	The emperor Theodosius I outlaws pagan worship (*C.Th.* 16.10.10). Aurelius becomes Catholic bishop of Carthage.	Elected priest in the service of Valerius, bishop of Hippo Regius.
392	Theodosius I issues an edict recognising limited right of asylum in churches (*C.Th.* 9.45.1), and one imposing a fine of ten pounds of gold on all clerics of heretical sects (*C.Th.* 16.5.21).	
395	Death of Theodosius I at Milan. Division of empire into West and East. Honorius becomes emperor of the West. Stilicho becomes *magister militum*, military commander-in-chief to Honorius.	Consecrated coadjutor bishop to Valerius at Hippo Regius.
395/396		Succeeds Valerius as bishop of Hippo Regius.

AD	Ecclesiastical and political events	Augustine
397	African Catholic bishops meet at Carthage (27–28 August).	
399	Honorius orders Jovius, an imperial commissioner, and Gaudentius, *comes* of Africa, to destroy pagan temples and idols at Carthage (19 March) (cf. *civ.* 18.54.1).	Preaches *serm.* 62 at Carthage, urging Catholics to show restraint in opposing pagan rituals.
	Emperors Arcadius and Honorius issue an edict to the proconsul of Africa, Apollodorus, decreeing the removal of idols from pagan temples (*C. Th.* 16.10.18) (20 August).	
	Destruction by Christians at Sufes in the African province of Byzacena of a statue of the god Hercules leads to riots in which sixty Christians are killed by pagans.	Writes *ep.* 50 to the municipal councillors of Sufes decrying the murder of Christians there.
401	Catholic bishops meet twice at Carthage in order to debate their response to violence against Christians by pagans, Donatists and Circumcellions (16 June/13 September).	Writes Letter 66 to Crispin, Donatist bishop of Calama, threatening to appeal to imperial authorities because the latter had rebaptised eighty tenant farmers and family members on an imperial estate in contravention of imperial edicts banning rebaptism.
	Tensions rise between pagans and Christians at Carthage over the recently re-gilded beard of a statue of the god Hercules. Christians wanted the statue destroyed (16 June).	Preaches *serm.* 24 at Carthage seeking to restrain Catholics from acts of provocation against pagans.
403	Crispin, Donatist bishop of Calama, blamed for an attack	

AD	Ecclesiastical and political events	Augustine
	on Possidius, Catholic bishop of the same city. Catholic bishops meeting at Carthage urge Donatist bishops to join them in a common council in order to debate their differences (25 August).	
404	Donatist attack against Maximian, Catholic bishop of Bagai. Catholic bishops meeting at Carthage send emissaries to the imperial court at Ravenna seeking greater protection against the Donatists.	
405	Honorius issues Edict of Unity (12 February) and several decrees, declaring the Donatist sect a heresy, banning their religious assemblies and confiscating those private homes which were used for such meetings, threatening the Donatist clergy with exile and their accomplices with harsh floggings. Donatists were also denied certain rights concerning contracts and inheritance (*C. Th.* 16.5.37, 16.5.38, 16.5.39, 16.6.3–5, 16.11.2).	
407	Honorius publishes an edict banning pagan religious ceremonies. Catholic bishops are given the right to prohibit pagan rites (*C. Th.* 16.5.43; 16.10.19 = *Sirm.* 12) (15 November).	

AD	Ecclesiastical and political events	Augustine
408	Honorius confirms *audientia episcopalis* but requires that each party agree in advance to take their case to the bishop's tribunal (*C. Th.* 1.27.2).	
	Civil disorder at Calama when the Catholic bishop, Possidius, intervenes against the celebration of a pagan festival (1 and 9 June).	Investigates riot at Calama (June/July).
	Possidius travels to imperial court at Ravenna in order to report on the Calama riot and seek imperial measures against the responsible parties.	Enters into correspondence with Nectarius concerning the riot at Calama (Letters 90; 91; 103; 104).
	Alaric blockades Rome.	
	Catholic bishops meet at Carthage and petition the emperor Honorius for stronger imperial measures against the Donatists (June and October).	
	Execution of Stilicho (23 August).	
	Honorius sends a rescript to the proconsul of Africa, Donatus, ordering him to punish any persons (meaning the Donatists) who endanger the Catholic Church (*C. Th.* 16.5.44) (24 November).	Writes Letter 100 to Donatus, the proconsul of Africa, urging him to avoid capital punishment in dealing with Donatists or Circumcellions convicted of injuring Catholics.
410	Alaric sacks Rome.	
	African Catholic bishops press the emperor Honorius to call a conference of Catholic and Donatist bishops to force an end to the strife between the two communities (14 June).	

AD	Ecclesiastical and political events	Augustine
	Honorius orders his military field commander at Carthage, Heraclian, to suppress heretical opposition to the Catholic religion by force (*C. Th.* 16.5.51 = 16.5.56) (25 August). Honorius appoints Marcellinus to convoke the requested conference.	
410/411		Writes *The sacking of the city of Rome*.
411	Conference of Carthage (1–8 June) results in condemnation of Donatism. Donatist worship banned, properties confiscated.	Participates as a major Catholic representative at the conference of Carthage.
	Church synod at Carthage condemns Celestius.	Composes first work in the Pelagian controversy, *pecc. mer.*
		Intervenes with the proconsul of Africa, Apringius, and with the tribune, Marcellinus, to spare the lives of Donatist clergy and Circumcellions convicted of murdering the Catholic priest Restitutus and of the maiming of another priest, Innocent (Letters 133; 134; 139).
412	Honorius orders Donatist bishops into exile outside north Africa and imposes fines and other penalties on Donatists (*C. Th.* 16.5.52) (30 January).	Begins to write *City of God*.
413	Heraclian defeated in his revolt against Honorius. Marcellinus and Apringius	Preaches *en. Ps.* 50 at Carthage (15 July) in an attempt to plead for clemency on behalf

AD	Ecclesiastical and political events	Augustine
413 (*cont.*)	executed at Carthage for treason (13 September).	of repentant rebels. Fails at attempted intervention with the imperial court at Ravenna on behalf of Marcellinus and Apringius.
413/414		Writes Letter 153 to Macedonius, the vicar of Africa, on the subject of capital punishment.
415	Synod of Diospolis (Palestine) acquits Pelagius of heresy. Imperial edict orders buildings for pagan worship to be handed over to the Catholic church (*C. Th.* 16.10.20).	
417	Innocent, bishop of Rome, condemns Pelagius and Celestius for heresy. Innocent dies and is succeeded as bishop of Rome by Zosimus, who rehabilitates Pelagius and Celestius.	Appeals to the emperor Honorius to outlaw Pelagius and his followers.
		Writes Letter 185 to the military tribune Boniface concerning Arian and Donatist heresies.
	Berber tribes cross over the frontier into the southern Roman province of Numidia	Writes Letter 189 to Boniface, encouraging him to resist the barbarians with military force.
	Catholic bishops meet at Carthage toward the end of the year and strongly protest Zosimus' rehabilitation of Pelagius and Celestius.	
418	Zosimus reverses himself and condemns Pelagius and Celestius for heresy. Over 200 Catholic bishops meet in synod at Carthage in	

AD	Ecclesiastical and political events	Augustine
	opposition to Pelagian teachings (1 May).	
419	The emperor Honorius condemns Pelagius and Celestius as heretics and bans the movement from the empire.	
	The emperors Honorius and Theodosius II issue an edict recognising the inviolable right of asylum in churches (*Sirm.* 13) (21 November).	
	Dulcitius, an imperial notary, seeks to enforce the imperial edict of 412 against Donatists at the Donatist stronghold of Timgad. Gaudentius, Donatist bishop of Timgad, threatens mass suicides in protest.	
419/420		Writes Letter 204 to Dulcitius concerning the action threatened by Gaudentius
		Writes *Contra Gaudentium* at Dulcitius' request.
423	Honorius dies. Valentinian III recognised as emperor of the West, but rules through his mother, Galla Placidia.	
427	Revolt of Boniface against the court of Galla Placidia.	Completes *City of God*.
427/428	Darius despatched to Africa from Italy to end the fighting between Boniface and imperial troops.	
428		Writes Letter 220 to Boniface, urging him to end his revolt against the imperial court.
		Writes a memorandum (Letter 10*) to Alypius concerning

AD	Ecclesiastical and political events	Augustine
428 (*cont.*)		worsening abuses in the slave trade at Hippo Regius.
429	Vandals cross into Africa from Spain. Imperial forces attempt to stop their migration across Africa.	Writes Letter 229 to Darius, congratulating him on his successful efforts at negotiating peace with advancing Vandal forces.
430	Vandals enter Numidia and lay siege to Hippo Regius.	Death at Hippo Regius with the Vandals at the city gates (28 August).

Bibliography

General abbreviations

ACW *Ancient Christian Writers: the Works of the Fathers in Translation*, ed. J. Quasten, *et al.* (Westminster, Md. 1946–)

AL *Augustinus-Lexikon*, ed. C. Mayer (Basel/Stuttgart, 1986–).

CCL *Corpus Christianorum, Series Latina* (Turnhout, 1949–).

C.J. *Codex Justinianus* = *Corpus Iuris Civilis*, vol. II, ed. P. Krueger (Berlin, 1954).

CSEL *Corpus Scriptorum Ecclesiasticorum Latinorum* (Vienna, 1866–).

C.Th. *Codex Theodosianus*, in *Theodosiani libri* XVI *cum Constitutionibus Sirmondianis*, ed. T. Mommsen (Berlin, 1904–5; repr. Dublin/Zurich, 1971), 27–906.

EDRL A. Berger, *Encyclopedic Dictionary of Roman Law* (Philadelphia, 1953).

EEC *Encyclopedia of the Early Church*, ed. A. Di Berardino (Cambridge, 1992).

FC *Fathers of the Church*, ed. L. Schopp, *et al.* (Washington, 1947–).

Nov. Val. *Novellae Valentiniani*, in *Leges Novellae ad Theodosianum pertinentes*, ed. P. M. Meyer (Berlin, 1905; repr. Dublin/Zurich, 1971), 73–154.

NPNF *A Select Library of the Nicene and Post-Nicene Fathers of the Christian Church*, ed P. Schaff (Edinburgh, 1886–8; repr. Grand Rapids, 1971–80).

PG *Patrologiae Cursus Completus, Series Graeca*, ed. J. P. Migne (Paris, 1857–66).

PL	*Patrologiae Cursus Completus, Series Latina*, ed. J. P. Migne (Paris, 1841–55).
Sirm.	*Constitutiones Sirmondianae*, in *Theodosiani libri XVI cum Constitutionibus Sirmondianis*, ed. T. Mommsen (Berlin, 1904–5; repr. Dublin/Zurich, 1971), 907–21.
WSA	*The Works of Saint Augustine. A Translation for the 21st Century*, ed. J. Rotelle (New York, 1989–).

Abbreviated titles of biblical books

Gen	Genesis
Exod	Exodus
Lev	Leviticus
Num	Numbers
Deut	Deuteronomy
Josh	Joshua
1 Sam	1 Samuel
2 Sam	2 Samuel
1 Kgs	1 Kings
2 Kgs	2 Kings
2 Chron	2 Chronicles
Ps	Psalms
Prov	Proverbs
Wisd	Wisdom
Ecclus	Ecclesiasticus (= Sirach)
Is	Isaiah
Jer	Jeremiah
Ezek	Ezekiel
Dan	Daniel
Hos	Hosea
Jon	Jonah
Hab	Habakkuk
Zeph	Zephaniah
Mal	Malachi
2 Macc	2 Maccabees
Mt	Matthew
Mk	Mark
Lk	Luke

Jn	John
Acts	Acts of the Apostles
Rom	Roman
1 Cor	1 Corinthians
2 Cor	2 Corinthians
Gal	Galatians
Eph	Ephesians
Phil	Philippians
1 Thess	1 Thessalonians
Col	Colossians
1 Tim	1 Timothy
2 Tim	2 Timothy
Tit	Titus
Heb	Hebrews
Jas	James
1 Pet	1 Peter
1 Jn	1 John
Rev	Revelation

Abbreviated titles of Augustine's works

References to Augustine's works which do not appear in this volume are indicated by abbreviation of the Latin title. Recommended English translations are listed whenever possible.

adult. coniug.	*De adulterinis coniugiis. CSEL* 41. *FC* 27.
bapt.	*De baptismo. PL* 43. *CSEL* 51. *NPNF* 1.4.
brevic.	*Breviculus conlationis cum Donatistis. CCL* 149A.
c. adu. leg.	*Contra aduersarios legis et prophetarum. PL* 42.
c. Don.	*Contra Donatistas. CSEL* 53.
c. ep. Parm.	*Contra epistulam Parmeniani. CSEL* 51.
c. Gaud.	*Contra Gaudentium Donatistarum episcopum. CSEL* 53.
c. Iul. imp.	*Contra Iulianum opus imperfectum. CSEL* 85.
c. litt. Pet.	*Contra litteras Petiliani. CSEL* 52. *NPNF* 1.4.
cat. rud.	*De catechizandis rudibus. PL* 40. *CCL* 46. *ACW* 2.
civ.	*De civitate Dei. PL* 41. *CSEL* 40. *CCL* 47–8. H. Bettenson, *Concerning the City of God against the Pagans* (London, 1972). R. W. Dyson, *The City of God against the Pagans* (Cambridge, 1998). *FC* 8, 14, 24.
conf.	*Confessiones, PL* 32. *CSEL* 33. *CCL* 27. R. S. Pine-Coffin,

	Saint Augustine, Confessions (London, 1961). *FC* 21. *WSA* 1.1.
cons. ev.	*De consensu evangelistarum. PL* 34. *CSEL* 44. *NPNF* 1.6.
Cresc.	*Contra Cresconium grammaticum partis Donati. CSEL* 52.
doct. chr.	*De doctrina christiana. PL* 34. *CSEL* 80. *CCL* 32. *FC* 2. *WSA* 1.11.
en. Ps.	*Enarrationes in Psalmos. PL* 36–7. *CCL* 38–40. Forthcoming in *WSA*.
ep.	*Epistula(e). PL* 33. *CSEL* 34, 44, 57, 58. *FC* 12, 18, 20, 30, 32.
ep.*	*Epistula(e)* 1*–29*. *CSEL* 88. *FC* 81.
haer.	*De haeresibus ad Quodvultdeum. PL* 42. *CCL* 46. *WSA* 1.18.
Io. ev. tr.	*In Iohannis evangelium tractatus. PL* 35. *CCL* 36. *FC* 78, 79, 88, 90, 92.
ord.	*De ordine. CCL* 29. *FC* 2.
pecc. mer.	*De peccatorum meritis et remissione et de baptismo parvulorum ad Marcellinum. PL* 44. *CSEL* 60. *NPNF* 1.5. *FC* 86. *WSA* 1.23.
qu. ev.	*Quaestiones evangeliorum. CCL* 44B.
retr.	*Retractationes. PL* 32. *CSEL* 36. *CCL* 57. *FC* 60.
serm.	*Sermo(nes).* For a listing of Latin editions, cf. *AL* 1.xxxviii–xxxix. To these should be added *Augustin d'Hippone. Vingt-six sermons au peuple d'Afrique*, ed. F. Dolbeau (Paris, 1996). *WSA* 3.1–11.
uita	Possidius, *Vita Augustini*, ed. A. A. R. Bastiaensen (Milan, 1975). T. F. X. Noble and T. Head, *Soldiers of Christ* (London, 1995). *FC* 15.

Latin editions of Augustine's works are indicated at *AL* 1.xxvi–xli. For a listing of English translations, consult the table prepared by A. Fitzgerald, *Augustine through the Ages: An Encyclopedia* (Grand Rapids, 1999). *WSA* plans to publish English translations of the complete works of Augustine.

Modern works cited in this volume

Buckland, W. and P. Stein, *A Text-Book of Roman Law from Augustus to Justinian* (Cambridge, 1921; rev. 1975).

Cameron, A., 'Earthquake 400', *Chiron* 17 (1987), 332–50.

Cameron, A. and J. Long, *Barbarians and Politics at the Court of Arcadius* (Berkeley, 1993).

Delmaire, R., *Largesses sacrées et res privata: l'aerarium impérial et son administration du ive au vie siècle* (Rome, 1989).

Dodaro, R., 'Church and State', in *Augustine through the Ages: An Encyclopedia*, ed. A. Fitzgerald (Grand Rapids, Mich., 1999), 176–84.

Ducloux, A., *Ad ecclesiam confugere: naissance du droit d'asile dans les églises* (Paris, 1994).

Hahn, T., *Tyconius-Studien* (Leipzig, 1902).

Huisman, H., *Augustinus' Briefwisseling met Nectarius* (Amsterdam, 1956).

Humbert, Michel, 'Enfants à louer ou à vendre: Augustin et l'autorité parentale (Ep. 10* et 24*)', in *Les Lettres de Saint Augustin découvertes par Johannes Divjak* (Paris, 1983), 189–204.

Lazewski, W., *La sentenza agostiniana: martyrem non facit poena sed causa* (Rome, 1987).

Lepelley, C., *Les Cités de l'Afrique romaine au bas-empire*, 2 vols. (Paris, 1979).

Nicholas, B., *An Introduction to Roman Law* (Oxford, 1962).

O'Brien, M. B., *Titles of Address in Christian Latin Epistolography to 543 AD* (Washington, 1930).

O'Reilly, M. V., *Sancti Aurelii Augustini De excidio Urbis Romae sermo. A Critical Text and Translation with Introduction and Commentary* (Washington, 1955).

Thomas, J. A. C., *Textbook of Roman Law* (Amsterdam/New York/Oxford, 1976).

Biography

Highly recommended is P. Brown, *Augustine of Hippo, A Biography* (London, 1967), which treats Augustine in historical and political contexts. G. Bonner, *St Augustine of Hippo, Life and Controversies* (London, 1963; rev. Norwich, 1986), presents a comprehensive account of Augustine's life, emphasising the theological side of his work. See also G. Bonner, 'Augustinus (uita)', *AL* 1.519–50. While not a biography, C. N. Cochrane, *Christianity and Classical Culture. A Study of Thought and Action from Augustus to Augustine* (Oxford, 1940; repr. 1980), retains its value as an introduction to the cultural shifts undergirding Augustine's thought. H.-I. Marrou, *Saint Augustin et la fin de la culture antique* (Paris, 4th edn, 1958; repr. 1983), remains essential for understanding the intellectual formation and cultural influences on Augustine's religious thought.

Political and social life in Roman late antiquity

Prominent among the many studies which merit mention in this area is the indispensable work of A. H. M. Jones, *The Later Roman Empire 284–602. A Social and Administrative Survey*, 3 vols. (Oxford, 1964). Economic and political aspects of Roman late antiquity are also discussed in detail by M. I. Rostovtzeff, *Social and Economic History of the Roman Empire*, trans. P. M. Fraser (Oxford, 1957). Less technical than these works, yet highly informative, is A. Cameron, *The Later Roman Empire, AD 284–430* (Cambridge, Mass. 1993). Our best source of information on Roman African cities at the time of Augustine is the two volumes of C. Lepelley cited above. *The Cambridge Ancient History*, vol. XIII, *The Late Empire, AD 337–425*, ed. A. Cameron and P. Garnsey (Cambridge, 1998), presents a large number of valuable and recent studies on the social, cultural, economic and political aspects of the Roman empire contemporaneous with the life of Augustine.

The *Theodosian Code* and other ancient collections of imperial edicts and constitutions, which are frequently mentioned in this volume, have been translated into English by C. Pharr, *The Theodosian Code and Novels and the Sirmondian Constitutions* (New York, 1952). Helpful introductions to the more technical aspects of Roman law can be found in the studies indicated in the notes to this volume, but see also R. P. Coleman-Norton, *Roman State and Christian Church* (London, 1966). The Roman educational system, with its emphasis on rhetoric, is ably described by H.-I. Marrou, *A History of Education in Antiquity* (London, 1956), and by S. Bonner, *Education in Ancient Rome. From the Elder Cato to the Younger Pliny* (London, 1977).

J. Matthews, *Western Aristocracies and Imperial Court AD 364–425* (Oxford, 1975), exposes the political atmosphere surrounding the imperial court of the Western empire during Augustine's life. P. Heather, *Goths and Romans 332–489* (Oxford, 1991), explains the more significant political and military consequences of Gothic migrations through the Western empire at this time. N. McLynn, *Ambrose of Milan: Church and Court in a Christian Capital* (Berkeley, 1994), describes the political and ecclesiastical situation at Milan during Augustine's sojourn in the city. R. A. Markus, *The End of Ancient Christianity* (Cambridge, 1990), reveals many of the difficulties in determining the elusive boundaries between Christian and 'pagan' in the early fifth century. P. Brown, *Religion and Society in the Age of St Augustine* (London, 1972), offers close case studies of the interrelationship of religion, politics and social class for the period. In *Power and Persuasion: Towards a Christian Empire* (Madison, 1992), Brown engages the political and social aspects of the role of the Christian bishop in the fifth century. His essay 'The Limits of Intolerance' in his *Authority and the Sacred. Aspects of the Christianisation of the Roman World* (Cambridge, 1995), 29–54, makes much historical sense of the fierce competition among the religions of the late classical period.

J. Merdinger, *Rome and the African Church in the Time of Augustine* (New Haven, 1997), discusses ecclesiastical politics in the relationship between Augustine, other African bishops and the bishops of Rome. Concerning the bishop's tribunal (*audientia episcopalis*) in the fourth and fifth centuries, J. C. Lamoreaux, 'Episcopal Courts in Late Antiquity', *Journal of Early Christian Studies* 3:2 (1995), 143–67, presents a useful, general introduction. On Augustine's relationship to this institution, see also the article by R. Dodaro, 'Church and State', cited above. A number of the letters of Augustine, which were first published in 1981 by J. Divjak, touch on matters related to aspects of Roman law. H. Chadwick, 'New Letters of St Augustine', *Journal of Theological Studies*, new series, 34:2 (1983), 425–52, provides a richly informative introduction to the letters. Many of the most valuable studies of these letters are contained in *Les Lettres de Saint Augustin découvertes par Johannes Divjak* (Paris, 1983). On the Donatist controversy, W. H. C. Frend, *The Donatist Church. A Movement of Protest in Roman North Africa* (Oxford, 1952; repr. 1985), though by now dated, remains the most comprehensive account available in English. Frend's studies can be profitably supplemented by F. Decret, *Le Christianisme en Afrique du nord ancienne* (Paris, 1996), 135–89. T. D. Barnes, 'The Beginnings of Donatism', *Journal of Theological Studies*, new series, 26 (1975), 13–22, is also helpful for understanding the complicated origins of the movement. Most useful as a source of documentation for the Donatist controversy is *Le Dossier du Donatisme*, ed. J.-L. Maier, 2 vols. (Berlin, 1987, 1989). M. A. Tilley, *Donatist Martyr Stories. The Church in Conflict in Roman North Africa* (Liverpool, 1996), assembles a rare collection of Donatist records of judicial proceedings (*acta*) against African Christian martyrs, as well as accounts of their torments (*pas-*

siones). These texts are valuable for what they tell us about the Donatist perspective on the fourth-century controversy. M. Edwards, *Optatus: Against the Donatists* (Liverpool, 1997), offers a superb translation of the theological treatise of the fourth-century bishop of Milevis, important as a source for Augustine's own work on the Donatist controversy. J. P. Burns, 'Augustine's Role in the Imperial Action against Pelagius', *Journal of Theological Studies*, new series, 30 (1979), 67–83, studies the historical evidence behind the African bishops' appeal for imperial intervention against the Pelagians. H. Chadwick, 'Augustine on Pagans and Christians: Reflections on Religious and Social Change', in D. Beales and G. Best (eds.), *History, Society and the Churches. Essays in Honour of Owen Chadwick* (Cambridge, 1985), 9–27, examines Augustine's perspective, reflected in his sermons, of the social tensions between Christians and pagans in north Africa during his episcopate. C. Munier, 'Carthage: Councils', *EEC* I.146–48, presents a clear, brief description of each of the African bishops' councils held at Carthage during and after Augustine's episcopate.

Augustine's political thought

R. A. Markus, *Saeculum. History and Society in the Theology of St Augustine* (Cambridge, 1970; repr. 1989), remains the essential starting point for any serious consideration of Augustine's social and political thought. It is complemented by R. F. Evans, *One and Holy. The Church in Latin Patristic Thought* (London, 1972), especially 65–128, on the key concept of church in Augustine's thought, and by G. B. Ladner, *The Idea of Reform. Its Impact on Christian Thought and Action in the Age of the Fathers* (Cambridge, Mass., 1959). The discussion of intellectual evil by G. R. Evans, *Augustine on Evil* (Cambridge, 1982), is outstanding, and the topic is crucial for understanding Augustine's anthropology. *The City of God: A Collection of Critical Essays*, ed. by D. F. Donnelly (New York, 1995), felicitously brings together numerous treatments of political themes in the *City of God* which are scattered throughout various journals and books. To Donnelly's collection R. Williams, 'Politics and the Soul: A Reading of the City of God', *Milltown Studies* 19:20 (1987), 55–72, should be added.

M. Ruokanen, *Theology of Social Life in Augustine's* De civitate Dei (Göttingen, 1993), offers a select bibliography of prominent studies on topics concerned with Augustine's political thought (pp. 166–76). R. A.

Markus, 'Saint Augustine's Views on the "Just War"', in *The Church and War*, ed. W. J. Shells (Oxford, 1983), 1–13, is still the best discussion of a complex issue. J. Rist, *Augustine: Ancient Thought Baptized* (Cambridge, 1994), offers a helpful overview of Augustine's treatments of social and political issues (pp. 203–55), which has the advantage of situating Augustine's thoughts on these issues in their historical and social contexts. Augustine's positions on lying, suicide and religious coercion are treated with care and clarity by C. Kirwan, *Augustine* (London, 1989), 196–218. Rhetorical mendacity is the subject of C. J. Swearingen, *Rhetoric and Irony. Western Literacy and Western Lies* (New York, 1991), especially 175–214, 'When the Rhetor Lies: Augustine's Critique of Mendacity'; and of E. Fortin, 'Augustine and the Problem of Christian Rhetoric', *Augustinian Studies* 5 (1974), 85–100. Augustine's views on slavery are examined by G. Corcoran, *Saint Augustine on Slavery* (Rome, 1985), and more recently by P. Garnsey, *Ideas of Slavery from Aristotle to Augustine* (Cambridge, 1996). Social conditions as they affected families during Augustine's episcopate are discussed by B. Shaw, 'The Family in Late Antiquity: the Experience of Augustine', *Past and Present* 115 (1987), 3–51. E. Pagels, *Adam, Eve and the Serpent* (London, 1988), provides a starting point for discussions of Augustine's attitudes to women and women's sexuality; however, the question remains controversial for scholars. E. A. Matter, 'Christ, God and Woman in the Thought of St Augustine' and M. Lamberigts, 'A Critical Examination of Critiques of Augustine's View of Sexuality', in *Augustine and his Critics*, ed. R. Dodaro and G. Lawless (London, 2000), 164–75 and 176–97, review recent scholarly viewpoints on these and related topics.

Closely tied to Augustine's views on political society is his theology of love, specifically the relationship which he conceived between love of self, other and God. Following Hannah Arendt's doctoral dissertation on the subject, and with the publication of A. Nygren, *Agape and Eros. Part I: A Study of the Christian Idea of Love, Part II: The History of the Christian Idea of Love*, trans. P. Watson (New York, 1930, 1953), considerable attention was paid during the twentieth century to ethical problems arising from Augustine's treatments of these related forms of love. See H. Arendt, *Love and Saint Augustine*, ed. J. Vecchiarelli Scott and J. Chelius Stark (Chicago, 1996). Given the crucial role of the self and its relationship to God in Augustine's thought, Arendt, Nygren and other scholars have enquired whether and to what extent, for Augustine, it is right for Christians to love other human beings for their own sake, that is, without immediate reference to the love of God. Among other important, recent discussions of these questions are J. Burnaby, *Amor Dei: A Study in the Religion of St Augustine* (London, 1939; rev. 1963); O. O'Donovan, *The Problem of Self-Love in St Augustine* (New Haven, 1980); T. van Bavel, 'The Double Face of Love in Augustine', *Augustinian Studies* 17 (1986), 169–81; R. Williams, 'Language, Reality and Desire in Augustine's *De Doctrina*', *Journal of Literature and Theology* 3:2 (July, 1989), 138–50; and R. Canning, *The Unity of Love for God and Neighbour in St Augustine* (Heverlee-Leuven, 1993).

The contemporary value of Augustine's political thought has become an object of serious debate. P. Bathory, *Political Theory as Public Confession. The Social and Political Thought of St Augustine* (New Brunswick, N.J., 1981), suggests the importance of Augustine's emphasis on public confession for just government. J. Milbank, *Theology and Social Theory. Beyond Secular Reason* (Oxford, 1990), holds that Augustine's social and political thought, with its emphasis on the role of the church in fostering forgiveness, uniquely succeeds in overcoming the ontology of violence still at work in modern and contemporary secular and theological social theories (pp. 380–438). Without responding to either Bathory or Milbank, W. B. Connolly, *The Augustinian Imperative. A Reflection on the Politics of Morality* (London/Newbury Park, California/New Delhi, 1993), argues from within the philosophical horizons of Frederick Nietzsche and Michel Foucault against the suitability for contemporary political morality of much of Augustine's insistence upon confession and conversion. R. Dodaro, 'Augustine's Secular City', in *Augustine and his Critics*, ed. R. Dodaro and G. Lawless (London, 2000), 231–59, examines Connolly's thesis and defends the validity of Augustine's approach to civic virtue through confession. Meanwhile, J. B. Elshtain, *Augustine and the Limits of Politics* (Notre Dame, Ind., 1995), prefers to see Augustine as a thinker whose contribution to contemporary, democratic, political life is to understand and to accept the limited scope of politics.

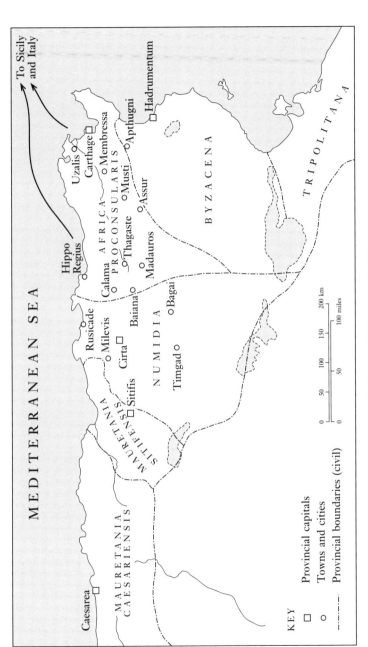

Map 1 Augustine's north Africa: some significant towns

KEY

□   Provincial capitals

○   Towns and cities

–·–·–   Provincial boundaries (civil)

Christianity and citizenship

Letters 90, 91, 103 and 104

The following exchange of letters between Augustine and Nectarius is concerned with a riot which took place during illegal pagan celebrations in Calama, Nectarius' home-town, not far from Hippo. Nectarius urges Augustine to intervene to protect his fellow-pagans from legal penalties.

Letter 90

408

Nectarius[1] to his notable lord and deservedly welcome brother, the bishop Augustine.

I need not describe the power of patriotic love, for you know it already: it alone could justly take precedence over affection for our parents. If a good man's service of his home-town had any limit or terminus, then by now I might deserve to excuse myself worthily from my duties to her. On the contrary, though, one's affection and gratitude for one's city grows as each day passes; and the nearer life approaches to its end, the more one desires to leave one's country flourishing and secure. That is why I am delighted before all else to be conducting this discussion with a man who is thoroughly well educated.

There are many things about the colony of Calama which deservedly win my affection: I was born there, and I have – it seems – discharged public duties of some significance on its behalf.[2] Now, my most excellent and deservedly welcome lord, the colony has lapsed through the serious misbehaviour of her populace.[3] Now it is indeed true that if we weigh matters according to strict public law, then quite a harsh sentence ought to be inflicted. But a bishop is sanctioned only to provide security for people, to stand in court on the more deserving side of the case, and to win mercy before almighty God for the misdeeds of others.[4] My request,

I

therefore, and my urgent plea, is that if the case must be defended, you will defend those not responsible, and protect the innocent from trouble.

Please do this; as you can well see, it is a request that suits your character. A limit for damages can easily be set; we simply beg to be spared the criminal penalty.[5]

May you live to please God more and more, notable lord and deservedly welcome brother.

Letter 91

408/409

Augustine to his distinguished lord and justly honoured brother Nectarius.[1]

(1) I am not surprised that your heart still glows with such warm love for your home-town, even though your limbs are now starting to be chilled by old age, and I praise you for this. Furthermore, I am not reluctant, but rather delighted, to see you not only recalling accurately, but also showing by your life and your behaviour, that 'a good man's service of his home-town has no limit or terminus'.[2] That is why we should love to count you too as a citizen of a certain country beyond; it is because we love *that* country with a holy love – as far as we can – that we accept hard work and danger among the people we hope to benefit by helping them reach it. If you were, you would consider there to be 'no limit or terminus' to the service of the small group of its citizens who are pilgrims on this earth; and in discharging your duties to a much finer city [cf. Heb 11.16], you would become so much finer a man. If you set no end to your efforts to serve that city for the present time, you would find no end to your enjoyment of her everlasting peace.

(2) Until this happens, however – we need not despair of the possibility of your finding that home-town, and perhaps even now you are wisely contemplating the prospect. After all, your father preceded you there, after giving you life here – but until this happens, forgive us if we cause some unhappiness to your home-town, which you are eager to leave flourishing, for the sake of our home-town, which we are eager never to leave.[3] We might argue with your wise self about its flourishing; but we should not worry that it will be difficult to persuade you how a city ought

to flourish – I am sure that will be easily obvious to you. The most famous poet in your literary tradition has mentioned the 'flowers' of Italy.[4] However, in your home-town we have had less experience of the land 'in flower' with heroes, than 'alight with weapons'; or perhaps I should say, not 'alight with weapons', but 'consumed with flames'. Do you think that leaving an outrage like that to go unpunished, or failing to reform the guilty as they deserve, will allow you to leave your homeland 'flourishing'? Flowers like that won't produce fruit, but thorns [cf. Mt 7.16; Lk 6.43–4]! Compare the choices: would you prefer your home-town to flower with piety or with licence, with reformed characters, or with atrocities unchecked? Compare the choices, and see whether your love for your home-town surpasses ours, and whether you, or we, are more fully and genuinely eager for it to flourish.

(3) Think a little about those volumes *On the Republic* (that was where you imbibed your devoted citizen's attitude that 'a good man's service of his home-town has no limit or terminus').[5] Please think about them; notice how they proclaim as praiseworthy simplicity and restraint, along with faithfulness to the marriage bond, and behaviour that is chaste and honourable and upright.[6] When a city is strong in such virtues as these, then it can truly be said to be 'flourishing'. In fact, though, such behaviour is being taught and learnt in the churches that are springing up all over the globe, like sacred lecture halls for the peoples of the world. Above all, they learn of the reverence that consists of worshipping the true and truthful God. All these virtues, which educate the human spirit and fit it for fellowship with God and for living in the everlasting city of heaven, he not only commands us to seek, but also enables us to acquire. That is why he predicted that the idols of the many false gods would be overthrown, and in fact ordered that they should be [cf. Lev 26.30; Ezek 6.4, 30.13; Hos 10.2; Num 35.52; 1 Kgs 15.12–13; 2 Chron 23.17, 31.15, 34.3–4]. For nothing renders people so unfit for human fellowship by corrupting their lives as imitating the gods in the way their characters are described (and recommended!) in their literature.

(4) When, then, our learned gentlemen were discussing the republic and the earthly city, and what they thought it ought to be like (and, incidentally, they sought it, and indeed described it, in private discussions, rather than actually founding and shaping it through public activity),[7] they did not offer the gods as examples for forming the characters of the young. Rather, they suggested men whom they considered outstanding and praiseworthy. Certainly Terence's young man, who looked at a wall-

painting depicting the king of the gods indulging in adultery,[8] found the feeling of lust which overcame him further inflamed when spurred by so authoritative an example. He would not have slipped into being tempted to his shocking deed, or sunk into perpetrating it, if he had chosen to imitate Cato rather than Jupiter! But how could he have done that, when in the temples he was compelled to worship Jupiter rather than Cato?

Perhaps, though, we oughtn't to offer examples like this from comedy to convict the impious of over-indulgence and idolatrous superstition. Read, or remind yourself, how the same volumes wisely argue that the words and the plots of comedies could not have been welcomed except by people whose characters corresponded to them.[9] Therefore these renowned gentlemen, who were outstanding in public life, when they were debating the republic lent their authority to the claim that depraved people become worse by imitating those gods, who are certainly not true, but false and fictional.[10]

(5) 'But', you might object, 'all the ancient written traditions about the gods' lives and characters ought to be understood and interpreted by wise readers in quite a different way'.[11] Yes indeed; just yesterday or the day before, we heard a wholesome interpretation of this sort being read out in the temples to the assembled people. I ask you: is the human race so blinded to the truth that it cannot grasp such clear and obvious facts? Jupiter is celebrated everywhere committing his acts of adultery: in paintings, in statues – cast, hammered or sculpted – in writing, in public readings, on the stage, in song, in dance. Why could he not have been described as prohibiting such behaviour, at least on his own Capitol?[12] If such wicked, such completely shameless and impious acts are allowed to blaze without prohibition among the people; if they are worshipped in the temples and laughed at in the theatres; if even the poor man's herds are wiped out as his animals become their sacrificial victims; and if the rich man's inheritance is squandered on actors to imitate them in plays and in dances – then, how can you say that the cities are 'flourishing'?

The proper mother of such 'flowers' is not the fertile earth; nor is it some opulent virtue. No, it is the goddess Flora: they celebrate in her honour a dramatic festival of such extravagant and unbridled shockingness that anyone can grasp the kind of demon she is;[13] she is not appeased by the deaths of birds or mammals or even human blood, but by nothing less than the sacrificial death, as it were, of human decency – a far greater outrage![14]

(6) I am saying all this in response to your writing that in as much as you are nearing the end of your life you are eager to leave your home-town

safe and flourishing. If so, all this deceitful idiocy must be done away with, and people must be converted to a true worship of God and to chaste and pious habits. Then you will be able to see your home-town flourishing, not merely in the opinion of fools, but in the true judgement of the wise. Then this home-town of the flesh where you were born will have become a part of the homeland into which we are born not physically, but by faith; there everyone who is holy and faithful to God will flower in everlasting eternity after their labours in the winter, as it were, of this life.

In short, we dearly wish not to abandon Christian gentleness; but also to avoid leaving any destructive examples in the city for others to imitate. God will be with us in doing this, if he is not too seriously angry with them. But perhaps obstacles will hinder both the gentleness that we are eager to preserve and the correction that we struggle to apply with moderation; for some other course may be pleasing to the hidden will of God. Perhaps he may judge that so great an evil ought to be punished by a harsher flogging; or if his anger is still fiercer, he may want to leave them unpunished in this life, so that they are not reformed and converted to him.

(7) Your wise self outlines for us something of a bishop's role, stating that your 'home-town has lapsed through the serious misbehaviour of her populace'. 'It is true indeed', you say, 'that if we weigh matters according to strict public law, then quite a harsh sentence ought to be inflicted. But a bishop is sanctioned only to provide security for people, to stand in court on the more deserving side of the case, and to win mercy before almighty God for the misdeeds of others.' In general we try to keep it the case that no one is punished too severely either by us or by anyone else with whom we might intercede; and we are eager to provide security for people. Security, however, lies in the happy condition of living rightly rather than in being safe to act wrongly. We also apply ourselves to winning mercy not only for our own misdeeds, but also for others'; but we can only achieve this on behalf of those who have been reformed. You also add the words, 'My request, therefore, and my urgent plea, is that if the case must be defended, you will defend those not responsible, and protect the innocent from trouble.'

(8) Listen briefly to what was done, and you yourself distinguish between innocent and guilty. In contravention of very recent laws an idolatrous ritual was celebrated on a pagan feast-day, the first of June.[15] No one prevented it; and it was performed with quite shameless bravado: an

outrageous group of dancers crossed right into the street where the church is and right up in front of it – something that did not happen even in Julian's time! When the clergy tried to prevent this utterly illegal and quite inappropriate behaviour, they threw stones at the church.

Next, about eight days later, the bishop made a formal appeal before the civic authorities to the very well-known laws,[16] and while they were arranging to implement the instructions of those laws, the church was stoned a second time. By the next day, our people's hope of deterring them by threats seemed vain; and we were denied our public rights when we wanted to speak on record for the official proceedings.[17] On the very same day a shower of hail fell in response to their hail of stones; perhaps they might at least fear the gods! But as soon as it was over, they immediately stoned the church for the third time, and then finally set the church roof on fire along with some of its personnel. One of the servants of God who lost his way and ran into them, they killed. The rest hid where they could or fled where they could; the bishop meanwhile was hiding, squashed in some cramped corner, and he heard the voices of men who were hunting him to kill him; they were reproaching themselves on the grounds that their outrages would have been committed for nothing if they failed to find him.

All this was happening from early evening[18] until late into the night. Not one person who might have carried weight and influence among them tried to control them, or to provide relief; none, that is, except for one foreigner. He enabled many of the servants of God to escape the hands of the men who were set on killing them, and he also forced the looters to return a lot of property. This man made it obvious how easily those events might have been prevented or nipped in the bud, if the citizens, and especially their leaders,[19] had intervened to stop them at the start or before the end.

(9) It might not be possible, then, for you to distinguish the innocent from the guilty out of the whole city, but only the less guilty from the more guilty. Certainly those who merely lacked the courage to offer help were guilty only of a minor sin; and in particular if they were deterred by fear of offending those powerful men in the town whom they knew to be enemies of the church. However, everyone was implicated in the outrages that were committed with their consent, even if they neither took part in them nor instigated them. Those who actually committed them are implicated more deeply; and those who instigated them most deeply of all. We ought, though, to treat the suggestions about the instigators as

suspicions rather than truth, and avoid discussing matters that can only be brought to light at the cost of torturing those who must be interrogated.[20]

We should also be merciful to those who are afraid, even if they have chosen to beg mercy from God on account of his bishop and his servants, rather than to offend the powerful enemies of the church. As for those who are left, do you really reckon that they should not be disciplined and restrained? Do you really think that we should offer such an example of appalling savagery to be allowed to go unpunished? We have no desire to nurse our anger by taking revenge over events that are past; rather we try to act mercifully with an eye to the future. There are ways of punishing evil men that are not only gentle, but even for their benefit and well-being, and Christians too can make use of these. They have been given three benefits: a life of bodily health; the means of staying alive; and the means with which to live badly. Let them keep the first two safe; in that way there will still be some potential penitents.[21] We pray for this, and we spare no possible effort in working for it. If God wishes to excise the third of these, as if it were a gangrenous and poisonous growth, then certainly he will, in his mercy, inflict punishment. If he wishes something more than this, or if he does not allow even this much – well, then, the rationale of his policy, which will be still more profound and, undoubtedly, more just, remains with him.

As for us, we must weigh our responsibility and our duty (as far as it is given to us to see it) beseeching him that our intentions may meet with his approval – for we intend and wish to act in the best interests of everyone – and that he may allow nothing to be done through our agency that might – as he would know far better than us – disadvantage both us and his church.

(10) When I went to Calama recently[22] to console those who were suffering because of this sorry and serious matter, and to calm those who were angry, I settled as well as I could with the Christians the courses of action that I judged most appropriate in the circumstances. After this, I received the pagans also, the source and cause of all this trouble, who had asked me to make myself available to them. I did so in order to advise them what it would be sensible for them to do in this situation, not only to relieve themselves of their present anxieties, but also to seek everlasting security. They listened for a long time, and they also spent a long time questioning us. Far be it from us, though, to be the kind of servants who are delighted to receive requests from people who are unwilling to make requests of our Lord.

You can see clearly, then – for your mind is still very lively! – that we must (while preserving gentleness and Christian moderation) make an effort in this affair to deter others from imitating the culprits' wickedness, or even to pray that others will imitate them once they are reformed. The losses that were inflicted are either being borne by Christians, or made good by Christians. The profits that we desire are souls: we are so eager to secure them that we are ready to risk shedding our own blood; we long for these profits to increase in your town, and not to be hampered in other places by your example.[23]

May the mercy of God allow us to rejoice over your security!

Letter 103

409

Nectarius sends greetings in the Lord to Augustine his justly and deservedly welcome lord and brother worthy of every type of honour.

(1) I read the letter sent by your distinguished self, with its assault on the worship of idols and the temple rituals. While doing so, I did not seem to be hearing the voice of the well-known philosopher who, they tell us, used to sit on the ground in some dark corner in the Academy's lyceum, sunk in some deep thought, with his head bent and his knees drawn up to his forehead, a sort of poverty-stricken critic, trying to attack the notable teachings other people had discovered and to find fault with their notable propositions, though he had nothing of his own to defend.[1] No – instead the *consularis*[2] Marcus Tullius Cicero was summoned by your eloquence and stood before my eyes; he it was who saved the lives of countless of his fellow-citizens and then, crowned as a victor, carried the victory standards from the battleground of the law-courts into the astonished schools of the Greeks; next he redirected his clarion, that sonorous voice and the tongue with which he had blasted guilty criminals and the parricides of his republic, and panting with the breath of righteous indignation, he flung back his toga itself, imitating the appearance of the folds of the Greek *pallium* in his flowing pages.[3]

(2) I was happy to listen, therefore, when you were pressing me towards

the worship and religion of the most high God. I gratefully welcomed your effort to persuade me to attend to our heavenly homeland. I did not take you to be speaking of the city that is enclosed by a circle of walls, nor of the city that philosophers' treatises call 'world-wide', and declare to be common to all.[4] Rather, you were talking about a city where the great God lives and dwells, along with those souls that truly deserve it, a city that is the goal at which all laws aim, by various paths and ways, a city that we cannot fully describe in speech, but can perhaps discover by contemplation.[5] This, therefore, should be our principal goal and our principal love.

However that may be, I do not think that we need to abandon the city in which we were born and brought into life, which first granted us the enjoyment of the light we see, which nourished us and brought us up; furthermore (to say what is specifically appropriate to the issue) for those heroes whose fine service to the city merits it, a home is being prepared in heaven – so the philosophers tell us – for after their bodily deaths.[6] In this way, the people who have served the town of their birth well are promoted to the city above; the people who are shown to have secured safety for their own homeland, by their advice or their efforts, are the ones who will live closer to God.

My next point is this: you thought to make a joke about our city burning not with arms, but with fire and flames, and growing thorns rather than flowers.[7] But that is not a very great criticism. After all, we know that flowers often grow from thorns. Everyone is aware that roses sprout from thorns and that even the fruit of corn is surrounded by a ring of spiky ears. In fact, pleasant and painful things are usually mingled together like this.[8]

(3) The final point in the letter from your excellent self was that the church does not demand in retribution either life or bloodshed. Rather, the guilty should be stripped of the possessions they are most afraid of losing. In my judgement (if my view is not mistaken) it is a more serious thing to be stripped of resources than to be killed. That is true at least if death entirely removes our perception of evil, while a life of poverty produces endless misfortune – claims which, as you know, are frequently found in literature.[9] It is a more serious matter to live a life full of evils than to put an end to those evils by dying. In fact, the principles behind your own work reveal this: you support the poor, care for the sick to ease their sufferings, administer medicine to those in bodily pain, and, in short, do everything possible to prevent the afflicted from suffering long-lasting misfortune.

Now in respect of the degree of sin, it makes no difference what kind of a sin has led to an appeal for leniency. In the first place, if repentance is able both to win mercy and to atone for the offence itself, then surely everyone who throws his arms around your feet and begs for pardon is repentant. Furthermore, if (as some philosophers agree) all sins are equal, then pardon ought to be granted in common to all.[10] If someone has spoken a little rudely, he has sinned. If he heaps abuse or accusations on you, he has sinned equally. If one person has stolen another's property, this should also be counted a misdeed. If he has violated secular places or sacred, still he should not be cut off from pardon. In the end, there is no room for mercy, unless sins are committed first.

(4) I have now replied for better or for worse, as they say, not as well as I ought, but as well as I could. Therefore, I beg and beseech you – if only you could be here to see my tears as well – I beg you to think again and again who you are, what you profess, and what you are doing, and to focus your attention on the sight of the city, as these people are dragged away from her to be led to punishment.

Imagine the grief of their mothers and their wives, of their children and their parents. Imagine the shame with which they must return to their home-town, set free, but only after torture. And thinking about their wounds and their scars will renew their pain and their tears. When you have studied all these points carefully, please think first of God and then consider your reputation among human beings, or rather the goodness of a friend and the bonds forged by affection. And then, please, win yourself praise for offering pardon and not retribution.

All that might already be said in the case of those who stand truly accused, implicated by their own confession.[11] To these people you have granted mercy, through reflection on the law;[12] I never fail to praise you for this. Now, though, it is almost impossible to explain how cruel it is to chase the innocent, and to summon to judgement on a capital charge those whom everyone agrees not to have been involved in the crime. Even if it happens that they are exonerated, please consider how they will win their freedom at the cost of hatred against their accusers, as having voluntarily allowed the guilty to go free, but left the innocent alone only once they had lost their case.[13]

May the highest God keep you safe and preserve you as a stronghold of his law and a jewel in our crown.

Letter 104

409

Augustine greets in the Lord his distinguished and justly honoured and welcome brother Nectarius.

(1) I have read the letter from your kind self, a reply which arrived rather a long time after the letter I had had delivered to you. I wrote back while Possidius my holy brother and fellow-bishop was still with me, and had not yet set sail.[1] However, I did not receive the letter you were good enough to give to him for me until 27 March, about eight months after I wrote.[2] I certainly do not know why my note took so long to reach you or yours to reach me; or perhaps your wise self only now wished to write back, and did not see fit to do so earlier.

If that is the case, I wonder what your reason was. Perhaps it was that you heard some news (which has not yet reached us) to the effect that my brother Possidius has had some success against your fellow-citizens. With all due respect to you, his love is better for them than yours is, in so far as his punishments are more severe.

Indeed, your letter shows that you are afraid of this, when you warn me to set before my eyes the sight of 'the city, as these people are dragged away from her to be led to punishment. Imagine the grief of their mothers and their wives, of their children and their parents. Imagine the shame with which they must return to their home-town, set free, but only after torture. And thinking about their wounds and their scars will renew their pain and their tears.' Far be it from me to press for such things to be inflicted on any of our enemies, at our own hands or anyone else's. However, as I said, if any rumour of such a thing reaches you, explain it more fully. Then we will know how to act to prevent it, or else how to reply to anyone who believes it.[3]

(2) I should prefer you to study my letter – the one to which you were reluctant to reply.[4] I expressed my mind clearly enough there. I think, however, that you have forgotten what I wrote back to you, and you have ascribed to me utterly different views, ones quite unlike my own. In fact, you slipped into your letter something that I never said, as if you were remembering something that I had in fact put in my letter. You said that the final point in my letter was this: 'the church does not demand in retribution either life or bloodshed. Rather, the guilty should be stripped of the possessions they are most afraid of losing.' Then, in order to show

what a great evil this is, you go on to add that, unless your view is mistaken, you judge it 'a more serious thing to be stripped of resources than to be killed'. Next, to clarify the type of resources you mean, you continue by saying that I know the claim made frequently in our literature that 'death entirely removes our perception of evil, while a life of poverty produces endless misfortune'. Then you conclude that it is a more serious matter 'to live a life full of evils, than to put an end to those evils by dying'.[5]

(3) I do not remember reading anywhere, either in our literature (to which, I admit, I applied my mind later than I should wish) or in yours (which I learned from my earliest youth) that 'a life of poverty produces endless misfortune'. Poverty with toil is surely no sin; and in fact it provides some restriction and check upon sin. There is no need to fear because of it that after this brief life the fact that someone lived as a pauper here will bring endless misfortune on his soul. In fact, no misfortune can be endless in the life we lead on earth, because that life cannot be endless. Indeed, it is not even very long, whatever age you reach, even old age.

On the other hand, I did read in your literature that the very life we enjoy is brief,[6] although you judge that it can have endless misfortune, and now advise me that your literature frequently claims so. Some – but not all – of your literature does indeed state that death is the end of all evils. That is the view of the Epicureans, and of anyone else who holds that the soul is mortal. However, the philosophers whom Cicero calls the 'consular philosophers',[7] because he considers their authority so weighty, believe that the soul is not destroyed when we complete the last day of our life, but departs. They also contend that it endures in a state of either blessedness or wretchedness, corresponding to its deserts, whether good or bad. This agrees with the view of holy scripture (and I try at least to grasp its basics).[8]

Death is, then, the end of evils, but for those only whose lives were chaste, devout, faithful and innocent; not for those who are inflamed by desire for the trifles and vanities of this temporary life, who although they think they are happy here are proved to be miserable by the fact that their wills are corrupt. After death they will be compelled not only to live in even more oppressive misery, but also to recognise it.

(4) Now that is said frequently both in some of your literature, which you hold in honour, and in all of ours, my excellent devotee of your hometown on earth.[9] What you ought to fear for your fellow-citizens, then, is a

life of luxury rather than a life of poverty. If you do fear a life of poverty
for them, you should warn them as a priority to avoid the sort of poverty
that is 'never reduced by plenty or by need', even though it is surrounded
by an abundance of earthly possessions – if I may borrow the words of
one of your writers for those whose grasping greed is insatiable.[10]

However, in the letter of mine to which you were replying, I did not say
that those of your citizens who are hostile to the church must be set
straight through poverty so extreme as to lack the necessities of nature.
It's that sort of poverty that we in our mercy must assist; you thought it
your duty to remind us of this, saying that 'the principles behind your
own work reveal this: you support the poor, care for the sick to ease their
sufferings, administer medicine to those in bodily pain'. Even then, one is
better off in this sort of need than having a surfeit of possessions to use to
indulge one's wickedness. But God forbid that I would take the view that
people with whom we are dealing should be restrained by being reduced
to that degree of distress.

(5) Look at my letter again. Even though you didn't think it worth
rereading when you had to reply to it, at least you may have thought it
worth putting somewhere so that it could be produced at your orders
whenever you wished. Take note of what I said in it. You will find the
words which you failed to answer – as I think you will admit – straight
away. I shall now include some words from that letter of mine:

'We have no desire', I said, 'to nurse our anger by taking revenge over
events that are past; rather we try to act mercifully with an eye to the
future. There are ways of punishing evil men that are not only gentle, but
even for their benefit and well-being, and Christians too can make use of
these. They have been given three benefits: a life of bodily health; the
means of staying alive; and the means with which to live badly. Let them
keep the first two safe; in that way there will still be some potential penitents. We pray for this, and we spare no possible effort in working for it. If
God wishes to excise the third of these, as if it were a gangrenous and poisonous growth, then certainly he will, in his mercy, inflict punishment.'[11]

If you had studied these words of mine when you thought to reply, you
would think it hostile rather than dutiful to beg me to avoid not just
putting to death the people whose cause you are pleading, but even
inflicting physical punishment on them. For I said that we wanted them
to be safe in this respect, to live free from bodily harm. Nor should you be
at all afraid of their living in poverty and having to be provided with food
by other people because of us. For the second respect in which I said we

wanted them to be safe was to have the means of staying alive. As for the third, that they should have the means to live badly, let me take just one example: the resources for making the silver statues of their false gods. And what have they done to serve and adore these gods, and to keep worshipping them still? They have even pounced to set fire to the church of God, and they have stolen and given to their wretched mob resources intended for supporting the devoutest of the poor; furthermore, blood has been shed.

You are concerned for your city's interests! Why are you afraid of wielding a scalpel to their audacious behaviour? Otherwise it will be nourished and strengthened by your leniency which is so destructive. Explain this to me, give me a careful argument to show where the harm lies. Give thought and attention to what I am saying to you in case your purported petition seems to be cloaking an implied accusation against my words.[12]

(6) We hope that your citizens will be honourable, upright in their behaviour, and without excessive resources; we do not wish them to be forcibly reduced because of us to Cincinnatus' plough or Fabricivs' hearth.[13] But those leaders of the Roman republic were not cheapened in the eyes of the citizens by their poverty. Far from it: they were particularly loved for it, and were better fitted to administering the wealth of their homeland. Nor is it our hope or our aim to leave the wealthy in your home-town with only the ten pounds of silver ornaments that the famous Rufinus, who was twice consul, possessed. The censors, who were at that time still laudably strict, decreed that this should be cut back, as if it were a vice to have it.[14]

Now, however, the habits of a rather degenerate age persuade us to deal more mildly with feeble souls; Christian gentleness, then, sees as excessive what seemed just to those censors. You can tell, therefore, what a difference there is between, on the one hand, its being a punishable offence simply to possess such an amount, and, on the other hand, permitting someone to keep only that amount because of other very serious offences. What was then a sin we should wish now to be at least the punishment for a sin. But this is what can and ought to be done so as to avoid both the former level of severity, and the guaranteed freedom from punishment that celebrates riotously and offers itself as an example for imitation, to lure other wretches into punishments that are heavy, but deeply hidden.[15]

Grant me this much, at least, that those who are fighting to destroy our basic necessities through arson might fear for their own superfluous possessions. Allow us also to give our enemies this benefit: while they are frightened of losing things which it will do them no harm to lose, they might avoid trying to commit deeds that will harm them. This should not be described as retribution for sin, but rather as safeguarding sensible policy. I am not calling for a penalty, but protecting them from incurring a penalty.

(7) If someone inflicts a degree of pain in order to prevent some fool from paying an awful penalty because he has got used to committing needless crimes, he is pulling a child's hair, as it were, to stop him from clapping at a serpent. Such love, by hurting him, ensures that his limbs are not damaged; but the thing we are deterring him from would put his life and his security at risk. It is no kindness for us to do anything that is requested of us; it is a kindness to do whatever does not harm the petitioners. On the whole, in fact, we would tend to help most by not giving what they want, and to do harm by giving it. Hence the saying, 'Don't give a boy a sword.' As Cicero says, 'You wouldn't give one even to your only son.'[16] Indeed, the more we love someone, the less we ought to present him with the possibility of sinning at grave risk to himself. Cicero was talking about wealth when he said this, if I am not mistaken. In general, then, if it is dangerous to entrust something to people who will misuse it, it is also safer for them if you take it away from them. When doctors see some gangrene that needs cutting and cauterisation, they often show mercy by shutting their ears to the patient's copious flood of tears. If, as little boys, or even as bigger ones, we had been let off by our parents or teachers whenever we pleaded for pardon after committing some sin, would any of us have been bearable as an adult? Who would have learnt anything useful? These things are done out of care, not cruelty.

Please, in this affair do not pay attention only to ways of winning from us whatever your townsmen beg of you. Consider the whole matter carefully. If you ignore the past, which cannot now be undone, look ahead a little to the future. Have the sense to concentrate on the real interests of your petitioners rather than their desires. Surely we cannot be held to love them faithfully if our only concern is to stop their love for us being weakened because we fail to achieve their demands. In that case where would the man be who is praised in your literature as 'ruler of his homeland', who pays attention to his people's interests rather than their wishes?[17]

(8) Next you argue that 'it makes no difference what kind of a sin has led to an appeal for leniency'.[18] You would be right about this if we were dealing with a case of punishing people rather than of reforming them. A Christian's heart will, I pray, never be driven to punishing anyone by a thirst for revenge. It will, I pray, when pardoning someone's sin, neither fail to anticipate the prayers of the petitioner, nor always respond to them directly. No, it should always be done without hating the person, without *returning* to him *evil for evil* [1 Thess 5.15; Rom 12.17], without a burning desire to harm him, without being eager to gratify vengeance, even if it is due by law. On the other hand, it should be done without failing to consult his interests, to look ahead, and to restrain him from evil. For it would be possible for someone to show extreme hostility to a person he strongly dislikes, by neglecting to set him on the right path. Alternatively, he might impose some painful restraint upon someone he loves greatly and thus make him a better person.

(9) Now it is true, as you write, that repentance wins mercy and atones for the offence itself.[19] But it is only that sort that is undertaken by true religion, with the future judgement of God in mind; not the sort that is displayed (or feigned) before human beings, just for the occasion, to free their ephemeral lives from immediate fear of trouble for the moment, rather than to cleanse the soul of its misdeeds for eternity. That is why we do believe that the pain of repentance will bear fruit for those Christians who have confessed their guilt and have begged for mercy, who were implicated in the offence either because they failed to provide assistance when the church was burning or because they stole something during the outrageous looting that took place.

We have taken the view that repentance suffices to reform them, because they have faith in their hearts, which will enable them to reflect on what they have to fear from the judgement of God.[20] But how can repentance heal those who not only fail to recognise the very source of forgiveness, but even continue to mock it and blaspheme against it? However, we do not harbour enmity against them in our hearts, because they are open and naked to the eye of God, and it is his judgement we fear, his assistance we are hoping for, both in this present life and in the life to come. In our judgement, though, we are showing our concern for them, if people who do not fear God have something to fear, which will not in fact harm their true interests, but might discipline their foolishness. Then it will prevent them from offending even more seriously the God they reject, because their damaging sense of security encourages them to behave with even more arrogance. It will also stop them offering that security as an example for others to imitate, something more destructive still.

Finally, while you plead with us on their behalf, we are pleading with God for them, that he might turn them towards him, and he might purify their hearts by faith and teach them to embrace true repentance, which will keep them safe.

(10) Notice how much more appropriate and more beneficial is *our* love for these people than *yours* (I say this with all due respect to you), although in your judgement we are angry with them. We are begging for them to avoid far more serious harm, and to win greater goods. If you too loved them out of God's heavenly gift[21] rather than from earthly human custom, and if you replied to me with sincerity that you were happy to listen to me pressing you towards the worship and religion of the most high God – then you would not just want this for them, but you would even beat them to it. That would mean that all our dealings about your petition could come to a very joyful and healthy conclusion. That would also enable you to reach the heavenly homeland. When I was encouraging you to attend it, you said that you were happy to embrace it. Now you could reach it through a true and devoted love for the home-town that gave you physical birth, by showing true concern for your citizens, bringing them not to empty and temporary enjoyment, nor to immunity from punishment for the outrage (which would be highly destructive) but to the grace of everlasting happiness.

(11) I have given you an exposition of my considered opinion on this issue, and of my deepest wishes. I admit that I do not know what is hidden in the plan of God: I am only human. However, I am absolutely certain that whatever it is, it is just and wise by comparison with any human mind, and very firmly established in incomparable excellence. The words that you can read in our scriptures are true: *There are many thoughts in the heart of a man, but the counsel of the Lord endures for ever* [Prov 19.21].

What time will bring, what will happen to help or hinder us, and, in short, how our wills might turn out as our immediate circumstances bring reform or sudden hope; whether God is so angry at these events that they will be punished more severely by being granted the immunity they are requesting, or whether he will in his mercy judge that they should be restrained in the way that we should like; or whether he will first employ some sharper, though more salutary, method of reforming them, and then when they undergo a true conversion, in accordance not with human mercy, but with his own, will avert the terror he was preparing, and transform it into joy – all this he already knows, but we do not know.

But until this happens, why should your excellent self and I struggle in vain with one another? Let us lay this concern aside for a while, as its hour is not yet come, and deal, if you will, with a matter that is always pressing. There is no moment when it is not fitting and proper to discuss how we may please God. In this life it is either impossible, or at least extremely difficult, to fulfil this so perfectly that no sin at all remains in a person. That is why we must abandon all hesitation and take refuge in his grace. We can truly address him in the words of the man who professed to have heard them from the Cumaean seer as a sort of prophetic ode, and delivered them in a flattering verse to some nobleman:

> With you as my guide, if any traces of our crimes remain,
> They will be rendered harmless and free the earth from perpetual fear.[22]

With him as our guide, indeed, all our sins are absolved and forgiven; and this path leads to our heavenly homeland. You were quite delighted to think of living there, when I recommended to you, as strongly as I could, that you should love it.

(12) The fact that you said that 'all laws aim, by various paths and ways, at the heavenly homeland' makes me nervous that you might be rather slow to grasp the only path that leads to it, if you think that the one on which you are established at present is going in that direction. Again, however, when I examine carefully the words you wrote, I think I am able to clarify your opinion reasonably sensibly. You did not say that all laws by various paths and ways 'achieve' or 'reveal' or 'find' or 'approach' or 'obtain' or anything else of that sort, but that they 'aim at' it.

The well-aimed and well-judged word you chose did not mean 'reach', but 'desire to reach'. In that way you did not rule out the true path, nor did you admit any other false ones. The path that leads there does indeed aim to do so; but not every path that aims to in fact leads there. Anyone who is led there is undoubtedly blessed. Again, we all wish to be blessed – that is, we aim at it; but not all of us who wish it are capable of it – that is, of reaching the place at which we are aiming. The person who is going to reach it is the one who keeps to the path that allows him not only to aim at it, but also to reach it. He leaves everyone else on the paths which aim at their target without in the end reaching it. For one would not be going astray either if one had no aim at all, or if the truth at which one were aiming were secured.

Perhaps, though, when you said 'different paths' you did not want us to understand these as incompatible, just as when we talk of 'different counsels', all of which however help to build a life of goodness, some concerning chastity, others patience, others mercy, and so on. In that case, not only do different paths and ways aim at this homeland, but they also find it. Thus in holy scripture we read both 'ways' and 'way'; for example, 'ways' in the sentence: *I will teach the unjust your ways and the impious will be turned to you* [Ps 51(50).13], and 'way' as here: *Lead me in your way and I will walk in your truth* [Ps 86(85).11].

The former 'ways' and the latter 'way' are not different; they are all one. Elsewhere holy scripture again says of them: *All the ways of the Lord are mercy and truth* [Ps 25(24).10]. Reflecting carefully on these words could produce a rich discourse and some delightful insights. This may need to be done, but I must put it off until another occasion.

(13) For the present, however, I think that I have done enough with regard to the duty I have assumed of replying to your excellent self. After all, Christ said, 'I am the Way'; and we ought to seek mercy and truth in him. Otherwise, if we look elsewhere, we will make the mistake of holding to a path that aims at, but does not reach; just as if we wish to hold on to the path that gives rise to the view you quoted, that 'all sins are equal', wouldn't it send us, like exiles, far away from our homeland of truth and blessedness?

Could anything be more irrational or more crazy than holding that someone who laughs a little excessively should be judged to have sinned as much as someone who savagely sets his home-town ablaze? In the view of certain philosophers, this path is not merely different, and still leading to a homeland in heaven, but is clearly distorted, and leads to very harmful error. However, you thought you should invoke it not out of personal conviction, but on behalf of your citizens, in the hope that we might pardon the violent men who lit the fires that burnt down the church, in the same way that we would pardon them if they were directing some wanton abuse at us.

(14) Look how you argued your case: 'If (as some philosophers agree) all sins are equal, then pardon ought to be granted in common to all.' Then when you were apparently labouring to show that all sins are equal, you continued with the words: 'If someone has spoken a little rudely, he has sinned. If he heaps abuse or accusations on you, he has sinned equally.'[23] This is not explaining, but simply stating a distorted view without arguing any proofs for it. When you say, 'he has sinned equally',

one can reply at once, 'he hasn't sinned equally'. Perhaps you will demand proof of this from me. Well, have you proved that he did 'sin equally'?

Perhaps we ought to listen to your next sentence: 'If one person has stolen another's property, this should also be counted a misdeed.' Here even you are embarrassed; you are ashamed to say that he has sinned in the same way; instead you say 'should be counted a misdeed'. But the question is not whether it should be counted a misdeed, but whether this misdeed is linked by equality to that one. If both are equal because they are both misdeeds, then mice and elephants are equal because they are both animals, and flies and eagles, because they both fly!

(15) Now you move on and draw this conclusion: 'If he has violated secular places or sacred, still he should not be cut off from pardon.' Here, surely, you have come to the atrocity your own citizens committed, when you mention violating sacred places. However, not even you make the insolent claim that their sin is equal. All you do is beg pardon for them; and it is quite proper to seek that from Christians because their pity is plentiful, and does not correspond to the size of the sin. Earlier, I quoted the words from our scriptures: *All the ways of the Lord are mercy and truth* [Ps 25(24).10]. They should therefore pursue mercy, unless they hate the truth. It is owed according to Christian justice not only to those who have sinned 'equally' (if, say, they have spoken a little insolently) but also to those who have repented of an appalling and impious outrage.

But you are a man worthy of praise; please do not teach your son Paradoxus to follow those Stoic paradoxes; we pray that he will grow up for you truly devout and happy. Could a well-born young man learn any 'wisdom' more wicked and more dangerous to you yourself than that of equating abuse directed at some stranger with, well, not parricide, but merely abuse directed at his father?

(16) It will suit you better when you intervene with us on behalf of your citizens to remind us of Christian mercy rather than Stoic hardness. That not only fails to favour the cause you have adopted, it even greatly hinders it. For if we do not possess that mercy, we will not be liable to being swayed by any petition of yours or by any of their pleas. The Stoics count mercy a vice, and drive it out completely from their wise man's mind; they want him to be as utterly unyielding as iron.[24]

The words you might quote from your Cicero may serve you better, therefore: he praised Caesar by saying, 'None of your virtues are more admirable or more welcome than your mercy.'[25] How much stronger ought this to be in the church, when they follow Christ, who said, *I am the way* [Jn 14.6], and when they read, *All the ways of the Lord are mercy and truth* [Ps 25(24).10].

Have no fear, therefore, that our efforts are directed to destroying the innocent; we do not even want the guilty to meet with the penalty they deserve, for we are prevented by the mercy that we love, along with truth, in Christ. However, if anyone spares and fosters vices so that they are encouraged, in order to avoid upsetting the wishes of the sinners, he is no more merciful than someone who does not want to take a knife away from a boy in case he should hear him crying, but is not afraid of grieving at his injury or his death. If you want to intervene with us on these men's behalf, save it for a suitable occasion. It is not just that you are only a little ahead of us in loving them (forgive me for saying so!); you are not yet even following us. Rather, please tell me in your reply what disturbs you about the way to which we hold. We are eager for you to proceed along it with us to our homeland above; for we know that that delights you, and are overjoyed at the fact.

(17) As for the citizens of your home-town in the flesh, even though you said that some but not all of them were innocent, you did not in fact defend them. You ought to notice that if you reread my letter. When I said that we saw thorns rather than flowers, in response to your writing that you were eager to leave your home-town flourishing, you thought that I was joking.[26] As if I would feel like joking in so bad a situation! Far from it. The burnt ruins of our church are still smoking, and we are cracking jokes about the issue? Now I cannot think of any 'innocent' except those who either were away, or lacked the necessary strength or influence to prevent the attackers.[27] Despite that, I made a distinction in my reply to you between the more guilty and the less guilty, and I said that the case of those who had been afraid to offend the powerful enemies of the church was different from that of those who had wanted the crimes committed, and different again from that of those who actually committed them, and different again from that of those who instigated them.[28]

I wished no action to be taken in the case of the instigators, because the matter perhaps could not be investigated without the use of physical torture, which is abhorrent to our way of thinking. Your Stoics, of course, accept that everyone is equally guilty, as they agree that all sins are equal. Those who unite with this opinion the hardness that makes them criticise mercy will not for a moment think that everyone should equally be pardoned, but that everyone should equally be punished. Remove them, then, as far as you can from the patronage of your cause. Instead pray that we will act as Christians. Then, as we pray, we will win the people we spare in Christ, without sparing them at the cost of destructive delinquency.

May the merciful and true God see fit to bless you with true happiness.

Letter 95

408

Augustine greets his beloved and honest lord Paulinus and lady Therasia, holy and fond and revered brother and sister and fellow-disciples of our master Jesus Christ.

(1) Brethren of ours who are very close to us are seeing you regularly; along with us you are able to reciprocate their affection and their greetings regularly. This comforts us in misfortune, rather than increasing our good fortune. For we do not like the pressing causes which force them to travel overseas; indeed we dislike them intensely, and make every possible effort to avoid them. For some reason, though – probably it is what we deserve – we cannot manage without them.

However, when they visit you and see you, the words of scripture come true: *Amid the multitude of sorrows in my heart, your encouragement has delighted my soul* [Ps 94(93).19, LXX]. Therefore when you hear from our brother Possidius himself what a sad cause has forced him to share the happiness of your company, you will recognise that what I say is absolutely true.[1] But if any of us were able to cross the sea solely for the purpose of enjoying your presence, could we find any reason more just or more worthy than that? However, the chains that bind me to the service of the weak in their sickness would not permit it. I cannot abandon them physically, unless they force me to by falling ill in a more dangerous, and therefore more demanding, way.

I do not know whether all this is given me to prepare me or to chastise me, except that *he does not deal with us according to our sins, nor repay us according to our iniquity* [Ps 103(102).10]. He mixes great solace with our sorrows, providing a wonderful medicine to prevent us both from loving the world and from weakening while in the world.

(2) In an earlier letter I asked you what you thought that the future everlasting life of the saints would be like. Your reply to me was a good

22

one: that we should also take thought still for the condition of this present life – except that you want to ask my advice, when you are as knowledgeable or ignorant as I am on this, or perhaps more knowledgeable than I am. Certainly you spoke very truly when you said that we must first die the death of the Gospel: 'by this we pre-empt our physical disintegration by dying voluntarily, leaving the life of this age not by our death, but by our decision'.[2] It is a single course of action, which does not float on the waves of doubt, when we reckon that we should live this mortal life so as somehow to adapt it to the life that is immortal. The question, though, that worries those such as I am, who are pondering this and asking questions, can be summed up completely as follows: how are we to live among those, or for those, who have not yet learnt to live by dying, not through physical disintegration, that is, but through an attitude of mind that turns itself away from physical temptations?

In general it seems to us that if we don't share with them to some extent the very things we wish to draw them away from, then we won't be able to have any salutary dealings with them. When we do this, though, the enjoyment of such things creeps subtly over us too, so that we often enjoy talking about foolish things, or listening to others talking about them; and we even enjoy not just laughing, but even being quite overcome and dissolving in laughter. Consequently, we burden our souls with the emotions of dust, or even of clay, and find ourselves struggling reluctantly to raise them to God, so that we can live the life of the Gospel by dying the death of the Gospel.

If on occasion this happens, then immediately we hear the comment, 'Well done, well done!' This doesn't come from a human being: no one human being can tell that another one has such things in his mind. Rather, the source of the cry, 'Well done, well done!' is some sort of inner silence. It was through this sort of testing, as the great apostle[3] confessed, that he was boxed by an angel [cf. 2 Cor 12.7]. See, then, how *human life on the earth is all a time of testing* [Job 7.1]. For a human being is tested even at the point where he is being conformed as far as possible to the life of heaven.

(3) On the subject of punishing or refraining from punishment, what am I to say? It is our desire that when we decide whether or not to punish people, in either case it should contribute wholly to their security. These are indeed deep and obscure matters: what limit ought to be set to punishment with regard to both the nature and extent of the guilt, and also the strength of spirit the wrongdoers possess? What ought each one to

suffer? What ought he to avoid, not just in case he doesn't progress, but even in case he regresses? Again, I don't know whether more people are reformed than slip into worse ways through fear of impending punishment (when they fear it coming from human beings, that is). What do we do when, as often happens, punishing someone will lead to his destruction, but leaving him unpunished will lead to someone else being destroyed? In all this I confess my sins and my ignorance every day.

When and how will I observe the words of scripture: *Condemn sinners before everyone that the rest will have fear* [1 Tim 5.20], and again: *Rebuke him between the two of you alone* [Mt 18.15]? Or *Do not judge anyone before time* [1 Cor 4.5]; and again: *Do not judge, lest you are judged* [Mt 7.1; Lk 6.37] (for here he does not add 'before time')? Or again: *Who are you to judge someone else's servant? He stands or falls to his own master. But he will stand. For God has the power to set him on his feet* [Rom 14.4]? These words confirm that he is speaking of those who are within; but again, Paul orders that they should in fact be judged, when he says: *What business is it of mine to judge those outside? Surely you judge those who are within. Therefore take the evil one from among you* [1 Cor 5.12–13].

Whenever it seems as if we must take this course, it inspires enormous concern and fear as to how far we should go, while avoiding the situation that Paul himself realises he must warn against in the second letter to the same congregation *that someone of this sort may not be engulfed by excessive sorrow* [2 Cor 2.7]. And again, in case anyone thinks this shouldn't be the object of great concern: *so that we are not possessed by Satan: for we are well aware of his intentions* [2 Cor 2.11].

How all this makes us tremble, my dear Paulinus, holy man of God! What trembling, what darkness! Surely we are to think that the following words apply here: *Trembling and fear have come upon me and darkness has covered me, and I said, 'Who will give me wings like a dove's?' Then I will fly away and be at rest. Behold, I have travelled far in my flight, and I have remained in the desert.* But perhaps he experienced this even in the desert, because he added: *I was awaiting him who would make me safe from weakness of spirit and from the storm* [Ps 55(54).5–8]. Yes, indeed, *human life on the earth is a time of testing* [Job 7.1].

(4) What then? Aren't we caressing the God-given discourses of the Lord instead of handling them – that is, while we are searching for what to believe in far more cases than we believe something fixed and definite? Moreover, although our cautiousness is full of anxiety, it's still far better than reckless assertion. Surely in many cases, if there's someone who

doesn't think according to the flesh (which the apostle describes as death) [cf. Rom 8.5–6], he will be a great stumbling-block for someone who still does think according to the flesh. For it will be very dangerous to say what you believe, very troublesome not to say it, and very harmful to say anything other than you believe.

Well then. As for the things which we do not approve in the speeches or writings of those who are within [the church] . . .⁴ We think it a part of the freedom of brotherly love not to conceal our judgement; it is a great sin against us to believe that we do this out of hatred rather than goodwill. Similarly, when we suspect that those who criticise our opinions wish to hurt us rather than reform us, we are sinning greatly against others. It is certain that hostility arises out of such situations even among very dear and intimate friends, as long as *one swells with conceit in favour of one against another, beyond what is written* [1 Cor 4.6]; and as long as they are *snapping and biting at each other* they must *fear being devoured completely by one another* [cf. Gal 5.15]. *Who* then *will give me wings like a dove's? Then I will fly away and be at rest* [Ps 55(54).6]. Perhaps it is because the dangers of which someone has experience weigh more heavily than those of which he's innocent – or perhaps it really is the way it seems – at any rate, a little weakness of spirit or a desert storm seems to me less troublesome than our sufferings and our fears in this crowded world of ours.

(5) That is why I much approve of your view that we should deal with the state of this life, or rather its course, not its state. I would further add that we should inquire into this and hold on to it before we inquire into the nature of the future, which is where the course of this life leads. That's why I asked you for your view, as one who already has a very safe grasp of and hold on the correct code for living this life; whereas I think that I struggle very dangerously in very many areas, and particularly in the points that I have mentioned as briefly as I could. However, all this sort of ignorance and inability seems to me to arise from the fact that we are in the middle of a great variety of characters and of spirits, among human beings who have deeply hidden wishes and weaknesses, and yet we are trying to engage in the affairs not of the earthly people of Rome, but the heavenly people of Jerusalem.

I was happier therefore to discuss with you on the basis of what we will be rather than of what we are. We do not indeed know what good things will be there; however, we are certain of one important fact, that there will not be any bad things there.

(6) As for the living of this temporary life in a manner that will allow us to reach eternal life, I understand that we must restrain our fleshly lusts and allow the physical senses only as much delight as suffices to sustain and live this life. I know that we should face all temporary hardships with forbearance and courage for the truth of God, and for our own eternal security and that of our neighbour. I know also that we should serve our neighbour with absolutely devoted love, with an eye to his living this life properly for the sake of everlasting life. We must also prefer spiritual things to fleshly, and unchangeable things to changeable; and human beings are able to do all this to a greater or lesser degree just as they are helped to a greater or lesser degree by the grace of God through Jesus Christ our Lord. I do not know why one person is helped or not helped in this way and another in that. I do know, however, that God acts with a fairness that is supreme and known to himself.

If, however, you have learnt anything else on the subject I have touched on above, how to live among human beings, please do instruct me. If these matters affect you as they do me, then discuss them with some other gentle doctor of the heart, whether you find one there where you are living, or when you go to Rome each year. Then please write and tell me what the Lord has revealed to you through such a person speaking to you, or when you converse with each other.

(7) You also asked me in turn for my view about our resurrected bodies and limbs with their condition of incorruptibility and immortality, and in their future roles. Listen to this briefly. If it is not sufficient, with God's help the discussion could be broadened. We must hold very firmly to the point that a true and unambiguous statement of holy scripture makes: these visible and earthly bodies, now described as *endowed with soul*, will be *endowed with spirit* [1 Cor 15.44] when the faithful and just are resurrected. Now we have no experience of what a spiritual body is like. I do not know how we could grasp or explain it. Certainly there will be no corruption there; therefore they will not then need the corruptible food that they now need. However, they will not be unable genuinely to consume it, but this will be through power rather than need. Otherwise the Lord would not have taken food after his resurrection [cf. Lk 24.30, 43; Jn 21.13]; here he provided us with a model of bodily resurrection, as the apostle says of this: *If the dead do not rise, then neither did Christ rise* [1 Cor 15.16]. He appeared with a complete set of limbs, and he employed them in their proper roles, and he showed the place where his wounds were [cf. Mt 28.9–10; Mk 16.9, 14–19; Lk 24.15–43; Jn 20.14–29]. I have always

understood this to mean scars rather than wounds themselves, and that it was power rather than necessity that explained them. He particularly showed the ease afforded by this power on the occasions when he revealed himself in a different form, or when he appeared, truly, to the disciples who were gathered in the house with the doors locked.

(8) Next there arises the question of whether angels possess bodies that suit their roles and their activities or whether they exist only as spirits. If we say they do have them, then this passage faces us: *He who makes his angels spirits* [Ps 104(103).4, LXX; cf. Heb 1.7]. However, if we say they don't have bodies, we have more difficulty in explaining the passages of scripture where angels present themselves to physical human senses (without a body), where they are welcomed with hospitality, where their feet are washed, and they are served with food and drink [cf., for example, Gen 18.2–9; 19.1–3; Mt 1.20–3; Lk 1.11–20, 26–38].

It might seem easier if angels are called 'spirits' in the way that human beings are called 'souls' (as when scripture says that so many souls went down with Jacob into Egypt [cf. Gen 46.27] – for they certainly had bodies!) rather than believing that all those actions were performed without bodies. Again, in the Book of Revelation an angel is defined as being of a specific height, using a measurement that is only possible for a body [cf. Rev 10.1–3]. Consequently, when they appear to human beings this should be attributed not to deception, but to the power and facility of spiritual bodies.

Now whether angels don't have bodies, or whether someone can show how they were able without bodies to do all those things, in either case, in the city of the saints those redeemed through Christ *from this generation into eternity* [Ps 12(11).7] will be joined with thousands of angels. Then indeed physical voices that no longer conceal the spirits will reveal that in that fellowship of God no thought can be hidden from one's neighbour. Rather, a peace harmonious in the praise of God will prevail, proclaimed not only through the spirit but also through spiritual bodies.

(9) That is how it seems to me at the moment. If you already know anything that fits the truth better, or manage to hear it from anyone more learned, then I eagerly await being informed by you. Read my letter again. I know you were made to reply very hastily because the deacon was in a hurry, and so I am not complaining. However, I do remind you so that you will make good what you left out then. Again, please do investigate and look at the question I was seeking to learn about from you: what you think about the leisure of a Christian, for the purpose of apprehending

and spreading Christian wisdom; and about your own leisure – as I thought it was – although I hear reports that you are amazingly busy.

Live happily, keeping us in mind, you who give us great joy and comfort, holy ones of God.[5]

Letters 136 and 138

Augustine replies here to some queries about pagan difficulties with Christianity, including the charge that Christians cannot be loyal citizens.

Letter 136

411/412

Marcellinus to his much revered father Augustine, whom he serves with unequalled devotedness.

(1) The illustrious Volusianus[1] read me the letter written to him by your blessed self.[2] Indeed, at my urging, he read it to several others; for, while everything that you say is truly admirable, my admiration for them was extreme. The grace of your divine discourse, inflated only by humility, deserved to win ready approval.

What pleased me most of all was your effort to support and strengthen the man's sometimes faltering footsteps, by encouraging him to adopt a worthwhile aim in life. For we argue with him daily, as far as our limited strength and feeble intelligence allow. I am moved by the entreaties of his saintly mother[3] to make it my concern to visit him frequently; and he indeed is good enough to return the compliment. When he received the letter from your revered self, he, a man seduced from a steadfast acceptance of the true faith by the persuasive tongues of the masses, who are plentiful in this city, was very impressed. So much so that (as he himself confirms) he would have conveyed to your blessed self every doubt that he entertains, if he weren't afraid of writing at inordinate length. However, he has requested you earnestly to solve certain of his difficulties, in a discussion quite polished and precise, and illuminated with the brilliance of Roman rhetoric, which you yourself will be happy to approve. The question he has raised is one that has been thoroughly exhausted, and we are very familiar with the cleverness with which the critics treat the dispensation of the Lord's incarnation.

However, I venture to add my entreaties to his, trusting that whatever reply you give will be useful to a number of people. We hope that you will be willing to give a careful reply to the passages where they falsely claim that the Lord's deeds were no greater than those which other men have managed to achieve. And here they might present us with their Apollonius and Apuleius and others skilled in magic, who, they argue, performed greater miracles.

(2) Furthermore, the illustrious man I have mentioned, when a few of us were present, raised many other problems that he might appropriately have added to this one, had not the brevity of his letter been one of his considerations.[4] But he could not restrain himself from speaking of the subjects he had not wanted to write about. Even if a reasoned account[5] of the Lord's incarnation were to be given to him today, he said, still it would hardly be possible to give a lucid account of God's rejection of the ancient sacrifices (for we insist that he is the God of the Old Testament) and of his delight in the new. Volusianus alleged that previous custom could only be corrected if it had been wrongly approved in the first place; or else, if it had once been correct, it ought to remain quite unchanged. He argued that correct behaviour could not be altered without injustice; in particular, God would be convicted of a foolish lack of consistency.[6]

Furthermore – and this is a common allegation – Christ's teaching and preaching must be incompatible with the ethics of citizenship.[7] For he told us – it is agreed – to *return to no one evil for evil* [Rom 12.17; 1 Thess 5.15], to *offer the other cheek to an assailant*, to *give our cloak to someone demanding a tunic*, and to *go twice the required distance* with someone who wants to requisition us [Mt 5.39–41]. He alleges that all these commands are contrary to the ethics of citizenship. Who would allow an enemy to steal something from him? Who would be unwilling to inflict evil, in the form of a just war, as recompense for the ravaging of a Roman province?[8] Your revered self will understand the kind of objection that could be raised against the other commands. Volusianus thinks that all these questions can be added to the previous one, especially because (though he himself does not mention this) it is obvious that under the Christian emperors the empire is in a very bad way, even though they have on the whole observed the Christian religion.

(3) Therefore, as your blessed self is willing to join with me in acknowledging, we need to reveal in all its splendour a detailed and laborious solution to all these problems. (The eagerly awaited reply from your holy self will without doubt be put into the hands of several people.) This is particularly true because a distinguished landowner and master from the region of Hippo[9] was here while all this was going on, and he was praising your holy self in flattering words, tinged with irony. He claimed that he himself had found little satisfaction when he asked about such matters. I have not forgotten your promise; indeed I insist upon it in begging you to provide written replies to these questions, replies that will be of exceptional value to the church, and especially at the present time.[10]

Letter 138

411/412

Augustine sends greeting in the Lord to the distinguished lord Marcellinus, his son, deservedly notable, beloved, and greatly missed.

(1) It was not proper to give our illustrious friend Volusianus, so eloquent and so dear to us, a reply that covered more than the questions he saw fit to raise. But as for the problems that you asked me in your letter to discuss and solve, whether it was Volusianus or others who laid them – or heaped them – upon you, it is to you that I ought to send such discussions or solutions as I can manage.[1] I shouldn't treat these questions laboriously as if in a book, but just adequately as one can do in the conversational style of a letter. Then, if you think it appropriate (for you know their state of mind through your daily debates) this letter may be read to others. But if my discourse is inadequate for ears that have not been well conditioned by a pious faith, let us first prepare a reply between ourselves that you consider adequate for them, and only then convey to them the fruit of our preparations. For in many cases they might eventually be persuaded, by a fuller or more subtle argument, or indeed by an appeal to an authority they think it improper to resist, of something that as yet their minds find abhorrent or repellent.

(2) And so to your letter. You said that some of them are disturbed by the question of 'God's rejection of the ancient sacrifices (for we insist that

he is the God of the Old Testament) and of his delight in the new. They alleged that previous custom could only be corrected if it had been wrongly approved in the first place; or else, if it had once been correct, it ought to remain quite unchanged. He argued that correct behaviour could not be altered without injustice.'[2]

I have taken this section of my letter verbatim from yours. If I wanted to reply at length, I would run out of time sooner than examples. For both the natural world and human activity are subject to change according to a system[3] fixed in accordance with appropriate seasons. However, the system that governs their changes is not subject to change itself. I shall mention just a few examples and allow them to arouse your attention so that you are alert to run through the many others like them. Doesn't summer follow winter, as the temperature gradually increases? Doesn't night turn into day? And look how often our time of life changes! Childhood yields to adolescence, never to return. Maturity follows adolescence, but it too will not last. Old age brings an end to maturity, and itself ends in death. These things all change, but the system of divine providence that governs their changes does not change.

If a farmer gives one order for summer and a different one for winter, it does not mean, it seems to me, that his system of agriculture has changed. Someone who rests at night may get up in the morning without altering his purpose in life. A teacher makes different demands of a child and of an adolescent. His teaching, though, is constant; it causes change as his instructions change, but remains unchanged itself.

(3) That great contemporary doctor Vindicianus was consulted by someone and he prescribed a remedy for a sickness that seemed suitable at that time. The man used it and was restored to health. A few years later his physical complaint flared up again. He decided to apply the same remedy. His health deteriorated further. He was surprised, and hurried back to the doctor to tell him what had happened. Vindicianus, a very clever man, replied, 'The reason that you are responding badly to this is that I did not prescribe it.' As a result, all those listeners who did not know him well thought that he didn't rely on his medical skill but on some forbidden powers.[4] Later on,[5] when some of those who had been amazed by him questioned him, he explained to them what they hadn't understood: he would not have prescribed that remedy for a man of that age. A remedy is only effective if it alters in accordance with different ages following a system of expertise that does not change.

(4) The claim that what was once correct action can never be altered is, therefore, untrue. Rather, when the circumstances of time have altered, true reason normally demands that actions that were previously correct now be altered. Consequently while they argue that an action can't be correct if it is altered, truth, by contrast, proclaims that the action will only be correct if it changes; each action will be correct precisely when it is adapted to each different period of time. The same may hold of different persons during the same period. Thus, 'He's allowed to do this without trouble, but he isn't. It's not what they do that's different, it's who's doing it.'[6]

Similarly, at different times one and the same person might have to do something now, but not now. It's not who is doing it that changes, but when he does it.

(5) Anyone who attends competently and carefully to those contrasts between the beautiful and the appropriate[7] which are found scattered all over the universe, as it were, will immediately see how far all this extends. The beautiful is assessed by itself and praised; its opposite is the shameful or misshapen. The appropriate, on the other hand, the opposite of which is the inappropriate, depends on something else as if it were tied to it. It isn't judged in itself, but with reference to the thing to which it's linked. The same is certainly true of 'fitting' and 'unfitting', or so it is thought.[8]

Come then, refer the actions under discussion to their source. Sacrifice was appropriate in primitive times because God had commanded it. Now that is not the case. For God has commanded something else, appropriate for the present period; and he understands far better than the human race what is most suitable to provide for each age, what and when he – the unchanging Creator, the unchanging governor of the changing world – should grant something or add something, take it away, remove it, increase it or diminish it. Then, finally, the beauty of the entire temporal universe, with its individual parts each appropriate to its time, will flow like a great song by some indescribably great composer; and those who worship God as they should even now, in this age of faith, will cross from there for ever to contemplating beauty.

(6) It is a mistake, therefore, to think that God gives such orders for his own benefit or pleasure. It is indeed right to be troubled by the idea that God could have ordered different offerings to be made to him in earlier and later periods, changing them to satisfy his own fickle fancy. This is false. God's orders never benefit himself, but rather their recipient. A

master is truly a master if he does not need his servants, but they need him. Indeed in those scriptures called the Old Testament, in the very period when those sacrifices that have now ceased were still being offered, these words are found: *I said to the Lord, 'You are my Lord, because you do not need my goods'* [Ps 16(15).2, LXX].

God, then, did not need their sacrifices, and is never in need of anything. However, certain actions function as signs of God-given gifts, whether they fill the soul with virtues, or secure everlasting salvation. When we celebrate and perform these, we are discharging duties of devotion that benefit not God, but ourselves.

(7) Now it would take too long properly to discuss the various different symbols that are called sacraments because they relate to matters divine.[9] It does not mean that God is changeable because he required a different offering in the morning from the evening or in one month from another, or in one year from another. Similarly, it does not mean that God is changeable if he required a different offering in the earlier stages of the unfolding of the world's history from the later; not if this enables him to arrange these as symbols of the life-giving teachings of our religion throughout the changing periods, without himself changing in any way. When people are disturbed by this, we must help them understand that it depends upon God's reason; new customs are not introduced because the old suddenly become distasteful, as if God's will is fickle. No, what is determined and what is established depends upon God's own wisdom. As scripture says of him, discussing even greater changes: *you will change them and they will be changed, but you yourself are always the same* [Ps 102(101).26–7].

We must help them understand this by showing them that the exchange of the sacraments of the Old Testament for those of the New was also predicted by the voices of the prophets. Then they will see, if they are capable of it, that whatever is new in time is not new for God, who established time, and who, while existing outside of time, contains all things, and assigns them to their respective times, corresponding to their differences.

Earlier I quoted a psalm to show that God does not need our sacrifices (for he was addressed in the words: *I said to the Lord, 'You are my Lord, because you do not need my goods'*). A little later in the same psalm, these words are given to the figure of Christ: *I will not gather their assemblies of blood* [Ps 16(15).4, LXX]; that is, of animal victims, which were used before to gather the Jews in their assemblies. Elsewhere we read: *I will not accept bullocks from your house, nor goats from your flocks* [Ps 50(49).9]. Another prophet says: '*Behold, the days will come*', says the Lord, '*when I will affirm a new covenant over the house of Jacob, not like that covenant that I granted to their fathers when I led them out of the land of Egypt*' [Jer 31.31–2]. There are many further testimonies that foretell this action of God's, but it would take too long to mention them all now.

(8) May we, then, consider the following as sufficiently established: that something that was properly decreed at one time might properly be altered at another, there being a change in the work, but not in the overall ordering of the person who brings about the change? (For the ordering is contained by intelligible reason; and here two things that cannot be simultaneous within time – for they occur at a different time – can be so outside of time.)

But still, an objector might expect us to provide an explanation of this change. You yourself know what an extended business that would be. We can, however, say something briefly that should perhaps satisfy a clever person. It was right that Christ should be heralded before he arrived by different symbols from those that announced him once he had arrived. Similarly, changing circumstances force us to use different words to say the same thing, if indeed 'herald' is different from 'announce', and 'before he arrived' from 'once he had arrived'.

(9) Let's now look at the next section of your letter. You added this objection of theirs:

> Christ's teaching and preaching must be incompatible with the ethics of citizenship. For he told us – it is agreed – to *return to no one evil for evil* [Rom 12.17; 1 Thess 5.15], to *offer the other cheek to an assailant*, to *give our cloak to someone demanding a tunic*, and to *go twice the required distance with someone who wants to requisition us* [Mt 5.39–41]. They allege that all these commands are contrary to the ethics of citizenship. 'Who would allow an enemy to steal something from him?' they say. 'Who would be unwilling to inflict evil, in the form of a just war, as recompense for the ravaging of a Roman province?'[10]

It might have been laborious to refute such objections (or such suggestions, perhaps, if they are put forward in a spirit of enquiry rather than criticism), if I were not debating these matters with men who possess a liberal education. Need I, then, toil at length over this when I could simply enquire of them how it was possible for the commonwealth to be governed and grow, for a small and poor city to be transformed into a great and wealthy one[11] by men who 'preferred to pardon those who wronged them than to pursue them'.[12] Take Caesar, a ruler of the commonwealth if ever there was one. Cicero heaped praise upon his character, saying that he 'used to forget nothing except the wrongs he received'.[13] Cicero spoke words of high praise, or perhaps of high flattery. If it was praise, then he recognised that Caesar was really like this; if it was flattery, though, his misleading declaration revealed what the leader of a city ought in fact to be like. For what is it 'not to *return evil for evil*' [Rom 12.17; 1 Thess 5.15] except to shrink from a passion for revenge, that is to prefer to pardon those who wrong you than to pursue them, and to forget nothing except the wrongs you receive?

(10) When they read such sentences in their own authors, they greet them with noisy applause. They see them describing and praising a type of character there that might give rise to a city worthy of ruling so many nations, in that 'they preferred to pardon those who wronged them rather than to pursue them'.

However, when they read the divinely authorised command not to *return evil for evil* [Rom 12.17; 1 Thess 5.15], when this precept, which is so beneficial, echoes from our pulpits around our congregations, as if they were at public lectures, open to both sexes and to every age-group or rank – then they charge our faith with hostility to the commonwealth. If we gave ear to this precept as it deserves, it would establish, consecrate, strengthen and increase the commonwealth far better than Romulus, Numa, Brutus and the other famous heroes of the Roman nation.

For what is 'commonwealth' other than the property of the people? Therefore it is shared property, the property precisely of the citizen body. And what is a city but a group of men united by a specific bond of peace? They can read in their authors that 'soon a varied and confused crowd was transformed, through peace, into a city'.[14] More to the point, have they ever decided to read aloud commandments to peace in their temples? Poor wretches – they were forced to ask how to worship their own gods, who were quarrelling among themselves, without giving offence to any one of them. If they wished to imitate their quarrelling gods they would undermine the city by shattering its bond of peace. Indeed this began to happen soon after in the civil wars, when their morals became depraved and corrupt.

(11) But is there anyone, even anyone unfamiliar with our faith, who is so deaf that he hasn't noticed how regularly we read out exhortations to peace in the churches of Christ? These haven't been discovered in human debate;

they were framed by divine authority.[15] Included in them are the commands that our critics prefer to criticise than to learn from, such as *offer the other cheek to an assailant* or *give our cloak also to someone demanding a tunic* or *go twice the required distance with someone who wants to requisition us* [Mt 5.39–41]. The result of such actions is that good overcomes someone evil [cf. Rom 12.21]; indeed the evil within an evil man is overcome by good, and so he is freed from an evil that wasn't external or foreign, but intimately his own.[16] That could ruin him more thoroughly and more destructively than any attack, however appalling, by an external enemy.

In overcoming an evil person through goodness, then, we patiently accept the loss of temporary benefits in order to show him how worthless we should consider them by comparison with faith and justice; after all, excessive love of such benefits makes him evil. In this way the wrongdoer might learn from the very person he's wronged what the things are really like that tempted him to do wrong. Then too he might repent and be won back to peace – the most beneficial thing there is for a city – not defeated by force and violence, but by patient goodwill. If something is done with the aim of helping someone to mend his ways and to embrace peace, then it's right to do it so long as it seems as if it will benefit him. And that must certainly be the intention, even if the result turns out differently, that is to say, if the patient, having medicine prescribed that ought to reform him and pacify him, to cure and heal him, as it were, is in fact unwilling to be reformed and pacified.

(12) In any event, if we attend closely to the wording, and think we should obey its precise meaning, we wouldn't turn our *right* cheek, if the *left* was struck. What he said exactly was: *'If anyone has struck you on the right cheek, turn the left to him.'* However, it's more usual for the left cheek to be struck, as it's easier for someone to hit it with his right hand. But the usual interpretation of these words is as follows: if anyone has attacked something more valuable of yours, offer him something less valuable. Otherwise, you risk making vengeance rather than patience your goal, and caring little for what is eternal by comparison with what is temporary. (Of course you should care little for the temporary by comparison with the eternal, as for left by comparison with right.)

This was always the aim of the holy martyrs. For vengeance can only be demanded justly at the end, when there is no more opportunity for reform, that is at the last and ultimate judgement. But here and now, we must be alert in case in our desire for vengeance we lose our forbearance – to mention nothing else[17] – which should be deemed more valuable than anything that an enemy can take from us, even against our will.

36

The other evangelist doesn't mention the right cheek when he reports this saying. He talks only of *one cheek* and *the other* [Lk 6.29]. Thus the other gospel gives scope for a more precise interpretation, but he recommends the same forbearance in a simpler way. Consequently someone just and pious ought to be prepared to endure the hostility of others patiently, while seeking to make them good. Then the ranks of the good may grow, instead of the ranks of the bad being swollen through his responding to them with similar hostility.[18]

(13) Finally, these instructions are more relevant to the training of the heart within than to our external activity. Consequently forbearance and benevolence should be kept secretly in one's own mind, while publicly we should do whatever seems likely to benefit those we should wish well. This is clearly shown by Christ, our outstanding example of forbearance. His response to being struck in the face was: *'If I have said something wrong, then reproach me for the wrong. If I have spoken well, why do you strike me?'* [Jn 18.23].

He failed to fulfil his own instruction, if we take it literally; for he didn't offer his other side to his assailant. Rather, he prevented the person who had injured him from increasing the injury. At the same time, he was prepared to accept not just blows in the face, but even death by crucifixion for the sake of people at whose hands he was suffering. For their sake, while hanging on the cross, he spoke these words: *'Father, forgive them, for they do not know what they are doing'* [Lk 23.34].

Again, it seems that the apostle Paul fulfilled the command of his lord and master when he was struck in the face and said to the chief priest: *'God will strike you, whitewashed wall! You are sitting to judge me according to the law, and yet you order me to be struck in contravention of the law.'* Those standing nearby said to him: *'You are committing an offence against the chief priest.'*

Paul chose to warn them of what he meant by mocking them, so that those who were wise enough might understand that the 'whitewashed wall', that is the hypocrisy of the Jewish priesthood, had now been destroyed by the coming of Christ. And so he replied: *'I did not know, my brothers, that he was the chief priest. For scripture says, "You shall not revile a leader of your people"'* [Acts 23.3–5; cf. Exod 22.28].

It is quite certain that Paul, who had grown up among this community and had been instructed there in law, could not have been unaware of the identity of the chief priest, and that those who knew Paul so well could not have been misled as to his ignorance.

(14) In short, we should always hold fast to the precepts of forbearance *in the disposition of our hearts* [cf. Ps 10.17, LXX]; and in our will we should always have perfect benevolence in case we *return evil for evil* [Rom 12.17; 1 Thess 5.15]. For people are often to be helped, against their will, by being punished with a sort of kind harshness. It is right to consult their interests rather than their preferences; indeed, in their literature we find lavish praise of a leading citizen for just this.[19] For example, a father doesn't lose his love for his son as soon as he tells him off, however harshly. However, it still happens that the son doesn't like it and is hurt, if he seems to need a cure that's painful, even against his will.

If the earthly commonwealth observes Christian precepts in this way, then even wars will be waged in a spirit of benevolence; their aim will be to serve the defeated more easily by securing a peaceful society that is pious and just. For if defeat deprives the beaten side of the freedom to act wickedly, it benefits them. Nothing, in fact, is less fortunate than the good fortune of sinners; the impunity that is their punishment is nourished on this, and the ill-will that is their inner enemy grows strong. But the hearts of mortals, perverse and contrary as they are, think that human life is happy if they can see rooftops shining splendidly – while they don't see that their minds are stained with sin; if massive theatres are being constructed – while the foundations of the virtues are being undermined; if crazy extravagance is a cause for boasting – while the works of mercy win mockery; if actors live in luxury at the expense of the very rich – while the poor can scarcely find what they need to live; if God, who cries out against such public evil through public declarations of his teaching, is blasphemed by impious communities – while they demand the sorts of gods who can be honoured by theatrical celebrations that bring shame upon mind and body.

If God allows that sort of thing to flourish, it shows that he is seriously displeased. By letting it go unpunished he inflicts a more savage punishment. But when he overthrows such aids to vice, and reduces their pampered passions to poverty, then his opposition is merciful. For the good would even wage war with mercy, were it possible, with the aim of taming unrestrained passions and destroying vices that ought, under a just rule, to be uprooted or suppressed.

(15) If Christian teaching condemned all warfare, then the soldiers in the gospel who were seeking guidance about their security would have been told to throw away their weapons and withdraw entirely from the army. But what was said to them was: *'Do not intimidate anyone; do not*

bring false charges against anyone; be satisfied with your wages' [Lk 3.14].
He instructed them to be satisfied with their due wages, but he didn't
prohibit military service in general.

So let those who say that the teaching of Christ is opposed to the commonwealth give us an army composed of the sort of soldiers that the
teaching of Christ would require. Let them give us provincials, husbands
and wives, parents and children, masters and servants, kings, judges, and
finally even tax-payers and tax-collectors, of the sort that the teaching of
Christ demands. Then let them dare to say that this teaching is opposed
to the commonwealth! Indeed let them even hesitate to admit that, if it
were observed, it would contribute greatly to the security of the commonwealth![20]

(16) What am I to reply to the charge that the Roman empire is in a very
bad way because of certain Christian emperors? This sweeping complaint
is slanderous! If they mentioned any clear and definite charges against
past emperors, I myself would have been able to mention similar, and possibly more serious, charges against non-Christian emperors. Then they
would realise that the faults lie not in the teaching, but in the men, or
perhaps not in the emperors, but in other men; for emperors can do
nothing without others. The moment that the decline of the Roman commonwealth began is clear enough. Their own literature tells of it.[21] Long
before the name of Christ shone out on earth, someone had said, 'O venal
city, ripe for destruction, if only it finds a buyer.'[22]

The same distinguished historian in his book about the Catilinarian
war (which was undoubtedly before the coming of Christ) did not fail to
mention the time when 'the army of the Roman people first began to
grow used to love and drink; to admiring sculptures, paintings and
engraved vases, to stealing them from private and public places, to
robbing temples, and in short to polluting everything sacred and
profane'.[23] These corrupt and dissolute characters in their greed and
their rapacity didn't spare either human beings or even those they
believed to be gods. That is when the acclaimed security and renown of
the commonwealth first began to be destroyed. It would take too long
now to describe the success of the worst vices, and the great cost to the
human race of the flourishing of such wickedness. They need only listen
to the truthful chattering of their own satirist:

> At one time, Latin womenfolk would be kept pure
> By humble fortune; and to stop vice tainting their small
> Abodes they had work, slumber brief, and hardened hands

Fretted with Tuscan fleece, and Hannibal beside
The city, and husbands standing on the Colline tower.
We suffer now the sores of long peace. Crueller than arms
Luxury has set in, avenging the conquered globe.
Not one crime has been wanting or one act of lust
Since Roman poverty expired.[24]

Do you expect me to exaggerate the evils introduced by wickedness with the assistance of good fortune? Why, even those who have examined events with a little more caution have realised that they should grieve more at the loss of Roman poverty than Roman wealth. For when they were poor, the Romans preserved their characters uncorrupted; but once they were wealthy, they allowed a terrible depravity, something worse than any enemy, to breach not the city walls, but the very minds of the citizens.

(17) Thanks be to God, who has sent us exceptional assistance against such evils. But for the cross of Christ, where would the dreadful torrent of humanity's wickedness have carried us? Would anyone have escaped its waves? How deeply would we have been submerged? But the cross was established, like a massive embankment of authority, high and strong. By grasping this solid support, we could steady ourselves, and avoid being snatched away and engulfed by the immense whirlpool of persuasion, of compulsion to evil, that this world contains.

It is in this cesspool of evil characters, where the ancient ethos has been abandoned, that the presence and assistance of heavenly authority is most needed. This exhorts us to voluntary poverty, to restraint, to benevolence, justice and peace, and to true piety, and to other splendid and powerful virtues. It doesn't do this only for the sake of living this life honourably, or only to provide a peaceful community for the earthly city. It does so also to win everlasting security for the heavenly and divine commonwealth of a people that will live for ever. Faith, hope and charity make us adopted citizens of this city, so that as long as we are on our pilgrimage, if we are unable to reform them, we should tolerate those who want the commonwealth to remain with its vices unpunished.

The first Romans indeed used their virtues to establish and enlarge the commonwealth, even if they failed to show the sort of true piety for the true God that could, through its saving religion, also lead them to the eternal city. However, they still protected their own sort of integrity, which was adequate for establishing, enlarging and preserving their earthly city.[25] For God revealed in the wealth and fame of the Roman empire how powerful are civic virtues even without true religion; to make it clear that with the addition of this human beings become citizens of the other city, whose king is truth, whose law is love, and whose limit is eternity.

(18) Doesn't it seem ridiculous that they seek to compare Apollonius and Apuleius[26] and other men skilled in the art of magic with Christ, and even to prefer them to him? However, we should put up with this comparison as more tolerable than their comparison of their own gods with Christ. We must admit that Apollonius was a finer man than Jupiter – as they call him – who initiated or committed countless acts of debauchery. They reply that all that is the stuff of myth. So let them continue to praise, in all its luxury, licence and manifest idolatry, the good fortune of the commonwealth that invented these divine scandals – and then not only allowed them to be listened to as stories, but even presented them for viewing in the theatres. Here the crimes outnumbered the divinities; and the gods were happy to have them displayed in their own honour, when they ought to have punished their worshippers for watching them with tolerance, if nothing more.

'But', they object, 'it isn't really the gods who are being celebrated in these deceitful myths.' Who is it, then, that their shameful celebrations aim to pacify? Because Christian teaching has exposed the perverse lies of the demons[27] who exploit the art of magic to lead human minds astray, because it has revealed this to the whole world, because it has shown the difference between their malice and the holy angels, because it has told us to be on our guard against them, and told us how to do this – because of all this Christian teaching is said to be hostile to the commonwealth. But in fact, any misfortune whatever would be preferable to temporary good fortune won at all by those means. And God didn't want us to be in doubt on this point: the first people to worship the one true God and to condemn the false gods he honoured with great good fortune on earth, for as long as the Old Testament, which contains the veil of the New, remained in its own shadow. This was so that people might understand that good fortune doesn't depend on the power of the demons, but on God, whom the angels serve and *before whom the demons tremble* [Jas 2.19].

(19) Let me speak primarily of Apuleius, for he is better known to us, as an African among Africans.[28] He was a man born to an honourable rank in his country, provided with a liberal education, and blessed with great eloquence. However, for all his magic arts he was unable to win a position as a

judge, let alone as a ruler. Perhaps, one might suggest, being a philosopher he voluntarily took no interest in such matters? But as the priest of a province[29] he was grand enough to provide entertainments, to dress up hunters, and to go to law over a statue that he wanted to place at Oea[30] (the city his wife came from) in opposition to several of the citizens. In case it were lost to posterity, he entrusted to future memory the script of the speech he delivered during the case.[31]

As far as earthly fortune goes, then, our magician was as successful as he was able. It seems then that he was never very important not because he didn't want to be, but because he couldn't be. However, he did defend himself with great eloquence against certain enemies of his who had brought a charge of magical practices against him.[32] That's why I am surprised that his admirers seem to want to act as witnesses against him by declaring that he used such arts to perform some great miracles or other. They should first examine whether the testimony they offer is true, and his defence is false. Indeed, this should be given close attention by anyone – if they've any sense – who pursues the art of magic (with no aim except earthly good fortune or, perhaps, reprehensible curiosity), or even anyone who's innocent of it, but still praises magic and admires it dangerously. They should also notice that our own David achieved royal rank from his position as a shepherd without employing any such techniques. Scripture faithfully tells us about his sins and his worthy deeds, so that we may learn both how to avoid offending God and how to placate him if we do offend him.

(20) Finally, what about the miracles that are produced to astonish the human mind? It's a great mistake to compare magicians with the holy prophets, whose great and glorious miracles far surpass their own. But how much greater a mistake to compare them to Christ! The prophets, who are incomparably greater than the magicians, foretold his coming both according to the flesh that he took from the Virgin, and according to the divinity that unites him continuously to the Father.

I see that my letter has become very long, and even then I have not said everything about Christ that could satisfy objectors, whether[33] it is their limited intelligence that makes theological matters difficult for them, or whether they are prevented from understanding despite their sharp minds by a delight in arguing, or because they have been possessed by error for some time. Take note, however, of anything that influences them to the contrary, and write back to me. Then I can make an effort to respond to every point, with God's help, whether in a letter or a treatise.

May you be happy in the Lord, through his grace and mercy, my distinguished and deservedly notable lord, my beloved son who is greatly missed.

Letter 10*

428

Memorandum from Augustine to his holy brother Alypius

(1) Our holy brothers and fellow bishops told me in a letter, while they were on their way back (I have not seen them), that if I wished to write to your holy self, I should send the letter to Carthage. I have therefore dictated these few words to greet you. My eagerness to see you in the very near future, my brother, has been reinforced by the hope for your return, indicated in your letter. I have already replied to you to say that the books by Julian and Celestius[1] have reached me, which you sent together with your memorandum with our son the deacon Commilito. I said too that I was very surprised that you had not bothered to report to me anything about the disciplining of Turbantius, the dedicatee of Julian's four books. I have heard from someone whose word I cannot doubt that he confessed humbly enough, condemned the heresy in question, and was received back into the peace of the Catholic church by Pope Celestine. But I ought to have guessed that you just forgot to mention this when you were writing to me.

I have already written all this once, but I wanted to mention it again now in case, by chance, your holy self receives this reply before the one that I wrote first. In the meantime, I found among some papers of my own a copy of a memorandum that you wrote to yourself when you were sent to the court the first time from the council. Having read it through I saw that it contained quite a few necessary jobs that you were not able to complete then; I thought I should send it to you (removing certain things that either have been done or do not seem very urgent) just in case they can be done now.

(2) There is something else to add: there is in Africa an enormous crowd of what are commonly called *mangones* [slave traders]. There are so many of them that they are draining the province of its human population on a huge scale by purchasing people and transporting them to provinces

overseas. Almost all of those purchased are free persons; a mere handful can be found who were sold by their parents.[2] Even these, however, they do not buy on the conditions allowed under Roman law, which are that they should give their labour for twenty-five years.[3] Rather, they buy them outright as slaves and sell them overseas as slaves. It is extremely rare for them to buy real slaves from their masters. And now this mob of merchants has spawned a mob of abductors and pillagers; these have the effrontery – so it is reported – to roam in gangs through regions that are wild, remote and sparsely populated, howling, and dressed in terrifying garb like soldiers or barbarians; and they carry off people by force to sell them to those merchants.

(3) I pass over the rumour that was recently reported to us of the men on a small farmstead being killed during one of these attacks so that the women and children could be stolen and sold. We were not told where this happened if it did really happen. However, I myself asked one girl how she had come to be sold to the slave-traders. (She was among those freed by the efforts of our own church from this pitiful state of captivity.) She replied that she had been snatched from her parents' house. I went on to ask whether the kidnappers had found her there on her own; she replied that they had done it when her parents and brothers were actually there. In fact, the brother who had come to fetch her was there too, and he explained to us – as she was quite small – how they had done it. He said that some of these bandits broke in at night. The family thought that they were barbarians, and hid themselves as best they could rather than daring to show them any resistance.

But if the merchants did not exist, these things would not be happening. I am quite sure that there must also be rumours there where you are, of this evil that has befallen Africa. It was incomparably much less extensive at the time when the emperor Honorius provided the prefect Hadrian with a law that checked this sort of trade.[4] He decreed that businessmen indulging in such impious practices should be beaten with whips tipped with lead, proscribed,[5] and sent into permanent exile. Honorius does not mention in this law those who buy free individuals who have been abducted and stolen (which is what these people almost always do); he deals rather in general with anyone transporting a group of slaves to an overseas province. Thus he ordered that the slaves in question should be claimed by[6] and become the property of the treasury, something that would certainly not be said of those who are free.

(4) I have enclosed this law along with my memorandum, even though

it may be easy enough to find it at Rome. It is useful; and it could provide a remedy for this plague. However, we have begun to exploit it only to the extent necessary to get people freed; but not in order to inflict its penalties on the merchants who are the cause of so many dreadful outrages being perpetrated. We are using the law to frighten those we can, but not to punish them. In fact, we are afraid in case others haul up the men we caught to face the penalty that this law prescribes – even though they are abominable and deserve every condemnation. I am writing this therefore to your blessed self in the hope that, if it is possible, our most pious and Christian emperors will decide that when prisoners are liberated from these men, through the efforts of the church, the culprits should not face the risk of the punishment defined by this law, and in particular beating with leaden whips, which can easily lead to the victim's death.[7] At the same time, it may be necessary to promulgate this law publicly in order to check them. Otherwise, if we hold our hand because we are afraid of all that, some free people, poor wretches, will be exported into permanent slavery. If we do nothing for them, it will not be at all easy to find any coastal authority who, as a Christian or as a human being, will take pity on any of them, whether by putting the poor wretches off the ship or by refusing to let them on – instead of accepting payment for providing them with so cruel a crossing.[8]

(5) Whichever authority or office has responsibility for this law, or for any other passed concerning this question, it is their job to ensure that it can be enforced.[9] Otherwise Africa will be even more completely emptied of its native inhabitants; and this vast crowd of people, male and female alike, whole groups and gangs of them in a continuous flood, will lose their personal freedom to a fate worse than barbarian captivity. Indeed, a great many captives have been ransomed from the barbarians; but once these people have been taken to provinces overseas they will not find assistance by way of ransom. Again, when the Roman army is fighting efficiently and successfully, the barbarians meet with resistance, to stop Romans being taken into foreign captivity. But who will resist these businessmen, who trade not in animals, but human beings, not in some barbarian tribe, but in Roman provincials? Since they are scattered all over the place, they can take captives from anywhere and everywhere, some forcibly abducted and some deceived by trickery, into the hands of anyone promising the price. Who will resist them, for the sake of Roman liberty, and I mean liberty not in the communal, but in the personal, sense?

(6) No, no one can tell you precisely the number of people who have succumbed to this wicked form of commerce, blinded to an astonishing extent by greed, or infected in some other way by this plague. Who could believe that we have found a woman here among us in Hippo who used to entice the women of Giddaba[10] on the pretext of buying wood, and then lock them up, beat them and sell them? Who could believe that a perfectly satisfactory tenant of our church actually sold his wife, the mother of his children? She had not even given him cause for offence; he was simply spurred by the fever of this plague. Again, a sensible young man of about twenty, a bookkeeper and clerk from our monastery, was abducted and sold. We managed to free him with great difficulty through the efforts of the church.

(7) Even the examples of this outrage that I personally have encountered are too many for me to list, if I wished to do so. Let me give you just one example, and you can estimate from it the total extent of their activity throughout Africa and along its coasts. About four months before I wrote this letter, a crowd of people collected from different regions, but particularly from Numidia, were brought here by Galatian merchants to be transported from the shores of Hippo. (It is only, or at least mainly, the Galatians who are so eager to engage in this form of commerce.) However, a faithful Christian was at hand, who was aware of our practice of performing acts of mercy in such cases;[11] and he brought the news to the church. Immediately, about 120 people were set free by us (though I was absent at the time), some from the ship which they had had to board, others from a place where they had been hidden before being put on board. We discovered that barely five or six of these had been sold by their parents. On hearing about the various misfortunes that had led the rest of them to the Galatians, via their abductors and kidnappers, hardly one of us could restrain his tears.

(8) It is now up to your holy and wise self to consider the extent to which the export of these wretched souls must be raging along other parts of the coast, if the Galatians exhibit such burning greed, such appalling nerve, even at Hippo Regius; for here, through the mercy of God, the church has kept a fairly watchful guard and succeeded in freeing some of these wretched people from this captivity; and also here the businessmen who engage in this commerce are punished, much less severely than this law prescribes, but at least by the loss of their profits. I beseech your loving self through Christian love, please may I not have written this to you in vain.

For the Galatians are not without patrons;[12] they are using them to demand back from us the people liberated by the Lord through his church, even when they have been returned to their families, who were already hunting for them and coming to me for the purpose, armed with letters from their bishops. Some of our children in the faith have been entrusted with the care of some of those rescued, who are staying with them, as the church does not have the capacity to feed all those liberated. The Galatians are beginning to harass them too, even as I dictate these words, despite the fact that a letter has arrived from an authority that they could be afraid of.[13] Nor have they abandoned their demands for restitution.

(9) In the love of Christ I return the greetings they have earned[14] to everyone who was kind enough to send me greetings in the letter from your reverend self. My fellow-servants who are with me join me in greeting your holy self.

Letters 250 and 1*

The following two letters both concern the same incident: Classicianus has been accused of forcing an asylum-seeker to leave a church, and has been excommunicated by his bishop. Augustine writes here to both Classicianus and the bishop.

Letter 250

412 or 427–30

Augustine greets in the Lord his dearest lord, revered brother and fellow-priest, Auxilius

(1) Our son, the *comes* Classicianus, a man ranked as 'admirable',[1] has made a serious complaint to me in a letter that he has suffered an unjust excommunication at the hands of your holy self. He relates that he came to the church accompanied by the small escort appropriate to his office, and that he requested you not to show favour, to the detriment of his own security, to men who swore falsely on the gospel, and then sought assistance in breaking faith in the house of faith itself.[2] However, he says that

47

they went on to reflect on the wrong they had done and did not need to be dragged forcibly out of the church, but left of their own accord.[3] Then your reverend self became so angry with him that you made an entry in the ecclesiastical records and struck him and his entire household with a sentence of excommunication.[4] When I had read his letter, I was more than a little perturbed. My heart was in turmoil and my thoughts tossed this way and that. I could not fail to say something to your beloved self. If you have a considered opinion on this matter, based on sure reasoning or the evidence of scripture,[5] then please be good enough to teach me too: how might it be right to excommunicate a son for his father's sin, or a wife for her husband's, or a slave for his master's – or someone not even yet born in the house, who may then be born while the whole house is bound by excommunication, and will be deprived of help from the washing of rebirth, even if he is in danger of death?[6]

For this is not a physical punishment; we read that certain men who despised God had all their families killed along with them, even though they did not share in their impious acts. But their mortal bodies, which would in any case one day die, perished for this purpose: to frighten the living. However, spiritual punishment, which leads to the words of scripture, *Whatever you bind on earth will be bound also in heaven* [Mt 18.18; cf. Mt 16.19] binds the soul. Here the following words apply: *The soul of the father is mine, and the soul of the son is mine. The soul which sinned will itself die* [Ezek 18.4].

(2) Perhaps you have cases of bishops whose names are important and who have excommunicated some sinner along with his entire household. However, if they were questioned, they might be found capable of giving an account of this. I, on the other hand, cannot find any reply to make to anyone who asks me whether it is right to act in this way. Therefore I have never dared to do this, seriously disturbed though I am when anyone perpetrates an appalling crime against the church. Perhaps, however, the Lord has revealed to you how this may be done justly. If so, I will not in the least look down on your youthfulness and your inexperience in ecclesiastical office.

Look, I am here: an old man, and a bishop of many years' standing, ready to learn this from a youngster and colleague of less than a year: how if we punish innocent souls with a spiritual penalty on account of another person's outrageous act, we may render a just account to God and to human beings. For they do not inherit such an act in the way that they can inherit original sin from Adam *in whom everyone has sinned* [Rom 5.12].[7]

Now the son of Classicianus may indeed have inherited from his father the liability of the first man, which must be expiated in the holy fountain of baptism. Yet surely everyone will agree that any sin his father has committed after begetting him does not affect him, when he himself had no part in it. What am I to say of his wife? What of the many souls in his whole household? What if a single soul were to perish by dying in the body without baptism, because of the harsh ruling that has excommunicated the entire household? What if countless innocent men were dragged violently from the church and executed? Even then their bodily deaths could not be compared with this loss. Therefore if you are able to give an account of this, please write back and provide it for me as well; then I too will be able to do the same. However, if you cannot, why are you acting in this thoughtless, emotional way? That is, if not capable of producing a correct explanation when you are questioned about the matter.

(3) I say all this to you if it is the case that our son Classicianus has committed an offence that could in all justice appear to you to deserve the punishment of excommunication. However, if the letter he sent to me was true,[8] not even he, alone of his household, ought to be bound by such a sentence. My purpose in discussing this matter with your holy self, though, is only this: to beg you to forgive him when he begs for your pardon, if he acknowledges that he has sinned. But you may, wisely, acknowledge that he has not sinned, on the grounds that he was quite just in demanding in the house of faith that faith should be kept. (For otherwise it would be broken in the very place that it is taught.) If so, then act as a holy man ought. Then if this matter touches you as a man – and the man of God everywhere in the Psalms says: *My eye is perturbed because of anger* [Ps 6.8] – may you cry out to God, *Have mercy on me Lord, because I am weak* [Ps 6.3]. Then he may stretch his right hand over you and restrain your anger and calm your mind so that you see and do what is just. As scripture says, *The anger of a man does not affect the justice of God* [Jas 1.20].

Nor should you think that we cannot be infiltrated by unjust emotions just because we are bishops. Rather, we should reflect that we live in great danger amid the traps of temptation just because we are human beings.

Remove the ecclesiastical records that you made when you were perhaps rather upset. Let love be restored between you; after all you shared this with him even as a catechumen. Get rid of your quarrel and summon back peace; for otherwise a man who is a friend will be lost to you, while the devil, an enemy, will rejoice over you both. However, the

49

mercy of God is powerful; may he hear me as I pray. Then instead of my sorrow over you both increasing, the wound that has been opened may be healed. May he by his grace direct you and make you joyful in your youth, yet not scornful of my old age. Farewell.

Letter 1*

412 or 427–30

Augustine greets in the Lord his notable and most excellent and dearest son Classicianus

(1) I was greatly grieved by the letter from your dear self; and I hesitated for a long time as to how to reply.[1] I must confess that I had no advice to offer, and the words of scripture came to my mind, *If you have advice, offer it to your neighbour. If not, let your hand be over your mouth* [Ecclus 5.14]. If only the bishops had used the opportunity of your case to make a decision that we would then have to follow in cases of this sort. As it is, though, there are no conciliar decrees; or if perhaps there are, they have escaped my notice. However, we are not short of examples of men who have been excommunicated; and not only of individuals themselves who were deemed to deserve this method of reform, but of their entire households as well, even though their families had done nothing wrong.[2] No bishop who has acted in this way has been charged or forced to defend himself on this count. (After all, he would have been acting within the flock of Christ in a way that he judged beneficial to the sheep entrusted to his supervision.)

As far as holy scripture is concerned, one can find cases where sinners have paid the penalty for their sin along with their whole family, even though they did not sin.[3] However, that was in the period of the old covenant, when the punishment was physical and not spiritual. Suppose that someone guilty of an outrage were killed in the flesh along with his family (who took no part in that outrage). Then it was their bodies, which were destined in any case to perish one day, that were put to death, in order to inspire great fear in all the rest, and thus prevent their dying and leaving no one to succeed them.

However, the punishment of the soul was always imposed only on the sinner himself, in accordance with the words of the Lord, speaking through the prophet: *The soul of the father is mine, and the soul of the son is mine, and the soul which has sinned will itself die* [Ezek 18.4]. In the period of the new covenant, spiritual punishment was clearly established in the church by the words of Christ: *Whatever you loose on earth will be loosed in heaven; whatever you bind on earth will be bound in heaven* [Mt 18.18; cf. Mt 16.9]. Therefore I do not know how it could be right to bind a father and son at the same time, when the father has sinned and the son has not. How much more so for the wife, slave, maid, and little children, indeed for the whole household. What about someone who had not yet been born when the household was excommunicated, and then was born? It is not enough for him to inherit the original sin, through which all have sinned in the one Adam [cf. Rom 5.12]. He will also discover new guilt through an injustice committed by someone else before he even saw daylight; and what is harsher still, if he is faced with the danger of death, he will not have the help of the sacrament of baptism.[4]

(2) Because I am influenced by these considerations, I have never done anything of this sort myself. I know that very many of my brothers and colleagues (whether senior, equal or junior to me in the episcopacy) share this view, which is also my own. However, we do know that certain men who stand on a peak of secular power even higher than yours have been excommunicated by the bishops along with their whole family, and that they neither raised any questions about this nor approached other bishops with complaints. Rather, they went to the bishops who had bound them with compensation for their offence, in order to receive mercy and be released.[5] I have explained to you, my deservedly notable and most excellent and dearest son, why I have no definite advice to offer your excellent self in reply to the point in your letter that even if you sinned, it is not only you, but your whole family who were excommunicated by the bishop.

(3) Now for the case that you put to me in your letter, which made me ask whether you would have deserved it, if you alone had suffered this constraint. If the story that you told me was true, I do not, upon reflection, find any blame in you. These men deceived you with their oath, betrayed their guarantor by despising promises sworn in the name of Christ, and then fled to the house of faith itself for the purpose of breaking faith with impunity. If they were led from the church without violence, and left of their own accord to put right that abominable and impious outrage of theirs, then you did not commit any sin – no, not even if you came to the church accompanied by soldiers (for you need them in

order to exercise your office) and then spoke to the bishop as your state of anguish drove you to do. For otherwise he would have been showing favour to those who deceived their guarantor; and moreover defending men who had perjured themselves against the gospel against you, the very person who believed them when they swore on the gospel. And they would have been being defended in the very place where the gospel itself is read with the maximum authority and reverence, for the very purpose of keeping and preserving faith.

(4) However, I beg you to forgive me if I also continue to listen impartially to the other side, and if I am not too ready to believe your exalted self against the holy person of the bishop. For surely you lose nothing – indeed, you will acquire a great deal of devout humility, and deservedly so – if you beg mercy from the bishop, just in case during the argument you had with him (as you indicate) you said something that you should not have said, and he should not have heard.

(5) Having said that, I am eager for a discussion in our council, with the help of God; and also, if necessary, for a letter to the Apostolic See[6] concerning these two matters:

(i) those who bind by excommunication an entire household, that is a large number of souls, because of the sin of a single soul. My particular concern is to prevent anyone in such a case dying without baptism; and

(ii) whether those who flee to the church with the aim of breaking faith with their guarantor should be driven out of there.[7]

In this way we can use the unanimous authority of all together to decide and confirm the path we should follow in such cases.[8] I would certainly not be rash in declaring this: that if any one of the faithful has been unjustly excommunicated, it will harm the person that inflicts the injustice rather than the one who suffers it. For the Holy Spirit, who dwells in the saints, and through whom each person is bound or loosed [cf. Mt 18.18], does not impose undeserved punishment on anyone. Indeed, through him love is poured into our hearts [cf. Rom 5.5], and love does not harm us.

(6) I have also written to my brother and fellow-bishop, your bishop, in the way I thought I must write. For a long time I was constrained by an anguished debate with myself over whether I ought to do this. If this is insufficient for your dear self, please pardon me. For I judged that I ought not to go further than this.

Sermon 335c[1]

*The sermon of the blessed bishop Augustine on the
feast of a martyr*

(1) The birthday of this blessed martyr[2] has dawned, and it is God's will that we share with you in celebrating it. With his assistance, then, let me say some words about the glory and the perseverance of the martyrs. Glory, they despised; perseverance they put to the proof. For their glory lay hidden in heaven, while they practised their perseverance on earth. If you're not frightened by their perseverance, may you attain their glory! We think of bodily suffering and hardship as deserving pity; for they are certainly something difficult to endure. If they were not difficult for human beings, they wouldn't bring the martyrs glory.

(2) Imagine, however, that you can see two different characters, the character of greed, and the character of charity.[3] By 'greed', I mean a desire to sin; though sometimes, of course, people talk of 'greed' for something good.[4] In the same way, I mean by 'charity' the love of living virtuously, even if sometimes people talk of charity in the context of something bad. That's why I wanted to define my terms. Those who have faith are 'greedy' for the kingdom of heaven. On the other hand, even bandits are said to feel charity for one another.[5] But charity doesn't really exist among people whose fellowship is founded on a bad conscience; it belongs to people who, within fellowship, find happiness in wisdom.

(3) Reflect on this, then (and see the differences). Think of all the evils that greedy men are prepared to face.[6] Think how they will put up with hardships, in order to win the things they are greedy for – things that seem unbearable to people who don't share their greed. But love makes them brave. Love of evil, though, is called 'greed', love of good is called 'charity'. There are many things that a greedy person might love; these are sometimes so different that they can even turn out to be incompatible. The miser wants to pile up money; the *bon vivant* wants to spend it freely. One of them tightens his belt, the other loosens his purse. At any rate, what could be more incompatible than saving money and squandering it? But even so, miserliness gives its orders. Think of what is done for it – the sufferings and hardships people endure, the pain they put up with . . . pleasure that delights you.[7] But it's possible even to love pleasure in a way that is shameful – for example when someone's madly in love – while bravely putting up with an awful lot for its sake.

(4) It is not surprising, then, my dear friends, if charity has the courage of its love. The martyrs were filled with charity, they endured all their suffering in charity. They weren't loving something they could look at. Rather, they put their trust in something that was certain, and they could see with their hearts as much as any human being clothed in flesh can see. Isn't it true to say that our flesh has its own beauty? And doesn't incorruptible wisdom have its own beauty? But the wicked can see the beauty of wisdom, and even they in the end are sometimes greedy for it. They also want to be wise, so long as they can hold on to the things they love, and have wisdom at the same time. It's quite certain that they would want them both, that they wouldn't reject wisdom. You can find people who love the pleasures of the flesh and who also want to be wise. Again, you can find wise men who despise the pleasures of the flesh. But it's extremely rare to find someone who desires pleasure but despises wisdom. If he can, he wants to have them both; however, he gives one priority over the other, and this leads the poor fool into deceiving himself. He cheats himself because his love for less valuable things makes him lose what is more valuable. But someone who revels in what is shameful is blind to being cheated of what is heavenly.

(5) Give me a lover of goodness.[8] In the words of the apostle Peter, *And who will be able to harm you if you are lovers of goodness?* [1 Pet 3.13]. Then, as far as your loves go, you cannot be harmed. Whatever an attacker might take from you, your Creator will not destroy you so long as you love him. Every reduction in earthly gifts allows an increase in heavenly ones, provided of course that the former are reduced through love for the latter. It matters, of course, why you give something up.

That's why it is not the punishment that makes a martyr, but the cause.[9] So we don't justify as martyrs anyone who has suffered a lot, without examining why he or she suffered. *'It is for your sake'*, we hear the voice of the martyrs say, *'It is for your sake that we are being put to death all day long'* [Ps 43.22; cf. Rom 8.36].[10] Take away *'for your sake'*, and what good is *'we are being put to death all day long'*? Add *'for your sake'*, and what harm is *'being put to death all day long'*? To be 'put to death all day long for your sake' doesn't merely not harm us, but even helps us a great deal. The cause lies in the words, *'for your sake'*, the suffering in the words, *'we are being put to death all day long'*. You construct your suffering on a solid basis if you don't deprive it of its foundations, your love for God.

(6) It also matters that you say, 'for your sake'. Take a lover full of lust, who's racing to fasten himself to a beautiful body. Imagine him boasting to his sweetheart like this:

For your sake, for your sake, I endured my father's rage. I was beaten by my strict father and by merciless teachers for your sake. I've spent absolutely everything I had for your sake; for your sake I'm now left without a penny.

Look how often you say, 'for your sake'! But wasn't any of it done for yourself? No! Not only was nothing done for yourself, but everything was done 'for your sake'.

(7) If money had ears, how many of its lovers would say to it: 'I endured a harsh winter at sea for your sake. I suffered so many shipwrecks for your sake. When I was in danger at sea for your sake, I had to throw my possessions overboard. In fact, for your sake I even lost you. I was greedy for even more, and having my eye on that, I lost even what I already had.' How many 'for your sake's! But you are speaking to someone that is deaf. He won't be able to hear you even if you destroy yourself for it. In any case, what is the good of dying for the sake of money? You die and you still do not find it. In fact, you say goodbye to the money you have simply by dying. You pass on; and another lover comes along. Think of all the lovers who have abandoned her, who have perished, desiring her and then passing on. *Although man walks in his image* [Ps 39(38).6, LXX], however, *he is troubled to no end* [Ps 39(38).11, LXX]. We ought to pity such people: although they certainly walk in the image of God, they are troubled to no end. *He stores up treasure and he does not know who he is saving it for* [Ps 39(38).6]. Why is he troubled except about storing up treasure? *Store up treasure*, then – but in the place where wisdom is saying [Mt 6.20; cf. Lk 12.33], not where avarice is staying.[11]

(8) On the question of money, the Lord gave some advice for preventing our possessions from being lost. He said, *'Make yourself friends by means of unjust mammon, so that they will welcome you into the eternal dwelling-places'* [Lk 16.9]. The martyrs endured so much for a worthy cause, indeed for the love[12] of God; and when they were hungry, they found people to welcome them, when naked, they were given clothes, as pilgrims, they were provided with hospitality. These were services provided for people in dire trouble. Friendships were forged through unjust mammon. The advice the Lord gave about money was excellent, if anyone listens to it. Surely, if you love your money, you ought to be careful not to lose it. In fact, if it has been lost to them, it will also have been lost to you. It slips away from you and it passes to someone else.

So put your money where you won't lose it. Before it's disappeared, *store up treasure in heaven* where *no thief can enter and no moth will consume*

it [Mt 6.20; cf. Lk 12.33]. The place is well defended! Why are you hesi-
tating to move your possessions? Send them on ahead, so that you can
follow them there. Buy yourself something, then, that can never be lost.
My dear friends, you know the policy that those greedy for money pursue
when they see that they've got a reasonable amount of capital. What do
they say to themselves? 'Possessions are like a wheel; it turns, and they
disappear. I must tie them down by buying some property.'

So they buy a country-house with the hope of tying down their money.
So, they've bought a country-house! They will own a country-house. But
surely the country-house won't always own them! No, it won't be long
before they will be moving immediately, and they will no longer own it.
You cannot tie up your soul in the place you've tied up your money. The
time will come when your soul is demanded back from you. Who will the
things you've bought belong to then? You will no longer own your
country-house, and it will no longer own you. Well, it might, of course,
own your body, if you are buried there after your death. Then we will have
a paradox! The house will own you, but you won't own it.

(9) The Lord gave excellent advice, golden advice, to the person to
whom he said, 'Move your things to where you will not lose them' [cf. Mt
6.19–21; Lk 12.33–34; Mk 10.21]. I can hear you objecting, 'What advice
to give! Then I will not be able to see them!'

You will see them later on. But you will not see what you've sent on.
You have lent that out at interest. You have given away one sum; a
different sum will be repaid. You've chosen to lend money to someone
omnipotent. He takes a little and he gives a lot. He accepts a small sum, he
will repay a very large one. He created this earth for you. If you send him
a few grains, you'll fill a granary. He created this earth for you. He created
heaven and earth. Think what he will keep for you if you sow good deeds.

(10) But the greedy people I am addressing are deaf, whether they're
lustful and desire beautiful bodies, or whether they're avaricious and are
piling up money and storing it up as treasure on earth. I'm addressing the
deaf, and they can't hear what I say. Lord, heal them so that they hear!
Nothing is impossible for you. There is no sickness you cannot heal; you
are a superb doctor. Especially so, since you showed us your pre-emptive
love[13] for us when you didn't even spare your own son, but handed him
over for the sake of all of us. Is there anything you have failed to give us,
along with him?

Miser, open your jaws wide! Put trivial sums beneath you; you'll have
so many possessions. For greed has been conquered, it's been trampled

on, it's been trodden into the ground by Christ, who spoke these words: *Having nothing and yet owning everything* [2 Cor 6.10].

(11) That is why many lustful and avaricious people thought that the holy martyrs were mad when they endured so much for the name of Christ, always putting their trust truly in him. They were urged to deny him; they confessed him [cf. Mt 10.32–3].[14] They were slaughtered, burnt, thrown to the beasts. In public, they suffered horribly, but in secret they were given crowns of indescribable beauty. Indeed, if they had had earthly ambitions, could they have added anything to the glory of their birthday celebrations? There are plenty of heroes who have acted crazily for the sake of glory; they have said that they must shed their blood for the sake of their country; and they haven't hesitated to shed it.[15] They knew that this life passes away, but their kind of glory lasts, perhaps for ever.[16] Did any of them win glory to compare with the glory of the martyrs?

In earthly glory, in the glory of human affairs, could anyone, even a dictator, find what a fisherman has managed to find?[17] At Rome there are the tombs of the brave heroes who died for the sake of their country. Has the emperor deigned to set foot in any of them? The martyrs' only goal was to be honoured among the angels. But even if they had been greedy for earthly glory, they would not have been cheated. We are amazed when we see how they are glorified on earth. What would we feel if we could see them in heaven? We can see the martyrs' birthdays being celebrated by different nations; imagine how utterly astonishing it would be to see them surrounded by the angels singing their praises.

(12) Still, my brothers, make the invisible goals of the martyrs your aim. Love the things they loved. Even though you don't need to endure what they endured, still prepare your spirits to endure it. Choose your cause first of all, as far as you can. Suppose that they had not chosen their cause: wouldn't the martyrs be receiving the treatment usual for bandits or adulterers or sorcerers or idolaters? If you look at the punishments, they are all similar. If you look at the different causes, the martyrs are a very long way from the rest. Nothing was closer or more similar or nearer than the three crosses of the Lord and of the two thieves. They were three. They were all crosses. They were all in the same place. All the bodies were hanging from a piece of wood. But their causes were forcing them apart.[18] In the middle hung the saviour, on either side, the culprits. His cross was a tribunal. He hung there and he delivered his verdict.[19] He hung there as one under judgement, and he judged the men hanging there.

Of the two defendants, one deserved to be punished, the other to be rewarded. Why did he deserve a reward? Because on the cross he changed his cause.[20] Hanging there, he put his trust in words aimed at a target far away. He wanted to be in the Lord's mind when he entered his kingdom. But what did the Lord reply to his words, *'Remember me, Lord when you come into your kingdom'* [Lk 23.42]? It was as if the thief was saying, 'I know my own case;[21] I know what I deserve, I must be tortured for what I have done – but please, pity me when you come!' He deferred his hopes; the Lord fulfilled them: *'In truth, I tell you, today you will be with me in paradise* [Lk 23.43]. Why are you looking so far ahead for my arrival? Today you will be with me in paradise. You hope that I will come; but I am never absent. I am everywhere, that is how I come. But *today you will be with me in paradise,* because you cannot be happy in the place where you will be happy, except with me.' And so, the souls of the blessed are happy with Christ even before they receive their bodies back;[22] without Christ they cannot be happy. They loved him, they held him dear, they kept in him their justice, their wisdom and their understanding; in him they kept hidden their treasures of wisdom and knowledge [cf. Col 2.3]. Think of all the things they considered completely unimportant, when they were suffering here. They certainly had no wish to be rich. For if a poor man has God, he has everything.

(13) Dear brothers, love what is really good. There is nothing more beautiful, even if only the eyes of our hearts can see it. Listen to me! Look at all the beautiful things you can see with your physical eyes: the sky, the earth, the sea, and all that they contain; the stars shining in the sky; the sun flooding the day, the moon softening the darkness of the night. Think of the birds, the fish, the animals; of human beings living among them all and made *in the image of* God [Gen 1.27], to praise the Creator[23] and to love his creation, provided that they love its Creator. If you ignore God in order to love something else – well, he made that too. Anything, I repeat, that you love at the cost of ignoring God, was created by him. If it wasn't beautiful, then you wouldn't love it. But where does its beauty come from if it wasn't created by God, whose beauty is invisible? You love gold. Well, God made it. You love beautiful bodies, you love flesh. God made them. You love your delightful estate. God made it. You love the precious light. God made it. If you ignore God in favour of something he made – well then, please love God himself as well. How much does he deserve to be loved, how much does he deserve to be loved, when he created everything that you love? Love him like this – and your love for him will grow.

I am not saying that you should have no loves; I simply want your loves to be properly ordered. Put heavenly things before earthly, immortal things before mortal, everlasting things before transitory ones. And put the Lord before everything, and not just by praising him, but also by loving him. It is easy enough to give him preference when it comes to praise. But then temptation comes along. Then, I ask you, do you show different priorities in your love from the preferences you showed in your praise?

If someone asked you, 'Which is better, money or wisdom, money or justice, or finally, money or God?' you wouldn't hesitate to answer: 'wisdom, justice, God'. You must hesitate as little when you're actually making a choice as when you're giving an answer. Which is better, justice or money? Of course, you all shout out 'justice!' as if you were children in class competing to answer the question first. I know you all; I can hear what you're thinking: 'justice is better'.[24] But then temptation comes along. It offers you some money from somewhere else. Now temptation is saying to you: 'Look, here's some money you could have; if you do a bit of cheating the money is yours.' But justice will ask you, 'What are you going to choose? Now's my chance to test your words.'

When you were listening to my questions just before, you preferred justice to money. But now – both of them are in front of you! Money on this side; justice on that side. You close your eyes against justice, as if you are ashamed, and you stretch out your hand to take the money. What an ungrateful idiot! When I questioned you, you preferred justice to money. You've acted as a witness against yourself. Will God call another witness when you've convicted yourself? You prefer justice so far as praising it goes; but when it comes to choosing you prefer money. Can't you see what it's a part of, the thing you prefer? It's a perishable part of something per-ishable. There's no doubt, of course, that money will perish, when *this world and all its lust will pass away* [1 Jn 2.17]. But make justice your choice: for *anyone who has done the will of God remains for ever, just as God too remains for ever* [1 Jn 2.17].

Bishops and civil authorities

Letters 133, 134 and 139

In the following set of letters Augustine writes to Apringius, proconsul of
Africa, and to his brother Marcellinus, urging mercy for the Donatists
who have been convicted of the murder and mutilation respectively of
two Catholic priests.

Letter 133

411

Augustine the bishop greets in the Lord his distinguished and
deservedly notable lord and beloved son Marcellinus.[1]

(1) I have been informed that the Circumcellions and clergy of Donatus'
sect who were taken from the diocese of Hippo by those responsible for
public order to stand trial for their activities have in fact been heard by
your noble self. Most of them have confessed to committing the murder
of Restitutus, the Catholic priest, and to beating Innocent, another
Catholic priest, and to gouging out the latter's eye and cutting off his
finger. Consequently, I am deeply stricken by the worry that your exalted
self might decide to have them punished so harshly by law that the
sufferings they will endure correspond to those they have inflicted. I
write, therefore, to beg you by the faith you have in Christ, through the
mercy of our Lord Christ himself, neither to do this yourself nor to allow
it to be done at all.

Now it might be possible for us to turn a blind eye to their deaths, when
they were clearly not summoned to trial because we accused them; rather,
those responsible for keeping an eye on the preservation of public peace
indicted them. However, we do not want a matching punishment to be
inflicted because of the sufferings of the servants of God, as if in retaliation.[2] We do not indeed want to prevent the suppression of a villain's

61

freedom to offend. However, we think this should be enough: if legal coercion can turn them from their present crazy restlessness to the peacefulness of sanity, or assign them away from harmful employment to serve useful work, while leaving them alive and physically unmutilated.[3] It is true that that is also described as condemnation; but surely everyone realises that it should be called kindness and not punishment when you refuse to give reckless violence its freedom, without withdrawing the medicine of repentance.

(2) Christian judge, fulfil the duties of your devoted father. Condemn injustice without forgetting to observe humanity. Do not indulge a thirst to revenge the horrors inflicted by sinners, but rather apply a willingness to heal the wounds of sinners. Do not abandon the fatherly care that you maintained in the investigation itself. Then you dragged from them a confession of their outrages without stretching them on the rack or scoring them with hooks, or burning them with flames, but only beating them.[4] That is a method of constraint that the teachers of the liberal arts use, and parents themselves. It is not infrequently employed even by bishops in their courts. Therefore do not punish too fiercely something you investigated rather gently. There is a greater need to investigate than to punish; in order to discover who should be spared, even the mildest of men will examine a hidden offence thoroughly and with urgency. In general, then, there is a need to give a cutting edge to the investigation in order to bring the outrage to light, at which point gentleness can come into play.

Now all good works love to be set in the light, not for the sake of human glory, but (as the Lord says) *so that they may see your good works and glorify your father who is in heaven* [Mt 5.16]. That is why it was not enough for the apostle to warn us to preserve gentleness; we were also to make this known to everyone. These are his words: *Let your gentleness be known to all people* [Phil 4.5]; and elsewhere *showing your gentleness to all people* [Tit 3.2]. Similarly, not even in the case of the holy David would his outstanding gentleness have stood out, when he mercifully spared the enemy who had been given into his hands [cf. 1 Sam 24.1–22],[5] were it not that his power were equally visible. Therefore do not let your power to punish harden you when the need to examine suspects did not shake your gentleness. Do not summon the executioner once you have discovered the offence, having refused to apply torture during its discovery.

(3) One final point: you have been sent to be useful to the church. I declare solemnly that this course of action assists the Catholic church, or

rather, in case I seem to be exceeding the boundaries of my jurisdiction, that it benefits the part of the church belonging to the diocese of Hippo Regius. Listen to me as a friend making a request; or if not, as a bishop consulting with you. In fact, as I am addressing a Christian, it would not be very presumptuous of me in such a situation to say, 'You should listen to me as to a bishop giving you orders', my distinguished and deservedly notable lord and beloved son. I know that ecclesiastical cases are assigned particularly to your eminent self. However, because I believe that here the specific responsibility falls to the renowned and admirable proconsul,[6] I have also written to him. I ask you not to think it a burden to hand the letter to him yourself, and lay the business before him, if necessary.

I beg you both not to think my intercession, or my advice, or my concern over-insistent; and not to bring shame on the sufferings of the Catholic servants of God, by inflicting retaliatory punishment on the enemies at whose hands they suffered. (Such suffering ought really to benefit the weak, to strengthen them spiritually.) Please, rather, soften the harshness of your judgements and do not forget to set an example of your faith (for you are sons of the Church) and of the gentleness that belongs to your mother herself.

May the almighty God increase your excellent self with all good gifts, my distinguished and deservedly notable lord and beloved son.

Letter 134

411

Augustine to Apringius,[1] his notable and deservedly exalted lord and most excellent son.

(1) I have no doubt that when you exercise the power that God has given you, a human being, over other human beings, you reflect upon the divine judgement, when judges too will stand to give an account of their own judgements.[2] I know that you are steeped in the Christian faith. That is why I have a greater confidence with respect to your eminent self, both when making requests and even when giving advice, for the sake of the Lord in whose family you are numbered along with us according to the law of heaven. We share an equal hope of everlasting life in him; and we pray to him on your behalf in the holy mysteries.

Therefore, my notable and deservedly exalted lord and most excellent son, I beg you first not to think me over-insistent in encroaching on your activities, because I am anxious, as I ought especially to be, on behalf of the church entrusted to me. It is her interests that I serve; and my desire is less to be first in her than to put her first. Secondly, I beseech you not to spurn the advice I offer or the requests I make, and not to delay in your assent.

(2) Those with the responsibility of serving public order issued an interdict to bring certain Circumcellions and Donatist clergy to the courts of law. They were heard by the renowned and admirable tribune and notary your brother Marcellinus.[3] They were tortured not with hooks and fire, but only a beating, and thus forced to confess the awful deeds they perpetrated against my brothers and fellow-priests: they caught the first in an ambush and butchered him; the second one they dragged from his house and mutilated by gouging out his eye and cutting off his finger.

Once I had heard that they had confessed to this, having no doubt that they would fall under the jurisdiction of your axe,[4] I hurried to send this letter to your noble self. I beg and beseech you now by the mercy of Christ (and then may we rejoice as your happiness increases in degree and in security) not to inflict equal treatment on them in retribution – though of course the laws are not able to punish them by stoning or chopping off their fingers or tearing out their eyes, as they themselves could do in their violence. Therefore I am not worried in case the men who have confessed to doing this suffer corresponding treatment in their turn. But I am afraid that these men, or others who are clearly guilty of murder, will be punished with a sentence that accords with your power. I beg you as a Christian to a judge, and I warn you as a bishop to a Christian, not to let this happen.

(3) We read that the apostle Paul said about you that you *do not wield a sword without reason*, and you are *ministers of God, and avengers on the evil-doer* [Rom 13.4].[5] However, the cases[6] of the province and of the church are distinct. The government of the former should be managed by deterrence; the gentleness of the latter should commend itself by its mercy. If I were speaking to a judge who was not a Christian, I would put it differently. I should still not abandon the cause of the church, and I should insist, so far as he saw fit to allow me, that the sufferings of the Catholic servants of God, which ought to bring benefit as examples of fortitude, should not be soiled with the blood of their enemies. If he were to refuse to assent, I should suspect him of resisting in a hostile spirit.

Now, however, I am discussing the matter with you. Therefore my reasoning and my method of consultation are quite different. We do indeed see that you are a governor endowed with elevated powers. However, we also recognise you as a son endowed with Christian piety. May your exalted self submit, and may your faith submit. The case I discuss with you is our shared concern. You, though, have powers here that I do not possess. Please consult with us, and offer us your assistance.

(4) It was very thorough work to persuade the enemies of the church to confess the awful crimes they have perpetrated against the Catholic clergy and to implicate themselves by their own words. After all, their usual habit is to worry inexperienced souls with their seductive nonsense, as they brag of the harassment that (so they boast) they are enduring.[7]

In order to heal the minds that they have poisoned with their venomous eloquence we have to read out the relevant proceedings. But surely you will not be happy if we are afraid of coming to the end of reading those proceedings, because that will lead to punishing them by shedding their blood? For then we lay aside even the conscience that tells us that victims should not be seen to return evil for evil. Now if there were no other established method of restraining the hostility of the desperate, then perhaps extreme necessity would demand the killing of such people. Even then, as far as we are concerned, if nothing milder could be done, we would prefer to have them set free than to have the sufferings of our brothers avenged by shedding their blood.

But now in fact something else is possible, and this will both bring credit to the mildness of the church, and restrain the recklessness of those who are far from mild. Why, then, will you not incline towards a more prudent role and a softer sentence? The law allows you to do this even in cases unconnected with the church. Join us in fearing the judgement of God the Father, and give credit to the mildness of our mother the church. For when you act, the church acts as you act on her behalf and as her son.

Fight evil men with goodness. They indulged in the appalling outrage of tearing the limbs from a living body. You should indulge in a work of mercy and ensure that the limbs they used for their unspeakable work should be put, undamaged, to serve some useful work. They did not spare the servants of God who were preaching reform to them. You should spare them when they are arrested, spare them when they are brought to you, spare them when they are convicted. They used an impious sword to shed the blood of Christians. You should prevent the sword of the law, for the sake of Christ, from shedding their blood. They killed a minister of the church and robbed him of time to live. You should allow the enemies of the church to live and have time to repent.[8] In cases concerning the church, you as a Christian judge ought to act thus: this is our request, this is our advice, this is the aim of our intercession.

It is usual for people to appeal against too mild a sentence when their convicted enemies are treated gently. However, we so love our enemies that we would appeal against your harsh sentence – if we were not relying upon your obedience as a Christian.

May almighty God keep your eminent self safe, increasing your fortune and happiness, my notable and deservedly exalted lord and most excellent son.

Letter 139

411/412

Augustine in the Lord greets Marcellinus, his deservedly notable lord and dearly beloved and much missed son.

(1) I am eagerly awaiting the proceedings[1] which your excellent self has promised; and I am longing to have them read in the church of Hippo as soon as possible, and if it can be done, also in all the churches established within the diocese. Then people will hear for themselves and know all about the men who have confessed their wickedness. It was not the fear of God that wrenched repentance from them, but judicial thoroughness that has opened the hardness of their cruel hearts – not only of those who confessed to murdering one priest and blinding and physically mutilating another;[2] but also of those who did not dare to deny that they could have known of all this, even though they said that they disapproved (they had fled the peace of the Catholic church on the grounds that they did not want to be polluted by other people's crimes; and yet they persisted in that blasphemous schism, surrounded by a great mass of appalling outrages); or again, of a third group who insisted that they would not return even once we had proved to them the truth of the Catholic claims, and the distortions of the Donatists.

It is no trivial thing that God has willed to be done through your efforts. If only you could hear such cases more often in this way. If only there were frequent opportunities to publicise their offences and their crazy stubbornness! If only these same proceedings could be published and brought to the notice of absolutely everyone.

Now your distinguished self wrote in your letter that you were not sure whether you ought to order the same proceedings to be posted in Theoprepia.[3] Do this, provided that a big crowd may gather there. Otherwise, you should look for some busier place; do not, though, in any way neglect to do this.

(2) As for the punishment of those who have confessed to such admittedly great outrages, I beg you to make it something other than the death penalty, both on account of our conscience and in order to set an example of Catholic gentleness. The fruit of their confession has accrued to us in the opportunity the church has found for maintaining and displaying her leniency towards the most appalling enemies. Indeed, in so cruel a case, the imposition of any punishment that avoids bloodshed will appear as great leniency. Now at the moment it may seem to some of us, who are upset by the shocking nature of the deed, that this is inappropriate and smacks of licence or negligence. However, when the emotions have calmed down (for they tend to be stirred up more excitably when events are fresh in the mind) the goodness of this will become transparently and conspicuously clear; and therefore much greater delight will be aroused by reading and publicising the proceedings in question, my deservedly notable lord, and dearly beloved and much missed son.

My holy brother and fellow-bishop Boniface is there; and I have sent an aide-mémoire through the deacon Peregrinus, who travelled with him.[4] Treat him as if I were with you. Then, whatever seems best to you both together for the benefit of the church, may that come to pass, with the help of the Lord, who has the power amid such evils to provide assistance in a merciful way.

Their bishop Macrobius, surrounded by packs of desperate supporters of both sexes, has been going about here and there and opening basilicas for himself when their true owners had closed them out of some slight fear. Now when Spondeus, the procurator of the renowned Celer, was present, then their recklessness was somewhat hampered. (He is the man I have commended, and continue to commend, to your affection.) Now that he has left for Carthage, however, Macrobius has opened basilicas on Spondeus' own estate, and is gathering crowds there. With him also is

Donatus, that deacon who was rebaptised when he was a tenant of the church. He was notably involved in that violent attack. If such a person is with Macrobius, who might not be with him?

It seems that the proconsul,[5] or both of you together, are about to pronounce sentence on them. Suppose that he persists in wanting to punish them with the sword, even though he is a Christian and not, so far as we can tell, inclined to that sort of bloodshed. Still, if it proves necessary, please give orders also to invoke my letters during the proceedings, the individual letters that I saw fit to send you on this topic.[6] For I am usually told that it lies in the power of the judges to soften a sentence or to punish more mildly than the laws suggest.

If despite this he does not agree with my letters on this point, please at least let him arrange for them to be held in custody. We have made[7] it our concern to appeal to the emperor's clemency to prevent the sufferings of the servants of God, which ought to bring glory upon the church, from being dishonoured by the blood of her enemies.[8] Indeed, I know that in the case of those clergy of Anaunia, who were killed by pagans and are now honoured as martyrs,[9] the emperor very easily granted the request that their killers, once they had been caught and were in custody, should not meet with corresponding punishment.

(3) I have forgotten why I took back the books on infant baptism, when I had already sent the volume to your excellent self.[10] Perhaps it was because I found them misleading when I was looking over them, and wanted to correct them. However, I have been so amazingly busy that I have not done so. You should also know that the letter that should have been written to you and attached to the books, which I had already begun to dictate when I was there, is still unfinished, though a little has been added. If I had the chance to render you an account of all the days and nights I have devoted to other necessities, you would be deeply sympathetic. You would be amazed at the amount of demanding business that I cannot possibly put off, which does not allow me to do the things you are pressingly requesting me and advising me to do; I want to do them, and I am inexpressibly sorry that I cannot.

Occasionally, I do have a little time free from attending to the needs of people who are commandeering my assistance in such a way that I can't avoid them and ought not to neglect them. Even then I have no shortage of things to dictate, and I must give these priority: for they are relevant to a critical moment and cannot be postponed. For example, I have composed a summary of the proceedings of our conference,[11] which required quite a lot of work, since I saw that no one was willing to devote himself to reading such a large amount of documentation. Again, I wrote a letter to the Donatist laity themselves about that conference of ours,[12] and this took several nights' work to complete. Also, there were the two substantial letters, the one to your dear self, the other to the illustrious Volusianus.[13] (I believe you have already received them.) Again, I have in my hands at this moment a book addressed to our friend Honoratus in reply to five questions that he put to me, communicating with me by letter.[14] You can see that it would be most inappropriate not to reply to him immediately. For love, like a nurse nurturing her children, puts the weaker before the stronger – in the order of helping them rather than of loving them. For she wants the weak to become like the strong; the strong she passes over for the time being, not out of contempt for them, but out of confidence in them.

In short, wherever I am allowed just a brief respite from the masses of preoccupations that demand my time and distract me because of others' desires or needs, then I cannot avoid the need to dictate the sorts of works I have described; and this keeps me away from the work that I ardently long to dictate. I simply do not know what I am to do.

(4) You have heard now why you should pray to the Lord with me. But I do not want you to stop giving me pressing and frequent reminders; you do not do so in vain.

A final point: I recommend to your eminent self the church established in Numidia. My holy brother and fellow-bishop Delphinus[15] has been sent to attend to her needs by my brothers and fellow-bishops who work together – and face dangers together – there. I shall not write any more about that, as you can listen to the man himself, who is with you. You will find everything else in the aide-mémoire that I sent to the priest,[16] whether now, or through Peregrinus the deacon. Then I do not need to repeat it all so many times.

May your heart ever be strong and rejoice in Christ, my deservedly notable lord, and dearly beloved and much missed son. I commend our son Rufinus, a leading citizen[17] of Cirta, to your distinguished self.

Letters 152, 153, 154 and 155

The following exchange of letters with Macedonius, vicar of Africa, includes Augustine's most extensive reflection on punishment.

Letter 152

413/414

Macedonius[1] to Augustine, his deservedly revered and uniquely cherished father.

(1) I have just received from Boniface,[2] the representative of the hallowed law, the letters from your holy self, for which I was hoping. I welcomed him lovingly all the more because he had brought me what I was longing for, words from your holy self, and assurance that you were well, my deservedly revered and uniquely cherished father. Consequently, he was given what he was hoping for without delay. However, since the opportunity has arisen, I do not want to remain unpaid for the favour – small as it was – that I granted on your advice.[3] I am eager to receive my pay; and I can be obliged without disobliging the payer. Indeed, I can be obliged to the glory of the payer.

(2) You say that it is your duty as a priest to intercede on behalf of the guilty and to be upset if you don't succeed, as if you are failing to carry out your duty. I am extremely doubtful here as to whether this duty derives from religion. If the Lord forbade sin so strongly that a sinner is offered no more than one opportunity to repent,[4] then how can we argue on the basis of religion that any crime whatsoever should be forgiven? For surely that is the course we are approving when we want the offender to go unpunished.

Again, if we argue that whenever sins are committed someone who approves of them is to be held as responsible as the perpetrator, it surely follows that whenever we want someone who is held blameworthy to go unpunished, we ourselves are bound to them in a fellowship of guilt. In addition to all that, there is something still more serious. All sins do indeed seem pardonable as long as the guilty party promises to reform. However, now with our current ways of behaving, those in question want both to have the penalty for their outrages mitigated, and to keep their ill-gotten gains. Speaking from your duty as a priest, you consider that you should intercede on behalf of such people. But there is no hope for them in the future, precisely because their criminal mentality persists unchanged in the present. For if someone so determinedly holds on to the gains that were the object of his crime, he makes it clear that he will commit similar sins in the future whenever he has the freedom to do so.

(3) These are the reasons why I am consulting your wise self. I am eager to be released from the doubts which burden me. Do not imagine that I am consulting you with any other motive. Rather, my resolve is to show gratitude to intercessors, especially when they are as deserving as you. In general, I do not want to seem to be doing this of my own accord (in case I mobilise others for crime by relaxing my strictness). I do, though, hope to be able to mitigate punishments in response to intercessions from good men. Consequently – and this I readily grant you – severity of judgement can be preserved at the same time as indulgence being granted thanks to the merits of someone else.

May the eternal God keep your holy self safe for a generous length of years, most revered lord and truly cherished father.

On the question of those writings of yours which your holy self promised me at some point and which I have not yet received:[5] please send them now along with a reply to this letter. Then – as the opportunity to see your holy self in the meantime is not given to me – at least I may be nourished by your words.

Letter 153

413/414

Augustine the bishop and servant of Christ and of his family greets his dear son Macedonius in the Lord.

(1) You are a man extremely busy with your involvement in public life[1] and very attentive to the interests of others rather than your own. I congratulate you, and human affairs too, on this; and in the light of it I must neither leave you deprived of my conversation, nor take up your time with preamble. Here, then, is the information that you wished to receive from me, or at least discover whether I knew it. If you were to judge it deficient or excessive in any way, you wouldn't consider it worth your attention when you are surrounded by such great and such pressing concerns.

Your question was this: why do we think that it is a part of our priestly duty to intercede on behalf of the guilty; and to be upset if we don't succeed as if we were failing to carry out a part of our duty? You say that you are extremely doubtful over whether this duty derives from religion. Then you add the reason why you feel this way:

'If the Lord forbade sin so strongly', you say, 'that a sinner is offered no more than one opportunity to repent, then how can we argue on the basis of religion that any crime whatever should be forgiven?'[2]

Then you press a more serious point: you argue that in wanting someone to go unpunished, we approve their behaviour. And if we agree that whenever sins are committed someone who approves of them is to be held as responsible as the perpetrator, it surely follows that whenever we want someone who is held blameworthy to go unpunished, we ourselves are bound to them in a fellowship of guilt.

(2) Anyone unacquainted with your gentleness and humanity would surely be terrified by these words! That's why I am replying to your point immediately, using other words of your own. For I know you, and have no doubt that you wrote with the aim of investigating the question rather than deciding it.

Indeed, either you did not want me to be hesitant over the issue, or else you have foreseen what my reply will be; or perhaps you have actually guided me as to how I ought to reply by saying: 'In addition to all that, there is something still more serious. All sins do indeed seem pardonable as long as the guilty party promises to reform.'

I will go on to discuss the 'more serious' point that follows in your letter. Meanwhile, however, I will accept this offering of yours and use it to break down the barrier which seems sufficient to block our intercessory activity. Indeed, this is precisely our reason for interceding on behalf of every sin (where we are given the opportunity), that 'all sins do indeed seem pardonable as long as the guilty party promises to reform'. This is your opinion; and it is also mine.

(3) Under no circumstances do we approve culpable behaviour; we want to reform that. Nor is the reason that we want wrong-doing to go unpunished that we are pleased with it. Rather, we pity the person, but hate the offence or transgression.[3] In fact, the more we dislike the vice in question, the less do we want the offender to die without correcting his vices.

It comes easily and effortlessly to hate the bad because they are bad. It is an uncommon mark of piety to love the same people because they are human beings, so that at one and the same time you disapprove of their guilt while approving of their nature. Indeed, you have more right to hate their guilt precisely because it mars their nature, which you love. Therefore if you take action against the crime in order to liberate the human being, you bind yourself to him in a fellowship of humanity rather than injustice.

Moreover, there is no space to reform character except in this life. After that, each person will have whatever he has won for himself here. That is why we are forced to intercede for the guilty, out of love for the human race. For otherwise punishment will end this life for them, and once it is ended, they will not be able to bring their punishment to an end.

(4) Do not doubt, therefore, that this duty of ours derives from religion, when God – as the gospel tells us – makes *his sun rise on the good and the evil, and rains on the just and the unjust* [Mt 5.45]. For with God there is no injustice; he possesses supreme power, he not only sees what everyone is like but even foresees what they will be like; he alone can judge infallibly, he cannot be deceived in what he knows.

The Lord Christ urges us to imitate his marvellous goodness, with the words: *Love your enemies, do good to those who hate you, pray for those who pursue you, so that you might be sons of your father, who is in heaven, who makes his sun rise on the good and the evil, and rains on the just and the unjust* [Mt 5.44–5; cf. Lk 6.27–8].

Everyone knows that many people abuse God's indulgence and leniency, with disastrous consequences for themselves. The apostle accuses them, rebuking them sharply with the words, *Do you think that you will escape the judgement of God, human being, whoever you are, when you judge others who behave like that, and behave the same way yourself? Are you scorning the riches of his kindness and patience and long-suffering? Do you not know that the kindness of God is leading you to repentance? Through your hardness of heart and your impenitent heart, however, you are storing up wrath for yourself on the day of wrath, and of the revelation of the just judgement of God. For he will render to each person according to his works* [Rom 2.3–6]. Surely God does not persevere in his patience because they persevere in their wickedness: he punishes very few offences in this life, in case no one believes in divine providence; and he keeps most of them back for the final assessment, in order to remind us of that future judgement.

(5) Our heavenly master does not, in my view, instruct us to love impiety, when he instructs us to *love our enemies, to do good to those who hate us, to pray for those who pursue us* [Mt 5.44]. For there is no doubt that if we worship God piously, the only enemies we can have, the only ones aroused by bitter hatred against us, our only pursuers, will be the impious. Should we then love the impious? Should we do them good?

Should we even pray for them? Clearly we should. It is God who gives these instructions. However, in saying this he is not associating us in fellowship with the impious, just as he himself does not become their ally when he spares them and bestows on them life and security. The apostle Paul explains his purpose (insofar as it is granted to a pious man to know this): *Do you not know that the forbearance of God is leading you to repentance?* [Rom 2.4]. When we intervene on behalf of others, we want them to be led to this; we are not sparing or supporting their sins.

(6) Indeed on some occasions when you have freed from the threat of severe treatment those whose crimes are openly known, we ourselves bar them from the fellowship of the altar.[4] In this way, having despised God by sinning, they are able to appease him by repentance, and at the same time by punishing themselves. A person who truly repents does nothing other than refuse to allow himself to go unpunished for his wrong-doing. That is how God, whose lofty and just judgement no one can despise and escape, spares the person who does not spare himself. For he shows patience even to the unjust and villainous by sparing them and by bestowing life and security even on the majority of those who he knows will not repent. How much more ought we to be merciful towards those who promise reform, when we are uncertain whether or not they will do as they promise. Consequently we intercede on their behalf to soften your harshness, and we also pray to God, whom nothing even of their future conduct escapes. This is not presumptuous, however, because he himself commands it.

(7) The injustice of human beings sometimes extends so far that even after they have performed penance, even after being reconciled at the altar,[5] they perpetrate similar or more serious offences. Yet God still makes *his sun rise* [Mt 5.45] over such people, and grants them no less than before the generous gifts of life and security. Even though the church does not offer them an occasion for repentance, still God does not forget his patience in their case.[6]

What if one of their number were to say to us: 'Please give me the same opportunity for repentance once more; or else declare me beyond hope so that I can do what I like – insofar as my resources allow me, and human laws do not prevent me – with prostitutes, and all sorts of luxurious living that are condemned in the eyes of God, but even deserve praise in the eyes of most people. Or else, if you must call me back from that kind of wickedness, tell me whether it will benefit me in my future life if I ignore the temptations of seductive pleasures, if I restrain the urges of my passions, if I abstain from much that is lawful and permissible in order to discipline my body, if I torment myself in penitence more fiercely than before, if I lament more sorrowfully, if I weep more abundantly, if I live a better life, if I support the poor more generously, if I burn more ardently with *love*, which *covers a multitude of sins*' [1 Pet 4.8]?

Would any of us be so crazy as to reply to him: 'All that will not help you at all in the future. Carry on and at least enjoy the delights of this life'? May God protect us from such appalling and idolatrous madness!

It is true that the cautious and salutary provision of allowing only one opportunity for humble repentance has been established in the church. The purpose of this is to avoid cheapening and thereby reducing the effectiveness of the medicine offered to the sick. For the less cheaply it is held, the more salutary its effects. However, no one would dare to say to God, 'Why are you yet again prepared to spare this person? He has already repented once, and now he has tangled himself up again in the net of injustice.'

Who would dare to say that the apostle's words, *Do you not know that the forbearance of God is leading you to repentance?* [Rom 2.4] ought not to apply to them? Or that the following words of scripture offer a definition that excludes them: *Blessed are all who trust in him* [Ps 2.12]? Or that this does not refer to them too: *Act manfully and let your heart be strengthened, all you who hope in the Lord* [Ps 31(30).24]?

(8) God's patience and mercy towards sinners is so great that they are not condemned everlastingly if they amend their behaviour in this temporary life. He himself does not wait for anyone to offer mercy to him, since no one is more blessed, no one more powerful, no one more just. And that is how we ought to be, as human beings one to another; however much we pile up praise in this life of ours, we can never describe it as sinless, because *if we say that we* are so, scripture says, *we deceive ourselves, and there is no truth in us* [1 Jn 1.8].

Now it is true that the roles of accuser, of defender, of intercessor and of judge are distinct, and it would take up unnecessary time to treat their respective duties in this discussion. But what about those even whose job it is to punish crime? In performing this duty they are not inspired by personal anger; rather they are executives of the laws, appointed to investigate and punish injustices committed not against themselves, but against others. That is what judges ought to be like, and God's judgement is there to inspire fear in them so that they remember that they stand in need of God's mercy for their own sins, and do not think that they have failed in their duty if they act at all mercifully towards those over whom they lawfully exercise the power of life and death.

(9) Think of the occasion when the Jews brought to Christ the Lord *a woman who had been caught in adultery and* said *to test him* that the law ordered that she should be stoned. Next they asked him what orders he would give in her case. He replied: *Who among you is without sin? Let him be the first to cast a stone at her.* In this way he avoided criticising the law, which commanded that women found guilty of this offence should be killed. He also frightened the men whose judgement could have her killed and so recalled them to mercy [cf. Jn 8.2–12].

It seems to me that if even the very husband who was demanding revenge for the broken faith of his marriage-bed had been present to hear the Lord's pronouncement, he would have been frightened into changing his mind from a desire for vengeance to a willingness to spare his wife. How clear a warning was issued to the accuser not to pursue vengeance for personal injuries. For the judges themselves were thus prevented from inflicting punishment, though they were under obligation to serve the law rather than personal grief in punishing the adultery [cf. Lev 20.10; Deut 22.22–4].[7]

Again, think of Joseph. He was betrothed to Mary, the Lord's mother. When he discovered that she was pregnant although he knew that he had not slept with her, he could draw no other conclusion than that she was an adulteress. However, he did not want her to be punished, even though he did not approve of her transgression. His wishes in this matter were counted as justice [cf. Rom 4.5]. Scripture says of him: *And since he was a just man and did not want to publicise her behaviour, he decided to send her away secretly. While he was thinking over these things, an angel appeared to him* [Mt 1.19–20], who explained to him that what he thought was a criminal act was in fact a divine one.

(10) If reflection on our common weakness[8] can soften the grief of the accuser or the harshness of the judge, what do you adjudge that the duty of the defender or intercessor to the accused demands? After all, you yourselves, good men who are now judges, have in the past engaged in arguing people's cases in the law-court; and you know that you used to be much happier to defend than to prosecute. Yet there is still a big difference between an advocate for the defence and an intercessor. The former puts all his effort into playing down or covering up the offence. The intercessor has as his concern the abandonment or mitigation of punishment even where there is agreement about the guilt. The just are urged to do this for sinners in the presence of God; and sinners to do this for each other on their own behalf. As scripture says: *Confess your sins to one another, and pray for yourselves* [Jas 5.16].

Every human being claims the role of humanity in someone else's house, if he can. He might punish an offence in his own home; but he is happy to leave it unpunished in the home of someone else. Indeed, if he is called to a friend's house, or if he happens to be present when a person with the power to inflict punishment is annoyed with someone, or if he comes by chance on someone who is in a rage, he is not thought very just, but rather very inhuman, if he fails to intervene. I know that you yourself, along with some of your friends, interceded for a cleric in the church of Carthage, when he had been deservedly disciplined by the bishop. You did this even though he did not have to fear the danger of bloodshed: the punishment was a bloodless one. You wanted the deed to go unpunished although you disapproved of it. But we did not conclude that you approved of his misdeed; rather we gave you a hearing, treating your intercession as something very humane. If it is allowable to intercede to mitigate ecclesiastical discipline, surely a bishop ought to intercede against your sword! The discipline is exercised so that its object will live well; the sword so that he will live no longer.

(11) In short, the Lord himself interceded with the men to save the adulteress from stoning, and by doing so he advocated the duty of intercession to us. The only difference is that he used fear to achieve this, whereas we use pleas; after all, he is the Lord and we are the servants. The fear he inspired, however, ought to make us all afraid. Is there any one of us who is *without sin*? When the men handed over to him the sinful woman to be punished and he told them that any one of them who knew that he was without sin should be the first to cast a stone, then their consciences shuddered and their violence collapsed. At that point they slipped away from the gathering, and left the pitiful woman alone with a man full of pity. Impious Jews yielded to his pronouncement; may pious Christians do so too. The pride of her pursuers yielded; may the humility of the obedient do so too. The deception of the tempter yielded; may the confession of the faithful do so too.

Good man, spare the wicked. The better you are, the gentler may you be. The more exalted you become in your power, the lowlier may you become in your piety.

(12) With an eye on your character, I have described you as a good man. However, you should keep an eye on the words of Christ and say to yourself: *No one is good except God alone* [Mk 10.18; Lk 18.19]. This must be true, as the truth spoke the words. However, do not conclude that when I

called you a good man, while the Lord says, *No one is good except God alone*, I was speaking in a deceitfully compliant manner, and setting myself in opposition to the words of the Lord. For didn't the Lord himself say something that contradicted his words: *A good man brings forth good things from the good treasury of his heart* [Lk 6.45; cf. Mt 12.35]? God, we conclude, is good in a unique way, and cannot lose this. He is not good because he participates in some other good;[9] he himself is the good which makes him good himself. When a human being is good, by contrast, his goodness depends on God, because he cannot acquire it from himself.

Those who become good do so by God's spirit; our nature is created with the potential to receive it, through its own will. In order for us to be good, we have to receive it and possess what is given us by God, whose goodness depends on himself. Anyone who abandons him becomes evil by depending on himself. In so far as someone acts rightly then – that is, does good in an informed and loving and religious manner – he is good. In so far as he sins, though – that is, turns from the path of truth and love and piety – he is bad. But who is there in this life who is completely sinless? We call someone good if goodness is predominant in his character, and we call someone excellent if he sins very little.

(13) Therefore the Lord himself describes the same people as good through participation in divine grace and as evil through the faults due to human weakness, until such time as our constitutions are completely healed of all failings and pass on to the life in which no sin is ever committed. Certainly he was teaching the good, not the evil, when he instructed them to say: *Our father, who art in heaven* [Mt 6.9]. They are good through being sons of God, not born by nature, but made so by grace; it is the same with those who *received him*, to whom he *gave power to become the sons of God* [Jn 1.12].

Scripture is also in the habit of using the name 'adoption' for this type of spiritual birth [cf. Rom 8.15, 23; 9.4], to distinguish it from the birth of God from God, of the coeternal from the eternal. Thus scripture says: *Who will tell of his generation?* [Is 53.8, LXX]. He showed that they were good because he wanted them to address God truthfully with the words, *Our father, who art in heaven*. However, he also instructed them to say in that prayer, among other things, *Forgive us our debts, as we also forgive our debtors* [Mt 6.12; cf. Lk 11.4].

It is clear that *debts* here means 'sins'. However, he made it still clearer later on when he said: *If you forgive the sins of others, your father will also forgive you your sins* [Mt 6.14].

The baptised pray this prayer; and indeed every one of their past sins is forgiven those who are baptised in the holy church.[10] However, if through living on in this frail, mortal life they did not commit further deeds requiring forgiveness, they would not be able to say truthfully: *Forgive us our debts*. They are good, then, in so far as they are sons of God; but in so far as they sin – and they witness that they do so by their own truthful confession – they are certainly bad.

(14) Now there might be some who argue that the sins of the good and of the bad are different. This is not a completely implausible thing to say. However, the Lord Jesus quite unambiguously called the same people bad, who, he said, had God as their father. Elsewhere in the very same discourse in which he teaches them that prayer, he encourages them to pray to God with the words: *Ask and you will receive; seek and you will find. Knock and it will be opened to you. For everyone who asks receives, and who seeks finds, and who knocks has the door opened* [Mt 7.7–8; Lk 11.9–10]. A little later he adds: *If you, then, who are bad, know how to give good gifts to your children, how much more will your father who is in heaven give good things to those who ask him?* [Mt 7.11; cf. Lk 11.13]. Surely God is not the father of bad men? Perish the thought! How can *your heavenly father* and *you, who are bad* be said to be the same people? Only if truth is showing two things, both what we are through the goodness of God, and what we are through the weakness of humanity.[11] The former he approves, the latter he improves.

Seneca, who lived in the apostolic period and whose letters to the apostle Paul are still read, rightly wrote: 'If you hate the bad, you hate everyone.'[12] However, we ought to love the bad precisely so that they will not be bad, just as we love the sick not so they remain sick, but so they will be cured.

(15) What about the sins we may commit in this life as we live on after our baptism, when all our sins were removed? They may not be such as to require our separation from the altars of God;[13] yet self-sacrificial mercy rather than barren grief may expiate them. If, then, we win any concession from you by our intercession, you must recognise it as an offering from you to God on your own behalf. For you are in need of the mercy that you are offering; and you can see his words *Forgive and it will be forgiven you; give and it will be given to you* [Lk 6.37–8].

On the other hand, if we really were to live so that the words *Forgive us our debts* did not apply to us, then the purer our souls were from wickedness, the more they ought to be filled with mercy. Consequently, if the

Lord's verdict, *If any of you is without sin, let him be the first to cast a stone* [Jn 8.7], were not to pierce our consciences, then we would follow his own example. For he, even though he certainly was *without sin,* said to the woman once the men had been frightened away: *Neither will I condemn you. Go, and do not sin any more* [Jn 8.11].

The guilty woman might well have been afraid that once they had left, sparing the sin of another because they were conscious of their own sins, she would be condemned quite justly by the man who was *without sin.* He, however, was not stricken by his conscience, but rather filled with mercy. When she replied to him that no one had condemned her, he said: *Neither will I condemn you,* as if to say: 'If hatred was able to spare you, why should you fear innocence?'

Moreover, to avoid appearing to approve rather than forgive her offences, he added: *Go, and do not sin any more.* This showed that he had spared the human being, but did not approve of her guilty deed. You can see now that our practice of interceding does indeed derive from religion and does not bind us in fellowship with them in their crimes. We intercede even for villains, if not as villains ourselves, still as sinners acting on behalf of sinners, and also, I think – please take this as truthful rather than insulting – with those who are sinners themselves.

(16) All this does not mean that institutionalised force has no point – the might of the emperor, the judge's[14] power of the sword, the executioner's hooks, the soldier's weapons, the correction a master gives his slave, and even the strictness of a good father.[15] All these have their own limits, causes, explanations and uses. They inspire fear and thus put a check on the bad, so that the good may live peacefully among the bad. The latter are not to be described as good just because they do not sin, out of fear of such penalties. One is good not through fear of punishment, but through the love of justice.

However, there is certainly much value in restraining human foolhardiness by the threat of law, both so that the innocent can live in security among the unscrupulous, and also for the unscrupulous themselves, that as long as fear of punishment might limit their opportunities, then appeals to God might heal their wills. However, the bishops' practice of intercession does not contradict this ordering of human affairs. Far from it. In fact, if the latter did not exist, there would be no cause or opportunity to intercede. The more just it is to punish sinners, the more welcome are the favours bestowed by those who intercede for them or spare them. In my view, the only reason that a harsher legal code of retribution was energetically put into effect in the Old Testament, in the time of the ancient prophets, was to show that it is right to establish penalties for the wicked. Consequently, when the New Testament, in its forgiveness, warns us to spare them, it must either be as a saving cure which might lead to our own sins being spared; or else in order to set an example of gentleness, so that by sparing them, Christians might allow the truth that is preached to be loved as well as feared.

(17) The spirit in which one person spares another makes a great difference. Sometimes indeed it is mercy that prompts punishment, and cruelty that prompts leniency. Let me demonstrate this clearly by an example. If someone were to spare his little boy when he insisted on playing with snakes, surely everyone would describe him, quite accurately, as cruel. If he prevented the boy and corrected him, even beating him if he ignored a verbal rebuke, surely everyone would describe him as merciful. That is why punishment should not be taken as far as death; if that happens, there is no one for it to benefit.

But even when one human being kills another, it makes a great difference whether this is done out of a passion to hurt someone, or in order to steal something unjustly say, by an enemy or robber; or within a system of retribution and obedience, as by a judge or executioner; or else, when it is necessary in order to escape or help someone else, as when a robber is killed by a traveller, or an enemy by a soldier.[16]

Sometimes the actual killer is less to blame than the person who caused the death, for example, if someone were to betray his judicial guarantor,[17] who then had to pay the lawful penalty instead of him. Again, it is not always the case that a person who causes another's death is guilty of it. What if a man was trying to seduce someone and then killed himself because he didn't get what he wanted? What if a son who was afraid of being beaten – even out of paternal love[18] – by his father, were to throw himself over a precipice and die? What if someone were to commit suicide because of, or in order to prevent, another's liberation? Surely we are not, in view of these examples of causing another's death, forced to assent to outrages? Surely we don't have either to abolish punishment for sin – even from a father – when it is imposed out of desire to reform rather than harm, or to restrict the work of mercy? We ought to feel human sorrow when such things happen; but we ought not, in order to avoid their happening, to curb the will to act correctly.

(18) Perhaps, though, when we intercede on behalf of a condemned sinner, other consequences follow that we regret. Take the very person

who has been liberated through our intercession. Perhaps his hot-headedness, having escaped punishment, will run riot in an appalling way, obedient only to his passions and ungrateful for his gentle treatment. Then the rescuing of one person from death might lead to the deaths of many others. Or again, perhaps he himself will be changed for the better through our service and reform his character, but someone else might live an evil life and perish through perpetrating similar or more serious offences, suggested to him by the other's escaping unpunished.

I do not believe that such evil consequences ought to be taken into consideration by us when we intercede with you, but only the good effects which are the aim and object of our action: setting an example of gentleness in order to win love for the word of truth; and enabling those who are freed from temporary death to live so as to avoid everlasting death (from which they will never be freed).

(19) Your strictness is, therefore, beneficial. Its exercise assists even our peace. But our intercession is beneficial as well. Its exercise modifies even your strictness. You should not object to being petitioned by the good, because the good do not object to your being feared by the bad.

The apostle Paul also inspired in wicked men the fear of your axes in the present,[19] as well as of judgement in the future, when he argued that they were a part of the provision of divine providence:

> *Every soul is subject to higher authorities. There is no authority except from God; all that there are are established by God. Anyone who resists authority resists what God has established. But those who resist that, bring judgement on themselves. Rulers do not inspire fear in those who do good, but in those who do evil. Do you want not to fear the authorities? Do good, and you will have praise from them; for the minister of God is there for your good. If you do evil, then fear him; for he does not wield a sword pointlessly. He is a minister of God, and avenger of his anger on the evil-doer. Therefore you must be subject to this necessity not only because of their anger, but also because of your conscience. That is why you also pay taxes: for they are ministers of God appointed to this very thing. Pay your debts to everyone: tax if tax is due to anyone, revenue if revenue, fear if fear, honour if honour. You should have no outstanding debts, except that of mutual love* [Rom 13.1–8].

These words of the apostle show the value of your strictness. Accordingly, just as those who are in fear are ordered to show love to those who inspire fear, so those who inspire fear are ordered to show love to those who are in fear. None of this should be done out of a desire to inflict harm, but everything out of love of serving others. Nothing appalling, nothing inhuman, should be done.[20]

In this way, the judge's punishment will be feared without the intercessor's religion being scorned. For both chastisement and pardon have a place in the successful reform of human life. Even if someone is so corrupt or impious that neither punishment nor mercy can help to reform him, still good men are to fulfil the duty of love, in their motives and in their consciences, which God can see, whether through strictness or through leniency.

(20) In the next part of your letter you say: 'However, now with our current ways of behaving, those in question want both to have the penalty for their outrages mitigated, and to keep their ill-gotten gains.'[21] Here you refer to the worst type of human being. The medicine of repentance does no good here at all. If someone is able to restore the stolen property which was the object of his sin, and does not restore it, his repentance is not real, but a pretence. If, however, he is really repenting, the sin cannot be forgiven before he returns what was stolen, but only if (as I said) this can be returned. Usually, someone who steals loses what he gains, either by suffering at the hands of other bad men or by living a bad life himself; in that case he will own nothing else to return instead. We certainly can't say to such a person, 'Return what you've stolen', unless we believe that he really does have it and is denying the fact.

Indeed, if he suffers further torment at the hands of the owner, who is wanting his goods returned and still thinks he has them to return them, then no injustice is committed. For even if he has nothing with which to pay back the stolen money, still he is paying the penalty that his sin – the cause of the money being stolen – deserves, when they use physical suffering to force him to return it. However, it is not inhuman to intercede also for such people (just as for those accused of crimes) not in order to prevent their returning other people's goods, but to avoid one human being using violence against another. I mean in particular the person who has forgiven the guilty deed, but who wants his money back and is afraid that he's being cheated; he is not still seeking vengeance.

Finally, in such cases we may be able to persuade them that those for whom we are interceding do not in fact have the required goods; then immediately we will get their sufferings alleviated. Moreover, sometimes the merciful, when the matter is in doubt, do not want to inflict on a human being punishment that is certain for the sake of money that is uncertain. It is fitting here too for us to appeal for this sort of mercy, and encourage it. It is better for you to lose the things even if he does have them, than to torture or kill him if he does not have them. In this matter, however, it is better to intercede with those who are wanting their goods returned than with the judges. Otherwise, the judge who has the power but does not force the man to return the goods might look as if he is taking them away; though in using force for this he must not, in observing probity, abandon humanity.

(21) On the other hand, I would say in utter good faith that someone who intercedes on someone else's behalf to avoid his returning stolen goods, and who, when someone has sought refuge with him, does not use every honourable means to force him to return goods, does indeed become a fellow-deceiver and fellow-criminal. It is more merciful for us to withdraw our support than to expend effort on such a person's behalf. Helping someone to sin rather than undermining or restraining their attempt gives them no real support. But surely we cannot and ought not therefore to exact the goods from him or hand him over for others to do this? We act as our episcopal powers allow us to;[22] we sometimes use the threat of human judgement; but emphatically and always we use the threat of divine judgement.

If we know that someone has stolen something and still possesses sufficient means to return it, but is reluctant to do so, we accuse, rebuke and curse him, sometimes privately, sometimes openly.[23] (The difference between characters seems to require different types of medicine, if it is not to be aroused[24] to greater madness with disastrous consequences for others.) Sometimes, if we aren't hindered by the risk of a more serious condition, we even deprive them of the communion of the holy altar.[25]

(22) It often happens, though, that we are taken in by people who either deny that they have stolen anything or insist that they have nothing which they can return. Conversely, you are often deceived when you think that we are not trying to get them to return goods, or that they have something they can return. In fact all or nearly all of us human beings love to call our own suspicions 'knowledge', or to believe them to be such, as soon as we are swayed by plausible indications. This is so even though some plausible beliefs are false, and some implausible ones are true.

That is why when you referred to some people who want both to have the penalty for their outrage mitigated and to keep their ill-gotten gains, you further added, 'Speaking from your duty as priest you consider that you should intervene on behalf of such people.'[26]

It can happen that you know something I do not know, and so I think that I should intervene on someone's behalf when he will be able to fool me but not you. I might believe that he did not have something that you know he did have. In such a case, consequently, we have differing opinions about the accused; yet neither of us wants stolen property not to be returned. As human beings we differ in our views of a human being, but we are at one on the question of justice itself.

In the same way it can also happen that I know that someone does not have something, while you do not possess absolutely certain belief, but rather plausible reasons for suspecting that he does have it. Therefore it would seem to you that I was interceding on behalf of someone who 'wants both to have the penalty for [his] outrage mitigated, and to keep [his] ill-gotten gains'.[27]

In short, then, I would not venture to say or believe or decide that I should intervene to help anyone keep his ill-gotten gains without being punished for the outrage he committed – whether I was interceding with you or others who – to our joy – are like you (if any can be found), or with the sort of men who 'pursue with great enthusiasm the possessions of others, which will do them no good, and often indeed prove dangerous and destructive',[28] or even with my own heart, of which God is witness. Rather my aim in this should be the return of the property taken unjustly, once the injustice has been forgiven, if, that is, the offender still has what he stole, or has other possessions to return instead.

(23) In fact, taking something from someone against their will does not always constitute unjust theft. Very often, people are unwilling to give due recognition to a doctor, or wages to a workman. If they receive their wages from employers who are unwilling, they do not receive them unjustly; rather, it would be unjust if they were not given to them. However, the fact that the advocate is paid for providing a just defence, and the legal expert for providing sound advice, does not mean that a judge ought to take money for a just judgement, or a witness for giving true evidence. The former appear for one side, the latter are engaged in investigating the issue between both sides.

If it is not right to be paid for just and true judgements or witness, it is certainly far more outrageous to take money for unjust and false ones; this is outrageous even if the money is given voluntarily. Usually indeed if someone pays for a just judgement he will end up demanding his money back as if it had been stolen; for the judgement ought not to have been for sale. But if anyone has given money for an unjust judgement, he would like to demand it back, if he were not afraid, and ashamed of having paid for it in the first place.

(24) There are others who have a less exalted public role and who receive money from both sides without impropriety, for example as each magistrates' official, as he receives and then advances the proceedings.[29] It is normal to demand repayment from them if they have exacted an excessive and dishonest amount, but not if their contribution was within acceptable and usual limits. We would be readier to criticise someone who, contrary to custom, demanded the return of such payment, than someone who accepted it in accordance with custom. For many roles necessary to human activity are filled by people who were attracted or held by benefits of this sort. If such people changed their way of life or advanced to a more exalted level of sanctity, they would more readily bestow the goods acquired in this way on the poor, as being their own to give, than return them as if they weren't their own to those who had given them. By contrast, anything taken in defiance of the customs of human fellowship, through theft, plunder, false accusations, force, or violent attack, must be returned – so we judge – rather than given away. Our example in the Gospels is Zacchaeus the tax-collector, who having welcomed the Lord hospitably, immediately adopted a life of holiness. *I give half of my goods to the poor*, he said, *and if I have robbed anyone of anything, I return it fourfold* [Lk 19.8].

(25) However, if we are honestly to serve justice, we will say to the advocate: 'Return what you received when you appeared against the truth and on the side of injustice. You deceived the judge, you opposed the just cause, you won your case through lies. And, of course, you see many highly honourable and eloquent gentlemen also doing this themselves, so it appears, without paying the penalty – and indeed to their own glory.' This is more just than saying to someone serving in some minor office: 'Return what you received when you obeyed the judge's order and kept hold of a man who was needed for some case, and tied him up so he didn't resist, and locked him up so he didn't run away, and finally brought him out during the trial, or sent him away when it was over.'

The reason that isn't said to the advocate is obvious: no one wants to demand back from his patron[30] the money he gave him for an unfair victory, any more than he wants to give back the money he received from his opponent after an unfair victory. Is it easy to find an advocate or former advocate who is so good a man that he will say to his client: 'Take back what you gave me when I represented you falsely, and give back to your opponent the money you took unjustly thanks to my work'?

· However, if someone very properly repents of his previously improper way of life, he ought also to do this: if the unjust litigant is unwilling, even when advised, to set the injustice straight, he at least oughtn't to keep the rewards of justice. Otherwise, one ought to return what belongs to another in cases where it was stolen secretly, but one needn't return it if it was won in the law-court itself (where sins are punished) by deceiving the judge and bending the law.

What ought I to say about interest on money, which even the law and judges require to be returned?[31] Is it more cruel to deprive or steal from someone rich, or to butcher someone poor by usury? To keep profits of this sort is certainly wrong, and I would want them returned. However, there is no judge to whom one can appeal for this restoration.

(26) Now, though, let us look wisely at the words of scripture: *The entire world of wealth belongs to the faithful person; the unfaithful does not have a penny* [Prov 17.6, LXX]. If so, surely all those who think that they are enjoying possessions they have acquired lawfully, but who don't know how to use them, can be convicted by us of keeping what belongs to someone else. They certainly do not belong to someone else if they are held lawfully; but lawfully implies justly, and justly implies well. If so, then everything that is possessed wrongly belongs to someone else; but if someone uses possessions wrongly, he possesses them wrongly. You can see then how many people ought in fact to return property that isn't theirs, and how few can be found who ought to have property returned to them! Wherever such people exist, the more justly they own property, the more they despise it. It is not possible for someone to possess justice wrongly; and if someone doesn't love justice, he does not in fact possess it. But money can be wrongly possessed by bad people, and as for the good, the less they love it, the more rightly they possess it.

In the meantime, however, there is toleration for the injustice of those in wrongful possession, and certain laws have been established among them, known as 'civil laws'. These are not intended to make them use possessions rightly, but rather to make them less oppressive in misusing them, until the time when the faithful and pious reach that city where their inheritance is eternity. (For by rights, everything belongs to the faithful; and they either come from among the bad or else live among them for a short time, and they experience their wrongdoing as a preparation rather than a hindrance.) In that city no one has a place except the just, no one rules except the wise. Whoever lives there, will truly own what he possesses.

However, even here we don't intercede to prevent the return of goods that belong to others according to earthly laws and customs. We do want you, though, to be conciliatory towards the bad. This isn't to keep them happy or help them remain bad, but because those who become good come from among them. Again, self-sacrificial mercy pleases God; moreover, if none of the bad ever found God well disposed, then no one good would exist.

I have taken my time, and seem to be adding a burden to your busy life by addressing you thus when I could have answered the questions of so clever and learned a man more quickly. I ought to have drawn to a close some time ago; and I would have done so if I thought that no one except you would read the reply you demanded from me.

May you live happily in Christ, my beloved son.

Letter 154

413/414

Macedonius to Augustine the bishop, his deservedly revered lord and truly welcome father.

(1) I am wonderfully impressed by the wisdom you showed both in your published works and in the letter that you took the trouble to send, intervening for those in distress. The former display unsurpassable penetration, knowledge and holiness; and the latter so much modesty that, if I failed to act as you advise, I should have to judge that the blame lay with me rather than with my job, deservedly revered lord and truly welcome father. You do not do as most men in your place do, and insist on exacting from me anything that any distressed person wants. Rather, you give whatever advice seems to you to be reasonable as a request to a judge who is constricted by so many concerns, and with a humble respectfulness that is particularly effective when difficulties arise among good men. Therefore I have immediately conceded to those you recommended the object of their desire; I had indeed previously cleared the way for hope.[1]

(2) I have finished your books.[2] They were not undemanding or ineffectual enough to allow me to attend to anything other than themselves. They laid their hands on me, snatched me from the bonds of other anxieties, and tied me up again in their own – may God be so kind to me! Consequently, I am torn as to what I should admire most in them: the

mature realisation of the priesthood, the teachings of philosophy, the wide knowledge of history, or the pleasant eloquence which is able so to seduce even the ignorant that they cannot stop reading until they finish, and still ask for more when they have finished. Your books have convinced even the shamelessly stubborn that worse things came out of the 'good generations' (as they call them) according to the inscrutable nature of things; and that everyone was mistaken, because of the delights laced with pleasure that they enjoyed, which led them not to blessedness, but to a precipice. On the other hand, these commandments of ours and the mysteries of the single and true God, as well as everlasting life, which is promised to those whose virtues are spotless, will indeed – they have been convinced – alleviate even this present age, and the unavoidable circumstances into which we have been born.

You used the powerful example of the recent disaster.[3] With this, you strengthened your case very vigorously; although I would have preferred you not to espouse that case if you had been allowed to choose freely. However, since those yet to be convinced, in their stupidity, had complained on that score, it was necessary to marshal the arguments for the truth of the matter.

(3) I write back to you, busy for the meantime with other concerns. They may be pointless if we reflect upon the end of things, but they are a necessary by-product, as it were, of the fact that we have been born. If I ever have the leisure, and if I live long enough, I will write again from Italy.[4] In that way your very learned work will be repaid with the services due to you, even if they fall somewhat short.

May almighty God keep your holy self in security and blessedness for a generous length of time, deservedly revered lord and truly welcome father.

Letter 155

413/414

Augustine the bishop and servant of Christ and of his family greets his dear son Macedonius in the Lord.

(1) Although I fail to recognise the wisdom which you assign to me, I still give thanks, as I ought, for your great and very genuine kindness towards me; and I am delighted that the strenuous efforts I have expended on

study have brought pleasure to so fine and great a man. This is all the more true because I can tell that your spirit is panting for God's heavenly commonwealth,[1] inspired by a love of eternity and of truth and of love itself. Christ is the ruler there, and there alone do all live in a permanent state of blessedness, if they have lived properly and piously here. I see you approaching near to it, and I embrace you as you burn to possess it. True friendship also flows from there; and this oughtn't to be weighed by temporary advantages, but drunk with freely given love. No one can truly be another's friend unless he has first been the friend of truth itself. If this does not happen freely, it can never happen at all.

(2) Philosophers have said a great deal on this topic. However, true piety, that is the truthful worship of the true God, is not found in them (and this is the source from which all the duties of a life rightly lived should be derived). This is the case, as far as I understand it, because they have wanted somehow to create the life of blessedness for themselves, and thought it something they should achieve rather than receive. However, it is given by no one except God.

No one makes a human being blessed except the maker of human beings. He has bestowed so many goods of his own creation on good and bad alike: their existence, their humanity, their flourishing senses, their health and strength, their overflowing wealth; he too will give himself to those who are good, that is, give them blessedness. For goodness is also his gift. Living in this wretched life, in these dying bodies, weighed down by the burden of their corruptible flesh, they still wanted to be the authors and founders, as it were, of their own life of blessedness. It is as if they were seeking this through their own virtues and already having hold of it, rather than asking for it from the source of all virtues and still hoping. They were quite unable to realise that God was resisting their pride.

That is why they fell into this absolutely absurd error: although they argue that a wise man is blessed even inside the bull of Phalarus,[2] they have to admit that the life of blessedness is sometimes to be avoided. For they give in to accumulated bodily evils and declare that if the latter prove seriously oppressive, one should abandon this life. I am unwilling to say here how impious it is for an innocent man to kill himself, when even a guilty man ought never to do this. I have already had much to say about this in the first of the three books which you have most kindly and devotedly perused.[3] Certainly, though, the following question demands careful thought, and sober rather than proud judgement: how can a life be blessed if the wise man does not preserve and enjoy it, but forces himself to lose it by laying hands on himself?

(3) There is a passage in Cicero, towards the end, as you know, of the fifth book of the *Tusculan Disputations*, which we should look at with respect to my present topic.[4] On the subject of physical blindness, he asserted that a wise man can be blessed even if he is blind, and then said that one could after all enjoy many things through hearing. Conversely, he transferred those enjoyments to the eyes for the case of someone who was deaf. What, though, if he were deprived of both senses, and became blind and deaf? Here Cicero did not venture to carry over the conclusion and pronounce him blessed. Rather, he added to the example further very serious physical sufferings. If these didn't kill the man, he was to kill himself, and thus reach the harbour of unconsciousness, set free by virtue of this sort.

The wise man gives in to appalling disasters, and collapses so completely under their weight that he is even forced to commit murder – against himself. If someone doesn't spare himself, will he spare anyone, in order to be rid of such evils? He is certainly permanently blessed. Undoubtedly no new disaster has the strength to deprive him of the life of blessedness. But look – either in his blindness, deafness, and grim torments he has lost the life of blessedness; or else, if his life is still blessed in the middle of such sufferings, then – according to the debates of the most learned men of this sort – there are times when the wise man cannot endure the blessed life. Alternatively – and even more absurdly – it may be that he ought not to endure it, and so should escape it, break it off, throw it away, removing himself from it with a sword or poison or some other means of voluntary death. Thus he ends up existing in the harbours of unconsciousness, or else not existing at all (as the Epicureans and any others of similar folly believed). Or thirdly, he is blessed just because he has fled from that life of blessedness as if he had been saved from some plague. What an excessively proud boast to make!

If the life of blessedness can exist in the middle of physical torment, why does the wise man not remain there and enjoy it? But if such a life is in fact miserable, then what, I beg you, except hubris prevents you from admitting this, from praying to God, from pleading with the just and merciful one who has power over this life, either to avert or to alleviate its evils or to arm you with the courage to endure them; or else to free you entirely from them, granting you after all this a life that is truly blessed? There no evil is present, and there the supreme good is never absent.[5]

(4) That is the reward of the pious. It is in the hope of gaining it that we lead this temporary and mortal life, with endurance rather than with delight. We face its evils bravely, relying on sound purpose together with divine assistance; while we rejoice in God's faithful promise of, and our faithful hope for, goods that will last for ever. The apostle encourages us with the words: *rejoicing in hope, patient in trials* [Rom 12.12]. He shows why he says *patient in trials* by putting *rejoicing in hope* first. I encourage you in this hope through Jesus Christ our Lord. God himself, our master, taught us this, when the majesty of his divinity was hidden but the weakness of his flesh manifest. He did this not only by his spoken word, but also by the example of his passion and resurrection. He revealed in the one what we ought to endure, and in the other what we ought to hope for.

They too would deserve his grace, if they were not, with all their proud over-confidence and conceit, pointlessly attempting to win the blessed life for themselves. For God alone has truly promised that he will bestow this on his worshippers after this present life. Indeed, Cicero's own opinion was more sound when he said: 'For this life is really death; if I wanted to, I could mourn for it.'[6]

Well, then, if it is right to mourn for this life, how can it be proved blessed? If it is right to mourn for it, aren't we rather convicting it of being miserable? Please, then, good man, for the mean time get used to being blessed in hope; then you may be so in fact when your unwavering piety is rewarded with everlasting happiness.

(5) If my lengthy letter is a burden to you, 'you are responsible for the mess yourself',[7] by calling me wise. That is why I have been bold enough to say all this to you, to display to you the wisdom not that I do in fact possess, but that I ought to. In the present age this consists in the true worship of the true God, so that in the future age you may enjoy its fruit secure and whole. Here it is steadfast piety, there everlasting felicity.

If I do possess any of the one true wisdom, I have received it from God. I did not receive it first from myself; and I hope in faith that it will be brought to maturity in me by God, from whom I have with humble joy received its seed. I am not distrustful because he has not yet granted the former, nor ungrateful now that he has already granted the latter. If I deserve any praise at all, it is not through my own abilities or merit, but through his gift. Indeed, many men of sharp and outstanding talents have more seriously lost their way the more that they have in their travels relied on their own strength and failed to beg God prayerfully and truthfully to show them the way. But what are the merits of any human being worth when he found us all sinners – he, the bringer of freedom who alone was freed from sin and came to bring not a reward that was owed, but grace that was freely given?

(6) So if true virtue pleases us, let us address to him the words we read in his own sacred writings: *I will love you, Lord, my virtue* [Ps 18(17).1].[8] If we wish to be truly blessed (something we cannot fail to wish) we should hold faithfully in our hearts the words of the same writings: *Blessed is the man whose hope is in the name of the Lord, and who has not gazed on foolishness and deceitful madness* [Ps 40(39).4, LXX].

What folly, what madness, what self-deception, for a mortal man to trust himself to win blessedness! After all, he is living out a grim life here, his flesh and spirit subject to change, burdened by so many sins, subject to so many temptations, exposed to such a variety of corruption, and destined for the justest of punishment. For not even the one outstandingly worthy part of his own nature, that is his mind and reason, can be acquitted of error unless God is present as a light to the mind.

Please, then, let us cast aside the *foolishness and deceitful madness* of lying philosophers: we will not possess virtue unless he is present with us to help us, nor blessedness unless he is present with us for us to enjoy, and unless he *swallows up* with the gift of immortality and *incorruption* the whole of our changeable and corruptible selves [cf. 1 Cor 15.53–4]; on their own they are simply weak, merely the stuff of which misery is made.

(7) Now I know that you are devoted to public affairs;[9] see then how clearly the sacred writings declare that the source of human blessedness is the same as that of civic blessedness. The psalmist in prayer, filled with the Holy Spirit, says there:

> *Rescue me from the hands of the sons of strangers, whose mouths have spoken folly and whose right hands are the right hands of injustice.*[10] *Their sons are like strong young plants in their youth, and their daughters dressed and adorned like a copy of the temple. Their storehouses are full, disgorging from one to another. Their sheep are fertile and multiply in their going forth; their cattle are fat. There are no falling walls, no traversing, no uproar on their streets. They have said that a people who has all this is blessed. Blessed is the people whose God is the Lord* [Ps 144(143).11–15, LXX].

(8) You can see that the people is described as blessed on account of accumulated earthly happiness only by 'the sons of strangers', that is, by those who have no part in the rebirth that makes us sons of God. The psalmist

is praying that he will be *rescued from their hands*, to avoid being dragged by them to their beliefs, and to impious acts of sin. They certainly did talk foolishly when *they said that a people who has all this is blessed* (referring to the things I listed above) which are the only things that lovers of this world seek. That is why *their right hands are the right hands of injustice*: they put first what ought to be put second, as right is put before left. One may have such goods; but the life of blessedness oughtn't to be thought to depend on them. They ought to be subordinate, not dominant; they ought to follow, not lead.

What might we say to the man who was praying in this way, and who longed to be rescued and separated *from the sons of strangers* who *have said that a people who has all this is blessed*? This perhaps: 'What do you think yourself? What sort of people do you call blessed?' He will not reply, 'Blessed is the people whose virtue belongs to their own spirit.' Now in saying that, he would, certainly, be distinguishing that people from the people who place the life of blessedness in visible and physical happiness.[11] However, he would not yet have risen above all *foolishness and deceitful madness*. For, as the same writings teach elsewhere: *Everyone who puts his hope in a human being is cursed* [Jer 17.5]. Therefore no one should place it in himself, as he is a human being himself. Consequently, in order to rise above the limitations of all *foolishness and deceitful madness* [Ps 40(39).4], and to establish the life of blessedness in its true place, he said: *Blessed is the people whose God is the Lord.*

(9) You can see, then, where you should look for the object of everyone's desire, whether they are learned or not. Many fail, through error or pride, to learn where to look for it, and where to receive it. Both types are criticised together in one of the divine psalms: *those who trust in their own virtue and who boast in the abundance of their riches* [Ps 49(48).6, LXX]. This refers both to the philosophers of the present age and also to those who shun even such philosophy as that, saying that a people is blessed if they have sufficient earthly wealth. Therefore we should seek virtue from the Lord our God who made us, so that we can overcome the evils of this life; we should also seek the life of blessedness, so that we may enjoy it after this life for eternity. Thus both in virtue and in the reward of virtue *whoever boasts*, to quote the apostle, *should boast in the Lord* [2 Cor 10.17].

That is what we want for ourselves and for the city of which we are citizens. The source of blessedness is not one thing for a human being and another for a city: a city is indeed nothing other than a like-minded mass of human beings.[12]

94

(10) Take all your virtues: all the good sense[13] with which you try to serve human affairs, all the courage with which you allow no enemy's wickedness to frighten you, all the moderation through which you keep yourself from corruption when surrounded by the rottenness of contemptible human habits, all the justice which you use to judge correctly in assigning to each his own.[14] Suppose that you employ all these virtues in toiling and struggling for the physical security of those you want to do well, and to allow them to be safe from anyone's unscrupulousness and in peace to enjoy *sons ... like strong young plants, and ... daughters dressed and adorned like a copy of the temple ... storehouses ... full, disgorging from one to another,* and *fertile sheep* with *no falling walls* to spoil their property, and *no uproar* from legal disputes echoing in *their streets* [Ps 144(143).12–15., LXX]. If so, neither your virtues nor the blessedness that comes from them will be real.

At this point I ought not to let the modesty which you were kind enough to praise in your letter prevent me from speaking the truth. I want to say this: if any of your governing, however informed by the virtues I listed, is directed only to the final aim of allowing human beings to suffer no unjust hardships in the flesh; and if you think that it is no concern of yours to what purpose they put the peace that you struggle to provide for them (that is, to speak directly, how they worship the true God, with whom the fruit of all peaceful life is found), then all that effort towards the life of true blessedness will not benefit you at all.[15]

(11) I appear to be rather shameless in saying this, as if I have somehow forgotten my normal practice when making intercession. Respectfulness, though, is nothing other than a sort of fear of arousing displeasure. If so, in this case fear causes me not to be too respectful. For I am justly afraid of displeasing, firstly, God and, secondly, the friendship which you have honoured me by initiating, if I fail to be free in giving the advice that I believe most salutary to give. I would certainly be more respectful when interceding with you for others. When I do so for your sake, though, the more I am your friend, the freer I should be; because the more your friend, the more faithful to you. However, I wouldn't say even that, if I weren't speaking respectfully. As you yourself wrote, respectfulness is 'particularly effective when difficulties arise among good men'.[16] I hope it will assist me with you, on your behalf, so that I may enjoy you in God, who has provided me with the opportunity to approach you with confidence. This is particularly so because I believe that the suggestion I am making is easy for you to accept, now that your spirit is supported by and furnished with so many God-given gifts.

(12) If you recognise the source of the virtues you have been given and give him thanks; if you use them even in your secular position of honour to contribute to his worship; if you inspire and lead those people under your power to worship him both by living an exemplary religious life and through the devotion you show to their interests, whether by support or deterrence; if the only reason that you want them, with your help, to live more securely is so that they might win God, in whose presence they will live blessedly; then, all your virtues will be real ones. They will develop and be perfected in this way through the assistance of God, whose generous gift they were. Then, without any doubt, they will bring you to the truly blessed life, which can only be everlasting.

In that place, there will be no sensible distinguishing of bad from good, because bad will not exist; there will be no brave endurance of difficulties, because there will be nothing for us to endure there except the things we love; in that place there will be no moderate restraining of the passions, because we will not feel them being aroused; and there will be no just use of our wealth to assist the needy because we will not have anyone poor or in need.

One virtue alone will exist there: both virtue and the reward of virtue. As the man who loves this says in the sacred discourse: *For me it is good to cling to God* [Ps 73(72).28]. Both complete and eternal wisdom, and also a life now fully blessed will consist in this. Now we will have reached the everlasting and supreme good; and it is the completion of our good[17] to cling to this for ever.

We might also call this good sense, because it will cling very prudently to the good that it will never lose; and courage, because it will cling very tenaciously to the good and will not be torn from it; and moderation, because it will cling in purity to the good, as it cannot now be corrupted; and justice, because it will cling very rightly to the good, which it deserves to serve.

(13) Moreover, even in this life there is no virtue except that of loving what ought to be loved. Good sense consists in choosing that, courage in allowing no hardships, moderation in allowing no temptations, justice in allowing no pride, to divert one from it. What should we choose to love particularly, if not the one thing we can find that is unsurpassed? This is God; and if in loving anything else we make it preferable or equal to him, we have forgotten how to love ourselves. The nearer we approach to him, the better it is for us; for nothing is better than him. We approach him, however, not by moving, but by loving.

We will have him nearer to us the more we can keep pure the love that carries us to him: he is not spread out or enclosed in physical space. He is present everywhere, and entirely everywhere; we can reach him then not by foot, but by character. However, our character is usually judged not from what we know, but from what we love. It is good and bad loves that make good and bad characters. Our crookedness takes us far away from the uprightness of God. But the latter reforms us when we love what is right; then, now made upright, we can cling to what is right.

(14) Let us do everything we can, then, to bring to him also those whom we love as ourselves; if, that is, we now realise that loving ourselves means loving him. For Christ himself (that is, the truth) said *on these two commandments hang all the law and the prophets*: to *love God with all our heart, and all our soul, and all our mind; and to love our neighbours as ourselves* [Mt 22.37–40; Mk 12.30–1; Lk 10.27; cf. Deut 6.5; Lev 19.18]. Surely we must count as our neighbour here not only our blood relatives, but our fellow sharer in reason; and all men are fellows in this respect. For if by reason of money we can be 'fellows', how much more so, then, by reason of nature – by the law, that is, of our shared birth, not our shared business?

For this reason the comic poet, whose shining wit contains rays of truth, wrote this line for one old man to address to another:

Do you have so much time off from your own affairs, that you concern yourself with someone else's, which have nothing to do with you?

The other one replied:

I am human, and I consider nothing human alien to me.[18]

They say that whole theatres, packed with ignorant and uneducated audiences, have burst into applause at this sentence. Indeed, the fellowship of all human spirits naturally touched the hearts of everyone, so much that everyone there thought of himself precisely as the neighbour of every other human being.

(15) A human being, then, ought to love God and himself and his neighbour with the love commanded by divine law. However, we were not given three commandments; he did not say, 'on these three', but *all the law and the prophets hang on these two commandments*, that is on the love of *God, with all one's heart and all one's soul and all one's mind*, and of *one's neighbour as oneself*. This is so that we grasp that the love with which

someone loves himself is exactly the same love as that with which he loves God. If he loves himself in any other way, we ought rather to say that he hates himself: for whenever someone, by turning away from a greater and more excellent good and turning towards himself, turns towards what is inferior and in need, he is deprived of the light of justice and becomes unjust. Then the very true words of scripture become true of him: *Whoever loves injustice, hates his own soul* [Ps 11(10).5].

No one, then, can love himself except by loving God. Thus there was no need, once he had given the commandment about loving God, to order human beings also to love themselves: one loves oneself precisely by loving God. We ought therefore *to love both God and our neighbour as ourselves*, so that we will lead anyone we can to worship God by comforting them with kindness, or educating them through teaching, or restraining them through discipline, in the knowledge that *all of the law and the prophets hang on these two commandments.*

(16) When anyone chooses this with sober discernment he is sensible. When hardships do not deter him he is brave; when pleasures do not, he is moderate; when self-esteem does not, he is just. We are divinely endowed with such virtues through the grace of the mediator, Christ Jesus, who is God with the Father, and human with us. Through him, we are reconciled with God in the spirit of love, after the enmity that wickedness created. Divinely endowed, then, with these virtues, we can lead a good life now; and afterwards our reward will be paid, a blessed life, which can only be everlasting.

Here we have the practice of the virtues, there their result; here their labours, there their reward; here their duties, there their goal. In this way all those who are good and holy can indeed be called blessed while suffering any torture you like, provided they rely on divine assistance in the hope of that end which will make them blessed. For if they were permanently to endure such tortures, or other agonising pains, no sane reasoning would hesitate to describe them as miserable, however virtuous they were.[19]

(17) Piety, therefore, that is the true worship of the true God,[20] is beneficial in every way. It protects against hardships in this life, or else softens them; and it brings us to that life and that security where we will suffer no more evil and enjoy the supreme and eternal good. I urge you to pursue it more perfectly and hold on to it with great tenacity; I urge this on myself also.

Unless you already shared in piety, and reckoned that your temporary position of honour ought to be put to its service, you would not have said the following to the Donatist heretics, in an edict aimed at bringing them back into the unity and peace of Christ: 'This is done for your sake. It is for you that the priests of unsullied faith, for you that the august emperor, for you that we his judges also, labour', and many other such things that you put in the same edict, so that even though you wore the belt [21] of an earthly judge you appeared to have your mind largely fixed on the heavenly commonwealth.[22]

I am sorry if I have wanted to speak to you at excessive length on this subject of the true virtues and the true life of blessedness; please don't think me a burden when you are so busy. Indeed, I trust that I am not, when you manage, in a great and wonderfully admirable spirit, to avoid abandoning those concerns, while at the same time involving yourself freely and familiarly with these.

Judicial authority

Commentary on the gospel of John, 33

419/421

On the gospel passage from: *When they heard his discourse some of the crowd* (Jn 7.40) to *Neither will I condemn you; go and do not sin any more* (Jn 8.11).[1]

(1) You will remember, my beloved friends, that when I was given the opportunity to preach by the gospel reading yesterday, I spoke to you about the Holy Spirit. The Lord invited those who believed in him to drink of the Spirit; he was addressing men who thought that they had him in their grasp, and were eager to kill him. They were not strong enough, because he himself was unwilling. While he spoke to them in this way, the crowd began to grow restless on his account: some thought that he was the Christ himself, others denied that the Christ was going to rise out of Galilee. The men who were sent to arrest him returned innocent of the crime, and filled with wonder. They also bore witness that his teaching was divine: when the men who had sent them in the first place asked, *'Why have you not brought him back?'*, they replied that they'd never heard a human being speak like that: *'Because no human being speaks in this way.'*

But he spoke in this way because he was both God and man. The Pharisees,[2] though, rejected their witness, and asked them, *'Surely you have not been led astray also? We can see how much you have enjoyed his speeches. Have any of our rulers believed in him, or any of the Pharisees? But this crowd, who do not know the Law, are accursed.'*

Those who didn't know the Law believed in the very person who had sent the Law; and the one who had sent the Law was condemned by those who were teaching the Law. In this way the Lord's own words were fulfilled: *'I came so that those who do not see might see, and the seeing might become blind'* [Jn 9.39]. The teachers, the Pharisees, indeed have become blind; while the people who did not know the Law, but believed in the author of the Law, have been enlightened.

(2) *Nicodemus*, however, was *one of the Pharisees, who had come to the Lord by night* [Jn 3.2]; he was not an unbeliever, but he was afraid.[3] He had come by night to the Light, because he wanted to be enlightened, but he was afraid of being recognised. He replied to the Jews, *'Surely our Law does not judge a person before it has given him a hearing and knows what he is doing?'*

In their perversity they wanted to condemn him before they had studied his case.[4] Nicodemus was well aware, or at least he believed, that if only they would be willing to listen to him patiently, they themselves might become like the men they'd sent to arrest him, who had chosen to believe. *They replied to him* just as they had to them, because they were prejudiced in their hearts, *'Surely you are not a Galilean as well?'*

That is to say, they were implying that he'd been led astray by the Galilean. The Lord was known as a Galilean because his parents were from the town of Nazareth. I said 'parents' with reference to Mary, not to the male seed.[5] He only needed a mother on earth, as he already had a Father above. In fact, his double birth was a double marvel: his divine birth didn't have a mother, his human birth didn't have a father. Well, then, what did those so-called teachers of the Law say to Nicodemus? *'Examine the Scriptures, and realise that no prophet rises from Galilee!'*

However, the Lord of the prophets has risen from there. *They returned*, the Evangelist says, *each to his own home.*

(3) *Then Jesus proceeded to the mountain.* The mountain, moreover, was the *Mount of Olives*, a mountain rich in fruit, a mountain rich in ointments, a mountain rich in oil for chrism. Where was more fitting for Christ to teach them than the Mount of Olives? For the name Christ comes from the word 'chrism'; in Greek it's called *chrisma*, and in Latin *unctio* [anointing]. He anointed us precisely by making us wrestle against the Devil.

And at daybreak he went again into the temple and all the people came to him, and he sat down and taught them. But they were not able to arrest him, because he didn't think it appropriate yet for him to suffer.

(4) Pay attention now to the part where the Lord's gentleness was put to the test by his enemies. *However, the Scribes and Pharisees brought to him a woman who had been caught in adultery, and put her in the middle. They said to him, 'Teacher, this woman has just been caught in adultery. Moses has instructed us in the Law to stone culprits of this sort. What would you say about this?'*

They said this to test him, so that they might be able to bring a charge against him. To bring a charge on what grounds? Surely they hadn't caught him in some criminal act! Or were they implying that the woman had some connection with him? What is meant by the words *in order to put him to the test, so that they might be able to bring a charge against him?* My brothers, we should realise that the Lord's marvellous gentleness is quite outstanding. They had noticed that he was exceedingly mild, exceedingly gentle. Indeed, an earlier prophecy had referred to him: *Gird your sword around your thigh, O mighty one. Press on in your splendour and beauty, march forward in prosperity, and reign, for the sake of truth, and gentleness, and justice* [Ps 45(44).3–4].

He brought the truth, then, as a teacher, gentleness as a liberator, justice as a judge.[6] That's why the prophet foretold that he would reign in the Holy Spirit.[7] When he spoke, his truth won recognition; when he wasn't roused against his enemies, his gentleness won praise. His enemies, then, were tormented by spite and hatred because of these two, his truth and his gentleness, and they put a stumbling-block in the path of the third, his justice.

Why? Because the Law had ordained that adulterers should be stoned;[8] and it was absolutely impossible for the Law to ordain something that was unjust.[9] If someone proposed an alternative to what the Law commanded, he would be convicted of injustice.

And so they spoke among themselves: 'He's thought to be truthful; he seems to be gentle; we must look for a way of slandering his justice. Let's present him with a woman caught in adultery; let's tell him what the Law instructs in cases like hers. Then, if he orders her to be stoned, he'll be lacking in mercy; but if he decrees that she should be released he'll lose hold of his justice.' 'However', they reasoned, 'he will undoubtedly say that we ought to release her, so that he does not destroy his gentleness, which has already won him the affection of the people. Here we have our opportunity to bring a charge against him and convict him of colluding against the Law.[10] We can say to him, "You are an enemy of the Law. Your reply contradicts Moses – or rather contradicts God, who gave the Law to Moses. You are guilty of a capital offence; you must be stoned along with her."'

Words and judgements of this sort would be capable of inflaming hatred, fanning accusations, and stirring up demands for condemnation. But against whom? Crookedness against uprightness, falsehood against truth, a corrupt heart against an upright one, folly against wisdom. Would they, though, even manage to prepare a noose without putting their own heads in it first? For look! – the Lord will both preserve justice in his reply and avoid abandoning gentleness. The trap was set for him and he wasn't caught; but they set the trap, and they were caught. This was because they failed to believe in him, even though he was capable of extracting them from the noose.

(5) What then did the Lord Jesus reply? What did Truth reply? What did Wisdom reply? What did Justice reply, the precise target of their false accusations? He didn't say, 'She should not be stoned.' So he avoided appearing to contradict the Law. Did he say: 'She should be stoned'? Perish the thought! He did not come to destroy what he had found, but to seek what had been lost [cf. Lk 19.10]. So what was his reply? Look how full of justice it was, how full of gentleness and truth! *'If any of you is without sin'*, he said, *'Let him be the first to cast a stone at her.'*

What wisdom in that answer! How did it open the door for them into themselves? They were engaging in false accusations out of doors, so to speak, but they failed to examine their own indoors. They saw an adulteress, they didn't notice themselves. It was as colluders against the Law[11] that they were eager to fulfil the Law; and to fulfil it by false accusation, rather than genuinely, by condemning adultery through chastity. You have heard him, Jews! You have heard him, Pharisees! Teachers of the Law, you have heard the guardian of the Law; but you haven't yet recognised him as maker of the Law. What else did you think it meant when he wrote on the ground with his finger? The Law was written by the finger of God, but it was written on stone because they were hard [cf. Exod 31.18]. And now the Lord was writing on the earth, because he was looking for fruit.

You have heard it then, 'Let the Law be fulfilled, let the adulteress be stoned.' But surely the Law shouldn't be fulfilled in having her punished, by men who deserve punishment themselves? Each one of you should reflect upon yourself, should enter within yourself, should mount the tribunal of your own mind, should arraign yourself before your own conscience, and should force yourself to confess. You know who you are; *for no man knows what belongs to him, except the spirit of the man which is within him* [1 Cor 2.11]. Each one of us discovers that he's a sinner when he attends to himself. It is clear, then: either release the woman, or else accept the penalty of the Law along with her.

If Jesus were to say, 'The adulteress shouldn't be stoned', then he would be convicted of injustice. If he were to say, 'She should be stoned', he'd seem to be lacking in gentleness. Let him say what he ought to say, as someone both gentle and just. *'If any of you is without sin'*, he said, *'Let him be the first to cast a stone at her.'*

This is Justice speaking: the sinful woman should be punished, but not by sinners.[12] The Law should be fulfilled, but not by those who violate the Law. This is certainly Justice speaking: and the others were hit by his justice as if it were a wooden club; they looked within themselves, and they discovered their own guilt; and *one by one they all left*. The two of them were left, pity and the pitiable. After the Lord had struck them with the weapon of justice, he didn't choose to focus on them while they were falling, but he turned his gaze away from them, and *once again wrote with his finger on the ground*.

(6) Then, when the woman was left there alone and they'd all gone, he lifted up his eyes to her. We have heard the voice of Justice; let's also hear the voice of Gentleness. It seems to me that the woman would have been more terrified still when she heard the Lord's words: *If any of you is without sin, let him be the first to cast a stone at her*.

The men, then, turned their attention to themselves, and confessed their guilt simply by departing; and they left the woman with her own grave sin to him, who was without sin.[13] Because she had heard his words, *'If any of you is without sin, let him be the first to cast a stone at her'*, she expected to be punished by him, *in whom no sin* could be found [cf. 1 Jn 3.5]. However, having rebuffed her opponents with the voice of justice, he lifted to her a look of gentleness and asked her, *'Has no one condemned you?'*

She replied, *'No one, Lord.'*

He then said, *'Neither will I condemn you.* Perhaps you were afraid of being condemned by me because you have found no sin in me. *Neither will I condemn you.'*

Why is this, Lord? Are you on the side of sinners, then? Surely not. Notice what comes next: *'Go, and do not sin any more.'* The Lord did, therefore, voice condemnation, but of the sin, not of the person.[14] For if he were in favour of sins, he would say, 'Neither will I condemn you; go and live as you want to. You can count on my setting you free. However much you sin, I'll free you from all punishments, even from Gehenna, and from the torments of hell.' But he did not say that.

(7) Those who love the gentleness of the Lord should take note, therefore, and also fear his truth. For *you are kind and upright, Lord* [Ps 25(24).8]. You love him because he is kind; fear him because he is upright. In his gentleness he said, *'I have kept silent'*; but in his justice he asks, *'Shall I keep silent for ever?'* [Is 42.14, LXX]. *The Lord is merciful and has pity*. That is clear; but add to it *patient*. And then add, *and very merciful*.

However, you should fear what comes at the end: *and truthful* [Ps 86(85).15]. Those he's supporting at present, despite their sins, he'll be judging eventually, because of their scorn.

Are you scorning the riches of his patience and gentleness, in ignorance of the fact that God's forbearance is leading you to repentance? Through your hardness of heart and your impenitent heart, however, you are storing up wrath for yourself on the day of wrath, and of the revelation of the just judgement of God. For he will render to each person according to his works [Rom 2.4–6].

The Lord is gentle, the Lord is patient, the Lord is merciful. However, the Lord is also just and he is truthful. He generously allows you room to reform yourself. You, however, are fonder of postponement than of improvement. You were wicked yesterday, were you? Then be good today. You've spent today indulging your spite, have you? Well, why not change for tomorrow? You're always waiting hopefully for something, and you've been promised so much by God's mercy. It's as if he has not only promised to pardon you if you repent, but has also promised you a longer life! How do you know what tomorrow will bring?

In your own heart you speak correctly: 'When I have reformed myself, God will disregard all my sins.' We can't deny that God has promised pardon to those who reform and convert. You can indeed read to me the passage from a prophet where God promised pardon to anyone who has reformed; but you can't read to me any passage from the same prophet[15] where God promises you a long life.

(8) We are in danger, therefore, from either side, from hope and from despair, contradictory things, contradictory emotions. Who is it that's deceived through hoping? The person who says, 'God is good, God is merciful, I will do whatever I like, whatever pleases me. Let me relax the reins of my passions and satisfy the longings of my soul. And why? Because God is merciful, God is good, God is gentle.' That is the sort who are in danger from hope.

On the other hand, people are in danger from despair when they fall into serious sins and think that they can't now be pardoned even if they repent. Then they decide that they're destined without doubt for condemnation, and say to themselves, 'As we're already condemned, why not do whatever we want?' They say this in the spirit of gladiators condemned to the sword. That's why desperate men are troublesome: they no longer have anything to fear, so they need to be strenuously feared themselves.

The one lot are killed by despair, the other by hope. The spirit vacillates between hope and despair. You need to be afraid of being killed by hope, in case by harbouring too great a hope of mercy you come under judgement. You need to be afraid on the other hand of being killed by despair, in case by thinking that it's too late for you to be pardoned for your serious offences, you fail to repent, and encounter the judge, Wisdom, who says, *'And I shall mock your affliction'* [Prov 1.26].

What does the Lord do, then, with those who are at risk from these two types of illness? This is what he says to those who are at risk from hope: *'Do not be slow to turn to the Lord, and do not delay from day to day. For his anger will arrive suddenly, and he will destroy you in the time of retribution'* [Ecclus 5.7].

What does he say to those who are at risk from despair? Every day that *the wicked man turns back, I will forget all his transgressions* [Ezek 18.21–2].

For the sake of those at risk from despair, he offers the haven of forgiveness; for the sake of those at risk from hope, who are cheating themselves by delaying, he makes the date of one's death uncertain. You do not know when your last day will arrive. Are you ungrateful because today you've been given the means to reform yourself?

This is the sense, then, in which he said to that woman, *'Neither will I condemn you.'* I have stopped you worrying about the past; beware of what's in the future. *Neither will I condemn you.* I have blotted out your offences; attend to my commands, so that you will come to find what I have promised you.

Sermon 302

On the feast of St Laurence

(1) Today is the feast-day of the blessed martyr Laurence.[1] The readings we have heard from holy scripture[2] were appropriate to this celebration. We heard them and we sang them, and we have listened attentively to the gospel reading.[3] Now we must follow in the footsteps of the martyrs by imitating them; otherwise our celebration of their feast-days is meaningless. Everyone knows the merits of the martyr we are commemorating. Has anyone prayed to him, and not had the prayer answered? Think of all the sick who have been granted temporary gifts through his merits – gifts

of the sort to which he was indifferent himself. They were not granted so that they'd remain sick. No, it was so that giving them earthly gifts might inspire them with a passion to seek something better. Sometimes a father with little children lets them have something small and unimportant, if they are going to cry unless they are given it. When he allows them or gives them these things, he is indulging them out of fatherly kindness, even though he won't want his children to keep them when they are older and more grown up. So he gives nuts to his children even while he is preserving their inheritance for them. The devoted father allows them to play and enjoy themselves with whatever silly toys they have, so as not to expect too much of them at their tender age. But that is not building them up, it is keeping them happy.

Now you have heard in the gospel what the martyrs have built, what they succeeded in winning, what their generous hearts won for them, why they shed their blood: *'Your reward will be great in heaven'* [Mt 5.12].

(2) My dear friends, there are two lives, one before death, the other after death. Both of these lives have had their lovers and still have them. Surely I needn't remind you how short life is. We know from experience that it is full of suffering and complaining. It is beset by temptations, it is filled with fears. It burns with passions; it is at the mercy of chance. It hurts in misfortunes; with success, it grows arrogant. It greets profit with unrestrained joy; and is tormented by losses. Even while someone is rejoicing over his profits, he is trembling in case he loses what he has already got, and has that to complain about. Though before he ever got it, of course, he wasn't complaining. In short, it is genuine unhappiness, or deceptive happiness.

While someone is at the bottom, he is keen to make his way up; when he gets to the top, he is afraid of slipping down. If someone hasn't got something, he envies whoever has it. If he has got it, he despises whoever hasn't. Now who could spell out in words quite how unpleasant, and how obviously unpleasant, this life is? But even this unpleasantness has its lovers. In fact, we would be lucky to find a handful of people who love everlasting life – which cannot end – as much as they love this life, which comes to an end so soon. Even while it lasts, every day we are afraid of losing it from hour to hour.

How am I to respond? What can I do? What can I say? Can I find any threats sharp enough to pierce hearts that are hard and apathetic, any encouragement fiery enough to burn hearts that are numbed and frozen by worldly preoccupations? To move them to shake off their earthly sleepiness at last, and to be fired with longing for something that lasts for ever? What can I do, I ask you? What can I say? But I do have something, which occurs to me from time to time: in fact, day-to-day experience gives me guidance, and suggests to me what to say. Move on from loving this temporary life, if you can, to loving everlasting life, the life that the martyrs loved, while counting this life as nothing. I entreat you, I beg you, I urge you, not only you, but those with you – and also myself: let's fall in love with everlasting life!

I don't expect us to love it enormously (although it is an enormous thing). No, just in the way that its lovers love this temporary life – though not in the way the holy martyrs loved their temporary lives! They had little or no love for them. They found it easy to put everlasting life first. I wasn't thinking of the martyrs when I said, 'Let's fall in love with eternal life in the way people love their temporary lives.' No, I meant the way lovers of this temporary life love it. Let's fall in love in the same way with eternal life. That is the love that Christians confess.

(3) That is why we became Christians, not for the sake of this temporary life. Think of all those Christians who are carried off before they grow up; and of the idolaters who survive this life and live to a frail old age. On the other hand, many of them also die young. Christians suffer many losses; the impious often make profits; but then again, Christians often make profits while the impious suffer losses. Many of the impious receive honours, and many Christians get rejections; but then again, many of the impious get rejections, and many Christians win honours. Success and failure are shared by both groups.

Did we become Christians then, my brothers, in order to avoid failure or to achieve success? Is that why we have enrolled with Christ, and presented our foreheads to receive this great sign? You are a Christian. You carry the cross of Christ on your forehead. This mark teaches you what it is that you confess. While he was hanging on the cross – the cross you carry on your forehead; it doesn't inspire you as a symbol of the wood, but as a symbol of him hanging on it – to repeat, while he was hanging on the cross, he looked at the violent people around him, he put up with their insults, and he prayed for his enemies. He was a doctor – even while he was being put to death, he was healing the sick with his own blood, by saying, *'Father, forgive them, for they know not what they do'* [Lk 23.34].

His prayer was not empty or in vain. Later on, thousands of people after them came to believe in the man they had put to death. Then they learned to suffer for his sake, as he had suffered for them, at their hands.

So learn from this sign, my brothers, learn from the mark that the Christian receives even when he becomes a catechumen[4] – learn from this why we are Christians. It is not for the sake of temporary and short-lived things, whether good or bad. It is in order to avoid evils that will never pass away, and to acquire goods that will never come to an end.

(4) But to continue what I started to say, my brothers, we must give our minds – please do this – to the subject I suggested and proposed just now: the way that the lovers of this temporary life fall in love with it. We human beings are so terrified in case we die – but we are going to die! You can see men shaking with fear, running away, searching for hiding places, hunting for protection, prostrating themselves, giving whatever they have in order to be granted their lives – if only it can be done – to live for one more day, to extend a little bit longer a tenure that can never be secure.

Those are the lengths to which people will go; but who does this sort of thing for the sake of eternal life? Let us have a word with a lover of this present life.

'Why are you doing all this? Why are you rushing around, why are you afraid, why are you running away, why are you looking for somewhere to hide?'

'In order to live', he replies.

'Are you sure you will live? That you'll never die?'

'No.'

'So you can't manage to get rid of death, but only to postpone it? If you're prepared to do all this so that you will die a little later, why not do something so that you'll never die?'

(5) Think how often we come across people saying, 'The tax-collector can take all my property, as long as I can die a little bit later.' But how rare it is to find someone saying, 'Christ can take all my property, as long as I never die.'

'But listen!', I would say to the lover of this temporary life, 'If the tax-collector takes everything, he'll leave you empty-handed in this world. If Christ takes everything, he will keep it safe for you in heaven. We want the means to live for the sake of this life; and for its sake we are willing to give up the means to live. If you have been storing up the necessities of life and you give them away in order to stay alive, well, maybe you will die of hunger. But you will still say, 'Let him take them: what does it matter to me?' You give it away to stay alive, and you're ready to beg to stay alive.

'You're prepared to give away even what you need and beg in this world. But you are not prepared to give out what you don't need and reign with Christ! Please, weigh the matter up. If you can find a fair set of weighing scales in the cupboard in your heart, bring them out. Then put these two options on it and weigh them: begging in this world and reigning with Christ. There's nothing to weigh. The one weighs nothing compared with the other one.'

Even if I said: reigning in this world and reigning with Christ, there would be nothing to weigh. I'm sorry that I said 'weigh'. There is nothing to weigh. *What does it profit someone if he gains the world but suffers the loss of his soul?* [Mt 16.26; Mk 8.36; Lk 9.25]. Anyone who has not suffered the loss of his soul will reign with Christ. Is there anyone, though, who reigns securely in this world? Even grant that he reigns securely; will his reign last for ever?

(6) Notice again the point I was making, that there are so many lovers of this present life – temporary, brief, unpleasant, yet it has so many lovers! Often enough, you end up a beggar, with no clothes because of this life. You ask him, 'Why?' He answers, 'To stay alive'.

'What have you fallen in love with? What do you love that's drawn you to it? You're a corrupt lover of a bad woman: what are you going to say to her? How are you going to address this life of yours that you've fallen in love with? Talk to her, chat her up, win her over if you can. What are you going to say? 'Your beauty has reduced me to this state of rags'? She shouts back, 'But I'm ugly. Are you in love with me?' I can hear her shouting, 'I'm a hard woman, and you're embracing me?' She's shouting again, 'I'm the flighty type – are you going to try and chase me?' Listen to the woman you love answering you: 'I won't stop with you; if I spend a bit of time with you, I won't stay with you. I could strip you of your clothes – but I couldn't make you happy.'

(7) Since we are Christians, then, let's beg the assistance of the Lord our God against the attractions of a life that it's stupid to love. Instead let's fall in love with the beauty of the life that *no eye has seen, and no ear has heard, nor has it reached the human heart.* For *God has prepared this for those who love him* [1 Cor 2.9]. And God himself is that life. I can hear you applauding, I can hear you sighing. We should be deeply in love with this life. May God allow us to love it. We should beg him in tears not just to let us win this life – but even to let us love it!

How do we give this warning? How can we prove it? Do I need to read out the scriptures to show them how insecure, how short-lived, how non-existent almost, are those other things, and how true are the words of scripture: *What is your life? It is a mist that appears for a short while, and then vanishes* [Jas 4.14]?

He was alive yesterday, he's gone today. We saw him a little while ago; now the man we saw no longer exists. They escort him to his tomb; they return in tears, and they quickly forget. The saying goes, 'Human beings are nothing!'; and it's a human being who says it. But humanity fails to reform itself so that it might become something rather than nothing.

And so the martyrs, in short, were lovers of that sort of life; it is that life that the martyrs have won. They possess the thing they loved, and they will possess it even more fully at the resurrection of the dead. And so, by suffering as much as they did, they have paved the way for us.

(8) St Laurence was an archdeacon. Somebody was pursuing him in order to get the church's money from him, so tradition tells us. As a result he suffered so many tortures that you would shudder to hear them. He was placed on a gridiron, he was burnt all over his body; he was tormented by the flames – what a horrific punishment. But he overcame all his physical anguish, with the help of God who had made him as he was, because his love was so strong. *For we are his handiwork, created in Christ Jesus for good works, which God prepared beforehand for us to walk in them* [Eph 2.10].

He managed to enrage his pursuer, although he wasn't intending to anger him. In fact, he was eager to make his own faith an example to those who would follow, and to show how little he cared about death. What he said was this: 'Let me have some carts so I can bring you the riches of the church in them.' The carts were brought, and he loaded them up with poor people. Then he ordered them to be taken back with the words, 'These are the riches of the church.'

And it is true, my brothers. The needs of the destitute amount to vast riches for the church, if only we understand where we ought to be storing our possessions. The destitute are in front of our eyes; if we look after them we won't lose them. We needn't fear that someone will take them away. God gave them to us and he looks after them. We could hardly find a better guardian, or a more trustworthy guarantor.[5]

(9) Let's keep all that in mind, and actively imitate the martyrs, if we want the feast-days we celebrate to be of help to us. I have always given you the same advice, my brothers. I have never stopped, I have never been silent on the subject. We must love eternal life, and we must count our present life as nothing. We must live well, and we must hope for what's good. If we are bad we must change; when we have changed, we must be

taught; when we've been taught, we need to persevere. *For whoever perseveres to the end will be saved* [Mt 10.22; 24.13].

(10) People say, though: 'So many evil people, so much evil!'[6] What would you like? Good coming from the evil? Don't look for *a grape on a thornbush* [cf. Mt 7.16]; you're not allowed to do that. *The mouth speaks from the overflowing of the heart* [Lk 6.45]. If you can, if you are not bad yourself, then pray for the bad person to become good. Why do you treat those who are bad violently? You reply, 'Because they are bad'. As soon as you treat them violently, you add yourself to them. Let me give you some advice. There's some bad person that you dislike? Well, don't let there be two. You criticise him, and then you join him? You swell the ranks that you're condemning. Are you trying to overcome evil with evil? To overcome hatred with hatred? Then there will be two lots of hatred, and both will need to be overcome. Can't you hear the advice your Lord gave through the apostle Paul: *Do not be overcome by evil, but overcome evil with good* [Rom 12.21]?

Now maybe he is worse than you; but you are still bad, and so there will be two of you who are bad. I'd rather that at least one were good. And in the end the violence leads to death.[7] Then what about after his death, when the one bad man can't be touched by punishment any longer, while the other one is taken up with hatred alone? But this is not punishment, it's madness.

(11) What can I say to you, my brothers? What can I say to you? That you mustn't approve of such people? But would it ever occur to me that you would approve of them? Don't let me even suspect you of that. But it's not enough for you not to approve of them, not enough at all. More than that is asked of you. No one should just say, 'God knows I didn't take part in it, God knows I didn't take part in it, God knows that I didn't want it to happen.'

Notice that you have said two different things: 'I didn't take part in it', and 'I didn't want it to happen.' That's still not enough. It's not even enough that you didn't want it to happen, unless you also tried to prevent it. Bad men have their own judges and their own authorities. As the apostle Paul said, *He does not wield a sword without reason. He is an avenger of his anger, but on the evil-doer* [Rom 13.4]. In anger, he is an avenger on the evil-doer. *If you do evil,* he says, *then fear him. For he does not wield a sword without reason. Do you want not to fear the authorities? Do good, and you will have praise from them* [Rom 13.3].

(12) Now someone could ask, 'What had St Laurence done wrong to be killed by the authorities? How were the words *Do good and you will have*

praise from them fulfilled in his case? He did good, and his reward for it was being horribly tortured.'

But if the holy martyr Laurence hadn't had praise from the authorities, we wouldn't be honouring him today, I wouldn't be preaching about him, he wouldn't be being praised so publicly. So he has had praise from them, even against their intentions. The apostle did not say, 'Do good and the authorities themselves will praise you'. All the apostles and martyrs did good, and the authorities didn't praise them, they killed them. So if he had said, 'Do good and the authorities will praise you', he would have misled you. But he chose his words with care, he examined them, he weighed them, measured them and kept them short.

Discuss the words you actually heard: *Do good and you will have praise from them*. If the authorities are just, you will have praise from them in that they themselves will praise you. But if they are unjust, if you die for your faith, for justice, and for truth,[8] you will have praise from them even though they treat you violently. You will have praise from them, even though they don't praise you themselves. They provide the opportunity for you to be praised. So do good, and you will have praise, and you will be safe.

(13) 'But', you might say, 'think of the things that that crook did, of the numbers of people he oppressed, the numbers of people he reduced to begging and poverty'.[9] He has his own judges, his own authorities. There is an established government: *all that there are are established by God* [Rom 13.1]. Why are you so violent? What authority have you been given? But, of course, this isn't public punishment, it's simply terrorism in the open.[10] Well then? Think about this: suppose that even under the established system of authority there is a condemned criminal, sentenced to death, with the sword hanging over him. Even then no one is allowed to strike him except the person who holds the appropriate office. This office belongs to the public executioner; it's his job to execute the condemned man. But suppose the judicial clerk[11] puts him to death when he is already condemned and sentenced to death. Certainly the person he kills has been condemned. But still, the clerk will be found guilty of murder. True enough the man he killed was already condemned and sentenced to punishment; but it still counts as murder if someone is attacked against the regulations.[12] Yet if it counts as murder to attack someone against the regulations, then please tell me what it counts as if you attack some crook who has not been given a hearing or been judged, and when you have no authority to attack him? I am not defending those who are bad, and I am

not denying that they are bad. But leave the judges to account for this. Why do you want the difficult task of accounting for someone else's death? The burden of authority isn't yours to carry. God has given you the freedom of not being a judge. Why take over someone else's position? You need to be giving an account of yourself.[13]

(14) Lord, when you said, *'If any of you is without sin, let him be the first to cast a stone at her'*, you certainly stabbed those violent men in their hearts. They felt your words penetrating their hearts, sharp and weighty.[14] They recognised the voice of their own consciences. Then they were embarrassed to be in the presence of justice. They began to leave, one by one, and they left the pitiful woman all alone. But she was not all alone, the defendant. The judge was with her, but he was not yet judging, he was offering pity. The violent men departed; pity and the pitiable were left. The Lord then said to her, *'Has no one condemned you?'* She replied, *'No one, Lord.' 'Neither will I condemn you'*, he said, *'Go, and do not sin again'* [Jn 8.10–11].

(15) 'But that soldier[15] did awful things to me.' I'd like to know whether you wouldn't have done the same, if you were a soldier. I certainly don't mean that I want soldiers to oppress the poor. I don't in the least want that. I want them too to hear the gospel. Soldiering doesn't prevent you doing good, but hating does.[16] Soldiers came to John for baptism and said to him, *'What are we to do now?'* He replied, *'Do not intimidate anyone; do not bring false charges against anyone; be satisfied with your wages'*[17] [Lk 3.14].

To tell you the truth, my brothers, if soldiers behaved like that, the empire would be a happy place, especially if not just soldiers, but also tax-collectors behaved as it says there. For the 'publicans', that is the tax-collectors, said: *'Then what shall we do?'* He replied, *'Demand no more than your set fee'* [Lk 3.12–13]. The soldier has been told off; the tax-collector has been told off. Now it's the turn of the ordinary citizen to be given a lesson. Here is a straightforward lesson for everyone. *'All of us, what are we to do?' 'Let anyone who has two tunics share with someone who does not have one at all. Let anyone who has food do the same'* [Lk 3.11]. If we want soldiers to listen to Christ's commands, then we should listen as well. Christ isn't just for them, and not for us. He's not their God only, and not ours.[18] We should all listen, and we should live in harmony and peace.

(16) 'But he took advantage of me when I was in business.' Have you always traded honestly yourself?[19] Have you never cheated anyone in business? Have you never sworn a false oath during negotiations? Have

you never said, 'In the name of God who carried me across the sea, I paid this much', when in fact you didn't pay that much? My brothers, I tell you explicitly, and as far as the Lord allows it, freely: only bad men use violence against other bad men.

The actions authorities need to take are a different matter. Usually a judge unsheathes his sword only when forced to. When he strikes, he does so unwillingly. Personally, he would have liked to have avoided bloodshed when sentencing; but maybe he did not want public order to collapse. He was obliged to act in this way by his office, by his authority, by the demands of his situation. But what are you obliged to do, except to beg God, *'Deliver us from evil'* [Mt 6.13]? You have said, 'Deliver us from evil.' God deliver you from yourself!

(17) To put it bluntly, my brothers, why do I keep going so long? We are all Christians. But I also carry a greater burden of danger.[20] People often ask about me, 'Why does he go to the authorities? What does a bishop want with the authorities?' But you all know that it's your needs that force me to go there, even though I don't want to. I have to wait my chance, stand outside the door, queue while they go in – worthy and unworthy alike – have my name announced – then sometimes I only just get admitted! I have to put up with the humiliation, make my request, sometimes succeed, sometimes leave disappointed. Who would put up with all that if he weren't forced to? Please do put me out of a job. Let me off it all! Please, don't let anyone make me do it. Look, just allow me this much – just give me a holiday from it all. Please, I beg you, don't let anyone make me do it.

I don't choose to have dealings with the authorities. God knows that I am forced into it. If we find Christians in authority we treat the authorities as we ought to treat Christians. If they are pagans, we treat them as we ought to treat pagans. We are well intentioned towards everyone. The critic objects, 'But he ought to warn the authorities to behave well.' And should we issue these warnings in front of you? Do you know whether we've issued a warning? You don't know whether we have or not. I know that you don't know, and that you're making a hasty judgement. However – my dear brothers, please – someone could say of me about someone in authority, 'If *he* had warned him, he would behave well.' My reply is this: 'I did warn him, but he didn't listen to me.[21] However, I gave him the warning when you couldn't hear me.'

Can you take a whole community on one side and give them a warning? But I could take one man aside to warn him and say, 'Do this', or, 'Do that', in front of no one else. But who could take a whole community on one side and issue a warning to them without anyone knowing about it?

(18) It is the demands of the situation that force me to speak to you like this. Otherwise, I will give a poor account of myself to God over my responsibilities for you. I do not want God to say, 'If you had warned them, if you had put down the money, I could have demanded the payment' [cf. Lk 19.23]. So keep out of it, keep completely out of all this bloodshed. When you see that sort of thing or hear about it, it's not your job to do anything – except feel pity for him.

'But the dead man was bad!' All right, then you should grieve for him twice as much, because he is dead twice over, once in this temporary life, and once in eternal life. If a good man had died, then we would be grieving out of human emotion, because he had left us, and because we wanted him to be living with us still. But we ought to grieve twice over for those who are bad, because after this life they are taken off into eternal punishment. It is up to you to grieve, my dear brothers, it is up to you to grieve rather than be violent.

(19) However, as I have already said, it is not enough to refrain from this sort of thing yourselves, and it is not enough to grieve, unless you also do your very best to prevent an action that ordinary people have no authority to carry out. I do not mean, my brothers, that one of you could go out and simply prevent the people from doing it. I couldn't do that either. But in your own homes you have each got your sons, your slaves, your friends, your neighbours, your dependants, your juniors.[22] Make sure that they don't behave like this! If you can persuade any of them not to, do so. As for the others, if they are under your authority, treat them severely. One thing I do know, and everyone else knows it as well. I can find plenty of houses in this city without a single pagan in them; I can't find a single house where there are no Christians. To put it more precisely, we won't find a single house where there are not more Christians than pagans. It is true; I can see you agreeing with me. You can see that this awful thing could not have been done if the Christians hadn't wanted it. You've got nothing to say in reply.

Now bad deeds might be carried out in secret. But if Christians weren't happy about it, and tried to prevent them, they couldn't be done in public. Then each of you would keep a hold on your son or your slave. The excesses of youth would be restrained by strict fathers, strict uncles, strict teachers, by the strictness of good neighbours, or by the strictness of that more serious punishment.[23] If all this had been done, we wouldn't be feeling so distressed now about this awful business.

(20) My brothers, I am afraid of God's anger. God has no fear of mobs. People are quick to say, 'What the crowd has done, it has done. Who can manage to punish a whole crowd?' I agree, who can? Not God? Was God afraid even of the entire universe? After all, he created the flood [cf. Gen 6.13ff]. Was he afraid of so many Sodoms and Gomorrahs? After all, he sent fire from heaven to destroy them [cf. Gen 19.1–29]. I don't want to go into the recent troubles; I don't want to remind you of their seriousness, of where they took place, and of what resulted, in case I seem offensive. Surely God, when he was angry, didn't distinguish those who were actually doing wrong from those who were not? No, rather he put together those who were doing wrong with those who were doing nothing to prevent them.[24]

(21) Let me now bring my sermon to a close at last. My brothers, I urge you, please, by the Lord and his gentleness, to live gently and peaceably; and to allow the authorities to do their job in peace. They will have to give an account of themselves to God and to their superiors.[25] Whenever you need to make some request, do so peaceably and respectfully. Don't get involved with wrong-doers, or with people who turn violent in an extreme and tragic way. Don't be eager to get involved in such things, or even in watching them. As far as you can, each of you in his own household and his own neighbourhood, whenever you are with anyone connected to you by ties of duty or love, warn them, persuade them, teach them, tell them off.[26] Even use threats in any way you can to restrain them from such horrific behaviour.

Then, at last, God may have pity on us and put an end to the evils of human life. He may cease dealing with us according to our sins, and not repay us according to our injustice, but put our sins as far away from us as east is from west. Then he may set us free for the honour of his own name, and be merciful towards our sins *in case the nations say, 'Where is their God?'* [Ps 79(78).10].

POSTSCRIPT (22)[27] *My brothers, don't be reluctant or hesitant about crowding into the church, who is your mother, or staying there a while, because of the other people who are seeking sanctuary with her, or because she is a refuge shared by everyone. The church is indeed worried about what the crowds might attempt: they are not well controlled. However, as far as the authorities go, Christian emperors have promulgated laws in the name of God that provide the church with enough protection and more,*[28] *and these people are unlikely to attempt anything against their mother that would end in humanity blaming them and God judging them. I pray that they don't. I don't believe they will, and I don't see evidence of it.*

But just in case the crowd does get out of control and attempt something, you ought to be thronging into your mother the church. For, as I said, she is not the refuge of one or two people, but shared by everyone. If anyone hasn't got a reason to come, he ought to be afraid in case he finds one. I tell your beloved selves the unjust flee to the church from the presence of those who live justly, and those who live justly flee there from the presence of those who live unjustly.[29] *Sometimes, too, the unjust flee from the presence of the unjust. There are three categories of refugee: the only exception is that the good don't flee from the good, the just don't flee from the just. However, the unjust flee from the just, the just flee from the unjust and the unjust flee from the unjust. But if we want to distinguish between them and remove wrongdoers from the church, then there will be nowhere for those who do good to hide. If we are willing to allow the guilty to be removed, there will be nowhere for the innocent to flee. It is better then that the church's protection includes the guilty, than that the innocent are dragged away. Hold to this advice: let them be afraid of your numbers (as I said) rather than your violence.*

Sermon 13

418

At the altar of Cyprian, 27 May[1]

On the words of Psalm 2.10, *Be instructed, all you who judge the earth.*

(1) *Be instructed, all you who judge the earth.* To judge the earth is to tame the body. Let us listen to the apostle[2] judging the earth: *I am not boxing as if I were beating the air; I pound my body and reduce it to servitude, in case in preaching to others I myself fail to win approval* [1 Cor 9.26–7]. Listen then, earth, to the earth's judge; and judge the earth in case you become earth yourself. If you judge the earth, you'll become heaven, and you will *proclaim the glory* of the Lord created in you. *For the heavens proclaim the glory of God* [Ps 19(18).1]. If, on the other hand, you fail to judge the earth, then you will become earth. But if you become earth, you will

belong to Adam, who was told, *You will eat earth* [Gen 3.14]. Those who judge the earth ought, then, to listen; they should chastise their bodies, put reins on their passions, love wisdom, overcome unruly desire. And they ought to be instructed so that they do this.

(2) This is a summary of their instruction: *serve the Lord in fear and rejoice in him with trembling* [Ps 2.11]. Rejoice in *him*, not in yourself, in him who is the source of your being what you are, a human being, and just – if indeed you are already just. However, if you think that the source of your being human is him, but the source of your being just is yourself, then you are not serving the Lord with fear, nor *rejoicing in him with trembling,* but in yourself with arrogance. Then what will happen to you, if not the thing that comes next: it then says *in case God is angry with you at some time, and you are lost from the path of justice* [Ps 2.12, LXX].

It does not say, 'In case God is angry with you at some time, and you do not set out on the path of justice'; but *you are lost from the path of justice.* You will be thinking yourself just already because you *do not steal* other people's possessions or *commit adultery* or *murder*, or *bear false witness by speaking against your neighbour,* and you *honour your father and mother,* and *worship the one God,* and serve neither idols nor demons [Exod 20.1–17; Deut 5.6–21]. This is the path from which you'll be lost if you claim all this for yourself, if you consider that these actions have their source in you yourself. The faithless don't even set out on the path of justice; the proud, though, are lost from the path of justice. What does it say, after all? *Be instructed, all you who judge the earth.* In case you attribute to yourself the strength and the power which enable you to judge the earth, in case you believe that they come to you from yourself – well, avoid this mistake.

Serve the Lord with fear, and rejoice, not in yourself with arrogance, but *in him with trembling, in case God is angry with you at some time and you are lost from the path of justice when suddenly his anger is kindled.*

What, then, ought we to do in order to avoid being lost from the path of justice? *Blessed are all who trust in him* [Ps 2.12]. If those who trust in him are blessed, those who trust in themselves are miserable. *Everyone who puts his hope in a human being is cursed* [Jer 17.5]. So do not place your hope in yourself, as you too are human. However, if you place your hope in another human being, you'll be excessively humble; if you place it in yourself, though, you'll be dangerously proud. What's the difference then? Both are destructive; both options should be refused. Someone who is excessively humble isn't lifted up at all; someone who is dangerously proud falls headlong to the ground.

(3) Finally, let me persuade your holy selves that the words *serve the Lord in fear and rejoice with him in trembling* were intended to disprove and dispose of the view that everyone trusts in himself by refuting it. Listen to the apostle Paul repeating these very words, and explaining the reason why they were spoken. Here is what Paul says: *Work for your security with fear and trembling* [Phil 2.12]. Why should I work for my security with fear and trembling if it lies within my power to work out my own security?[3] Do you want to hear why it says *with fear and trembling? For it is God who works in you* [Phil 2.13]. Hence *with fear and trembling*: the humble person gains what the proud person loses.

If, then, it is God who is at work in us, why does it say *work for your security?* For this reason: he is at work in us in such a way that we too are at work: *be my helper* [Ps 27(26).9, LXX]. By invoking a helper, the speaker marks himself also as a worker.

'But my will is good', my interlocutor objects. I agree, it is yours. But who gave you even that? Who stirred it into action? Don't listen to me; ask the apostle Paul. *For it is God who works in you, both your willing and your acting in good will* [Phil 2.13] – he also works in you your willing. Why, then, were you claiming this for yourself? Why were you walking so proudly, and being lost? Return to your own heart, discover that you are bad, and pray to the one who is good that you may become good. For nothing in you is pleasing to God except what you have from God. Anything you have from yourself is displeasing to God.

If you think about your goods, *what do you have that you did not receive? But if you received it, why do you boast as if you hadn't received it?* [1 Cor 4.7]. He alone knows only how to give. No one gives to him, for there is no one better. If you, then, are less than he – indeed, since you are less than he – congratulate yourself on being made in his image [cf. Gen 1.27]. Then you might find yourself in him, as you have lost yourself in yourself. For in yourself, you had no power except to lose yourself; and you don't know how to find yourself unless God who made you also looks for you.

(4) But now let us address those who judge the earth in the everyday physical understanding of the phrase. Kings, leaders, rulers, judges, they judge the earth; each one of them judges the earth in accordance with the office he has been given on earth. What is meant by 'judge the earth' except 'judge the people who are on the earth'? For if you are only willing to understand earth in the strict sense as the soil you tread on, then 'You who judge the earth' must be addressed to farmers! But if kings also judge

the earth, and anyone under them who receives power from them, then they too ought to *be instructed*; the earth itself is judging the earth, and when earth judges earth it ought to fear God who is in heaven. It is indeed judging its own equal, a human judging a human, a mortal judging a mortal, a sinner judging a sinner.

If the Lord's verdict *If any of you is without sin; let him be the first to cast a stone at her* [Jn 8.7] were to step forward[4] surely everyone who is judging the earth would feel the earth quake! Let us call to mind once more that chapter of the gospel. The Pharisees,[5] trying to tempt the Lord, brought before him a woman caught in adultery. The punishment for this sin was determined in the Law, that is the Law given through Moses, the servant of God [cf. Lev 20.10]. The Pharisees approached the Lord with the following crafty and deceitful reasoning in mind: if he were to order that the disgraced woman be stoned, he would abandon his gentleness; if, however, he were to forbid the punishment commanded by the Law, he would be convicted of sinning against the Law.

Again, on a similar occasion, they asked him about paying tribute to Caesar, and he took the words out of their own mouths by offering them a coin and asking them in their turn whose image and inscription were on it. The questioners themselves answered: the image on the coin was Caesar's. He turned their own words against them: *Give to Caesar's what is Caesar's and to God what is God's* [Mt 22.15–22; Mk 12.13–17; Lk 20.22–5].[6] In this way he was able to warn them to restore to God the image of God in the human being, just as the image of Caesar on the coin is restored to him. Similarly in the case of the adulteress he interrogated the interrogators, and thus pronounced judgement on the judges. 'I do not forbid the stoning of whomever the Law orders', he said, 'I merely ask who will do it. I am not opposing the Law, but I am looking for someone to execute it.'

In short, listen to this: 'Do you want to cast stones according to the Law? *If any of you is without sin, let him be the first to cast a stone at her.*'

(5) Moreover, when he heard what they said, *he began writing with his finger on the earth*, in order to judge the earth. However, when he addressed these words to the Pharisees, he raised his eyes, and examined the earth and made it tremble. Then, after he had spoken, he began to write on the earth once more. Pierced by remorse and trembling with fear, they left, one by one. A true earthquake! The earth was moved so much that it changed its place!

When they were gone, the two of them remained: the sinner and her

Saviour, the sick woman and her doctor, the pitiable and pity himself. He looked at the woman and said, '*Has no one condemned you?*'

And she replied: '*No one, Lord.*'

However, she was still anxious. The sinners, indeed, hadn't dared to condemn her; they hadn't dared to stone a sinner, once they'd looked at themselves and discovered that they were the same. However, the woman was still in great danger, because he had remained with her as her judge, and he was without sin.

'*Has no one condemned you?*', he asked.

She replied, '*No one, Lord. If you do not either, then I am safe.*'

The Lord replied silently to her anxiety: '*Neither will I condemn you. Neither will I* even though I am without sin *condemn you.* Conscience inhibited the others from vengeance; pity persuades me to come to your help' [Jn 8.3–11].

(6) Listen to these things, and *be instructed, all you who judge the earth.* It says 'all', because we should understand this passage to refer to the same people as the apostle's words: *Every soul is subject to higher authorities. There is no authority except from God; all that there are were established by God. Anyone who resists authority resists what God has established . . . Rulers do not inspire fear in those who do good, but in those who do evil. Do you want not to fear the authorities? Do good, and you will have praise from them* [Rom 13.1–3].

And if not given by them, still from them. For either you act justly, and a just authority will praise you, or else, when you act justly, even if an unjust authority condemns you, God, who is just, will crown you. Hold on to justice yourself, then, live a good life yourself. Whether the authorities condemn you or whether they absolve you, you will have praise *from them.*[7] Think of the blessed man whose blood was shed on this very spot[8] – hasn't he found praise from the very authority before whom and by whom, as it seemed, he was being judged? He made a public confession, he stood by his faith; he had no fear of death, he shed his blood, he overcame the devil.

(7) If, then, you don't want to exercise your authority unjustly, all you human beings who wish to have authority over human beings, well, *be instructed,* so that you avoid judging corruptly, and perishing in your soul before you manage to destroy anyone else in the flesh. You want to be a judge, and you can't be on merit – only by spending money.[9] I'm not criticising you yet. For perhaps you're eager to be of assistance in human affairs, and you're buying your way into being of help. You're not sparing

your money so that you'll be able to serve justice. But first, for your own sake, act as judge on yourself. Judge yourself first, then you'll be able to leave the inner cell of your conscience in security and go out to someone else.

Return to yourself, observe yourself, debate with yourself, listen to yourself. I should like you to prove yourself an honest judge there, where you don't need to look for a witness. You want to step forward with authority, so that one person will tell you things you didn't know about another. First judge yourself within. Is there nothing that your conscience has told you about yourself? It certainly told you something, unless you've refused to admit it. I don't want to hear what it told you: you yourself must be the judge of what you have heard. It's told you about yourself – what you've done, what you've received, what sins you've committed. I should like to know what sentence you have pronounced. If you listened well, if you heard aright, if you were being just as you listened, if you climbed up to the judgement seat of your mind, if you stretched yourself out in front of yourself on the rack of your heart, if you applied to yourself the heavy torture of fear – if that is how you listened, then you listened well, and there is no doubt then that you have punished your sin by your repentance. See how you interrogated yourself and listened to yourself and punished yourself, and yet you spared yourself. [10] Listen to your neighbour in the same way, if you are being instructed as the Psalm says, *Be instructed, all you who judge the earth.*

(8) If you listen to your neighbour in the same way that you listen to yourself, then your target will be the sin, and not the sinner. And if someone happens to be hardened against his sins being reformed, if he has turned away from the fear of God, well, you must make that element of him your target, you must try to reform that, and work to lose and remove precisely that, so that the sin is condemned, but the human being himself preserved.[11] There are in fact two nouns, 'human' and 'sinner'. God made the human being, but the human being himself made the sinner. May the human creation perish, but God's creation be set free!

Do not, therefore, when you are attacking the sin, put the human being to death. Avoid the death penalty, so that there's someone left to repent. Don't allow the human being to be killed; then someone will be left to learn the lesson.[12] You are a man judging other men; foster love of them in your heart, and judge the earth. Love to instil fear in them, but do so out of love. If you must be arrogant, be arrogant towards the sin, not towards the person. Vent your rage on the failing, which you dislike as much in yourself, and not on the person, who is created just as you are. You both came from the same workshop, you both had the same crafts man, the stuff you are both made of is the same clay. Why are you destroying the person you judge by failing to love him? For you're destroying justice, by failing to love the person you're judging. Punishments should be imposed; I don't deny it; I don't forbid it. But this must be done in the spirit of love, in the spirit of concern, in the spirit of reform.

(9) After all, you do not refrain from instructing your own son. In the first place you try, as far as possible, to instruct him by using shame and generosity, wanting him to be ashamed of offending his father rather than afraid of a harsh judge. You're delighted to have such a son. However, if he happened to take no notice of this, you would also apply the rod. You punish him and inflict pain on him, but your aim would be his security. Many people have been reformed through love, and many through fear; the latter, though, have progressed through the horror of fear to reach love. *Be instructed, all you who judge the earth.* Love, and then make your judgement; I do not mean that you should seek to avoid hurt at the cost of losing discipline. Indeed, scripture says: *Whoever abandons discipline is unhappy* [Wisd 3.11]. We could well add to this maxim: just as anyone who abandons discipline is unhappy, so anyone who withholds discipline is cruel.

Now I have dared to say this, my brothers, the very difficulty of the matter forces me to explain it to you a little more fully. Let me repeat what I said: *Whoever abandons discipline is unhappy.* This, then, is quite plain. But I further hold that 'whoever does not apply discipline is cruel'. I hold this, and I will show you someone who shows devotion by applying the rod, and cruelty by sparing it: let me put an example before your eyes. Where can I find someone who shows devotion by applying the rod? I need go no further than a father and a son. When the father strikes him, he does so out of love. The boy doesn't want to be beaten; but his father takes no account of his wishes; his concern is for his benefit. Why is this? Because he is his father; because he is training his heir; because he is nur-turing his successor.[13] Note then how a father shows his devotion and his pity by beating the boy.

Well, give me an example now of someone who shows cruelty by sparing the rod. I needn't abandon my characters; I have them before your eyes. Imagine though this time that the boy is never punished,[14] and lives without discipline in such a way that he is ruined. The father averts his gaze. He spares the boy, if he's afraid of offending the son who has been ruined by applying harsh discipline. Then isn't he, in fact, in sparing him, being cruel?

Well then, *be instructed, all you who judge the earth*; and do not expect your reward for honest judgement from the earth, but from God, who made heaven and earth.

The Donatist controversy

Some time before 312, Caecilian, an archdeacon of Carthage, was elected and consecrated bishop. There is evidence of a pre-existing dispute which began during the persecution under the emperor Diocletian, from 303. Some Christians refused any compromise with the authorities, and even courted martyrdom; others, to whom Caecilian seems to have been sympathetic, recommended evasive action short of directly betraying the faith. At any rate, the election was opposed by certain Carthaginians, and a council of bishops from Numidia and elsewhere investigated. This council deposed Caecilian and elected Maiorinus in his place, on the grounds that the former's consecration had been invalid. This was because of the participation of Felix, bishop of Apthugni, who, they alleged, had been guilty during the persecution of handing over the sacred scriptures to the authorities to be burnt. Caecilian refused to accept the council's decision and remained as bishop. The Carthaginian church was divided, and the Donatist controversy had begun.

In 313, the opponents of Caecilian requested the proconsul, Anulinus, to forward their charges against him to Constantine for his judgement (see Letter 88). Constantine left the matter to the church authorities, and a council in Rome ruled in favour of Caecilian. His opponents appealed, and the matter was referred to a second council, in Arles in 314, which repeated the decision of the Roman council. However, the decision was not accepted by Maiorinus' supporters. Maiorinus was succeeded on his death by Donatus, after whom the Catholics named the sect. In 315, Felix was tried at Carthage on the charge against him and was acquitted. Donatist and Catholic communities, each with their own bishops, continued to live side by side in many cities of north Africa.

By the middle of the fourth century, theological differences between Donatists and Catholics had hardened, and were centred on the nature of the church. The Donatists saw themselves as inheriting the African tradition of a rigorously disciplined church, 'without stain or wrinkle' (Ephesians 5.27): the purity of the church's witness set it apart from the world. That was why sacraments such as baptism were invalid when performed by Catholic priests; for the Catholics, connected historically to the traitor Felix, stood outside the one, holy church. Catholic bishops resented the Donatist practice of rebaptising Catholics who joined them.

The Donatists identified themselves with the African church against the Roman authorities, and there were close links between Donatism and social opposition to the wealthy landowners of north Africa. Groups of men known as 'Circumcellions', Donatist devotees with no respect for Roman laws, gave violent expression to this alliance, and caused both the imperial authorities and the Catholic communities much anxiety.

In about 345, two imperial legates, Macarius and Paul, were sent to Africa to investigate the controversy. They quickly decided against Donatus, and called in the troops to quell the resulting resistance. Several Donatists died, and severe punishments were imposed, including executions, which provided the Donatist church with much-revered martyrs. Subsequently, the Donatists called the Catholics 'Macarians', to emphasise their collaboration with what they saw as imperial persecution.

By the turn of the fifth century, the Donatists were openly opposing the Roman occupation of north Africa. At the same time, they were weakened by internal tensions. The Catholic bishops seized the opportunity to appeal for support against them to the emperor Honorius. In 405, Honorius issued the Edict of Unity, which outlawed the Donatists by prohibiting their assemblies, confiscating their places of meeting, and threatening their clergy with exile. However, the imposition of these and subsequent laws still failed to bring peace.

In June 411, a council of more than 500 bishops, Donatist and Catholic, met at Carthage under the presidency of Marcellinus, a lay imperial official and Catholic, eventually a close friend of Augustine's. Augustine played an important role in the debates, which covered both the history of the dispute and the resulting theological disagreements. Finally, and to no one's surprise, Marcellinus ruled in favour of the Catholics, thus reinforcing the existing legislation against their opponents.

Letter 51

400

(1) I am opening my letter as I do, because your side has criticised my humble self.[1] It might seem as if I had done this to insult you; but I am

assuming that you will write back to me in the same manner. Need I dwell long on your promise about Carthage, or on my insistence upon your keeping it?[2] Let whatever arrangements we made then be a thing of the past – so they may not provide obstacles for us with regard to the future. Now, however (if I am not mistaken), there is, with God's help, no excuse. We are both in Numidia, and we find ourselves no distance from one another. A rumour has reached me that you are still willing to examine in debate with me the issue that is destroying the communion between us.

See how quickly all the confusion may be removed. Send me a reply to this letter, if you will; and perhaps that will be enough not only for us, but also for the people who are longing to listen to us. If it is not enough, then we will send letters back and forth until it is enough. For things could hardly be more convenient for us when we are living in cities so near to one another. In fact, I have decided to discuss this matter with you by letter alone. That will allow us to avoid both letting anything we say slip from memory, and disappointing those who are very interested in the question, but who might be unable to be present.

You tend to make rather over-blown claims, as it suits you, based on past events. This is not perhaps because you like telling lies, but because you have been misled. I should prefer, therefore, if you agree, that we measure these claims in the light of the present. Doubtless it has not escaped your notice that in the days of the 'former people'[3] they committed the sacrilege of idolatry; and also a haughty king burnt the prophet's book [cf. Exod 32.1–6; Jer 36.23]. The evil of schism would not have been punished more fiercely than these two crimes, had it not been counted a more serious offence. I am sure that you will recall how the earth gaped open and swallowed alive the initiators of the schism, and how fire came rushing down from heaven on those who supported them [cf. Num 16.31–5]. Neither the making and worshipping of idols nor the burning of the sacred book merited such a punishment as that.

(2) It is your habit to reproach us not simply with crimes not proven against us, but, more to the point, with crimes that have been proven against your side – I mean the crimes committed by those who were pushed by fear of legal action into handing over[4] the books of the Lord to be burnt in the fire. Well, then – what about the very men whom you condemned for the crime of schism 'with the truth-bearing voice of a plenary council'? (I quote what is written there.) Why do you welcome them back into the very same episcopates which they were holding when you condemned them? I am talking about Felicianus of Musti and Praetextatus of Assur.[5]

Your council did indeed adjourn itself and set a date by which one group should return to communion with you or else be liable to the same sentence. But they did not belong to that group (which is what you tell the uninformed). Rather, they belonged to the group which you condemned on the same day without any of the delay that you offered to the others. I can prove this, if you deny it. Your own council has spoken. We have the records of the pro-consul[6] in our hands; and there you affirmed this more than once. Prepare yourself a different defence then if you can, if we are not to waste time while you deny something that I can prove.

If, then, Felicianus and Praetextatus were innocent, why were they condemned as they were? If they were guilty, why were they welcomed as they were? If you have proved that they are innocent, why shouldn't we believe that other innocent men may have been condemned by a far smaller number of your predecessors, on a false charge of handing over sacred books? After all, 310 of their successors were capable of condemning innocent men on a false charge of schism, and this, too, was grandly recorded for us 'with the truth-bearing voice of a plenary council'.

If, on the other hand, you have proved that they were rightly condemned, do you have any further defence against the charge of welcoming them back into the same bishoprics? Only by emphasising the importance of peace for success and for well-being, to show that even that sort of thing must be tolerated for the sake of the bond of unity. And if only you would do that with all your heart, not just with all your voice! Then you would realise immediately that if in Africa it is acceptable to welcome back for the sake of the peace of Donatus those condemned even for the impiety of schism, then the peace of Christ himself throughout the whole world should not be violated by any slanders.

(3) Similarly, you are in the habit of reproaching us with using worldly powers to pursue action against you. In this matter I do not propose to argue either about what you deserve for your monstrous impiety or about the extent to which Christian gentleness ought to moderate this. I say simply this: if it is a crime, why have you used judges sent by the emperors (who, incidentally owe their birth by the gospel to our communion) for the purpose of putting pressure upon these same Maximianists[7] in order to drive them from the basilicas which they held when their separation occurred?

Why have you routed them, using as weapons the din of quarrels, the power of imperial decrees and the force of the military? Fresh traces of recent events testify to their sufferings in this conflict in various places;

official documents show the relevant decrees; and as for what was done, the land itself cries out, the very land where the holy memory of your own notable tribune Optatus is proclaimed.[8]

(4) Another allegation that you are in the habit of making is that we do not possess the baptism of Christ, which is to be found nowhere except in your communion.[9] I could at some point expand upon this topic rather fully. However, there is no need at the moment to argue against you; you have accepted the baptism even of the Maximianists with Felicianus and Praetextatus. What about all those they baptised when they were actually in communion with Maximian, even while you were engaging in a daily battle of lawsuits in your efforts to expel them by name, Felicianus and Praetextatus that is, from their basilicas? (The records attest to this.) They now join with each other and with you in recognising everyone whom they baptised during that same period, even though they were baptised outside under the outrage of schism; and this not simply when they were at risk from illness, but during the solemn celebrations of Easter, in a great number of churches that were attached to their cities, and even in the great cities themselves.[10]

But none of them have been rebaptised. I wish that you could show that after they had been baptised 'to no avail' by Felicianus and Praetextatus, when they were still outside under the outrage of schism, they were baptised again by them once they had been welcomed back this time internally and 'validly'. For if they had to be baptised afresh, then Felicianus and Praetextatus ought to have been ordained afresh. Surely when they abandoned you, they lost their episcopacy, if they were unable to baptise when not in communion with you.

If when they left they did not lose their episcopacy, they were capable of baptising anywhere; if on the other hand they did lose it, they ought to have been reordained on their return in order to receive again what they had lost. Have no fear, though. Just as it is certain that they came back with the same episcopacy with which they left, so it is certain that everyone whom they baptised while in schism with Maximian has been reconciled with your communion without any need for rebaptism.

(5) Have we tears enough to lament your welcoming the baptism of the Maximianists, while tossing aside the baptism of the whole world? You condemned Felicianus, you condemned Praetextatus, with or without a hearing, whether justly or unjustly. Tell me then, which bishop of Corinth have any of you heard or condemned? Which bishop of Galatia, Ephesus, Colossae, of Philippi, of Thessalonika,[11] or of any of

the other cities referred to in the words, *All the countries of the nations will worship him in his sight* [Ps 22(21).27]? And so you have welcomed the baptism of the Maximianists, but you have tossed aside that of the nations, which belongs neither to the former, nor to the latter themselves, but to Christ, of whom scripture says: *It is this man who baptises* [Jn 1.33].

But I am not arguing on those grounds. Look rather at the matter near at hand. Give your attention to things that could strike the eyes of a blind man. Those who were condemned possess baptism; those who have never been heard do not. The former were excluded by name and expelled in a state of outrageous schism; they have it. The latter are unknown, travellers from afar, who have never been accused and never judged, and they do not. The former were a segment of a segment of Africa, and they have it. The latter are the source from which the gospel reached Africa, and they do not. Do I need to labour the point? Give me a reply to these arguments. Note that your council charged the Maximianists with impiety; note that you demanded that judicial powers be employed to pursue action against them;[12] and note then that you have accepted their baptism along with them, although you had condemned them. Then answer me, if you can: do you have some way of clouding the issue for the uninformed as to why you are separated from the whole world by the outrage of a schism far greater than that of the Maximianists which you are proud of having condemned?

May the peace of Christ be victorious in your heart.

Letter 66

401

(1) You ought indeed to fear God. However, when you rebaptised the Mappalians,[1] you wanted to be feared as a man. Why then does the emperor's decree have no force in the province, if a provincial decree has so much force on an estate? If you compare roles, you are the owner, he is the emperor; if you compare places, you are on a farm, he in an empire; if you compare motives, his was to heal a division, yours to divide a unity. However, we do not want to use human means to frighten you.

We could if we wished ensure that you paid ten pounds of gold in accordance with the emperor's orders.[2] But perhaps the reason that you do not have enough to pay the amount that rebaptisers are ordered to pay is that you spent so much on buying people to rebaptise! However, as I said, we do not want to use human means to frighten you. Rather, let Christ inspire fear in you. I should like to know how you would reply to him if he said to you:

> Crispin, was your price dear enough to buy the fear of the Mappalians, but my death too cheap to buy the love of every race? Was the money counted out from your purse[3] worth more for rebaptising your tenants than the liquid that flowed from my side for rebaptising my nations?

If you do lend an ear to Christ, I know that you will be able to hear even more, and be warned by the very possessions themselves, how impiously you are speaking against Christ.

If you take it for granted that you are by human law firmly in possession of whatever you buy with your silver, how much more firmly is Christ, by divine law, in possession of whatever he bought with his blood. Indeed, his possession of the whole world will be unshaken, for scripture says of him, *He will rule from sea to sea, and from the river to the ends of the globe* [Ps 72(71).8]. How can you be assured of not losing what you appear to have purchased in Africa, when you contend that Christ has lost the entire globe, and Africa alone remains his?

(2) Need I write at length? If the Mappalians transferred to your communion of their own free will, then let them listen to each of us through our writing down what we say, signing it and having it translated into Punic.[4] Then let them choose what they will, free from fear of their master's authority. For our words will reveal whether they are remaining in error under compulsion, or are willingly holding to the truth. If they do not understand them, then how have you had the nerve to convert them without their understanding? However, if they do understand, then let them listen to us both, as I suggested, and do whatever they wish.

Again, if any ordinary people have come over to our side and you think that they were compelled by their masters, then let us do the same for them. Let them listen to us both and choose what they prefer. If on the other hand you are unwilling for this to happen, then it will be obvious to anyone that you are not relying on the truth. But we must beware the anger of God, both here and in the age to come. I beseech you through Christ to respond to these suggestions.

Letter 86

406/409

Augustine the bishop greets in the Lord his distinguished lord Caecilian,[1] a son truly and deservedly honoured and welcome in the love of Christ.

Your uncorrupted[2] exercise of government, your reputation for the virtues, and furthermore the admirable assiduity and faithful single-mindedness of your Christian piety – these are all gifts of God, and in your delight at what he has already granted, you put your hope in his promise of still greater things. It is these that have inspired me to communicate with you by letter to allow your eminent self to share my own disturbed circumstances.

We rejoice that in other parts of Africa you have been marvellously effective in serving the unity of the Catholic church. Equally, however, we grieve that the region of Hippo Regius and the neighbouring area on the borders of Numidia have not yet deserved to benefit from the vigour with which you as governor have applied your edict,[3] my excellent lord and son truly and deservedly honoured and welcome in the love of Christ.

I thought it necessary to speak to your magnificent self about this because I did not want it to be attributed to my own neglect, as the burden of the see of Hippo is mine to bear. Perhaps you will be good enough to listen to my brothers and colleagues, or the priest whom I have sent with these letters. They can relate to your exalted self the degree of presumption and recklessness the heretics show even on the plain of Hippo. Then, with the help of the Lord our God, you will no doubt see to it that their blasphemous folly, like some tumour, is healed by deterrence, rather than punished by surgical removal.

Letter 100

408

Augustine greets in the Lord Donatus,[1] his distinguished lord, and deservedly honoured and outstandingly praiseworthy son.

(1) I should be happier if the church in Africa were not so troubled as to need the help of any earthly authority. However, as the apostle said, *there*

is no authority except from God[2] [Rom 13.1]. There is no doubt, therefore, when assistance comes to your mother the Catholic church through you, her most single-minded sons, that *our help is in the name of the Lord, who made heaven and earth* [Ps 121(120).2]. Would not anyone count this a God-sent comfort amidst such troubles, and indeed a significant one, that a man like you, who deeply loves the name of Christ, has been elevated to the dignity of proconsul?[3] The consequence is a union of power with your good will that might restrain the enemies of the church from their outrageous and sacrilegious assaults, my distinguished lord and deservedly honoured and outstandingly praiseworthy son.

Finally, there is one thing only about your justice that we fear: that you might decide to constrain them with the appalling nature of their offences rather than Christian gentleness in view. (For whatever evil is inflicted upon the fellowship of Christians by the impious and ungrateful, it is certainly more serious and shocking than if similar things are inflicted upon others.) We pray to you through Christ himself to avoid the former course.

We do not ask for vengeance on our enemies on this earth. Our sufferings ought not to constrict our spirits so narrowly that we forget the commandments given to us, for whose truth and in whose name we suffer. We love our enemies and we pray for them [cf. Mt 5.44; Lk 6.27–8]. That is why we desire their reform and not their deaths, through the intervention of judges and laws that inspire fear, so that they will not meet with the punishment of everlasting judgement. We do not want you to neglect their correction; but neither do we want you to impose the punishments they deserve. Restrain their sins, therefore, in such a way that they will live to repent of having sinned.

(2) Consequently, we beg you that when you hear cases involving the church, even if you learn that horrific injuries have been attempted against or inflicted upon her, you will forget that you have the power to kill, but you will not forget our plea. My honoured and dearest son, it is no trivial or negligible request that we make of you, to avoid killing those for whose reform we are petitioning the Lord. Even leaving aside the fact that we ought never to waver from the goal of *overcoming evil through good* [Rom 12.21], your wise self also might reflect that no one except those in the church has any concern with introducing cases concerning the church. Therefore if it is your opinion that these should lead to human deaths, you will deter us from bringing any such case by our own efforts before your court. When they learn this, they will proceed with still less restraint in their reckless attempts to destroy us; and we shall be driven to

the necessity of choosing to be killed by them rather than arraign them before your courts to be killed.

I beg you not to spurn my warning, my request, and my pleading. I believe that you recall that I might have had great confidence in approaching you even if I were not a bishop and if you were much more exalted than you are already. Meanwhile, let the Donatist heretics recognise through the edicts issued by your excellent self that the laws passed against their errors remain in force;[4] at present they reckon them a dead letter, and boast of this, and consequently are unable to show us any mercy even for that reason.

Furthermore, you will help us most greatly in our labours and in the risks that make them fruitful, if you take care not to restrain their sect – foolish and full of impious pride as it is – by using imperial legislation in such a way that they see themselves as suffering whatever hardships for the sake of truth and justice. Rather, you will help us by allowing them, when you are petitioned, to be persuaded and informed in proceedings before your excellent self or lesser judges, using the very clear documentation of those indubitable events.

Then, those very men who are in custody at your orders might, if it is possible, bend their hardened will to a better course, and read this salutary material to the others. For when people are led through force alone and not through teaching even to abandon a great evil and embrace a great good, the efforts expended prove burdensome rather than profitable.

Letter 87

405/411

Augustine to his dear and fond brother Emeritus.[1]

(1) Whenever I hear of someone who is equipped with a high intelligence and a liberal education,[2] whose view on some straightforward matter is, however, at odds with the truth – of course the security of one's soul does not depend upon such advantages, but still, the more I wonder at someone like that, the more eager I am to meet him and talk with him. Or if I cannot do that, then I find myself longing to reach his mind with letters – for they cover distances – and to be reached in turn by him. I hear

that you are such a man, and I am distressed that you are separated and cut off from the Catholic church, which (as the Holy Spirit prophesied) is spread throughout the world.[3]

I do not know the reason. It is quite clear that Donatus' sect is unknown to the greater part of the Roman world, not to mention the barbarian races (to whom the apostle Paul acknowledged his obligations) [cf. Rom 1.14]. Our communion is bound to them in the Christian faith. It is clear too that they are entirely unaware of the date or the causes of the origin of this dispute. If you will not confess that all these Christians everywhere else are innocent of the crimes of which you accuse those in Africa, then you will be forced to admit that included in those liable on account of everyone else's wicked deeds are all of you yourselves – for you are contaminated as long as desperate characters (to put it mildly) succeed in hiding among you.

After all, you do occasionally expel someone from your communion; and you do not do so before he has first committed the offence for which he is expelled. In such a case aren't you condemning someone only after he has escaped your notice for a while before being discovered and then convicted? My question is this: has he contaminated you during the period he was lying low? 'Not at all', you will answer. In that case, he would not contaminate you if he escaped your notice permanently. Quite often we discover that people who are now dead committed certain crimes, but that does not mean that the Christians who were in communion with them when they were alive were deluded. But if so, why have you broken away so recklessly and impiously, and cut yourselves off from communion with the countless churches of the east? They have never even noticed, and are still unaware of, the events that you teach – or imagine – happened in Africa.

(2) For this is a further question: is what you say true? We are able to find far more persuasive documentation to prove it false. Even from your own documents we are able to show evidence for the very positions you attack. But this, as I said, is a further question which we should address in debate when the need arises. At the moment I ask you to attend with an alert mind to this point: no one can be contaminated by the unknown crimes of unknown persons. From that it follows clearly that your separation from communion with the rest of the world constitutes an impious schism; for they are completely unaware of the charges you press against the Africans (whether they are true or false) and they have always been so.

However, we must also state that even well-known wrongdoers in the church do not harm its good members, if the latter have no power to prevent them from sharing communion, or if considerations of preserving peace provide a reason against this. The prophet Ezekiel tells us that before the damned are destroyed, there are some individuals who merit being marked out and escaping unharmed while the others are destroyed [cf. Ezek 9.4–6]. Who can these be except (as is clearly shown there) those who sorrowfully lament their sins, and the injustices of the people of God committed in their midst? But who can sorrowfully lament something he does not know about?

For the same reason the apostle Paul puts up with false brethren. When he says, *They all seek what belongs to them rather than to Christ Jesus* [Phil 2.21], he is not talking about individuals unknown to him. He makes it clear that they had been in his company. But surely the sort of people who preferred to burn incense or hand over the sacred books to idols rather than die must be counted among those who *seek what belongs to them, rather than to Christ Jesus*.

(3) I shall leave out many other pieces of evidence from scripture, because I don't want to make the letter longer than necessary. In any case, I can leave it to your learned self to reflect by yourself on other examples. I do beg you, however, to look at this, which is quite sufficient. If so many unjust individuals within the one people of God did not make [the prophets] who witnessed against them like themselves; and if the mass of false brethren did not turn the apostle Paul into someone who *sought what belonged to himself rather than to Christ Jesus*, even though he was a member with them of a single church [cf. Gal 2.4; 2 Cor 11.26]; then it is obvious that a man is not made bad[4] just because some bad person approaches Christ's altar with him. This is so even if he knows about him, so long as he disapproves of him, and by his disapproval distances him from his own clear conscience. It is obvious then that 'running with a thief' consists only of either helping him to steal or welcoming his theft with heartfelt consent. (We make this point to forestall endless and unnecessary questions about human actions that do not constitute a problem for our argument.)

(4) Unless you share this view, you too will have to be the same sort of people as Optatus.[5] While he was in communion with you, you were aware that his behaviour was very unlike that of Emeritus or of others among you who, I have no doubt, have no connection at all with the sort of thing he did. Furthermore, our only charge against you is the crime of schism, which, by obstinately persevering with it, you have in fact made

into a heresy. You should read how seriously this transgression is measured by the judgement of God; I have no doubt that you have read it. You
will discover that the earth gaped open to devour Dathan and Abiron, and
that all the others who had supported them were burnt up by a fire that
arose from their midst [cf. Num 16.31–5]. The Lord God, then, marked
out this outrage for immediate punishment as an example to warn us to
avoid it. In this way he shows us what kind of a final judgement he is
reserving for such people, even though he spares them so patiently the
while.

We do not criticise your reasons if you were unwilling to excommunicate Optatus at the time when his insane and raging abuse of power was
on everyone's lips, when the whole of Africa stood to accuse him, groaning in chorus with your own groaning. If you are indeed the man that
general opinion proclaims you to be (and God knows that I believe so, and
hope so), we do not blame you if you were unwilling to excommunicate
Optatus at that time, for fear of his drawing many others with him into
excommunication, and splitting your communion with the madness of
schism. However, it is this point, brother Emeritus, that will convict you
in the court of God: although you saw that it would be such an evil thing
to divide Donatus' sect that you deemed it better to tolerate being in communion with Optatus than to allow that, you still persist in the evil that
your predecessors wrought by dividing the church of Christ.

(5) At this point you will perhaps attempt to defend Optatus, as you
have so little room for reply. Do not, please, my brother, do not. It would
be unworthy of you; even if it were worthy of someone else (if anything
can be worthy of those who are bad) it is certainly not worthy of Emeritus
to defend Optatus. And neither, perhaps, to accuse him. Let that be so.
Take the middle course and say: *Let every man carry his own burden* [Gal
6.5]. *Who are you to judge someone else's servant?* [Rom 14.4].

Faced with the witness of the whole of Africa, indeed of every land in
which stories about Gildo were rife (for Optatus shared his notoriety),
you hesitated even to judge Optatus, in case you made a rash judgement
without knowing the facts. If that is so, are we able, and ought we, to pronounce a rash sentence on those who lived before us, when we do not
know the facts, faced with your testimony alone? Is it not enough that you
should accuse them in ignorance, without us also making ignorant judgements? It is not Optatus whom you are defending (though it may be a mistaken hostility that endangers him) but you yourself when you say, 'I do
not know what he was like.' The Africans whom you accuse are less well

known to you still; how much more unknown, then, are they to the world of the east? Yet you allow a shocking dispute to disassociate you from those churches, even while you recite their names which are in your bibles.

If the bishop of, not even Caesarea, but, say, Sitifis[6] was ignorant of his colleague and contemporary, your notorious bishop of Timgad, with his evil reputation, then however could the churches of Corinth, Ephesus, Colossae, Philippi, Thessalonika, Antioch, Pontus, Galatia, Cappadocia[7] and all the other parts of the world, founded in Christ by the apostles, how could they know which Africans were guilty of handing over? How could they deserve your condemnation when they could not have known it? Yet you refuse to share communion with them, you deny that they are Christians, you attempt to rebaptise them. What can I say? How can I object? What protest can I make? If I am speaking with a sensible man, I can be sure that you share with me in feeling a sharp edge of outrage. You can see immediately, surely, what I would say if I were wanting to say anything.

(6) Perhaps you will say that your predecessors held a council among themselves at which they condemned the entire Christian world except themselves? So is our judgement of events to be reduced to this, that the council of the Maximianists, who are a segment of your segment, does not have any power against you because they are tiny compared to you, but your council has power against *the nations that are* Christ's *inheritance and* his *possession, the ends of the earth* [Ps 2.8]?[8] If anyone failed to blush at that, I'd be amazed to find a drop of blood in his body!

Please do write back to me. I have heard from certain people whom I cannot fail to trust that you would write back if I wrote to you. I have already sent you one letter.[9] I do not know whether you received it; perhaps you have replied to it and I did not receive your answer. Meanwhile I ask you not to be reluctant to reply to this one, giving me your view. But please don't take yourself off into other issues: this is the starting-point of an orderly enquiry into why the schism took place.

(7) Even worldly powers defend themselves using the rule given by the apostle Paul when they pursue action against schismatics. What he said was: *Anyone who resists authority resists what God has established. But those who resist that, bring judgement upon themselves. Rulers do not inspire fear in those who do good works, but in those who do evil. Do you want not to fear the authorities? Do good, and you will have praise from them; for the minister of*

God is there for your good. If you do evil, then fear him; for he does not wield a sword pointlessly. He is a minister of God, and avenger of his anger on the evildoer [Rom 13.2–4].[10]

The entire issue, then, amounts to this: is a schism nothing evil? Or did you not in fact bring about a schism? If not, then the resistance you offer the authorities is for *good works* and not for evil (which would lead you to bring judgement on yourselves). That is why our Lord said, with infinite foresight, not simply *Blessed are those who suffer harassment* [Mt 5.10], but in addition, *for the sake of justice*. I am eager to know from you, therefore, with reference to my earlier arguments, whether the way you have acted during the feud you are maintaining constitutes justice.

Is it not unjust, then, to condemn the whole world without a hearing, either because it has not heard the things you have heard, or because the things you have believed hastily and the accusations you have made without solid documentation have not been proved to them; and then for this reason to wish to rebaptise so many churches which were founded by the labour and preaching of the Lord himself, when he was still here in the flesh, and by his apostles? Is this not unjust, when you are free to be ignorant of your wicked colleagues in Africa (who live as your contemporaries and handle the sacraments with you) or even to know about them but tolerate them so that the Donatist sect is not split, while they, who live in distant parts of the globe, are not allowed to be ignorant of the things that you know or believe or hear or imagine concerning Africans? If so, it is exceptionally perverse to embrace one's own injustice while yet criticising the harshness of the authorities.

(8) 'But Christians are not permitted to pursue action even against the wicked.' Let us take it that they're not. Still, surely, it is not right to criticise the authorities who are ordained for this purpose. Are we to rub out the apostle's words? Or perhaps your copies of the Bible do not include the bits I quoted a little earlier?

'But', you will say, 'you should not be in communion with such people'. Well, then. Were you not in communion with Flavianus, who was once *vicarius*, a member of your sect?[11] He used to execute the guilty when he discovered them, in service of the laws.

'But', you will say, 'you have appealed to the Roman rulers against us'. Indeed not. You have appealed to them against yourselves; it was you who were bold enough to split and tear apart the church, the church of which they, in accordance with ancient prophecies, are now members. (For the

words, *And all the kings of the earth will adore him* [Ps 72(71).11] referred
to Christ.) Our people, moreover, are seeking from the ordained authorities protection from illegal and personal violence inflicted by your
members.[12] You yourselves, who do not do such things, are very sorry
about them, and greatly regret them. Our people do not do this to pursue
action against you, but to defend themselves. Similarly, the apostle Paul
managed to be provided even with an armed guard to protect himself
from the Jews who were plotting to kill him. And that was before the
Roman empire became Christian.

Our rulers, however, whatever chance acquainted them with your
godless schism, decide to act against you as they wish, bearing in mind
their own responsibilities and authority. For they do not *wield a sword
pointlessly:* they are *ministers of God, and avengers of his anger on the evil-
doer* [cf. Rom 13.4].

Finally, if any of our members are pursuing this course with a lack of
Christian moderation, we do not approve of it. However, we are not going
to abandon the Catholic church on their account, just because we are not
able to purge away the chaff before the final period of winnowing. Neither
did you abandon Donatus' sect on account of Optatus, when you were
afraid to expel him.

(9) 'But why do you wish us to be united with you, if we are implicated
in this outrage?' You are still alive, and you can still be reformed, if you
are willing. When you rejoin us, that is, the church of God, the heritage of
Christ (to whom the ends of the earth belong) [cf. Ps 2.8], you will be
reformed so that you draw life from the root. The apostle has this to say of
the broken branches: *God has the power to graft them on once more* [Rom
11.23].

You will then change from that sect in whose name you dissented
from us; the sacraments which you possessed were, however, holy, as
they were the same for all of us. So we wish you to change from the error
of your ways, in order, that is, for your cut branch to be regrafted into
the root.

The sacraments you have not indeed altered, and we approve of them
as you have them; otherwise in wishing to reform your perverseness, we
would be inflicting damage impiously on those mysteries of Christ which
you have not, despite your own perverseness, perverted.

Similarly, Saul did not pervert the anointing which he received, and
king David, a devout servant of God, treated his anointing with extreme
respect [cf. 2 Sam 1.1–16]. That is why we do not rebaptise you. We are

eager to restore you to the root, but we approve of the shape of the severed shoot, as long as it hasn't been altered. But even if it is whole, it cannot bear any fruit without its root.

The issue of legal action is one thing; you say that you suffer from this, even when our people are so gentle and mild, and although yours inflict heavy injuries on them, illegally and as private individuals. But the issue of baptism is something different: our question is not where it is, but where it is beneficial. For everywhere that it exists, it is the same. But the person who receives it is not the same wherever he is. Consequently, we hate the individual impiety of human beings in schism; but the baptism of Christ we honour everywhere. If military deserters take the imperial standards with them, whether they are condemned and punished, or reformed in a merciful way, the standards are welcomed back as unharmed, provided they remain unharmed. If there is need to investigate this matter more thoroughly, it is, as I have said, a separate issue; for we have to observe in these matters whatever the church of God observes.

(10) The question is, then, whether your church or ours is the church of God. That is why we need to investigate from the beginning why you created a schism. If you do not write back, my case is easy to defend before God, as I believe, as I have written letters aimed at peace, to a man who is, I have been told (the schism apart), both good and liberally educated. You must imagine what you would respond to God, whose patience we must at present praise, but whose sentence we must fear in the end.

If you reply with the concern with which, as you can see, I have written to you, then the mercy of God will be with you; and at some time the error which is dividing us will succumb to the love of peace and to reasoning about the truth.

Bear in mind that I have not discussed the 'Rogatists' who, it is said, describe you as 'Firmians' (just as you call us 'Macarians').[13] Nor have I discussed your bishop of Rusicade,[14] who is supposed to have made an agreement with Firmus about the security of the latter's flock, on condition that they open the gates to him and yield the Catholics up to destruction. And there are countless other examples. So do stop using rhetorical commonplaces to exaggerate the human deeds that come to your ears, or your notice. For you can see that I am keeping silent about your side, in order to deal with the origin of the schism, where the whole burden of the issue lies.

May the Lord God inspire you in peaceful reflection, my dear and fond brother. Amen.

Letter 88

406/408

From the Catholic clergy of the region of Hippo Regius, to Januarius.[1]

(1) Your clergy and your Circumcellions are savagely harassing us in a manner unheard of, and with unprecedented cruelty. Even if they were only returning *evil for evil*, they would still be breaking the law of Christ [Rom 12.17; 1 Thess 5.15; 1 Pet 3.9]. But in this case, when we take into account all your actions and ours, we find ourselves in the situation that scripture describes: *They were returning to me evil for good* [Ps 35(34).12]; or as another psalm puts it, *I was a peacemaker among those who hated peace; when I spoke with them, they waged war against me unprovoked* [Ps 120(119).7, LXX].

Since you yourself have reached such a great age, we considered that you would know that the Donatist sect (which was at first known at Carthage as the sect of Maiorinus) took the initiative in accusing Caecilian (who was at the time bishop of the Carthaginian church) before the great Constantine, emperor so long ago. But in case your respected self has forgotten this (or you are pretending not to have known) or even (which we doubt) in case you do not know, we enclose in this letter of ours a copy of the report by the then proconsul, Anulinus. The sect of Maiorinus on that occasion made an appeal to him that as proconsul he might pass on to the aforementioned emperor the charges they were laying against Caecilian.

(2) To A. GGG. NNN. from Anulinus V.C., proconsul of Africa.[2]

The heavenly letters your majesty sent to Caecilian and those acting under him, who are called priests, are welcomed and reverenced, and I, your devoted servant, in my lowliness, have taken care to include them in my proceedings.[3] I have also urged their addressees, now that unity has, with everyone's agreement, been restored, and they, through the comprehensive generosity of your majesty's pardon, appear to be set free, to observe the sanctity of Catholic law, and put themselves at the service of due reverence and sacred affairs.[4]

However, a few days later certain individuals appeared who had united to themselves a crowd of the populace, and were intent on contradicting Caecilian They presented to my venerable self a bundle wrapped in leather and a stamped and an unstamped pamphlet, and they begged me earnestly to have these sent to your sacred majesty's holy and revered court. Your lowly servant has ensured that these have been sent to you and the proceedings of these events have also been enclosed, so that your majesty may judge all the evidence. Caecilian meanwhile remains in his position. I have sent you two booklets; the one in leather has written on it 'A book of the Catholic church containing charges against Caecilian, handed over by the party[5] of Maiorinus'. The other has no seal, and is attached to the same piece of leather wrapping.

Dated the 17th day before the calends of May, at Carthage, in the third consulship of our Lord Constantine Augustus.[6]

(3) After this report had been sent to him, the emperor ordered the two parties to come to the city of Rome for the bishops to give judgement. The records of the church show how the case was heard and concluded, and how Caecilian was adjudged innocent. And now, after the peacemaking measures of the bishops' judgement, all persistent strife and hostility ought to have been quenched.

However, your predecessors returned to the emperor once more. They complained that the judgement had been mistaken and that the case had not been heard in its entirety. Consequently, the emperor allowed a second episcopal trial to be held in the city of Arles in Gaul.[7] There this false and devilish dissension was condemned, and many of your associates returned to peace with Caecilian. However, others who were more stubborn and more litigious made an appeal to the same emperor. After this he himself was driven to judge and bring to a conclusion the episcopal proceedings between the parties. Then he introduced for the first time a law against your party which ordered the public confiscation of the buildings that belong to your assemblies.[8]

If you wanted us to enclose all the documentation concerned with this, our letter would be far too long. However, I certainly cannot omit the case of Felix of Aphthugni. Your predecessors claimed at the council of Carthage, which was held under the primate Secundus of Tigisis, that he was the source of all evils. His case was debated and concluded as a public lawsuit,[9] when your members were exerting pressure upon the emperor. Indeed, the aforementioned emperor attested in his own letter to the fact that it was your side who, in this very case, brought the accusations before him, and tirelessly presented their complaints. We quote from a copy of this letter below.

> (4) From the Flavian emperors Constantine Maximus Caesar
> and Valerius Licinianus Licinius Caesar to Probianus, proconsul
> of Africa.

Whilst the most perfect Verus, who was at the time vicar of prefects in our Africa,[10] was in the grip of ill health, your predecessor Aelian consequently took over his duties. These included dealing with the business of – or rather the hostility which, it seemed, had been aroused against – Caecilian, the bishop of the Catholic church. Aelian believed that this ought to be submitted once more to his investigation and his jurisdiction. He therefore summoned Superius the centurion, Caecilian the magistrate of Apthugni, Saturninus the former city-clerk, the younger Calibius, the present city-clerk of the same town, and Solus, a public servant of the aforementioned town.[11] He gave them a hearing whose result was to establish the innocence of Felix in the matter. For the objection made against Caecilian was that he appeared to have been ordained bishop by Felix, when Felix had been accused of handing over and burning the holy scriptures.

Finally, Maximus maintained that Ingentius, a decurion of the town of Ziqua, had forged a letter supposedly from Caecilian as former *duumvir*.[12] We saw from the proceedings before us that this same Ingentius had been put on the rack, and had in fact hardly been tortured, for the reason that he claimed to be a decurion of the town of Ziqua.

We wish you therefore to send us the same Ingentius, with a suitable escort, to our court of Constantine Augustus. The matter can be decided in the hearing and presence of those who are at the present time carrying on the business, who continually, day after day, present their complaints; then it might be possible to make it clear to them and impress upon them the fact that in wishing to encourage hostility to the bishop Caecilian and to attack him violently they are acting to no avail.

In this way, strife of this sort may be laid aside, as it should be, and consequently the people will devote themselves to their own religious duties without disagreement and with due reverence.

(5) When you realise that the situation was like this, how can you possibly arouse hostility against us on account of those imperial decrees that are

aimed at you? You were the ones who initiated all this. If it is wrong for the emperors to make rulings in such cases, if it is wrong for Christian emperors to involve themselves in such concerns, then who pressed your predecessors into referring the case of Caecilian through the proconsul to the emperor? Who pressed them to accuse the bishop a second time before the emperor, when you had already somehow pronounced sentence on him in his absence? And then, when he was declared innocent, to contrive slanders against Felix, the man who ordained him, on yet another occasion before the same emperor? Surely the only judgement that is operative against your sect at present is the one given by the elder Constantine himself; and this your own predecessors chose, extorting it from him by their tireless complaints, and preferring it to the judgement of the bishops.

If the imperial judgements do not satisfy you, who was it who first compelled the emperors to activate them against you? You protest against the Catholic church because of decisions the emperors have made against you; it is as if Daniel's opponents wanted to protest against him because after he was freed they were sent to be eaten by the same lions that they had originally hoped would eat him. As scripture says, *There is no difference between the threats of a king and the anger of a lion* [Prov 19.12].

Daniel's enemies slandered him and forced him to be sent into the lion's den. His innocence defeated their malice; he was lifted out of there unharmed and they were sent back there to their deaths [Dan 6.16–24]. Similarly, your predecessors cast Caecilian and his companions into the fury of the king to be consumed. His innocence caused him to be set free, and now you are suffering at the hands of those very kings under whom your side wished them to suffer. For scripture says: *Whoever prepares a pit for his neighbour will fall into it himself* [Ecclus 27.26].

(6) Therefore you have no right to make complaints against us. However, the gentleness of the church would have restrained it from making any use even of imperial decrees, if your clergy and Circumcellions had not ruined and destroyed our peace with their appalling atrocities and their insane violence, thus forcing us to resume activating these measures against you. Indeed, before the more recent laws about which you are now complaining reached Africa,[13] they had set ambushes for our bishops when they travelled; they had battered our fellow-clergy and wounded them horribly; they had inflicted serious wounds also on our lay people, and had set fire to their buildings. There was another priest also who had, of his own free will,

chosen unity with our communion; he was dragged from his house, beaten savagely at their whim, then rolled in a muddy pool, dressed in rushes, and displayed by them to show off their crime, an object of pity for some and of mockery for others. Then he was taken from there to wherever they wished to take him, and released with difficulty after twelve days.[14]

As a result, Proculianus[15] (according to the municipal records) was prosecuted by our bishop. When the case was examined and he pretended[16] to innocence, and then he was immediately prosecuted once more, he declared in the records that he would say nothing more. Even today the perpetrators of this crime remain as priests among you, still free, moreover, to terrorise and to harass us as much as they ever could.

(7) Neither is it the case that our bishop complained to the emperors about the injuries and harassment that the Catholic church in these parts suffered at that time. Rather, we preferred to call a council[17] and summon you to it peacefully, so that, if it could be done, you might hold a conference among yourselves; then, error might be eradicated and brotherly love might rejoice *in the bond of peace* [Eph 4.3].

As to the details of that meeting, the records themselves should inform your reverend self of them: of the reply that Proculianus made at the beginning, that you were going to hold a council and examine there what reply you should make; and of his subsequent statement in the proceedings, once he had been summoned again on the strength of his promise, that he rejected a conference aimed at peace.

Finally, when the notorious atrocities committed by your clergy and Circumcellions did not stop, another trial was held. This time, Crispin[18] was condemned as a heretic; but through the mildness of the Catholics he was let off the imposition of a fine of ten pounds of gold (the amount that the emperors had determined as the penalty for heresy).[19] Despite that, he decided to appeal to the emperors. As to the response given to that appeal, was it not the previous iniquities of your members and his own appeal that wrung it out of them?[20] Yet even after the answer was returned, the fine of gold to which he had been sentenced was not enforced, because our bishops interceded with the emperors on his behalf. Moreover, after the council our bishops sent delegates to the court to request that the fine of ten pounds of gold (which had been set for heretics) should not be imposed upon all of the bishops and priests of your sect, but only on those in whose areas your members were inflicting violence on the Catholic church.[21]

However, when these delegates arrived at Rome, the emperor was so upset by the awful scars freshly inflicted upon the Catholic bishop of Bagai[22] that he had laws despatched of the kind that were despatched.[23] When these arrived in Africa and pressure began to be put upon you (not to your harm, but to your good) then surely what even you ought to have done was contact our bishops with the aim of summoning them to a meeting (just as they had summoned you); then, perhaps, a conference might reveal the truth of the matter.

(8) However, not only did you fail to do this, but now your side are inflicting even worse harm on us. They are not just beating us with sticks, or stabbing us with knives; their extraordinary imagination for wickedness has led them to use vinegar mixed with chalk to blind their victim's eyes. They have also pillaged our homes; and they have made themselves a number of enormous and frightening weapons. They arm themselves with these, and run around all over the place breathing threats of slaughter, pillage, arson and blindness.

All this has driven us to complain first of all to you, in the hope that your reverend self might reflect on this situation: a large number of your side – or rather all of you – who you claim are being harassed are in fact sitting safely on your own property and on that of others, under those supposedly fearful laws imposed by the Catholic emperors; and meanwhile we are enduring unprecedented evils at the hands of your side.

You allege that you are suffering harassment; we meanwhile are being battered with clubs and knives by your armed men. You allege that you are suffering harassment; meanwhile our houses are being ruined by the pillaging of your armed men. You allege that you are suffering harassment; meanwhile our eyes are being blinded by the chalk and vinegar of your armed men. On top of all that, if they take it into their heads to kill themselves, they want their deaths to bring hatred on us, but glory on themselves. They don't hold themselves responsible for the actions they commit against us; while those they commit against themselves, they hold us responsible for! They live as bandits, they die as Circumcellions; they are honoured as martyrs. However, we have never heard even of bandits who blinded the victims of their robbery; bandits remove their dead victims from the light,[24] rather than removing the light from their living victims.

(9) Meanwhile, if we ever catch any of your side we keep them unharmed and treat them with great affection; we discuss with them, and

we read them anything that might overcome the error that divides brothers from one another. We do as the Lord commanded when he spoke through the prophet Isaiah: *Hear the word of the Lord, you who fear it. Say to those who hate you and revile you, 'You are our brothers.' Then the name of the Lord may be glorified and revealed to them in joy; but as for them, let them be ashamed* [Is 66.5, LXX]. In this way, by reflecting upon the clarity of the truth and the beauty of peace we are uniting some of them into the love of the Holy Spirit and the body of Christ, not in baptism (for they had already received this royal sign, so to speak, although they were deserters) but in faith, which was where they were lacking. For scripture says: *cleansing their hearts by faith* [Acts 15.9]; and again: *Love covers a multitude of sins* [1 Pet 4.8].

However, extreme hardness of heart; or shame which makes them unable to endure the mockery of those who used to be their allies in boasting untruthfully so often against us, and in dreaming up so many evils to inflict on us; or else fear of suffering (now that they are on our side) the sort of thing they used to inflict on us before, may make them reluctant to assent to the unity of Christ. In that case, we send them away unharmed just as we held them unharmed. We also, so far as we are able, advise our lay people to hold them without harming them, and to bring them to us for correction and instruction. Some of them listen to us, and do this if they can. Others treat them as they would treat bandits, because, to speak the truth, they have been treated by them as if they were. Some deflect the blows that threaten their own bodies by striking them before they are struck by them. Others present those they have caught to the judges and do not spare them even when we intercede, so long as they are afraid of suffering appalling harm at their hands. But in all these cases they will not abandon the ways of bandits, although they demand for themselves the honour due to martyrs.[25]

(10) This, therefore, is what we desire, and we plead with your reverend self by means of these letters, and through the brethren whom we send to you: in the first place, if at all possible, that you should hold a conference with our bishops for the sake of peace. In this way we may remove the error itself rather than those individuals where it is found; they themselves might be reformed rather than punished; and you might now summon the council as you previously despised their invitation.

How much better indeed if you do this among yourselves, and then write down what you have enacted, sign your names, and send it to the emperor; rather than this happening before the earthly authorities, who are only able to observe the laws already given against you! Indeed, your colleagues who had made the voyage[26] said that they had come to be heard before the prefects, and they nominated our holy father the Catholic bishop Valentinus, who was then at the court, saying that they wished to be heard in his presence.[27] The judge was not able to grant them this; by now he was making his judgement in accordance with the laws that had been established against you.[28] Again, that bishop had not come with this in mind, and he had received no instructions to this effect from his fellow-bishops.

How much better a judgement, therefore, could the emperor himself pronounce on the whole matter, once the proceedings of your conference had been recounted to him; for he is not subject to the same laws, and he has the power of introducing other laws. (Of course, though, the case has already been heard and concluded long ago!) But our reason for wishing you to hold a conference is not to close the issue once more, but to show to those who are unaware of it that it has already been closed. If your bishops are willing[29] to do this, how will you lose by it? Will you not rather gain, as your willingness becomes well known to save you from the criticism you deserve for your hesitation?

But perhaps you think that it should not take place because you fail to notice that Christ our Lord debated even with the devil [cf. Mt 4.1–10; Lk 4.1–13], and that not only the Jews, but even pagan philosophers of the Stoic and Epicurean sects discussed things with Paul [cf. Acts 17.17–18]? Or perhaps those very imperial laws prevent you from inviting our bishops? Come now! Invite in the mean time those bishops of ours from the region of Hippo, where we are suffering so badly at the hands of your side. How much more freely and more easily will your letters be brought to us by your men than their weapons!

(11) To conclude, then, please write back in a similar vein to us via the same brethren whom we have sent to you. If, however, you are unwilling to do that, at least listen to us as well as to those of your side at whose hands we are suffering so. Show us the truth for whose sake you are, as you claim, suffering harassment, while we suffer such cruelty at the hands of your side. If, then, you persuade us that we are in error, perhaps you will allow us not to be rebaptised by you. We consider it just that you should offer us this; for we have been baptised by people who have never been tried and condemned by you; and after all you offer this to those baptised over so long a period by Felicianus of Musti and Praetextatus of Assur, even though you were attempting to use the judges' rulings to

drive them from their basilicas on the grounds that they were in communion with Maximian;[30] moreover they had been condemned by you along with him, specifically and by name, at the council of Bagai. We can prove all this from the judicial and municipal records. According to these you both appealed to your own council, as long as you were trying to show the judges that you were expelling your own schismatics from their basilicas; and yet, having yourselves created a schism from the very seed of Abraham, in which *all races are blessed* [Gen 22.18], you are not willing to be driven out of your basilicas not only through the judges (which is how you treated your own schismatics) but through the very *kings of the earth* [Ps 2.2], who (now the prophecy has been fulfilled) adore Christ. It was in their presence that you accused Caecilian, but once defeated there, you withdrew.

(12) However, if you are willing neither to teach us nor to listen to us, then at least come to the district of Hippo, or send to us someone to have a look at your side's armed troops (though no soldier includes among his weapons chalk and vinegar for blinding barbarians). If you are unwilling to do even this, then at least write to them and tell them to stop behaving like this, and to begin to restrain themselves from slaughtering, looting and blinding our people. We don't want to say, 'Condemn them.' For you will have seen that you are not polluted by the bandits whom we have now uncovered within your communion, just as we are not polluted by those whom you could never prove to have handed over [the sacred books].

Choose what you will out of all this. But even if you have contempt for our complaints, we will still not regret our wish to deal with the matter in a peaceable and orderly way. The Lord will be with his church, so that you, rather, will regret having despised our humble request.

Letter 173

411/414

Augustine, bishop of the Catholic church, to Donatus,[1] priest of Donatus' sect.

(1) Perhaps if you could see my heart-felt sorrow and concern for your security, then you would have some pity *on your own soul: you would please God* [Ecclus 30.24, Latin] by listening to the word that is not ours, but his;

and you would not nail the scriptures into your memory in just the way that locks your heart against them. You are unhappy about being dragged to security; though you have dragged many of our people to disaster. After all, are we asking for anything except to get hold of you, bring you in, and keep you from dying? But if you are a little battered physically, you have done this to yourself. A horse was quickly provided for you. You refused to use it; and then you dashed yourself hard against the ground. Your companion was brought along with you, and he arrived quite unhurt, because he did not treat himself like that.

(2) Now you don't think that this should have been done to you. You reckon that no one should be forced to accept what is good for him. But note the words of the apostle Paul: *If anyone desires to be bishop, he covets a good work* [1 Tim 3.1]. However, very many individuals are held against their will to force them to accept the episcopate. They are taken away, locked up, and put under guard; and they have to put up with a great deal that they do not like, until they begin to want to undertake this good work.[2] Surely it is far more appropriate to drag you away from your disastrous errors, which make you your own enemy, and lead you to recognise and choose the truth. Then you will not only retain your honour[3] along with your security, but also avoid a miserable death.

Your argument is that God has given human beings free choice and that therefore they ought not to be forced to accept what is good. If so, why are the people I have just mentioned forced to accept what is good? Just notice this point, which you are reluctant to bear in mind: good will spends itself in merciful efforts to guide another's evil will.

Everyone knows that a person cannot be condemned unless his evil will deserves it, and cannot be set free unless he acted out of good will.[4] That is no good reason, however, to abandon those one loves to their evil will, by cruelly neglecting to punish them. Rather, if we have the power, we should both keep them from what is bad, and push them towards the good.

(3) You might argue that an evil will is always allowed its own freedom. If so, what about the Israelites when they were being disobedient and complaining [cf. e.g. Exod 15.24]? Why were harsh blows inflicted on them to keep them away from evil, and to force them towards the promised land? If an evil will must always be allowed its own freedom, then why was Paul not allowed to indulge his wicked will to pursue action against the church? Instead, he was knocked to the ground only to be blinded, blinded only to be transformed, transformed only to be sent

away, and sent away so that he would suffer for the sake of the truth the very hardships that he had in his error inflicted on others [cf. Acts 9.1–9]. If an evil will must always be allowed its own freedom, then why does sacred scripture advise a father faced with an obdurate son not just to rebuke him with words, but also to beat him *on his sides* [Ecclus 30.12]? This is to guide him by bringing him under control and forcing him into well-disciplined behaviour. That is why scripture also says: *You strike him with a rod, but you will free his soul from death* [Prov 23.14].

Again, if an evil will is always to be allowed its own freedom, then why are negligent pastors rebuked with the words, *You have failed to call back the straying sheep, you have not searched for the lost sheep* [Ezek 34.4]? You too are Christ's sheep; you bear the Lord's stamp in the sacrament you have received.[5] However, you have gone astray and become lost. Please, then, do not take offence at us because we call you back when you are straying, and look for you when you are lost. Surely it is better for us to carry out the Lord's will – he advises us to force you to return to his sheepfold – than to go along with the wishes of the straying sheep and allow you to be lost. Please, then, do not repeat the words that I hear you repeating continually: 'I want to stray this way, I want to be lost like this.' For it is better for us not to allow that at all, in so far as we can stop it.

(4) Recently you threw yourself into a well trying to kill yourself.[6] You certainly acted with free will then. But it would have been extremely cruel of the servants of God[7] if they had abandoned you to this evil will of yours and not rescued you from such a death. Everyone would have blamed them, and deservedly so. Everyone would have adjudged them impious, and rightly.

Then you threw yourself into some water of your own free will, to kill yourself. They lifted you out of the water, against your will, to stop you dying. You acted according to your will, but to bring disaster on yourself. They acted against your will but for your security. It seems then that you ought to protect the physical security of those you love even to the extent of saving them against their will. If so, how much more their spiritual security! For if they abandon that, they must fear death that lasts for ever. However, in inflicting death on yourself, you would have died not just temporarily, but eternally. For suppose that you weren't being com-pelled towards security, the peace of the church, the unity of the body of Christ, holy and indivisible love – no, even if you were being forced into something evil, still it would not have been right to inflict death on your-self.

(5) Reflect on holy scripture; examine it as thoroughly as you can, and see whether any of the just or faithful have ever performed this act, even when they were suffering terribly at the hands of men who were driving them not towards everlasting life (which is where you were being pushed) but towards everlasting death. I have heard your story that the apostle Paul meant to approve this act when he said, *And if I hand over my body for me to be burnt*. Doubtless Paul was giving a list of good things which were of no benefit without love, for example *the tongues of men and angels, all mysteries, all knowledge, all prophecy, all faith strong enough to move mountains, the distribution of one's possessions to the poor* [1 Cor 13.1–3]. Therefore, in your view, he also counted self-inflicted death among the goods.

Concentrate carefully, and understand what scripture means by saying that someone may hand over his body to be burnt. Certainly not that he should throw himself into a fire when he faces an enemy pursuing him. Rather it means this: if someone has the option of either doing something evil or suffering something evil, he should choose not to do, rather than not to suffer, evil. In this situation, he should hand over his body into the power of his killer. That is what the three men did who were being forced to worship a golden statue, while their oppressor threatened them with the flames of a burning furnace if they failed to obey [cf. Dan 3.13–21]. They refused to worship the idol. However, they did not throw themselves into the fire. But scripture does also say about them that *they handed over their bodies rather than serve or adore a god other than their God* [Dan 3.28]. Now look at what the apostle means by *If I hand over my body for me to be burnt*.

(6) Look at what follows next: *If I have no love, it does not help me*. That is the love to which you are called; that love refuses to allow you to perish. You think that it can help you to throw yourself headlong to your death; but it cannot benefit you even if someone else kills you as an enemy of love. No – if you have set yourself up outside the church, separated from its bond of unity, its chain of love, you are due to suffer everlasting punishment even if you are burnt alive for the name of Christ. That is what the apostle means when he says: *And if I hand over my body for me to be burnt, but have no love, it does not help me* [1 Cor 13.1–3].

Summon your mind back to healthy reflection and sober thought. Attend carefully to the question of whether we are urging you towards error and impiety; and then be prepared to endure any amount of trouble for the sake of the truth. If in fact you are now involved in error and impiety, while truth and piety are to be found in the place where we are urging you to go, because that is where Christian unity and the love of the Holy Spirit are – if that is so, then why continue your efforts to be your own enemy?

(7) That is why the merciful nature of God provided for us together with your bishops to go to Carthage for that packed and crowded conference, and to discuss among ourselves the actual dispute in a really orderly manner.[8] The proceedings of the conference were written down, and our signatures are appended. Read them or have them read to you. After that make your own choice. I have heard that you would be able to deal with us over these proceedings if we leave out the following words spoken by your bishops: 'Do not let one case bind[9] another, nor one person another.'[10]

You want us to leave out these words, precisely where truth itself spoke through them without their knowing it. You are going to argue that they made a mistake here, and unwarily slipped into a false position. It is our claim that they spoke the truth here, and we can prove this very easily using you yourself.

Your bishops were elected by the whole of Donatus' sect to defend the common cause on the understanding that the rest would accept and welcome whatever they did. Despite this, you seem reluctant to let their judgement bind yours on the specific point where you consider their words hasty and incorrect. But if so, then for that very reason they must have spoken the truth in saying 'Do not let one case bind another, nor one person another.' Moreover, you ought to recognise this: you are reluctant for the collective person of so many of your bishops, represented by these seven,[11] to bind the person of Donatus, priest of Mutugenna. How much less, then, ought the person of Caecilian[12] – even if they had found some evil in him – to be allowed to bind the universal unity of Christ, which is not enclosed in the single village of Mutugenna, but spread throughout the whole world?

(8) Look, though. We are doing as you wanted. We are dealing with you as if they had never said, 'Do not let one case bind another, nor one person another.' But you must find something that they ought to have said instead at this point. The objection made against them concerned the case and person of Primian. He had both along with the rest condemned his condemners, and also welcomed back those he had condemned and cursed, each to his own position of honour. As for the baptism which had been administered by 'dead men' – for it was to them that the famous pronouncement referred: 'the shores are full of the corpses of dead men'[13] – as for this baptism, Primian preferred to recognise and accept it rather

than nullify and reject it. Indeed, he completely dismantled your customary misinterpretation of the words, *whoever is baptised from a dead man, how does the washing benefit him?* [Ecclus 34.30].[14]

Therefore, if they failed to say, 'Do not let one case bind another nor one person another', they would be found guilty with reference to the case of Primian. However, as they have said this, they have protected the Catholic church from charges concerning the case of Caecilian, just as we contended earlier.

(9) Read and examine the rest, though. Look and see whether they actually succeeded in proving anything evil against Caecilian; for they try to bind the church with reference to his person. Look and see whether they did not rather do a great deal on his behalf, and in fact confirm that his case was entirely sound, using the many passages that they produced and read, effectively against themselves. Read all this or have it read to you. Think it all over, review it all carefully, and choose which course you will pursue – to rejoice with us in the peace of Christ, in the unity of the Catholic church, in brotherly love; or else – for the sake of vicious disagreement, for the sake of the sect of Donatus, for the sake of sacrilegious division – to continue to endure the persistent demands that we make out of love for you.

(10) You have noticed, and – so I hear – you repeatedly remark, that the gospel relates how seventy disciples[15] left the Lord and were allowed the choice of their evil and impious withdrawal. Furthermore, the following reply was given to the twelve who remained: *Do you not want to go also?* [Jn 6.67]. However, you fail to notice that the church at that time was just beginning to sprout from a recent seed, and this prophecy was not yet fulfilled in her: *And all the kings of the earth will adore him; all nations will serve him* [Ps 72(71).11]. Certainly the more nearly this is fulfilled, the greater the power at the church's disposal. Consequently she cannot only invite others to embrace what is good, but also compel them.

That is what the Lord intended that incident to signify; for even though he possessed great power, he preferred to recommend humility. He also indicated the point quite clearly in the parable of the banquet, when he summoned the invited guests and they refused to come. Then he said to the servant, *'Go out into the roads and streets of the city and bring here the poor and the weak and the blind and the lame.' And the servant said to his lord, 'Your orders have been carried out, and there is still room.' Then the Lord said to the servant, 'Go out into the pathways and hedgerows and compel them to come in, until my house is full'* [Lk 14.16–24].

Now look at the way in which it was said about the first group 'bring here'. 'Compel' was not said. This shows the beginnings of the church, when it was still growing to be strong enough to use force. But then, because it was right that people should be forced to come to the banquet of everlasting security once the church was strong and sturdy in numbers, there followed the words, *'Your orders have been carried out and there is still room.' 'Go', he said, 'into the pathways and hedgerows and compel them to come in.'*

Therefore, even if you were walking quietly outside the banquet of the holy unity of the church, we would still find you in the streets, as it were. As it is, however, you are full of prickly thorns, so to speak, since you inflict so many evil acts of cruelty on our people. Consequently, we find you in the *hedgerows* and *compel* you *to come in*. If one is forced to go where one does not want, one goes under duress. Once having entered, though, one grazes willingly. Come now: curb your spirit of injustice and rebellion; and then you will find the banquet of salvation within the true church of Christ.

Letter 204

419

Augustine greets in the Lord Dulcitius,[1] his distinguished lord and honoured son.

(1) I must not neglect your request: you have begged me eagerly to teach you how you ought to respond to the heretics; and you are urgently and energetically seeking their security in the mercy of the Lord. Now it is true that great crowds of them realise the benefits bestowed on them (and we congratulate you warmly for this). Some of them, though, are inspired by a deplorable madness and show no gratitude to God or to mankind. If they cannot devastate us by slaughtering us, then they believe that they can terrify us by dying themselves. Their goal is either their own joy at our deaths, or else our sorrow at their deaths.

However, the crazy mistakes of a handful of people ought not to get in the way of saving so many big communities.[2] Our wishes concerning them are known of course to God and sensible men, but also to them, despite their being so hostile to us. When they decide to threaten us by destroying themselves, they have no doubt that we will be afraid in case they perish.

(2) What are we to do, though? We can see that many people, with God's help, are finding the path of peace through your intervention. Surely we cannot and should not restrain your urgent promotion of unity, while we are afraid that a few particularly hard men – and particularly cruel to themselves – should lose their lives at their own wish (and not ours).

Our hope would be that all those who carry the standard of Christ against Christ, or who boast against the gospel using the very words of the gospel (which they fail to understand), should abandon their mis-guided ways and celebrate sharing his unity with us. However, God whose providence is certainly hidden, and yet just, has predestined some of them to the ultimate punishment. There is no doubt therefore that it's better for a few to have perished in their own flames, while the majority – an incomparably large number – have been rescued from being separated and scattered by the plague of schism, and have been reabsorbed. The alternative is for the whole lot alike to burn in the everlasting fires of hell, as the desert for their idolatrous rebellion.

The church grieves for them when they are lost, just as the holy David grieved for his rebellious son,[3] when he had given instructions for his security to be preserved, out of a concern born of love [cf. 2 Sam 18 and 19]. The son died as his heinous act of impiety deserved; and yet David lamented him and paid a tearful tribute to him. However, as the son's proud and unkind spirit left for its appropriate place, the people of God, who had been divided by his tyrannical rule, recognised their king. Their complete reunion provided solace for the father as he grieved for the son he had lost.

(3) I am not therefore criticising you, my distinguished lord and hon-oured son, for deciding to make use of the edict first at Timgad to warn people of that sort. However, by saying there, 'You know that you will meet with the deaths you deserve', you led them to think (as is shown by the letter they wrote in reply) that you were threatening to kill them your-self if you caught them.

They did not realise that you were referring to the death that they will-ingly inflict on themselves. Indeed, you have not been granted by any law the right to use the sword against them; and those imperial ordinances which it is your duty to execute[4] did not include the instruction to have them killed. In the second edict issued by your beloved self, you made your wishes quite clear. Moreover, you thought it right to write to that bishop of theirs[5] in an extremely civilised tone. By doing so, you revealed the gentleness that moderates even those members of the Catholic church who are charged with using the authority of the Christian emperors to reform those in error, by deterrence and by punishment. Perhaps, though, you addressed him in language that implied more honour than was appropriate for a heretic.

(4) Now you wanted me to reply to his reply to you. I suppose you were thinking that my reply ought to be made available to the citizens of Timgad. Then his misleading teaching, which was leading them astray, might be carefully refuted. However, I am extremely busy. Moreover, I have devoted a large number of other treatises to refuting this sort of foolishness. I do not know how many times I have already shown in debate and in writing that no one can die a martyr's death who does not live a Christian's life: it is not the punishment, but the cause, that makes a martyr.[6] This has been our teaching: free will was given to human beings, but in such a way that it is quite right for the punishment for serious sins to be laid down by human laws as well as by divine ones. It is the job of God-fearing *kings of the earth* [Ps 2.2] to restrain with suitable harshness idolatry just as much as adultery, murder and other transgressions and wrongs of that sort.[7]

I also argued that very often people make the mistake of thinking that we accept those people just as they are because we do not rebaptise them. But how can we be accepting them just as they are, when at present they are heretics, but they will become Catholics by coming over to us? It's not true that a corrupt heart may not be reformed, just because the sacraments, once bestowed, may not be repeated.

(5) What about the utterly crazy deaths that some of them inflict upon themselves? Even many of their own side, if they haven't succumbed to such an extreme degree of madness, find these abhorrent and horrible. We frequently answer them in accordance with the scriptures, and with Christian reasoning: scripture says, *If anyone is worthless to himself to whom will he be good?* [Ecclus 14.5]. If someone thinks it useful and acceptable to kill himself, then surely he will kill his neighbour whenever he is subject to similar trials and wishes to die. As scripture says: *You will love your neighbour as yourself* [Lev 19.18; cf. Mt 22.39; Mk 12.31; Lk 10.27]. But unless the laws or the legitimate authorities order it, you are not allowed to kill anyone else, even if he wants you to and begs you to, and no longer has the strength to live. Scripture makes that clear enough

when, in the book of Kings, David orders the killer of king Saul to be put to death [cf. 2 Sam 1.1–16].[8] The man reported that Saul had been wounded and half-dead and had begged him to do the deed, and free his spirit from its torments with a single wounding blow; for it was struggling in the bonds of its body and longing to be set free.

Therefore, if anyone kills a human being without any authorisation from a legitimate authority, he is a murderer. If anyone kills himself, he is not a murderer only if he is not a human being. We have argued this both in speech and in writing on many other occasions and in innumerable ways.

(6) I remember, though, that I haven't yet answered them on this point: what account should we give of the elder, Razis?[9] Limited by the extreme shortage of examples to the book of Maccabees, after they have scoured all the church's authorities they can just about boast of having found him – as if they had found authorisation for their outrageous practice of self-destruction. However – and this should be sufficient for your loving self or any sensible person to refute them – if they are ready simply to take over any exemplary deed from the Jewish race and their literature into the Christian life, then let them take over this example also [cf. 2 Macc 14.37–46].

On the other hand, it may be the case that the men who were quite truthfully praised in their literature still very often performed deeds that wouldn't be appropriate in our age, or even that shouldn't have been done in their own time. If so, this is true also of Razis' treatment of himself. Among his own people, he was indeed a noble man, and he was far advanced in the practice of Judaism (although the apostle Paul described that as *loss and dross* in his view by comparison with Christian justice) [cf. Phil 3.8]. As a result, Razis was called the father of the Jews. Despite all that, is it any surprise if pride and arrogance so crept over the man that he preferred to die by his own hand? Otherwise, after enjoying such eminence in the eyes of his own people, he would have endured an undignified slavery at the hands of his enemies.

(7) It is normal for this sort of behaviour to be praised in Gentile literature. In the book of Maccabees, though, the man himself was praised, but his action was merely described and not praised. It should be set before our eyes for us to judge rather than to imitate. Not to judge it, that is to say, by our own judgement – the sort that we who are also human possess – but by the judgement of sober teaching, which can be clearly seen in those ancient books also. Razis was certainly a long way from the words

we read there: *Accept everything that is brought on you; endure in pain and when you are humiliated show forbearance* [Ecclus 2.4]. In short, Razis was not so wise that he chose death; rather, he was too weak to accept humiliation.

(8) Scripture says that he wanted *to die in a noble and manly fashion*: but does it also therefore say 'wisely'? *In a noble fashion* indeed, because although a captive, he didn't lose his kind of freedom. *In a manly fashion* indeed, because he had such great strength of spirit that he was capable of killing himself. For when he was unable to finish the job with a sword, he threw himself headlong from a wall; and alive still, he ran to a rock and there, by now covered in blood, he pulled out his own innards, then scattered them with both hands, spattering the people with them. Finally, he was exhausted and fell down dead.

These were grand actions, but they were not good ones: not every grand action is a good one, and many are bad. God has said, *Do not kill anyone who is innocent and just* [Exod 23.7]. If Razis was not *innocent and just*, why is he held up as a model for imitation? But if he was *innocent and just*, then he killed an *innocent and just* person, that is, himself, Razis. If so, why is he considered to deserve further praise?

(9) I don't want to go on too long: this is enough to fill my letter for the time being. I owe this sort of service of love to the inhabitants of Timgad. They found favour with me, through your request and through my honoured and beloved son Eleusinus, who served as tribune among them; consequently I replied to the two letters of Gaudentius, the Donatist bishop, and in particular to the second one, where he thinks that he has written in accordance with sacred scripture, in such a way that no point would be thought to have been omitted.[10]

Letter 105

409/410

To the Donatists from Augustine, the Catholic bishop.[1]

(1) The love of Christ, for which we wish to win every person, in so far as this is down to our will, does not allow us to remains silent. If you hate us because we preach Catholic peace to you, we are only serving the Lord, who said: *Blessed are the peacemakers, for they shall be called the sons of God*

[Mt 5.9]. Again, it is written in the psalms, *I was a peacemaker among those who hate peace; when I spoke with them, they waged war against me unprovoked* [Ps 120(119).7, LXX].

That is why certain of the priests of your sect have sent us the following instructions: 'Keep away from our congregations, if you don't want us to kill you.' Our words to them were far more just: no, do not keep away. Rather be pacified and approach not *our* congregations, but *his*, to whom we all belong. Or if you are unwilling to, and remain unpacified, withdraw yourselves from the congregations for whom Christ shed his blood. You want to make them yours so that they will no longer be Christ's; though you do try to own them under his name, as if a servant were to steal sheep from his master's flock and brand the lambs born to them with his master's mark, so that his theft would not be noticed. Your predecessors did just this: they separated from the church of Christ those marked by the baptism of Christ, and baptised the children born to them with the baptism of Christ. However, a master both punishes thieves, if he hasn't reformed them, and also calls sheep back to his flock when they wander, without erasing his mark on them.

(2) You claim that we are guilty of 'handing over',[2] something that your predecessors were not able to prove against our predecessors and you cannot in the least prove against us. What do you want us to do? When we request you to listen patiently to your case and ours, you seem capable only of arrogance and madness! For we would certainly show you that it was the ones who condemned Caecilian[3] and his associates on a charge of handing over who were in fact guilty of that offence.

You say, 'Keep away from our congregations', while you are teaching them to believe you and not to believe Christ. You tell them that the church of Christ has survived only in Africa within the Donatist sect, because of the handers over (and you cannot prove that). The story you tell is not from the Law, not from the prophets, not from the psalms, not from the apostle, not from the gospel, but from your own hearts and the false accusations of your ancestors.

However, Christ said that one should *preach in his name repentance and the forgiveness of sins throughout all the nations, beginning from Jerusalem* [Lk 24.47]; yet you are not in communion with the church that is revealed by Christ's own words; while you drag others into ruin along with you, and refuse to let them go free.

(3) If you don't like us because you are being forced into unity by the imperial decrees, well, you have brought this about yourselves. Whenever

we were happy simply to preach the truth and let each person listen to it in security and choose of his own free will, you have always prevented us from doing this by your violence and terrorism. Now don't start shouting and getting yourselves worked up. Study our words patiently, if it is possible, and bear in mind the behaviour of your Circumcellions and your clerics (who have always led them on); then you will see what has stirred all this up against you. You are complaining simply because you yourselves have forced all these orders to be imposed upon you.

I will avoid repeating many details from the distant past. Consider at least your recent activities. Marcus was a priest of Casphaliana. He had become a Catholic without anyone forcing him, of his own free will. Your side pursued him because of this, and would almost have killed him if the hand of God had not made use of some passers-by to restrain their violence.

Restitutus of Victoriana converted to the Catholic church without anyone forcing him. For this he was snatched from his home, beaten, rolled in water, dressed in straw and kept in captivity for I don't know how many days; and perhaps he would not have been restored to his freedom if Proculianus[4] had not now realised that he himself might be threatened with summons because of Restitutus' case.

Marcianus of Urga chose Catholic unity of his own free will. He himself fled; but his subdeacon was nearly beaten to death on his account by your clergy, and then stoned. For this crime they had their houses destroyed.

(4) Need I expand on the subject? Recently you sent us a messenger, to announce at Sinitus that 'if anyone has been in communion with Maximinus, his house should be burnt down'. What is this? Before Maximinus converted to the Catholic church, when he hadn't yet returned from overseas, we had sent a priest to Sinitus whose only purpose was to visit our people, without troubling anyone, and to remain in the house that was lawfully his and preach the Catholic peace to those willing to listen. You proceeded to drive him out, which was deeply unjust.

Again, when Possidius, the bishop of Calama, one of our people, went to the estate of Figula, what were we doing except allowing our people there, few as they were, to be visited, and allowing those who wished to hear the word of God and convert to the unity of Christ to do so? But while he was walking on his way, they laid an ambush for him. They behaved just like bandits. Because he managed to avoid falling into their ambush, they used open violence against him, setting fire to him along with the house on the estate of Oliveta where he had fled. He would scarcely have lived if the tenants of the farm had not put out the flames because of the risk to their own security. The place was set on fire three times.

Despite all this, when Crispin was deemed a heretic for doing this in the proconsul's court, the same bishop Possidius interceded for him so that he was not fined the ten pounds of gold. Far from being grateful for his kindness and gentleness, Crispin had the nerve to appeal to the Catholic emperors.[5] That is how he provoked against you a far more oppressive and fiercer example of God's anger, which you are now grumbling about![6]

(5) You can see that the violence you arouse against us is contrary to the law of Christ, and that you are not suffering for his sake, but because of your unjust behaviour. What madness is this? You are living wickedly and acting as bandits; yet when you are punished justly, you demand the glory of martyrs?[7] You exploit the recklessness of your private troops so violently to force people to embrace, or to remain in, error. How much more ought we to use the ordained authorities (which God has subjected to Christ, as his prophet foretold) to resist your madness, in order to free wretched souls from your control, and to uproot them from long-standing falsehood, and let them grow used to the clear light of truth? Many of those who, so you claim, have been forced by us against their will, confess to us before and afterwards that they want to be forced, so that they can avoid your bullying.

(6) In any case, which is better, to promulgate the true decrees of the emperors for the sake of unity? Or, as you have done, suddenly to fill all of Africa with your lies, and promulgate a false leniency for the sake of perversity? In this business you have nothing to show us except the Donatist sect ever ready to take falsehood for granted and to be tossed and swayed by every breeze. As scripture says, *Whoever trusts in falsehoods, feeds the winds* [Prov 10.5, LXX].

This leniency of yours is 'true' in just the same way as the crimes of Caecilian and the handing over carried out by Felix of Apthugni (who ordained him) were 'true', and for that matter anything of your other usual accusations against the Catholics, which led you to separate yourselves and others from the church, to the misfortune of both. We do not rely on any human authority, however much more honourable it may be to rely on the emperors rather than the Circumcellions, and the law rather than riots.

However, we keep in mind the words of scripture: *Everyone who puts his hope in a human being is cursed* [Jer 17.5]. If you want to know what it is that we rely on, then think of Christ, whom the prophet heralded with the words: *All the kings of the earth will adore him; all nations will serve him* [Ps 72(71).11]. That is why we make use of this authority of the church, which God promised her and has granted her.

(7) If the emperors were indeed in error (heaven forbid!) then they would be passing laws on behalf of their own error and against the truth. These would enable the just to be tested, and crowned if they refused to do what the emperors were commanding, because God was forbidding it. This was the situation when Nebuchadnezzar ordered everyone to worship a golden statue. Those who were unwilling to do so found favour in the eyes of God, who forbids such things.

However, when the emperors are in possession of the truth, the orders they give are on truth's behalf against error. Whoever despises these calls judgement upon himself. For he not only pays the penalty on the human level, but will also have no way to face God. For he will have refused to obey orders that truth had given him through *the heart of the king* [Prov 21.2]. Similarly, even Nebuchadnezzar himself was so moved and altered by witnessing the miracle that saved the three lads that he issued an edict on behalf of truth against error. This said that *Anyone who should blaspheme the God of Shadrach, Meshach and Abednego will meet his death, and his house will be scattered* [Dan 3.29]. Are you unwilling for the Christian emperors to issue some similar command against you, when they are aware that you are rejecting Christ in those whom you rebaptise?

If, though, the rulings of kings do not extend to preaching religion or to prohibiting idolatry, then why did you mark yourself as bound to the king's edict when he issued commands of that sort? Do you not know the king's words: *the signs and portents which the Lord God on high has given me I am pleased to report in my sight: how great and powerful is his reign; his reign lasts for ever and his authority from generation to generation* [Dan 4.2–3]? Or when you hear this do you not reply 'Amen'; and mark yourselves by saying this in a loud voice and with sacred ceremony as bound to the king's edict?[8] But now that you have no influence with the emperors, you want to arouse hostility towards us from that quarter. But if you did have influence there, how far would you go, when even without influence you never let the matter drop?

(8) Be sure of this: your predecessors took the initiative in referring the case of Caecilian to the emperor.[9] Force us to prove it to you, and do with

us whatever you can if we don't succeed. However, because Constantine didn't dare to judge the case of a bishop, he delegated it to the bishops to discuss and bring to a conclusion. This was done in the city of Rome under the presidency of Miltiades, bishop of that church, assisted by a large number of his colleagues. They declared Caecilian innocent, and gave the decision against Donatus, who had caused the schism at Carthage. After this your side went to the emperor once more and grumbled about the bishop's judgement, which had defeated them. Indeed, is a worthless plaintiff ever capable of praising the judges whose decision has defeated him? However, the emperor very mercifully provided another set of bishops at Arles, a town in Gaul; then your side appealed from their council to the emperor himself, until he examined the same case, and declared Caecilian innocent, and them slanderers.

Even when they had been defeated as often as this they did not rest, but wearied the emperor by making daily complaints about Felix of Apthugni, who had ordained Caecilian. They alleged that he was guilty of handing over and that therefore Caecilian could not be a bishop as he had been ordained by such a man. Eventually, the case of Felix himself was examined by the proconsul Aelian, at the emperor's command, and he was shown to be innocent.[10]

(9) It was then that Constantine first provided a very severe law against Donatus' sect.[11] His sons followed him in making similar rulings.[12] Julian succeeded them, a deserter and enemy of Christ; your Rogatianus and Pontius pleaded with him and he granted Donatus' sect the liberty to ruin themselves.[13] In the end he returned the basilicas to the heretics, at the same time as he returned the temples to the demons. He thought that through this action the name of Christianity might disappear from the earth, if he was hostile to the unity of the church from which he had lapsed, and allowed free rein to impious disputes. This was his much-vaunted 'justice', which Rogatianus and Pontius praised when they pleaded with him, telling a man who was an apostate that it was only with him that justice found a home! He was succeeded by Jovian, who issued no instruction on these matters because he died so quickly. Then came Valentinian: read the orders he gave against you.[14] Then came Gratian and Theodosius: read, when you wish to, their decisions concerning you.[15]

In the light of all this, why should you be surprised by the sons of Theodosius, as if on this issue they ought to follow anything other than the judgement that Constantine made, which has been steadfastly protected during the reigns of so many Christian emperors?[16]

(10) It was your predecessors, then, as we have argued and as we can prove to you whenever you like, if you are still unaware of it, who took the initiative in referring the case of Caecilian to Constantine. Constantine is dead; however, his judgement against you lives on. But your own side directed the case to him, having criticised to him the bishops when they first gave judgement, and appealed to him from the bishops when they judged again, and wearied him with their accusations about Felix of Apthugni; and then after being left defeated and embarrassed by him so often, they still did not abandon their destructive madness and their hatred, but left it as an inheritance for you, their successors. The result is that you are shameless in arousing hatred against the orders of Christian emperors; by contrast, if you were free, not to complain against us as now to the Christian Constantine (who favours the truth), but rather to rouse Julian the apostate from the dead, it seems as if that, if it could happen, would be a dreadful thing for everyone except you! For what is more deadly to the soul than freedom for error?

(11) But let's put all this aside. Let us love peace; everyone, learned or otherwise, realises that peace ought to be preferred to discord. Let us love and embrace unity. This is what the emperors command, and Christ too commands it, since whenever they command something good, none other than Christ commands it through them. He begs us also through the apostle all to say the same thing; and that there should be no schisms among us, and we should not say: *I belong to Paul, I to Apollos, I to Cephas, but I to Christ* [1 Cor 1.10, 12]. Rather, all of us at once should belong to none other than Christ, because *Christ* has not *been divided*, nor was *Paul crucified* for us, let alone Donatus [1 Cor 1.13]. Neither have we been baptised in the name of Paul, let alone of Donatus.

The emperors also say the same, because they are Catholic Christians, not servants of idols like your Julian, nor heretics, as some were who did pursue action against the Catholic church. At that time true Christians endured what was not a very just punishment for heretical error, but rather glorious suffering for Catholic truth.

(12) Notice how in this law God himself has spoken with lucid truthfulness through *the heart of the king*, which lies *in the hand of God* [Prov 21.1]. You say this law was passed against you; however, if you can understand this, it was passed on your behalf. Notice the force of the ruler's words:

> For if the rite of baptism is adjudged invalid in those who have been initiated before, on the grounds that those at whose hands they received it are considered sinners, then it will be necessary to renew a

sacrament that has been handed down to us every time that a minister who has conferred baptism is found to be unworthy; then our faith will hang not on the decision of our will, nor on the grace of God's gift, but on the deserts of the priests and the quality of the clergy.[17]

Let your bishops hold a thousand councils, but let them reply to this one verdict; and we will then agree to whatever you want. For you can see how wrong-headed and impious is the claim you are in the habit of making: that if a person is good, he sanctifies whomever he baptises; but if he is bad and the person baptised is unaware of this, then God sanctifies him. If this is the case, then everyone ought to hope to be baptised by bad men without knowing it, rather than by men they know to be good: for then they can be sanctified by God rather than by a human being! But we want nothing to do with such madness. Why, though, is the following version untrue? Why isn't this view sensible? That is, that the grace is always God's, and the sacrament God's, but the ministry alone belongs to a human being. If he is good, then he cleaves to God and co-operates with him; if, however, he is bad, then God effects the visible form of the sacrament through him, while he himself bestows the invisible grace. Let us all hold this sensible view and let there be no schisms among us.

(13) Make peace with us, my brothers. We love you; we want for you what we want for ourselves. If you hate us more deeply because we do not allow you to go astray and be lost, then tell that to God; for we are afraid of him when he threatens unworthy shepherds, and says: *You have failed to call back the straying sheep, and you have not searched for the lost sheep* [Ezek 34.4]. It is God himself who does this through us, whether by entreaty or threat or censure; by fines or by hard work; whether through secret warnings and visitations, or through the laws of the temporal powers. Try to understand how he is dealing with you. God does not want you to be lost in impious dissent, estranged from your mother the Catholic church.

You were not able at any time to prove anything against us. Your bishops were summoned by us: were they willing to hold a conference with us that was aimed at peace? They behaved as if they were fleeing from discussion with sinners. Who can put up with that sort of pride? As if the apostle Paul did not debate with sinners and, indeed, with idolaters – read the *Acts of the Apostles* and see for yourself. As if the Lord himself did not hold a conversation on the law with the Jews who were to crucify him, and reply to them appropriately. Finally, the devil is the foremost among sinners, and can never be converted to justice; yet the Lord himself did not scorn replying to him about the Law [cf. Mt 4.1–10; Lk 4.1–13]. Consequently you may realise that the reason they don't want to hold a conference with us is that they know that their cause is lost.

(14) We do not know why people boast to their own discredit, and rejoice in disagreements born of slander. We have learnt of Christ in the scriptures, we have learnt of the church in the scriptures. We share these scriptures with you: why don't we hold Christ and the church in them in common with you? The apostle said of him: *Promises made to Abraham and to his seed; it does not say 'and to his seeds' as if in many, but as if in one, 'and to your seed', which is Christ* [Gal 3.16 (Gen 13.15; 17.8)]. Wherever we recognise him, we also recognise the church. God said about the church to Abraham, *All nations will be blessed in your seed* [Gen 22.18].

Again, we recognise Christ in the psalm that prophesies of him, *The Lord said to me, 'You are my son: today I begot you'*; and we recognise the church in the words that follow, *Ask me and I will give you the nations as your inheritance and as your possession the ends of the earth* [Ps 2.7–8]. We recognise Christ when scripture says, *God, the Lord of gods, has spoken*, and there too we recognise the church, because there follow the words, *And he summoned the earth from the rising of the sun to its setting* [Ps 50(49).1]. We recognise Christ when scripture says, *And he, as a bridegroom going forth from his chamber rejoiced like a giant running his course*; and we recognise the church there also because a little earlier it said, *Their voice has gone out to all the earth and their words to the ends of the globe; he has placed his tent in the sun* [Ps 19(18).4–5]. This is the church herself, placed *in the sun*, that is, known by revelation to all peoples as far as the ends of the earth.

Again, we recognise Christ in the words of scripture, *They have pierced my hands and my feet; they have counted my bones; they have looked on me and gazed at me; they have divided my clothing and cast lots for my robe* [Ps 22(21).16–18]. And there we recognise the church too, because a little later in the psalm it says, *All the ends of the earth will remember and will be converted to the Lord, and all the countries of the nations will worship him in his sight; for the kingdom belongs to the Lord, and he will rule the nations* [Ps 22(21).27–8].

We recognise Christ when scripture says, *Be exalted above the heavens, God* [Ps 57(56).5]; and we recognise the church also in the words that follow: *And your glory over all the earth.* Again, we recognise Christ in the words of scripture, *God, give your judgement to the king, and to the king's son your justice* [Ps 72(71).1]; and we recognise the church also when the same psalm says of him, *He will rule from sea to sea, and from the river to the ends of the globe; the Ethiopians will fall prostrate before him and his enemies will lick the dust; the kings of Tarsis and the islands will offer him presents; the kings of Arabia and Saba will bring him gifts; and all the kings of the earth will adore him; all the nations will serve him* [Ps 72(71).8–11].

(15) We recognise Christ also when scripture relates that a stone from the mountain, cut not by human hands, has broken all the kingdoms of the earth, all those which were relying upon the worship of demons; and there we recognise the church too, because it says that this very stone grew and became a vast mountain, and filled all the earth [cf. Dan 2.34–5]. We recognise Christ when scripture says, *The Lord will overwhelm his enemies and will annihilate all the gods of the nations of the earth*; and we recognise the church too in the passage that follows, *And all the islands of the nations will worship in his sight, each from his own place* [Zeph 2.11].

We recognise Christ in the words of scripture, *God will come from the south and the Holy One from the shady mountain; his power will cover the heavens* [Hab 3.3, Latin]; and we also recognise the church in the words that follow, *and the earth is filled with praise of him.* Jerusalem comes from the south, as we read in the book of Joshua, son of Nun[18] [Josh 15.8; cf. 18.5],[18] and the name of Christ was spread abroad from there; and the shady mountain is there, that is, the Mount of Olives, from where he ascended into heaven in order to *cover the heavens with his power*, and to fill the church, throughout all the earth, with praise of him.

Again, we recognise Christ, when scripture says, *He was like a sheep that was led to be sacrificed, and like a lamb before the shearer, without a voice; thus did he not open his mouth* [Is 53.7], and so on, referring here to his passion. And we recognise the church in the same passage where it says: *Rejoice you barren, who do not bear children; cry out, shout aloud, you who are not in labour. For the woman who is alone has many more sons than her who has a husband. The Lord declares this. Enlarge the place of your tent, and fasten your curtains. There is nothing that you should spare. Stretch the cords longer and strengthen the strong stakes. Extend again and again to the right and to the left. For your seed will inherit the nations and you will inhabit cities that are deserted. There is nothing for you to fear: you will prevail and you should not be ashamed because you were once an abomination. For you will forget your humiliation for ever, and you will have no memory of the reproach of your widowhood. For I am the Lord who made you – the Lord is his name – and he the God of Israel who delivered you will be called* [God of] *the entire earth* [Is 54.1–5].

(16) We do not know what you mean about those who handed over [the sacred books];[19] for you have never been able to prove them guilty, or even offer evidence. I am not saying this because it was really members of your side who were clearly detected in such a crime and confessed it. Why are other people's burdens any concern of ours? Only that we should reform those whom we can, by rebuking them, or disciplining them in whatever way, in a spirit of gentleness, with conscientious love; and if we are not successful in reforming them, even if necessity requires (for the security of everyone else) that they should share in the sacraments of God in communion with us, we should still not share their sins (something that can only be done by assenting to them and supporting them). For we tolerate them in this world, in which the Catholic church is dispersed throughout all nations. The Lord calls this his field, as if darnel were growing among the wheat, or as if on this threshing-floor of unity the chaff were mixed in with the corn, or as if in the nets of word and sacrament bad fish were caught along with the good [cf. Mt 13.24–30, 36–43, 47–9]; we tolerate them until the time of harvest or winnowing, or the time when the boats reach the shore. For we do not want because of them to uproot the corn or remove the bare grains from the threshing-floor by cleansing them before time, and rather than send them to the barn, collect them and scatter them to the birds; nor even, once our nets have been broken by schisms, to swim out into the sea of ruinous freedom out of fear of the bad fish.

That is why the Lord used these and other similes to encourage tolerance in his servants, to avoid them destroying *little ones*, or to avoid *little ones* [Mt 18.14] being lost through reckless human disputes, because the good were thinking that they would be blamed because they were mixed in with the wicked. Our heavenly master warned us to beware of this in order to secure his flock against bad rulers, in case the seat of saving doctrine were abandoned because of them; for even bad men are forced to speak good words when they are sitting there. For they do not speak their own words, but those of God, who established the teaching of truth in the seat of unity. Accordingly, he, who is truthful, and indeed truth itself, said the following of rulers who perform their own evil deeds, but speak the good words of God: *Do as they say; do not do as they do. For what they say they do not do* [Mt 23.3]. He would not say, *Do not do as they do*, unless their evil deeds were obvious.

(17) Let us not, therefore, be lost in wicked disputes because of the wicked – even though we could, should you wish it, show that your predecessors were accusing the innocent rather than cursing the wicked. But

whoever they were and whatever they were like, let them bear their own burdens.

See the scripture we share, see where we come to know Christ, see where we come to know the church. If you hold on to Christ, then why don't you hold on to the church itself? If you believe in Christ because of the truth of scripture, although you can read of him, but not see him, why do you deny the church, which you can both read of and see? We have become your enemies by saying this to you, and by forcing you into this good of peace and unity and love. You report that you are going to kill us when we are only speaking the truth to you, and preventing you, so far as we can, from being lost through error. May God rescue us from you by killing this error of yours in you. Then you may rejoice with us in the truth. Amen.

Letter 185[1]

c. 417

(1) I am filled with praise, congratulations and admiration, my dearest son Boniface, that in the middle of the cares of warfare and weaponry, your desire to know the things of God is so powerful. Truly this shows that you rely on a soldier's courage in serving the faith that you possess in Christ. So let me briefly inform your dear self of the difference between the errors of the Arians and those of the Donatists. The Arians hold that the substances of Father, Son and Holy Spirit are different. The Donatists do not hold this; they confess a single substance of the Trinity.[2]

It may be that some of them say that the Son is less than the Father; however, they have not denied that he is of the same substance.[3] But the majority of them say that they believe just what the Catholic church believes about the Father, Son and Holy Spirit. Furthermore, this is not the question that is being debated with them. Their unfortunate legal battles are on the question of communion only; it is against the unity of Christ that they, with their distortions and errors, are fostering their rebellious hostility.

Occasionally, as we have heard, some of them, who are wanting to be reconciled with the Goths, see that they are getting somewhere, and claim to believe what the Goths believe.[4] However, they are refuted by the authority of their predecessors; for Donatus himself is not alleged to have believed this, and they boast of belonging to his sect.

(2) However, these matters should not trouble you, my dearest son. It was foretold that there would be heresies and scandals, so that we might learn from being surrounded by enemies [cf. 1 Cor 11.19]. In this way both our faith and our love might be better tested: our faith, in avoiding being deceived by them; and our love, in our concern to reform them, as far as we are able. Here we should both push hard to prevent them from harming the weak, and to free them from this dreadful error, and also pray for them that the Lord might open their minds so that they understand scripture. For in the sacred books, wherever Christ the Lord is revealed, his church is also proclaimed. They, though, are remarkably blind: despite knowing Christ only through scripture, they fail to recognise his church on the authority of the sacred writings, and instead create their own idea of it on the strength of idle human slanders.

(3) Along with us, they recognise Christ in the words: *They have pierced my hands and my feet, they have counted my bones; they have looked on me and gazed at me; they have divided my clothing and cast lots for my robe* [Ps 22(21).16–18]. But they are unwilling to recognise the church in the passage that follows a little later: *All the ends of the earth will remember and will be converted to the Lord, and all the countries of the nations will worship him in his sight; for the kingdom belongs to the Lord, and he will rule the nations* [Ps 22(21).27–8].[5] They recognise Christ when they read: *The Lord said to me, 'You are my son; today I bore you.'* But they are unwilling to recognise the church in the words that follow: *Ask me and I will give you the nations as your inheritance and as your possession the ends of the earth* [Ps 2.7–8]. They recognise Christ in the words of the Lord himself in the Gospel: *Christ must suffer and rise from the dead on the third day.* However, they are unwilling to recognise the church in the words that follow: *And preach in his name repentance and the forgiveness of sins throughout all the nations, beginning from Jerusalem* [Lk 24.46–7].

There are countless pieces of evidence in the sacred books which I don't need to cram into this volume. In these, just as Christ the Lord appears (whether according to his divinity, in which he is equal to the Father, as one who, *'In the beginning was the Word, and the Word was with God, and the Word was God'* [Jn 1.1], or according to the flesh which he assumed in humility, as *the Word became flesh, and dwelt among us*) [Jn 1.14] in the same way, the church appears, not only in Africa (as they claim, but this is foolish and insolent raving!) but rather spread throughout the whole globe.

(4) But they prefer their lawsuits to the witness given by God. For through the case of Caecilian, who was once bishop of the church of Carthage, when they charged him with crimes that they neither could nor can prove, they separated themselves from the Catholic church, that is from the unity of all nations. Even if the charges against Caecilian were true, and they were at some time able to demonstrate this to us, maybe we would anathematise him (he is already dead). Still we ought not to abandon the church of Christ on account of any human being. For the church is not a fiction created by litigious opinions, but a reality, demonstrated by God-given evidence. *It is indeed better to trust in the Lord than in a human being* [Ps 118(117).8].

Moreover, if Caecilian was guilty of sin (I say this without prejudicing his innocence) Christ has not on that account lost his inheritance. It is easy for one human being to believe things of another, whether they are true or false, but to wish to condemn the communion of the whole world because of one human being's crimes betrays quite outrageous arrogance.

(5) Whether Caecilian was ordained by men guilty of handing over the sacred books, I do not know. I was not there to see it; I heard of it from his enemies. I have not heard it read from the Law of God, nor the proclamations of the prophets, nor the holy words of the Psalms, nor the apostle of Christ, nor the discourse of Christ himself. By contrast, the witness of the entire scriptures proclaims in unison the church spread over the whole globe, the church with which the Donatist sect is not in communion. *All nations will be blessed in your seed* [Gen 26.4], states the Law of God. *From the rising of the Sun to its setting, a pure sacrifice is offered in my name; for my name is glorified among the nations*, as the Lord says through the Prophet [Mal 1.11]. *He will rule from sea to sea, and from the river to the ends of the earth* [Ps 72(71).8], as the Lord says in the psalm. *Bearing fruit and growing through the whole world* [Col 1.6], as the Lord says through the apostle. *You will be my witnesses in Jerusalem and in all Judaea and in Samaria and to the ends of the earth* [Acts 1.8], as the Son of God spoke out of his own mouth.

Caecilian, bishop of the church of Carthage, was accused in a lawsuit of human origin. The church of Christ, established among all nations, is recommended by God-given pronouncements. Piety itself, and truth and charity, do not allow us to accept the witness of these men against Caecilian; for we do not see them in the church to which God bore witness. And those who fail to follow God-given testimony have forfeited the respect due to human testimony.

(6) A further point is this: they themselves sent the case of Caecilian for the emperor Constantine to judge when they accused him. Or rather, they brought Caecilian himself to be investigated by the aforementioned emperor by persistently pursuing action against him, after having failed to overwhelm him at the bishops' court.[6] As for the fact that they are now criticising us (with the aim of deceiving the uninformed) and saying that Christians ought not in opposing the enemies of Christ to make any demands of the emperor – well, they were the first to do this! They have not dared to deny that this was the case too at the conference which we held at the same time at Carthage.[7] Rather, they dare to boast that their predecessors assailed Caecilian in a criminal way before the emperor. On top of this they add the lie that they defeated him there and had him condemned.

How can they deny their pursuit of us? They pursued action against Caecilian in accusing him, and were defeated by him; they then wanted to claim false glory for themselves by telling the most insolent of lies. Then, they didn't just think it blameless if they proved that Caecilian had been condemned on the accusation of their predecessors; they even boasted of it for their own glory!

If you want to know how they were comprehensively defeated during that conference, perhaps you will be able to read the summary of this. (For the proceedings are very extensive and there is a lot to read when you are busy with other matters crucial to the peace of the Roman empire.) I believe that my brother and fellow-bishop Optatus has a copy; or if he does not, you will be able to get it very easily from the church at Sitifis. Indeed even that volume will seem tiresomely lengthy to you at the moment, when you are so preoccupied.

(7) The same thing happened to the Donatists as to the men who accused the holy Daniel [cf. Dan 6.24]. The lions which they had wanted to use to crush an innocent man were turned against the latter, the laws, similarly, against the former; except that through the mercy of Christ the laws that seem to oppose them are in fact on their side. For many of them have been reformed as a result of the law, and every day many more are being reformed. Furthermore, they give thanks that they have been reformed and freed from this disastrous madness. Those who used to hate now love; after regaining their sanity, they give thanks for the very beneficial laws that had oppressed them, just as much as they had cursed them when they were mad. And now they feel inspired to love as much as we do those left behind, in whose company they would have perished; and they share equally in our efforts to prevent their perishing now.

To a raging lunatic a doctor seems oppressive, and a father to a badly behaved son, the one when he ties him down, the other when he beats him. But both are acting out of love. However, if they neglect them and let them perish, their misguided gentleness is in fact cruelty. *A horse or a mule, which has no intelligence* [Ps 32(31).4], may hinder the people who are treating its wounds by biting and kicking them. Despite frequently being threatened, and occasionally harmed by their teeth and hooves, the men don't abandon them before they succeed, despite the pain and trouble, in restoring them to health.[8] How much more should one man not abandon another, or one brother another? Otherwise, he may perish for ever, whereas if he is reformed he will be able to understand how much help he was being given even while he was complaining of suffering harassment!

(8) To quote the apostle: *While we have the time, let us work tirelessly for the good of all* [Gal 6.9–10]. Some, if they can, should do this using the sermons of Catholic preachers; others, if they can, using the laws of Catholic rulers; then, through some obeying God-given warnings, through others obeying imperial decrees, may everyone be restored to security, and all recalled from destruction.

Emperors, indeed, when they establish bad laws on the side of false-hood against the truth, allow those with good beliefs to be tested, and to be crowned if they persevere. When they establish good laws on the side of truth against falsehood, those who are violent are frightened by this, while those with understanding are reformed. Therefore anyone who refuses to obey the imperial laws that are passed in opposition to the truth of God wins a grand reward. On the other hand, anyone who refuses to obey those imperial laws that are passed on behalf of the truth of God wins a grand punishment. For all the kings who, during the period of the prophets, failed to outlaw or overturn the practices of the people of God in breach of the commandments of God received blame. Those who out-lawed or overturned them won praise beyond that that others deserved.

Again, king Nebuchadnezzar, when he was a slave to idols, established an idolatrous law ordering the worship of an image. However, some people refused to obey his sacrilegious ruling, and acted in accordance with religion and faith. The same king, however, once reformed by a God-given miracle, established on behalf of truth a law that was religious and praiseworthy, that *anyone who should utter blasphemy against the true God of Shadrach, Meshach and Abednego should be destroyed along with his house* [Dan 3.1–30]. Any who dismissed this law and deservedly suffered the set penalty would have had to make the same claim as the Donatists make, that they were just in that they were suffering harassment through a royal law. And they would, surely, say this, if they were crazy, as indeed people who divide the limbs of Christ are crazy: they toss aside the sacraments of Christ, and they brag about suffering harassment, because they are forbidden to do these things by the imperial laws that were established to defend the unity of Christ. They boast untruthfully of their innocence, and they try to win from men a martyrs' glory, though they cannot win it from the Lord.

(9) The true martyrs are those referred to in the Lord's words: *Blessed are those who suffer harassment for the sake of justice* [Mt 5.10]. Not, then, those who suffer harassment for the sake of injustice, or for the sake of the impious rupturing of Christian unity; rather those who *suffer harassment for the sake of justice* are the true martyrs.

Indeed, even Hagar suffered harassment at the hands of Sarah [cf. Gen 16.6]; and she who did this was a holy woman, while she who suffered was unjust. Surely the harassment suffered by Hagar cannot be compared with the case of the holy David, who was harassed by the unjust Saul [1 Sam 18.8–9]? His case is certainly very different, not in so far as he was suffering, but in so far as he was suffering for the sake of justice. The Lord himself was crucified in the company of robbers; but while their suffering united them, their cause divided them [cf. Mt 27.38; Mk 15.27; Lk 23.33]. Again, the following verses in the psalm must be taken as referring to true martyrs, who wish to be differentiated from false martyrs: *Judge me, God, and differentiate my cause from the nation that is not holy* [Ps 43(42).1, Latin]. It does not say, 'differentiate my punishment', but 'differentiate my cause'.⁹ The impious may suffer a similar punishment, but their cause is different from that of the martyrs.¹⁰

Again, the following cry belongs to the latter: *they have pursued me unjustly; help me!* [Ps 119(118).86]. The speaker thought that he deserved to be assisted justly, because he was being pursued unjustly. If indeed he had been being pursued justly, he would not have needed assisting, but reforming.

(10) But perhaps they are of the opinion that one person cannot justly pursue action against another – for during the conference they said that the true church was not the one that pursues, but the one that suffers legal action.¹¹ If so, I will not bother to repeat what I said above, that if the case is as they claim, then Caecilian belonged to the true church when their predecessors pursued action against him by continuing to accuse him

until he was judged by the emperor himself. For we say that he belonged to the true church not on the grounds that he suffered legal action, but because he suffered for the sake of justice. On the other hand, they were estranged from the church, not because they were pursuing action against him, but because they were doing so unjustly.

This, then, is what we say; but as for them, if they do not examine the causes why someone pursues legal action or suffers it, but take it to be a sign of a true Christian that someone suffers rather than pursues legal action, then undoubtedly on that definition they must include Caecilian as a true Christian. He certainly did not pursue action, but suffered it. Moreover, on their same definition they consign their own predecessors to being outside the church, as they pursued action and did not suffer it.

(11) I will not, however, as I said, restate that point. I will, though, say this: if the true church is the one that suffers harassment rather than inflicting it, they should inquire of the apostle which church Sarah was symbolising when she was harassing her maid. For he said that that woman, who was ill-treating her maid [cf. Gal 4.21–31 (Gen 16.6)], prefigured our free mother, the heavenly Jerusalem, that is the true church of God. But if we are to raise the level of argument, then she was harassing Sarah by her pride, more than Sarah was harassing her by using force. For she was harming her mistress, while Sarah was disciplining her [Hagar's] pride.[12]

My next question is this: if good and holy people never pursue anyone, but are only pursued, who do they think uttered the cry in the psalm, where we read: *I will pursue my enemies and I will catch them, and I will not be turned back until they collapse* [Ps 18(17).38, LXX]? If we want to state the truth and recognise it, there is such a thing as unjust pursuit, which the impious inflict on the church of Christ, and there is such a thing as just pursuit, which the churches of Christ inflict on the impious. Therefore she is blessed, as she suffers pursuit on behalf of justice; while they are wretched, as they suffer pursuit for the sake of injustice.

Again, she pursues action in love, they in rage; she in order to reform people, they to ruin them; she to recall them from error; they to hurl them into error. Finally, she pursues her enemies and holds them until they retreat from their lies, so they can advance in truth; while they return evil for good. Our concern indeed is their everlasting security, while they are trying to take from us even our temporary security. Moreover, they delight in murder so much that they inflict it on themselves when they cannot inflict it on others! The church, out of love, struggles to free them from ruin so that none of them will die; and they, out of madness, struggle either to kill us, to indulge their passion for cruelty, or even to kill themselves, for fear of appearing to have lost the power to kill people.

(12) People who are ignorant of their habits think that they are only killing themselves now that the introduction of the laws established for unity has freed so many communities from their crazy rule. However, people who know them and the way they used to act even in the time before these laws remember their previous behaviour, and are unsurprised at their deaths. In particular, when the worship of idols was still practised, they used to come in huge crowds to very well-attended pagan ceremonies, with the intention not of smashing the idols, but of being killed by their worshippers. If they were aiming to do the former, and had been legitimately authorised, and something had happened to them, they might be granted some shadow of the name of martyr. However, they used to go only for the purpose of dying themselves, leaving the idols unharmed. (Indeed, the toughest individual youths among the idol-worshippers used to consecrate to the idols themselves however many of them they managed to kill.)[13] They flung themselves on passers-by who were armed, hoping to be slaughtered, and threatening horribly to attack them if they themselves didn't die at their hands. Sometimes they even used force to compel judges who were passing through to have them put to death by the executioner, or at least officially flogged. One of these, consequently, succeeded in fooling them by ordering them to be bound and sent away as if for execution. That is how he managed to escape their attack, unbloodied and unhurt.

Now, however, they are playing a daily game of killing themselves from steep precipices, or in water or flames.[14] The devil has taught them these three types of death: consequently when they want to die and cannot find anyone to terrorise into turning his sword on them, they cast themselves onto rocks, or throw themselves into fires or floods. Who else can we believe taught them this and *took possession of their hearts* [Ecclus 51.20], other than the devil? He it was who quoted the law to suggest to our Saviour that he should throw himself down from the pinnacle of the temple [Mt 4.5–7; Lk 4.9–12].

If they bore their master Christ in their hearts, they would, surely, protect themselves from such suggestions. However, instead they have given the devil room inside themselves. Consequently, they either die like that herd of pigs which the mob of demons drove from the hill into the sea [cf. Mt 8.32, Mk 5.13]; or else they are rescued from such a death and gathered into the devoted lap of their mother the Catholic church, and in this way set free. Then they are like the man who was set free by the Lord when his father brought him to be cured of demonic possession; he had been in the habit of falling into water sometimes, and sometimes into fire [Mt 17.14–18; Mk 9.17–27; Lk 9.37–42].

(13) All this arouses a lot of pity for them. This is so even though these imperial laws are actually the means of rescuing them from the sect where they have learnt these evil ideas from the teachings of lying demons. At first this is against their will; but this is so that afterwards, within the Catholic church, they might grow used to good rules and good habits and be healed. Indeed many of them, now that they are within the unity of Christ, arouse our admiration by their pious fervour for the faith and their love; and they themselves thank God with great joy that they are free of the error of thinking such evils good. Surely they wouldn't be giving thanks willingly like this, if they had not first unwillingly abandoned their previous dreadful alliance.

What are we to say of the people who confess to us every day that they formerly wished to be Catholics, but they were living with men amongst whom they could not be what they wanted to be? Their fear made them weak: for one word spoken on behalf of the Catholic church would have led to them and their houses being completely destroyed.

Who is so crazy as to deny the correctness of using imperial decrees to come to the aid of these people, and to rescue them from such evil? And at the same time the men they feared are forced to be afraid themselves. Indeed they are either themselves reformed by that fear, or at least, if they only pretend to be so, they spare those who really have been reformed, those who previously had been afraid of them.

(14) But what if their hope in killing themselves was to prevent those due to be liberated from being liberated? What if they hoped to make their pious liberators so afraid, that in their fear of allowing even the desperate to die, they would fail to rescue from ruin those who didn't want to die? Those, that is, who, faced with compulsion, would be able to avoid death.

How does Christian love act in such a situation? Especially when the men who are using the threat of crazy, voluntary suicides are very few in number compared to the population due to be liberated? How does brotherly affection act here? Does it, out of fear of the ephemeral fires of a furnace, send all the rest to the everlasting fires of Hell? Does it abandon to permanent death so many who now have the will to use Catholic peace to head for eternal life, and later may be too weak? And this out of concern to avoid the voluntary deaths of people whose lives constitute a hindrance to the security of others. For they refuse to allow others to live following the teaching of Christ, so that eventually they can instruct them, following the custom of the teaching of the devil, to rush into a voluntary death. Yet their own voluntary death is what we are afraid of at present!

Is it not rather that Christian charity, that brotherly affection, save those they can, even if those they cannot save die of their own accord? They hope passionately that everyone will live; they struggle still more that not everyone will die.

Thanks be to God that among us, not indeed everywhere, but certainly in most places, and also throughout the rest of Africa, Catholic peace continues to progress unhampered by the deaths of any of these crazy men. However, wherever that mad and worthless set of men exist, these fatal acts take place. (And even in earlier times they were in the habit of behaving like this.)

(15) Furthermore, even before those laws were despatched by the Catholic emperors,[15] the teaching of the peace and unity of Christ was gradually gaining strength, and individuals were crossing over from their sect into it, as they each learnt more, began to want to and were able to. Meanwhile in their midst, crazed gangs of those desperadoes were, for various reasons, disturbing the tranquillity of the innocent. Was there a master who was not forced to fear his own slave, if the latter fled to their protection? Did anyone dare even to threaten a rebel?[16] Who could force a wasteful steward, or a debtor, to settle up, if he begged help and protection from them? The deeds relating to slaves of the worst sort were being smashed for fear of cudgels and fires and imminent death;[17] they then disappeared as free men. IOUs were being extorted and returned to the debtors.

If anyone took no notice of their harsh words, they were beaten more harshly and forced to do as they were told. Innocent men who crossed them had their houses razed to the ground. Heads of households, nobly born and with a cultured education, were carried away scarcely alive after being beaten by them; some were even tied to a millstone and forced under the whip to turn it, like some miserable beast of burden. Even if the civil authorities can offer a little help against them, is that of much use?

Has any officer even breathed in their presence? Has any debt-collector enforced payment if they did not want it? Has anyone attempted to avenge the victims of their murders? Only indeed when their own madness has led them to demand punishment from them. Then some of them have thrown themselves on the swords they had turned against themselves by terrorising their owners with death-threats into striking them. Others have hurled themselves all over the place to voluntary deaths, some over various precipices, others into water and others into fire. And so, they inflicted a self-imposed punishment on their death-loving souls.

(16) Even most of those committed to their heretical superstition were horrified by such things. They thought that their own innocence was adequately protected by their disapproval of such actions. And then the Catholics were able to say to them: 'If these awful things don't contaminate you in your innocence, why do you allege that the whole Christian world is contaminated by the unreal, or at least unknown, sins of Caecilian? How can you separate yourselves in this dreadful and outrageous way from Catholic unity, as if from the Lord's own threshing-floor? For it is necessary that both parts should remain there until the time for winnowing, the corn that is due to be stored in the granary, and the chaff that will be burnt in the fire' [cf. Mt 3.12; Lk 3.17].

That is how reason was restored to some of them; as a result, some crossed over into Catholic unity, prepared to face even the hostility of the desperadoes. Most of them, although they would have liked to do that, did not have the courage to make enemies of men who had such unlimited freedom for violence. And indeed, some of the former group, when they did transfer to our side, suffered very cruelly at their hands.

(17) Let me move on to another incident. There was a certain deacon at Carthage called Maximian.[18] He showed arrogance towards his own bishop; there was a schism, and the Donatist sect among the populace of Carthage was divided. Then certain bishops on his side ordained him a bishop in opposition to his own bishop. This offended the majority of them, and they condemned Maximian, along with twelve others who had attended his ordination. Others who belonged to the same alliance they granted the opportunity of returning on a specified day. Later, however, both some of that twelve, and others of those who had been granted a delay, but who returned after the appointed day, were received back by them into their own positions of honour, for the sake of peace among them.

They did not dare to rebaptise any of those the condemned men had baptised when out of communion with them. Their action began to win great support for the Catholic church against those others, and consequently their mouths were completely stopped. The matter was spread around more persistently (as was right) in order to cure human minds of schism, and the Catholics exploited sermons and debates to publicise the fact they had welcomed back to their former positions of honour even those they had condemned, and that they had not dared to invalidate the baptism administered by individuals condemned by, or perhaps suspended from, their church; and that they had done this for the sake of the peace of Donatus.[19] At the same time they were charging the whole world with being contaminated by some alleged sinners or other, and nullifying the baptism granted even to the churches from which the gospel came to Africa, and this against the peace of Christ.

As a result, very many of them were thrown into confusion, embarrassed by the evident truth, and were reformed in greater numbers than usual, and this far more so wherever they enjoyed the respite of a certain freedom from their opponents' violence.

(18) As a result of this, their anger, driven by the goad of hatred, burnt so fiercely that hardly one of the churches of our communion could feel secure against their ambushes, their violent attacks, or their quite open robbery. There was hardly a safe road on which to travel for anyone who was preaching Catholic peace against their insanity, and using the lucid truth to refute their madness. They went so far as to offer the following harsh conditions not only to the laity, but also to any Catholic clerics and even, in a way, to the bishops: keep quiet about the truth, or else face our atrocities!

But if they kept quiet about the truth, then not only would they fail to liberate anyone by keeping silent, but also many more people would be led astray by their opponents and perish. However, if they were to preach the truth and arouse their opponents' fury to violence, then though some would be freed and our people strengthened, on the other hand, fear would again deter the weak from following the truth. These are the difficulties that constrain the church. Those who reckon that we should put up with anything before asking for God to assist us through the Christian emperors ought to pay more attention to this: that they cannot render a good account of such neglect.[20]

(19) Those who do not want just laws to be established against their own impiety object that the apostles did not make such requests of earthly kings. They do not take into account that that was a different time, and everything is done at its own proper time. Which emperor then believed in Christ, and would serve him by passing laws in defence of piety against impiety? *Why have the nations raged, and the peoples imagined*

empty things? The kings of the earth are at hand, and the rulers have come together as one against the Lord and against his Christ [Ps 2.1–2]. The events described a little later in the same psalm were not yet taking place: *And now, kings, understand; be instructed, you who judge the earth. Serve the Lord in fear and rejoice in him with trembling* [Ps 2.10–11].

But how can kings serve the Lord in fear, except by forbidding and punishing breaches of the Lord's commandments with devout severity? As a man, he serves in one way, as a king in another. As a man, he serves by living faithfully, as a king by sanctioning with suitable vigour laws that order just behaviour and prevent its opposite. This is how Hezekiah served by destroying the groves and temples that were sacred to idols, and the high places whose establishment had contravened the commandment of God [cf. 2 Kgs 18.4]. This is how Josiah served by doing the same himself [cf. 2 Kgs 23.4–20]. This is how the king of Nineveh served by forcing his whole city to appease the Lord [cf. Jon 3.6–9]. This is how Darius served by giving the idol into Daniel's power for him to break it, and by casting his enemies to the lions. This is how Nebuchadnezzar served (I spoke of him earlier) by imposing a terrifying law that forbade everyone living in his kingdom to blaspheme God [cf. Dan 6.24; Dan 14.22, 42; Dan 3.29]. All kings serve the Lord in this way in so far as they are kings, performing in his service deeds that they could not perform unless they were kings.

(20) Therefore in apostolic times, when kings were not yet serving the Lord, but were still *imagining empty things* against Christ (so that all the prophetic predictions might be fulfilled) [e.g. Ps 2.1], surely it was not possible then to forbid acts of impiety by law. They could only practise them! For the ages were succeeding one another in order, so that first the Jews, the preachers of Christ, also killed him (as Christ had predicted) under the impression that they were doing their duty to God, then the nations raged against the Christians; while the forbearance of the martyrs overcame them all.

However, once the following words of scripture began to be fulfilled, *And all the kings of the earth will adore him; all nations will serve him* [Ps 72(71).11], what sober-minded person would now say to the kings, 'Don't worry about those within your kingdom who are restraining or attacking the church of your Lord. It should be no concern of yours whether someone chooses to be devout or sacrilegious'? For one could hardly say to a king, 'It should be no concern of yours whether someone chooses to be chaste or unchaste.' Why, indeed, even when free choice has been granted to human beings, should adultery be punished by law, but sacrilege permitted? Or is it less important for a soul to keep faith with God than a woman with her husband? Admittedly, offences committed through ignorance of religion rather than contempt for it ought to be punished rather mildly; but surely they should not for that reason be ignored?

(21) Does anyone doubt that it is preferable for people to be drawn to worship God by teaching rather than forced by fear of punishment or by pain? But because the one type of people are better, it does not mean that the others, who are not of that type, ought to be ignored. Experience has enabled us to prove, and continue to prove, that many people are benefited by being compelled in the first place through fear or pain; so that subsequently they are able to be taught, and then pursue in action what they have learnt in words.

Some people suggest the following maxim from a secular author: 'I am sure it is more satisfactory to restrain a child by shame and generosity, than by fear.'[21] This is certainly true. However, just as boys guided by love are better, so boys reformed by fear are more numerous. Indeed, if we want to reply to them by quoting the same author, they can also read in him: 'You can't do anything properly, unless trouble makes you do it!'[22]

Moreover, holy scripture also said, with the better sort in mind: *There is no fear in love; rather perfect love casts out fear* [1 Jn 4.18]; and with the poorer, but more numerous sort in mind: *The hard servant will not be improved by words; even if he understands them he does not obey* [Prov 29.19]. In saying that *he will not be improved by words*, it is not telling us to abandon him; rather it implicitly warns us that he ought to be improved. Otherwise it wouldn't say, *he will not be improved by words*, but would instead say just, *he will not be improved*. Indeed, elsewhere we read that not only a servant, but even a son who lacks discipline ought to be controlled with a beating, and this will prove very fruitful: *You strike him with a rod*, it says, *but you surely free his soul from death* [Prov 23.14]. And again, *Whoever spares the stick, hates his son* [Prov 13.24].

Give me a man, then, who is able to say with sound faith and true understanding, and with all the strength of his soul, *My soul thirsts for the living God: when shall I enter and appear before the face of God?* [Ps 42(41).2]. Such a man does not need the fear of temporary punishment or of imperial laws, or even of Hell. For him, *to cling to God is* so attractive a good [Ps 73(72).28] that not only does he shudder at the thought of being estranged from such happiness, as if that were a great punishment in itself, but he even finds it hard to accept the delay. However, before good sons are able to say, *We desire to be dissolved and to be with Christ* [Phil 1.23], first many who are like bad servants, as it were, or even worthless runaways, need to be summoned back to their Lord by the blows of a temporary flogging.

(22) Is anyone able to love us more generously than Christ, who *laid down his life for his sheep* [Jn 10.15]? Now when he called Peter and the other apostles, he did so with a single word. However, Paul, formerly known as Saul, who was to become a great builder of his church, was at first a fearsome destroyer of it; and Christ did not restrain him with a single word. Rather, he used his power to knock Paul down: with the aim of encouraging a man who had been raging in the dark of faithlessness to long for light in his heart, he first struck him with physical blindness. If that was not a punishment, he wouldn't have been healed later on; and if his eyes had been sound (when he could see nothing with them open) scripture would not have described how something like scales, which had been covering them, fell from them when Ananias laid his hands on Paul, so that their gaze was opened up [cf. Acts 9.1–18]. Where do they get that cry of theirs? 'We are free to believe or not to believe: did Christ apply force to anyone? Did he compel anyone?' Look – they have the apostle Paul! They should realise that Christ first used force on him and later taught him, first struck him and then consoled him. It is amazing, moreover, how Paul, who came to the gospel under the compulsion of a physical punishment, afterwards struggled more for the gospel than all of those who were called by word alone; although a greater fear drove him to love, still his *perfect love casts out fear* [1 Jn 4.18].

(23) Why shouldn't the church, then, force her lost sons to return, when her lost sons have themselves compelled others to be lost? As a devoted mother she embraces more affectionately those who were not forced, but only lured, if they are recalled to her bosom by frightening but salutary laws. Yet she gives far warmer thanks for the latter than for those whom she has never lost. Is it not the duty of a devoted pastor also to find those sheep who have strayed from the flock and come into someone else's possession not because they were forcibly stolen, but because they were lured away gently and seductively? And then when he finds them to call them back to their master's sheepfold threatening them with whips or even hurting them if they try to resist? And especially so since, if they are fruitful and multiply while with the runaways or robber servants, he has more right in that the mark of their master on them is recognisable. This

is dishonoured less if we welcome them back without, however, rebaptising them. That is how one ought to reform a straying sheep, so that the sign of its redeemer upon it is not spoilt. Similarly, if someone is branded with the king's mark by a deserter who is similarly branded, and if the two are then granted pardon,[23] the one returning to the army and the other joining the army to which he had never belonged, on neither of them should the mark be erased. Should it not rather be recognised on them both, and approved with due honour, since it belongs to the king?

In short, since they aren't able to show that they are being compelled in a direction that is bad for them, they argue that they should not be forced in a good direction. However, we indicated that Christ used force on Paul; the church imitates her Lord in using force on the people in question, having waited without using force on anyone until the prophetic predictions about the faith of kings and nations were fulfilled.

(24) Furthermore, the saying of the blessed apostle Paul makes complete sense in this context: *Prepared to avenge all disobedience, once your earlier obedience is fulfilled* [2 Cor 10.6, Latin]. In this spirit too the Lord himself ordered guests first to be invited to his great feast, and subsequently compelled to come. For when his servants replied to him *Lord, your orders have been carried out, and there is still room*, he replied, *Go out into the pathways and hedgerows and force everyone you find to come in* [Lk 14.16–24].

The *earlier obedience* then is fulfilled in those who were, first of all, gently invited. Disobedience was forcibly checked, though, in those who were compelled. After all, what does, *Force them to come in* mean? For in the first place he said *invite*, and then they answered, *Your orders have been carried out, and there is still room*.

Maybe he wanted them to take this as meaning that they should be forced by terrifying miracles? But many divine miracles were performed among those who were first called, in particular among the Jews (it was said of them, *The Jews seek signs* [1 Cor 1.22]). Among the gentiles too in apostolic times such miracles lent credibility to the gospel; if therefore the command was to force people by means such as that, then we should, properly speaking, believe that the first set of guests (as I said) were forced.

Therefore if the church receives power through God's generosity and at the appropriate time, because of the king's religion and faith, and uses this to force anyone to come in who is found on *the pathways and in the hedgerows* (that is, in heresies and in schisms), they should not criticise the fact that they are being compelled, but concentrate on *where* they are being compelled to go. The Lord's banquet is the unity of the body of Christ, not only in the sacrament of the altar, but also *in the bond of peace* [Eph 4.3]. Now we are certainly able to say of *them* very truthfully that they would force no one in a good direction; for anyone they force, they force only in a bad direction.

(25) Admittedly before the laws which are used to force them to come to the holy banquet were despatched to Africa, several of the brethren – and I was one of them – thought otherwise. It seemed that although the madness of the Donatists was raging left, right and centre, we should not petition the emperors to order this heresy to be entirely suppressed by imposing a penalty on those who wanted to embrace it; rather they ought to decree that anyone who preached Catholic truth by word of mouth, or chose it by their decision, should be protected from the violence of their fury.

We were of the opinion that this could be achieved to a certain extent by using the law of Theodosius (of most pious memory), that was promulgated against all heretics. According to this, any bishop or cleric of theirs discovered anywhere could be fined ten pounds of gold.[24] This could be reaffirmed, so we thought, specifically against the Donatists (although they were denying that they were heretics) not so that all of them would be penalised by fines, but only those in areas where the Catholic church was suffering various acts of violence at the hands of their clerics or Circumcellions or congregations. In this way once the Catholics who had suffered all of this had made a protest, the bishops or other ministers could be held liable to pay the fine, on account of the responsibility of their orders.[25]

We used to think that once they were frightened by this, they wouldn't dare to behave so badly, and we would be able to teach and hold the Catholic truth in freedom, without anyone being forced into it, but so that anyone who so wished could follow it without fear; for we didn't want to have people pretending falsely to be Catholics.

Others of the brethren, on the other hand, were of a different opinion. They tended to be of greater age, or in charge of the many examples of cities and towns where we could see the Catholic church strongly and truly established. However, it had been established and strengthened there by similar God-given benefits, when the laws of earlier emperors were still forcing men into Catholic communion.[26] However, we had our way, and the scheme that I described above was requested from emperors. Our council passed a decree, and we sent delegates to the court.

(26) However, God knew how much the corrupt and icy souls of so many needed the terror of these laws, a sort of painful medicine, and he knew that their hardness of heart could not be *improved by words* [Prov 29.19], but only by the application of a little hard correction. In his greater mercifulness, he arranged it that our delegates failed to achieve the commission they had been given. For we were pre-empted by some very serious complaints from bishops in other places, who had suffered very badly at their hands, including being expelled from their sees. In particular, the awful, scarcely credible, assault on Maximian, the Catholic bishop of Bagai, ensured that our delegation did not achieve their end.[27] A law had already indeed been issued to the effect that the appalling Donatist heresy – it now seemed that to spare them was even crueller than was their own savagery – would not only not be allowed to remain violent, but would not be allowed to exist unpunished at all. The only reason that a capital penalty was not set was to preserve Christian gentleness, even towards those unworthy of it. However, financial penalties were established, and their bishops and ministers were made liable to exile.

(27) Now the bishop of Bagai mentioned above had, in a hearing between the parties in a civil court,[28] regained by its verdict a certain basilica, which they had seized although it was Catholic. When he was standing at the altar, they rushed on him, attacking him horribly, brutal in their fury; they beat him viciously, with clubs and any other sort of weapon, and finally even with wood broken off from the altar. They also stabbed him in the groin with a dagger, and the blood flowing from the wound would have killed him if their further savagery hadn't served to keep him alive. For they dragged him, seriously wounded as he was, over the ground, and the dust, sticking to his spurting artery, staunched the wound, whose flow was bringing him near death.

Finally, they abandoned him, and then some of our people tried to carry him away to the accompaniment of psalms. Their opponents then were inflamed with even greater anger and snatched him from their hands as they were carrying him. They overwhelmed the Catholics with their vast numbers, they were so violent that they easily terrified them, and they chased them off much the worse for wear.

Next, under the impression that Maximian was already dead, they lifted him into a tower, and then threw him down from it, while he was still alive. He landed on a heap of something soft, and some night-time travellers spotted him by lamplight, and recognised him. They picked him up and took him to a religious house, where he was given a great deal of care, which enabled him to recover from this desperate condition after some days. However, rumour carried the story that he had been outrageously killed by the Donatists even across the sea. When he turned up after this, and there could be no doubting the plain fact that he was alive, he was still able to show by his many scars, which were large and fresh, that the rumour of his death had not been groundless.

(28) Therefore he requested assistance from the Christian emperor, not so much to avenge himself, as to protect the church entrusted to him. If he had omitted to do this, we ought not so much to have praised his patience as, quite properly, blamed his negligence. Indeed, the apostle Paul also was not concerned for his own ephemeral life, but for the church of God, when he arranged to betray to the tribune the plans of the men conspiring to kill him [cf. Acts 22.12–32]. As a result, an armed soldier brought him to the place where he had to be taken, so that he could avoid their ambush. He had no hesitation in appealing to Roman laws, and declaring himself a Roman citizen (for it was not allowed at that time to beat a Roman citizen) [cf. Acts 22.24–9]. Again, he begged help from Caesar to escape being handed over to the Jews who desired to put him to death, when Caesar was a Roman ruler but not a Christian one [cf. Acts 25.11].

Here he showed clearly enough what the stewards of Christ ought to do later on when they found emperors who were Christians, and when the church was in danger. As a result, once such cases had been brought to the notice of the devout and pious emperor, he chose to reform their impious error altogether by applying extremely pious laws, and chose to use fear and compulsion to bring into Catholic unity those who were bearing the standards of Christ against Christ, rather than to suppress only their freedom for violence, and leave them the freedom to stray and be lost.

(29) Now once the relevant laws had arrived in Africa, those people in particular who were looking for the opportunity, or who were afraid of the violence of the madmen, or who were merely ashamed to upset their relatives, immediately came over to the church. Many of them were simply in the grip of a custom passed down by their parents; and they had never previously considered, or wanted to examine and consider, the sort of cause that gave rise to the heresy. Once they began to apply their minds to this, and to discover nothing in it for which it was worth suffering such large penalties, they soon became Catholics without any problems. Anxiety educated them, while freedom from care had made them

neglectful. Where such people set a precedent, many others followed, impressed by their authority and persuasiveness: these were less capable of understanding on their own the differences between Donatist error and Catholic truth.

(30) Although in this way the true mother received great crowds of people joyfully into her lap, the tough mobs still stayed outside, and in their sickness they remained regrettably hostile. Many of them also received communion to keep up a pretence. Others were few enough to escape notice. Those who kept up a pretence gradually got used to it, and listened to the preaching of the truth. Consequently, and in particular after the conference and debate between us and their bishops held at Carthage,[29] a large number of them were reformed. In some places, however, where a more stubborn and less peaceable crowd held sway, and a smaller group (whose views on communion were sounder) either were unable to stand up to them, or else had to obey, for the worse, a mob that was under the authority of a powerful few, then the struggle lasted a little longer.

In some of these places, the struggle continues still, and Catholics, especially bishops and clergy, have suffered many grim and ghastly experiences in this struggle. It would take a long time to enumerate all these – but some of them have had their eyes put out, another bishop has had his hands and tongue cut off, a few have been slaughtered. I pass over in silence the cruellest murders, the pillaging of houses in attacks by night, and the arson not only of private dwellings but even of churches. There were even some who threw the Lord's books into those flames.

(31) However, when we have been afflicted by such troubles, our consolation has been their fruit. Wherever the lost have perpetrated such deeds, there Christian unity has progressed with greater fervour and perfection, and the Lord has been praised more fully; for he has seen fit to allow his servants to gain their brothers by their sufferings, and by their blood to gather his sheep, scattered by this deadly error, into the peace of everlasting security. The Lord is powerful and merciful, and we pray to him daily to grant also to others *to repent and recover their sense, away from the snares of the Devil, by whom they are held captive according to his will* [2 Tim 2.25–6]. For these others seek only the means of slandering us and returning evil for good. They have not learnt to understand the loving attitude we maintain towards them, and the way in which we wanted to call them back from their wanderings, and to find the lost in accordance with the Lord's commandment, which he gave to pastors through the prophet Ezekiel [cf. Ezek 34.5–6].

(32) By contrast, they – as we have said elsewhere before[30] – both refuse to attribute to themselves what they do to us, and attribute to us what they do to themselves! For which of us wants any one of them, I do not say to be lost, but even to lose anything?[31] Even though the house of David could expect no peace unless his son Absalom were killed in the war he was waging against his father, still David instructed his men with great concern to keep Absalom alive and safe if they possibly could [cf. 2 Sam 18.5–15, 33]. In this way he would be there to repent and to be forgiven by his affectionate father. In the event what was left for him to do except weep over his lost son, and comfort his own grief with the thought of the peace regained for his kingdom [cf. 2 Sam 22.1–51]?

The same, then, is true of our mother the Catholic church. She finds none other than her sons waging war against her.[32] For in Africa, this shoot has been completely snapped off the great tree which spreads itself, stretching out its branches, through the whole globe. She bears them in love, for them to return to the root; they cannot have true life without it. But if the loss of some allows her to gather in so many others, especially since (unlike Absalom) they are not dying in accidents of war, but by suicide, then she may soothe and ease the grief of her maternal heart with the thought that so many peoples are being set free.

If only you could see the joy they have in the peace of Christ, their gatherings, their enthusiasm, their frequent and joyous assemblies to listen to hymns, to sing them, to grasp the word of God! If you could see how many among them recall their former error with great sadness and reflect with joy on the truth they have come to recognise. Then there is their angry dislike of their untruthful teachers, as they now realise how they spread lies about our sacraments. Again, many of them confess that previously they did want to become Catholic, but lacked the courage to do so when surrounded by men who were so crazy. Imagine that you took in a single gaze the congregations of all these peoples throughout the region of Africa, now set free from such destruction. Then you would call it excessively cruel to abandon them to perish eternally and be tormented in fires that last for ever, out of fear of whom? Of a negligible number compared with the countless mass of the rest who were burning to death in fires they had chosen themselves.

(33) Suppose that there were two people living in one house, and we knew for certain that it was going to fall down, but when we announced this to them they refused to believe us and insisted on remaining in it. If we were then able to drag them out of there, even against their will, and if

later on we would be able to prove to them that the collapse was imminent, so that they would not dare to return again to the area of danger – well, I think we would quite rightly be adjudged cruel if we did not do this. Again, suppose that one of them said to us, 'If you come in to drag us out, I will slaughter myself immediately!' but the other one neither wished to leave or be dragged out, nor dared to kill himself, what ought we to decide to do? To leave both of them to be crushed when the house collapsed? Or to rescue at least one of them in a work of mercy, while the other died not through any fault of ours, but rather his own? No one is so unfortunate that he doesn't find it easy to judge the right course of action in such a situation. In the analogy I offered, there were two men, and one was lost, while the other was set free. What then should we think when only a few are lost, while a countless mass of communities are set free? For the number of men who die of their own free will are fewer than the number of estates, settlements, villages, garrisons, towns and cities set free by the laws in question from that deadly and everlasting ruin.

(34) Let us now reflect a little more carefully on the matter under discussion: it seems to me that if there were a lot of people in the house that was going to collapse, but at least one of them could be freed from it, and if while we were trying to help him, the others killed themselves by jumping from a height, then we would console ourselves in our grief about the others by thinking that at least one was safe. However, we would not allow them all to die without freeing anyone, just to avoid the others destroying themselves. What, then, ought we to judge about the work of mercy that we need to perform to help others win eternal life and avoid everlasting punishment? For in the case of the men in the house, true and kindly reason compels us to come to their aid and to free them even for a brief time, since their security is not only temporary, but indeed short-lived.

(35) They also object that we are coveting their possessions, and stealing them! As for that, I only wish they would become Catholics and thus own not only the possessions they call 'theirs', but also ours, together with us in peace and charity. Their passion for slander so blinds them that they fail to notice how they are contradicting themselves in what they say. For they certainly allege, and they think they are complaining bitterly about it, that we are forcing them into communion with us, using the authoritative force of the laws. But surely we wouldn't be doing this if we wanted to own their possessions! Do misers look for people to share their possessions? Do those inflamed by lust for power, or elated by pride in

exercising it, long for a partner? They should notice their former allies, now ours, joined to us in brotherly affection, how they have not only their own things (which they had before) but also ours (which they did not have before). In the case where we are poor along with them, such possessions belong to us and to them alike. However, if we individually own sufficient for ourselves, then such things belong not to us, but to the poor; in some way we have the responsibility for administering them, but we do not seize them and claim them ourselves (which would be unforgivable).

(36) The Christian emperors, therefore, ordered under the laws of religion that whatever was owned in the name of the churches of the Donatist sect should be transferred along with the churches themselves to the Catholic church.[33] Consequently, the ordinary populace of their churches now joined us, as paupers along with us, when before they used to be supported by the same paltry possessions. Our opponents, therefore, who are standing outside, should stop coveting the things that belong to others, and rather enter into the fellowship of unity. Then we will be able to share equally in managing not only the possessions they claim are 'theirs', but also those that are called 'ours'.

Indeed, as scripture says, *Everything is yours, and you are Christ's and Christ is God's* [1 Cor 3.22–3]. Let us then be one, in single body, under him as our head [cf. Gal 3.28; Eph 1.22–3, 4.15, 5.23; Col 1.18]; and let us in such matters follow the lead of the Acts of the Apostles, where it is written: *There was among them one soul and one heart, and no one used to call anything his own; rather everything among them was held in common* [Acts 4.32]. Let us love the thing we sing, *Behold how good and pleasant it is to live together in one as brothers* [Ps 133(132).1], and do so in such a way that they learn from experience how truly their mother the Catholic church is crying out to them in the words of the blessed apostle to the Corinthians, *I do not seek your possessions, but you yourselves* [2 Cor 12.14].

(37) Now if we reflect upon the words of the book of Wisdom, *Therefore the just have taken the spoils of the impious* [Wisd 10.20], and again, as we read in Proverbs, *The riches of the impious are laid up as treasure for the just* [Prov 13.22], then we shall see that we should not ask who holds the property of heretics, but who dwells in the fellowship of the just. Indeed, we know that they usurp for themselves so much justice that they boast not only of having it, but of handing it out to other people. Indeed, they claim that someone they have baptised is justified; after this, where can they go from there but to say to the person they have baptised that he should believe in his baptiser? Why indeed shouldn't he do so,

when the apostle tells us, *To the one who believes in him who justifies the impious, his faith is counted as justice* [Rom 4.5]. Let him believe in his baptiser, then, if he in fact justifies him, *so that his faith is counted as justice*. It seems to me, however, that they would be horrified by the idea of their even considering such thoughts as that. For God alone is just and justifies [cf. 2 Macc 1.25; Rom 8.33]. However, we are able to say of them too what the apostle said of the Jews, that *not recognising the justice of God and wanting to establish their own justice, they were not subject to the justice of God* [Rom 10.3].

(38) Far be it from any of us, then, to call himself just. Then he would want to establish his own justice, that is one granted to himself by himself; for the words, *What do you have that you did not receive?* [1 Cor 4.7]. are addressed to him. Or else, he would dare to boast of being sinless in this life, just as during our own conference they said that they were in a church that already has *no spot or wrinkle or anything of that kind* [Eph 5.27]. They do not realise that at present this word is fulfilled in individuals who leave their bodies either immediately after baptism, or after the forgiveness of their trespasses, for which forgiveness we plead in prayer.[34] However, for the whole church, it will not be the case that it is completely without *spot or wrinkle or anything of that kind* [Eph 5.27] before it is the time to say, *Where is your victory, O Death? Where, O Death, is your sting? For the sting of death is sin* [1 Cor 15.55–6].

(39) In this life, when the *body, which decays, weighs the spirit down* [Wisd 9.15], if their church is already as they claim, then they should not address to God the words that the Lord taught us to pray: *Forgive us our debts* [Mt 6.12; cf. Lk 11.4]. For if all sins have been forgiven in baptism, and if already in this life the church has no *spot or wrinkle or anything of that kind* [Eph 5.27], then why does the church make this plea? They ought also to disregard the cry of the apostle John in his letter: *If we say that we have no sin, we deceive ourselves, and there is no truth in us. But if we have confessed our sins, he who forgives us our sins and cleanses us from all injustice is faithful and just* [1 Jn 1.8–9].

This is the hope that inspires the church to say, *Forgive us our debts*, so that the Lord Christ may *cleanse us if we are trusting and not arrogant, from all injustice*, and thus reveal for himself on that day a glorious church that *has no spot or wrinkle or anything of that kind*. Now he cleanses her with *the washing of water in the word* [Eph 5.26–7]. Firstly, nothing else of our past sins remains after baptism, that is not forgiven (that is, if the baptism does not take place in vain outside the church, but is either given within, or if it is given outside, returns to the church along with the baptised).[35] Secondly, if anything culpable is perpetrated through human weakness by those who live here after they have received baptism, it is forgiven through the same washing. And indeed, it does not help the unbaptised to say *Forgive us our debts.*

(40) Let him cleanse his church now in this way, *with the washing of water in the word* [Eph 5.26] so that then, when *death will be swallowed up in victory* [1 Cor 15.54], he may reveal her for himself with *no spot or wrinkle or anything of that kind* [Eph 5.27], that is, utterly beautiful and complete. At the present time, therefore, in so far as he is strong in us, because we were born of God and live from faith, we are just. However, in so far as we carry around the traces of mortality from Adam, we are not sinless. It may be true that *anyone who is born of God does not sin* [1 Jn 3.9], but it is also true that *if we say that we have no sin, we deceive ourselves, and there is no truth in us* [1 Jn 1.8]. Therefore, the Lord Christ is just and justifies; we by contrast, are *justified freely through his grace* [Rom 3.24]. However, he only justifies *his body, which is the church* [Col 1.24]. Therefore, if the body of Christ takes the *spoils of the impious* [Wisd 10.19] and if the body of Christ has *the riches of the impious laid up as treasure* for it [Prov 13.22], then the impious ought not to remain outside and slander others, but rather to enter within, and be justified themselves.

(41) Consequently, we have the words of scripture on the day of judgement, *Then the just will stand in great steadfastness against those who have afflicted and frustrated their labours* [Wisd 5.1]. We should certainly not interpret this to mean that, say, Canaan will stand against Israel (as Israel has frustrated the labours of Canaan) [cf. Josh 17.12–13], but rather that, say, Naboth will stand against Ahab since Ahab frustrated the labours of Naboth [cf. 1 Kgs 21.1–16]. Similarly, the pagan will not stand against the Christian, who has frustrated his labours, by plundering or destroy-ing[36] his temples; rather the Christian will stand against the pagan, who frustrated his labours by laying low the bodies of the martyrs. Similarly, then, the heretic will not stand against the Catholic, who frustrated[37] his labours when the laws of the Catholic emperors prevailed against him. Rather the Catholic will stand against the heretic, who was frustrating his labours as long as the fury of the impious Circumcellions was prevailing. Indeed, scripture itself answers our question by saying not, 'then people will stand', but *then the just will stand*, and also *in great steadfastness*, to indicate 'in good conscience'.

(42) Moreover, no one is just through his own justice, that is through

justice that he has made for himself, as it were, but rather, to quote the apostle, *just as God has bestowed a measure of faith on each one*. He follows this by adding, *For just as we have many members in one body, but all our members do not have the same activities, so we who are many are one body in Christ* [Rom 12.3–5]. As a result, no one can be just as long as he is separated from the unity of this body. Just as one member cannot preserve the spirit of life once it is cut off from the body of a living man, so a person who is cut off from the body of the just Christ cannot possibly preserve the spirit of justice, though he may preserve the shape of a member, which it had when part of the body. Let them, then, become part of the framework of this body; and let them keep up their labours, but not out of desire for domination; instead, for good and pious purposes.

As for us, we are purifying our wills (as I have already said)[38] from the stain of such desire – and let any enemy be our judge! – since with all our power we are seeking the very people whose labours I mentioned, in the hope that they will make use of their own labours and of ours, along with us within the fellowship of the Catholic church.

(43) 'But', they object, 'this is what troubles us: if we are unjust, why are you searching for us?' Our reply to this is, 'We search for you while you are unjust, so that you won't remain unjust; we seek the lost so that we may rejoice over them when we have found them and say, "My *brother was dead and now he is alive, was lost and now he is found*"' [Lk 15.32].

'Well, why don't you baptise me, then?', he asks, 'to cleanse me from my sin?' I reply, 'So as not to harm the brand of the emperor while I am reforming the error of the deserter.' 'Well, why need I not even do penance among you?', he asks. 'Indeed, unless you do, you cannot be saved. For how will you rejoice at being reformed, unless you have felt sorrow at your previous state of corruption?' 'Well, then', he asks, 'What will we receive from you when we transfer to you?' I reply, 'you won't receive baptism, to be sure. That you are able to possess while you are outside the framework of the body of Christ, although it cannot benefit you.[39] However, you receive *the unity of the Spirit in the bond of peace* [Eph 4.3], without which *no one will be able to see God* [Heb 12.14]; and also love, which (as it is written) *covers a multitude of sins* [1 Pet 4.8]. This is indeed a great good, and without it – as the apostle bears witness – neither *the tongues of men nor of angels, nor the knowledge of all mysteries, nor prophecy, nor faith great enough to move mountains, nor the bestowing of everything one owns on the poor, nor the suffering of one's body in the fire* [1 Cor 13.1–3] is of any use. So if you count this great good as little or nothing, you will stray from the path and deserve your unhappiness, and, if you do not cross over to Catholic unity, deserve to be lost.

(44) Next they object, 'But if we need to repent of having been outside the church and against the church if we are to be saved, how come that after our penance we may remain as clergy and even bishops, among you?'[40] This would not happen (for to be truthful – and I ought to say this – it should not happen) if the resulting peace didn't compensate by helping to heal the wound.[41] They should tell themselves this, and be extremely humble in their sorrow; for while they are cut off from us, they lie sunk so far in death that their mother the church needs to be wounded to bring them back to life. When a branch has been cut off, and is regrafted, one needs to make another wound in the tree, to receive the branch so that it can live; without life from the root it would have died. However, when the branch introduced becomes one with the tree that receives it, it then becomes strong and fruitful. If on the other hand it does not become one with it, the branch withers, but the tree will remain alive. There is also another method of grafting, as follows: if no branch from the tree has been cut off, the one that is separate can be grafted on, by inflicting a cut, though a very light one, on the tree.

Similarly, when they return to the root of the Catholic church without being stripped of the honour of their priesthood or episcopacy, despite the error of which they have repented, then it is as if there were a cut in the bark of the mother-tree, breaching her unbroken discipline. However, since *neither he who plants nor he who waters is anything* [1 Cor 3.7], through the mercy of God, once our prayers are poured out and the newly grafted branches begin to become one with the tree in peace, their *love covers a multitude of sins* [1 Pet 4.8].

(45) The decision within the church not to allow anyone who had done penance for some crime to receive clerical ordination or to return to, or remain in, the priesthood, was not taken in despair of the possibility of pardon; it was for the sake of strict discipline.[42] Otherwise, people would object to the keys given to the church, as mentioned in the words, *Whatever you loose on earth, will be loosed also in heaven* [Mt 16.19; 18.18]. However, for fear that even if someone had been convicted of a crime, the prospect of ecclesiastical honours might make him do penance arrogantly and in a spirit of pride, a severe decision was taken: anyone who had completed penance for a condemnable offence would not be a priest; in this way, in the absence of temporal promotion, the medicine of humility might prove truer and more effective.

Now it is also the case that the holy David did penance after his death-dealing crimes, while remaining in his position of honour [cf. 2 Sam 12.13–20; 24.17]. Again, the blessed Peter certainly repented, with a flood of bitter tears, of having denied the Lord, and he too still remained an apostle [cf. Mt 26.69–75; Mk 14.66–72; Lk 22.55–62]. However, all these cases should not lead us to think that their successors are being excessively cautious when they add something to humility without detracting from security, indeed, with the aim of protecting security. For I think that they have found through experience that some people, aspiring to the power of positions of honour, have feigned their repentance: the experience of many illnesses forces them to discover many cures.

However, in the sort of cases in question, disputes that cause serious divisions are not just threatening this person or that one. Whole communities are devastated and lie in ruins. That's why we should mitigate the harshness of the discipline; so that unadulterated love may help to heal such serious damage.

(46) They should, then, feel bitter sorrow for their abominable former errors, just as Peter did for his lying cowardice; and they should approach the true church of Christ, that is their mother the Catholic church. Let them be priests in her, and let them be bishops to her benefit, when they were previously her opponents to her harm. We will not be hostile to them. No, we embrace them, we hope for them, we encourage them and *force them to enter*, when we find them in the *pathways and hedgerows* [Lk 14.23]. Even so, there are still some we have as yet failed to persuade that we want them, and not their property!

When the apostle Peter denied his saviour, and wept, and remained an apostle, he had not yet received the promised Holy Spirit.[43] They, though, are further from having received him; they are separated from the framework of the body, and it is this body alone that the Holy Spirit brings to life. They have maintained the sacraments outside the church and in opposition to the church, and they have fought us in civil war, as it were, raising standards and arms against us. Let them come; let there be peace in the strength of Jerusalem, the strength which is love; as it is said of the holy city: *Let there be peace in your strength, and abundance in your towers* [Ps 122(121).7, LXX]. They should not elevate themselves against their mother's concern, the concern that she had and continues to have for gathering in them, together with all the many communities whom they have been misleading. They must not be proud because she welcomes them. They should not attribute what she does for the good end of peace instead to the bad end of their own promotion.

(47) This is the way that the church has habitually come to the aid of the vast crowds who were perishing through schisms and heresies. Lucifer disapproved when the same approach was used in welcoming and healing those who were dying from the Arian poison, and having disapproved, he fell himself into the darkness of schism, abandoning the light of love. The Catholic church in Africa has maintained this approach towards these people from the beginning, in accordance with the decision of the bishops who judged in the church of Rome between Caecilian and the party of Donatus. When one specific person, Donatus, was condemned, as he had been proved the originator of the schism, they decided that the rest, if they reformed, ought to be received back into their own positions of honour even if they had been ordained outside the church.[44] They did not do this because it was possible for them to have the Holy Spirit even outside the unity of Christ's body; it was especially for the people who might have been deceived by those placed outside, and prevented from receiving that gift.[45] Secondly, they did it so that even the latter's weakness might prove curable, if they were received back into the church on gentler terms, once obstinacy could no longer close their eyes to the obvious truth.

After all, did they think differently themselves when they condemned the Maximianists for sacrilegious schism and ordained others in their place (as their own council proves)?[46] For afterwards they saw that their communities didn't abandon them, and to avoid losing everyone, they received them back into their former positions of honour. Moreover, they didn't contradict or question the baptism that had been administered outside the church by men condemned by them. So why are they amazed? Why do they complain and slander us, because we accept them in a similar way, for the sake of the true peace that is Christ's? Do they not remember what they themselves did for the sake of the false peace of Donatus, which is opposed to Christ? If this action of theirs is held up against them, and insisted upon with intelligence, they will have no answers at all to make to it.

(48) What, then, of this objection of theirs? 'If we have sinned against the Holy Spirit in rejecting your baptism, how come you are seeking us? For this sin cannot be pardoned at all. The Lord said, "If anyone has sinned *against the Holy Spirit, he will not be pardoned either in this age or in the age to come*"' [Mt 12.32].[47] They fail to notice that on their interpretation no one can be set free. Surely everyone speaks against the Holy Spirit

and sins against him either before he is a Christian, or as a heretic – Arian or Eunomian or Macedonian (they assert that the Spirit is a creature) or Photinian (they deny that he is a substance at all, saying that there is only one God, the Father) – or various other heretics it would take too long to mention.[48] What about the Jews themselves? After all, the Lord's reproach was aimed at them. If they believed in him shouldn't they be baptised? Our saviour did not say, 'Will be pardoned in baptism'; he said *will not be pardoned either in this age or in the age to come* [Mt 12.32].

(49) They need to realise, then, that not every sin against the Holy Spirit is meant here as being unable to be pardoned, but only a specific one. Similarly, when he said, *If I had not come, they would not possess sin* [Jn 15.22], he certainly did not wish us to understand *every* sin (as they were, certainly, full of many great sins). Rather, he meant a certain specific sin, such that if they did not possess it, they could be pardoned of all the sins they did possess; this was their failure to believe in him when he came. If he had not come, they would not have had this sin. In this way, when he says, 'If anyone has sinned *against the Holy Spirit, or has spoken a word against the Holy Spirit*' [Mt 12.32], he certainly does not want us to understand every sinful word or deed committed against the Holy Spirit, but a certain specific and particular one. This in fact is the hardness of heart that lasts until the end of this life, which leads a person to refuse to accept pardon for his sins within the unity of the body of Christ, to which the Holy Spirit gives life. Indeed, when he said to his disciples, *Receive the Holy Spirit*, he continued immediately, *If you forgive anyone's sins, they will be forgiven; if you retain them, they will be retained* [Jn 20.22–3]. If anyone, then, resists or opposes this gift of God's grace, or in any way becomes alienated from it before the end of this temporary life, *he will not be pardoned either in this age or in the age to come* [Mt 12.32].

We cannot prove that anyone has committed this sin (so vast that all other sins are retained on its account), unless he has already left his body. But as long as a person remains alive, *God's forbearance is leading* him *to repentance* [Rom 2.4], as the apostle declares. However, if he himself (to continue the apostle's next words) through obstinate wickedness, *through* his *hardness of heart and* his *unrepentant heart*, stores up wrath for himself *on the day of wrath, and of the revelation of the just judgement of God* [Rom 2.5], he will not be pardoned either in this age or in the age to come.

(50) We ought not, therefore, to despair of our opponents in debate, and indeed the subject of our debate: they are still in their bodies. However, they should not seek the Holy Spirit except within the body of

Christ. They keep the sacrament of his body outside; but they do not hold the reality itself within – the reality of which it is the sacrament.[49] Therefore they eat and drink judgement for themselves [1 Cor 11.29]. The one bread is the sacrament of unity: *Since there is one bread, we who are many are one body* [1 Cor 10.17], as the apostle says. The Catholic church alone, then, is the body of Christ, and he, her head, is the saviour of the body. The Holy Spirit does not give life to anyone outside this body, because (to quote the apostle) *the love of God is spread in our hearts through the Holy Spirit, who is given to us* [Rom 5.5].

An enemy of unity cannot share in God-given charity. Those who are outside the church do not have the Holy Spirit. Scripture refers to them in the words, *Those who separate themselves have souls, but not spirit* [Jude 1.19]. Someone who merely pretends to be in the church does not acquire the Spirit; for scripture says in reference to this, *the Holy Spirit of instruction will flee deceit* [Wisd 1.5]. If anyone, then, wishes to possess the Holy Spirit, he should take care not to remain outside the church and he should take care not to pretend that he has entered within; or else, if he has entered her in this way, he should take care not to persist in his pretence. Then he might be truly united with the tree of life.

(51) I have sent you this lengthy volume, which may be rather a burden for you when you are so busy. Perhaps it can be read to you in sections; then, the Lord will grant you understanding so that you will be equipped to reply to those in need of reform and healing. For our mother the church commends them to you also as a faithful son of hers; wherever and however you are able, you are to help reform and heal them with the Lord's help, whether by speaking to them and answering them yourself, or by bringing them to the teachers of the church.

War and peace

The sacking of the city of Rome

The sacking of the city of Rome by Alaric in 410 led pagans to blame Christianity for the loss of the gods' favour. Even some Christians sympathised with this view, while others were led to question the justice of God. Augustine's *City of God* will eventually provide an extensive reply to the first problem; here he deals more immediately and more concisely with the second.

The sacking of the city of Rome

410/411

(1) Let us now turn our attention to the first reading, from the holy prophet Daniel.[1] There we heard him praying; and we were amazed to hear him confessing his own sins, and not just the sins of the people. Now after this prayer – and his words show that he was not simply pleading but also confessing – after this prayer, then, he said, *When I was praying and confessing my sins, and the sins of my people, to the Lord my God* [Dan 9.20]. Can anyone claim to be sinless when Daniel confesses his own sins? Surely it was to a proud man that the following words were addressed through the prophet Ezekiel: *Are you wiser than Daniel?* [Ezek 28.3].

Again, God placed Daniel among the three holy men whom he used as symbols of the three types of human beings he intends to free when the great trial comes upon the human race; he added that no one would be set free from it except Noah, Daniel and Job [Ezek 14.14]. And it is certainly clear that God uses those three names to symbolise three types of human beings (as I have said). For those three men have fallen asleep by now; their spirits are with God, while their bodies have decayed in the earth. They have been placed at the right hand of God. They could not desire to be freed from any trials in this world: they have no such thing to fear.

How is it, then, that Noah, Daniel and Job will be freed from such trials? When Ezekiel spoke those words only Daniel, possibly, was in his body. Noah and Job had long since fallen asleep and were laid near their forefathers in the sleep of death. How then could they be freed from the trials that threatened them, when they had already long since been set free from their flesh?

Noah, though, is used to symbolise good men in positions of responsibility who govern and rule the church, just as Noah steered the ark during the flood. Daniel is used to symbolise all holy people who are celibate; Job, all who are married and live well. God sets free these three types of men from the coming trial.[2] It is clear from the fact that Daniel deserved to be named as one of the three how highly he has been commended. Despite that, he is confessing his own sins! Even Daniel can confess his sins! Wouldn't anyone's pride, then, be shaken, anyone's self-importance collapse? Wouldn't anyone feel his arrogance and conceit being checked? *Who could boast of having a chaste heart? Who could boast of being cleansed from sin?* [Prov 20.9].

People are also amazed (if only they would be amazed without also blaspheming!) when God rebukes the human race, when he subjects it to a lashing, chastising it as a devoted father.[3] He imposes discipline before he executes judgement;[4] and he is not usually selective about those he will lash; for he does not want to find anyone to condemn. Indeed, his lash falls upon the just and the unjust alike; although if Daniel confesses his own sins, who is there who is just?

(2) You have also heard the reading from the book of Genesis.[5] If I am not mistaken, it made us all very attentive when Abraham asks the Lord whether if he finds fifty just individuals in the city he will spare the city for their sake, or if he will destroy the city with them in it. The Lord replies to him that if he finds fifty just men in the city he will spare it. Then Abraham pressed his inquiry and asked whether, if there were five less, and forty-five just individuals remained, he would spare the city in the same way. The Lord replied that he would spare it for the sake of forty-five. Need I say more? By asking questions and reducing the number step by step, he reached ten, and asked the Lord whether if he found ten just individuals in the city, he would destroy them along with the countless others who were bad, or whether he would spare the city for the sake of ten just individuals. God replied that even on account of ten just individuals he would not destroy the city.

So what are we to say, my brothers? We are confronted forcefully and powerfully with this question, especially by those who are laying siege to our scriptures out of unbelief, rather than asking questions of them as believers. Particularly in view of the recent sack of so great a city, they ask us this:

> So weren't there fifty just individuals in Rome? The vast number of the faithful, all those consecrated women, all those celibates, all those servants and handmaids of God – and yet not fifty, not forty, not thirty, not twenty, not ten, could be found who were just? But if that can't be believed, then why didn't God spare the city for the sake of those fifty, or even those ten?

Scripture does not deceive anyone, unless human beings deceive themselves. Now we are asking questions about the justice of God, and God's reply is about justice. Surely then he is looking for people who are just according to divine rules, not human ones.

And so I reply at once, 'Well, either he did find enough people there who were just, and spared the city; or else, if he didn't spare the city, he didn't find enough who were just.' But they answer me that it's obvious that God did not spare the city. I reply, 'No, it is not obvious to me.'

Indeed the city of Rome has not been destroyed in the way that Sodom was destroyed. When Abraham questioned God the city under examination was Sodom. Moreover, God's words were, 'I will not *destroy* the city'; he did not say, 'I will not lash the city.' He did not spare Sodom, he destroyed it. He swallowed Sodom up completely in flames. He didn't postpone dealing with it until the last judgement, but executed on Sodom the sentence reserved until the judgement for other bad cities. Not a single person from there survived [cf. Gen 19.24–5]. Nothing was left of their animals, nothing of their people, nothing of their homes: the fire consumed absolutely everything. You see what it is like when God does destroy a city!

Contrast the city of Rome: look how many left there, and will return; how many remained there and escaped; how many more were in holy places and could not be touched! 'But', they object, 'there were many taken captive'. That happened to Daniel too, not to punish him, but to provide comfort for the others.

'But', they object once more, 'many people were killed'. That happened to a lot of just prophets *from the blood of Abel the just to the blood of Zachariah* [Mt 23.35; Lk 11.51]. That also happened to a lot of the apostles; and it even happened to the Lord of the prophets and apostles himself, Jesus.

'But', they object, 'many people suffered a variety of cruel tortures'. Do we think that anyone suffered as much as Job did?[6]

(3) The most awful things have been reported to us: slaughter, arson, looting, murder, human torture have taken place. It is true; we have heard many reports, we have grieved about it all, we have often been in tears; it is hard for us to be comforted. I deny none of this; I accept that we have heard many such reports and that many such things have been done in the city.

Despite that, my brothers, please may your loving selves attend to what I am saying. We have heard from the book of the holy Job how his property was destroyed, and his children were destroyed, and then he could not even keep safe his own flesh which was all he had left. For then he was afflicted with painful sores from head to foot. He sat there on some dung, rotten with ulcers, flowing with pus, teeming with worms, tortured by bitter and agonising pain.[7]

If we had heard reports that the entire city was enduring this sort of thing, that no one there was healthy, that it was suffering from painful sores and that living men were rotten and worm-ridden, decaying as if they were dead – well, which would be more serious, that or the war? It seems to me that the violence of iron on human flesh is gentler than that of worms, that it is easier to endure blood flowing from wounds than pus dripping from gangrene. You may look at a corpse rotting and shudder; but the corpse's suffering is lighter, indeed it is no suffering at all, because the soul is gone. As for Job his soul was present, and capable of feeling; it was tied down so that it couldn't escape; it was subjected to pain, and goaded to blaspheme. Despite it all, Job endured his trials and it *was counted* to him as great *justice* [Gen 15.6; cf. Rom 4.3, 5, 9; Gal 3.6; Jas 2.23]. And so no one should concentrate on what he suffers, but rather on what he does. Power over what you suffer is not yours to have: you are human. What is yours is the will in what you do, whether it is guilty or innocent.

Job was suffering; his wife, left all alone, stood at his side, a temptation, though, rather than a comfort. She was not so much bringing medicine as prescribing blasphemy: *Say something against God, and die!* [Job 2.9].

You see how death would have been a boon for him, yet no one offered him that boon. Despite this, throughout all the suffering that his saintly soul endured, he put patience to use, he put his faith to the test, he put his wife to shame, he put the devil to defeat. His virtue provided an outstanding spectacle, shining with beauty through the ugliness of his physical decay.

The enemy causes widespread devastation; his feminine accomplice openly advocates evil; she assists the devil rather than her husband. She is the new Eve; but he is not the old Adam. She says, '*Say something against God, and die!* Blaspheme, and extort what you can't obtain through prayer.' He replies, *You have spoken like a foolish woman. If we accept good things from the hand of the Lord, why do we not also put up with the bad?* [Job 2.9–10].

Note the words of this brave man of faith. Note the words of someone who is rotten on the outside, but whole within: *You have spoken like a foolish woman. If we accept good things from the hand of the Lord, why should we not also put up with the bad?* He is our father; surely we should not love him when he caresses us, and then reject him when he corrects us? Surely he is our father both when he promises us life and when he imposes discipline? You have forgotten the following:

> *My son, when entering the service of God, stand in justice and fear; prepare your soul for testing. Accept everything that is brought on you; endure in pain, and when you are humiliated show forbearance. For gold and silver are tested in the fire, but the acceptable are tested in the furnace of humiliation* [Ecclus 2.1, 4–5].

You have also forgotten this: *If the Lord loves someone, he corrects him; he lashes every son whom he receives* [Prov 3.12, LXX; Heb 12.6].[8]

(4) Think of any torment you like, cast your mind over any human pain you like. Compare that with hell, and all your suffering is light. In the one case both tormentor and tormented are temporary, in the other, everlasting. Surely the victims from the time that Rome was devastated aren't still suffering? However, that rich man [cf. Lk 16.19–31] is still suffering among the dead: he has been burning, he is burning, he will burn.[9] He will come to judgement, and he will receive back his flesh not as a benefit, but for punishment. If we fear God, that is the penalty we should fear.

Anything a person has suffered here counts as amendment if he is reformed. If he is not reformed, his condemnation is doubled. He will pay a temporary penalty here and endure an everlasting one there.

My brothers, I say this to your loving selves: we certainly praise, glorify and admire the holy martyrs. We celebrate their feast-days with devoted solemnity; we revere their merits; if we are able, we imitate them. In short, the martyrs have great glory; but I am not sure that the glory that belonged to the holy Job was any less. It is true that he was not told, 'Burn incense to idols, sacrifice to foreign gods, or else deny Christ.' However, he was told, 'Blaspheme God'. This wasn't said to him meaning, 'If you blaspheme him all your gangrene will disappear and your health will return', but rather, 'If you blaspheme' (as his incompetent and dull wife put it), 'you will die, and by dying you will be rid of your agony'. As if, when a blasphemer dies, no everlasting pain follows!

The foolish woman was horrified by the cruel decay that was before her, but gave no thought at all to the everlasting flames. But he was enduring his present suffering to avoid facing suffering in the future. He was keeping his heart from evil thoughts, and his tongue from cursing; he was preserving his soul uncorrupted while his body rotted. He was able to see what he was escaping in the future, and that is why he bore his present sufferings.

Every Christian should meditate on hell in this way when he is suffering some physical hardship; then he may see how lightly he is suffering. He should not mutter against God; he should not say, 'My God, what have I done to you? Why should I suffer like this?'

No. Rather he should speak as Job himself spoke, although he was a saint: *You have sought all my sins, and you have sealed them as if in a bag* [Job 14.16–17]. He didn't dare to say that he was without sin, even though his suffering was not a punishment but a test. Each of us should say the same whenever we are suffering.

(5) There were indeed fifty just people in Rome. In fact, if you consider human standards, there were thousands of just people. If you examine the rule of perfection, then there is no one just in Rome. If anyone is bold enough to call himself just, he should listen to the truth: *Are you wiser than Daniel?* [Ezek 28.3]. Listen to him then confessing his sins. Or perhaps he was lying when he made his confession? Well, if so, then he did sin, because he lied to God about his sins! Sometimes there are people who reason as follows: 'A just person ought to say to God, "I am a sinner"; and even if he knows that he has no sin, he should say to God, "I am sinful."' I'd be amazed if that should be called sane advice.

Who made you sinless? If you have no sin at all, surely it is God who has healed your soul. (If in fact you do have no sin: reflect a little, and you will find not *a* sin, but rather sins.) But if you really have no sin, then surely that is a gift from God. As you prayed to him, *I said, Lord have mercy on me; heal my soul, for I* [10] *have sinned against you* [Ps 41(40).4].

If, then, your soul is sinless, your soul has been completely healed. If your soul has been completely healed, then why are you ungrateful to the doctor, saying that you are still wounded, when he has already restored you to full health? If you were to show a doctor that your body was weak or wounded, and ask him to make it his concern to cure you, and then he were to restore you to health and fitness, and you still said you were not very well, surely you would seem ungrateful, and insulting toward the doctor?

Similarly, God has healed you, and you still have the nerve to say, 'I am wounded.' Aren't you afraid of his replying to you: 'Well, then, didn't I do anything?'[11] Or have I wasted everything I did? I receive no pay; don't I deserve some praise?'

May God spare us from such madness, from this sort of empty reasoning! When someone says, 'I am a sinner', let him do so because he is a sinner; let him say, 'I am sinful', because he is sinful. For if he is not, he is wiser than Daniel.

Well, then, my brothers, I should conclude this debate at some point. If the just are to be named in this way (being called just by certain human standards, because they live irreproachable lives among other people) then there are many such in Rome; and God spared the city for their sake. Many escaped; but God also in fact spared those who are dead. Look, if the dead lived good lives that were truly just and faithful, then aren't they now free from human uncertainty and misery? Haven't they reached their God-given place of refreshment?

'But they died after various trials.' What of the poor man at the rich man's gate? Were they hungry? So was he. Were they wounded? So was he, and perhaps the dogs licked them less. Are they dead? So is he. But listen to the end of his story: *It happened that the poor man died, and was carried by angels into the bosom of Abraham* [Lk 16.22].

(6) If only we could actually look at the souls of the saints who died in that war. Then you would see how God has spared the city. Indeed there are thousands of saints in the place of refreshment. They are rejoicing and saying to God, 'Thanks be to you, Lord, because you have rescued us from physical hardship and agonising injuries. Thanks be to you that we now fear neither barbarians nor the devil, that we do not fear hunger on earth, that we do not fear enemies or pursuers or oppressors. But on earth we are dead; in your presence, though, God, we will not die. This is by your gift, not by our own merits.' What sort of a city is it, with its humble citizens, that speaks such words? Or perhaps, my brothers, you think that what counts in a city is its walls, and not its citizens?[12] In short, suppose God were to say to the Sodomites, 'Flee, because I am going to burn down this place!' If they did flee, and the flames swept down from the sky and

flattened only the city-walls and buildings, then we'd be tempted to say that they had won a great reward. Surely God would have spared the city, if the city had moved out and escaped the havoc wreaked by the fire?

(7) Didn't something happen a few years ago in Constantinople when Arcadius was emperor?[13] (Perhaps some of you listening to me know about it. Some of our local people were present at the event.)[14] Didn't it happen that God wanted to frighten the citizens, and by frightening them to chasten them and convert them, cleanse them and change them? Don't they say that he appeared in a vision to one of his faithful servants, an official, and told him that fire was going to fall from heaven and ruin the city? God warned him to tell the bishop; he did so, and the bishop did not make light of it, but addressed the people. The city was converted to a penitential state of mourning, as once was the case with the ancient city of Nineveh [cf. Jon 3.5].

However, God didn't want people to think that the man who had spoken up had been deceived by a false vision, or was telling lies so as to deceive them. The day arrived with which God had threatened them. With everyone waiting for the end intently, and very fearfully, a fiery cloud appeared from the east at nightfall, when the world was growing dark. It was small at first, then gradually, as it approached the city, it grew, until a vast and terrifying threat menaced the entire town. A dreadful flame was seen hanging from the sky; the smell of sulphur was in the air. Everyone fled to the church, which was too small to hold such a big crowd. People were wringing baptism out of anyone they could. They begged for the saving sacrament not only in the church, but in their homes, in the streets, in the squares, wanting to escape the wrath of God – not in the immediate present, of course, but in the future.

However, after this great trial, once God had proved his servant's trustworthiness, and his servant's vision, the cloud began to shrink, just as it had grown, and gradually disappeared. The people were safe for a short while; then they heard once more that they must evacuate the city, because it would be destroyed the following Saturday. The entire city left with the emperor. No one remained at home; no one locked his house. As they moved far away from the walls, they looked back at their sweet roofs, and said farewell in sorrowful voices to the dear homes they had abandoned.

The enormous crowd advanced a few miles and gathered together in one place to pour out prayers to the Lord. Suddenly they saw a huge billow of smoke; and they cried out to the Lord in a loud voice.

Eventually, when they saw that peace was restored, they sent scouts to report back to them. Once the anxious hour predicted had passed, and the scouts had reported that all the city-walls and buildings stood undamaged, everyone returned home giving profound thanks. No one lost anything from his house; everyone found it just as he had left it, though it had been left open.

(8) What are we to say? Was that an example of God's anger, or of his mercy? Does anyone doubt that our very merciful father wanted to use fear to reform rather than punish, when the great disaster that was present and threatening in fact harmed none of the people, none of the houses and none of the walls? Yes – just as you might well lift a hand to hit someone, but when your victim reacts with terror withdraw the blow out of pity. The city was dealt with in the same way. But what if it had been devastated during the time when it was abandoned, when all the population had left? What if the entire city had been destroyed, like Sodom, leaving not a single ruin standing? Even then no one could doubt that God had saved the city: for the city would have been forewarned and frightened, it would have departed and moved away, and only then would the place have been swallowed up.

Similarly, we should have no doubt that God spared the city of Rome: in many places much of her population had moved away before the enemy set fire to it. Those who had fled had moved away; and those who had left their bodies prematurely[15] had moved away. Many of those who remained hid as best they could; many were kept alive and safe within the shrines of the saints.[16] Consequently we should say that the city was corrected by the improving hand of God rather than destroyed,[17] just as a servant who knows the will of his master, yet behaves in a way that deserves a beating, will suffer for it heavily.

(9) If only this served effectively as an example and deterrent. The Lord demonstrates how unsteady and fragile are all worldly trivialities and all deceitful madness. If only evil desires, in their thirst for the world and their quest to enjoy the most destructive pleasures, might be restrained instead of muttering against the Lord at the lashes they thoroughly deserve.

However, the threshing-floor bears a single threshing-sledge to remove the stubble and purge the grain. Again, the furnace of a goldsmith accepts only one fire for the dross to be reduced to ash, and the gold to be freed from impurities.[18] Similarly, Rome too has endured a single time of trial. The pious have been chastened by this, but the impious have been condemned. I say condemned, whether they were snatched from this life to pay the justest penalties elsewhere, or whether they remain here to blaspheme and invite greater condemnation. For surely God, in his indescribable mercy, would preserve those whom he knew were to be saved, so that they could repent.

The burden borne by the pious should not, then, disturb us: its role is to train them.[19] Or do we perhaps shudder at the sight of someone just facing hard and undeserved suffering on this earth, while failing to remember what the justest of the just, the most saintly of the saints, suffered? Everything that the city as a whole has suffered was suffered by one man. You can see who that one is: *The king of kings and lord of lords* [Rev 19.16] arrested, bound, whipped, treated to all kinds of insults, hung from a plank and crucified, and killed.

Weigh Rome against Christ; weigh the whole earth against Christ, weigh heaven and earth against Christ. No creature balances its creator, no handiwork bears comparison with its craftsman. *Everything was made through him and without him nothing was made* [Jn 1.3]; yet still he was handed over to his pursuers. Let us, then, endure whatever God wishes us to endure. He sent his own son to care for us and bring us healing; and like a doctor, he knows which pains are beneficial. Indeed, we find in scripture: *Let patience have a perfect work* [Jas 1.4]. What will the work of patience be if we suffer nothing adverse? Why, then, do we refuse to endure temporary ills? Are we perhaps afraid of being made perfect? But, surely, we should pray in sorrow to the Lord, in the hope that the words of the apostle may hold true in our case, *a faithful God, who does not allow you to be tested beyond your capacity; but when you are tested, he will provide an escape so that you may be able to endure it* [1 Cor 10.13].

Letter 189

417

Augustine sends greetings in the Lord to Boniface,[1] his distinguished, deservedly illustrious, and honoured son.

(1) I had already written to your beloved self;[2] however, when I was looking for the opportunity to get my letter to you, my dearest son Faustus arrived on the scene, on his way to your distinguished self. When

he agreed to carry the letter that I had already written to your kind self, he intimated to me that you were very eager to have me write you something that would fortify you for the everlasting security³ for which you hope in Christ Jesus our Lord. Although I was busy, he pressed me not to postpone doing this, with an urgency that you will recognise, as his affection for you is indeed single-minded. In order therefore to meet his haste, I preferred to write something to you rather hurriedly, than to hamper your eagerness for matters religious, my distinguished and deservedly illustrious and honoured son.

(2) Briefly, then, I am able to say the following: *Love the Lord your God with all your heart and with all your soul and with all your strength, and love your neighbour as yourself* [Mt 22.37, 39; Mk 12.30–1; Lk 10.27; cf. Deut 6.5; Lev 19.18].

That is the saying which the Lord gave us as a summary when he was on earth; as he said in the Gospel: *On these two commandments hang the whole of the Law and the prophets* [Mt 22.40]. Make daily progress, then, in this love, both through prayer and through doing good. Then, with the help of God, who both commanded and granted that love, it may be nourished and grow, until it is perfect, and makes you perfect. For it is charity itself, which (as the apostle says) *is spread in our hearts through the Holy Spirit, who is given to us* [Rom 5.5]. This is also what he referred to in the words, *Charity is the fullness of the Law* [Rom 13.10]. It is charity again through which faith works, to quote the apostle once more: *Neither circumcision nor the foreskin has any value, but faith, which works through love* [Gal 5.6].

(3) In this love all our holy forefathers and patriarchs and prophets and apostles found favour with God. In it all the true martyrs fought against the devil to the point of shedding their blood; and they were victorious just because it neither failed nor *grew cold* [cf. Mt 24.12]. In it all the worthy faithful make daily progress in their desire to reach not a kingdom of mortals but the kingdom of heaven, not a temporary but an everlasting inheritance, not gold and silver but the incorruptible riches possessed by angels, to attain not a few of this world's goods – which cause you fear while you are alive and which you cannot take with you when you die – but rather the vision of God.

The sweetness and delight of the vision of God surpasses in beauty not only earthly bodies, but the heavenly bodies also; it surpasses in splendour every single just and holy soul; it surpasses in loveliness the angels and powers above. It surpasses anything that we can say of it – or rather anything that we can imagine. However, we oughtn't for that reason to lose hope in so great a promise – for it is a great one; rather, because the promise was made by someone very great, we ought to trust that we shall be granted it. As the blessed apostle John said: *We are sons of God, and what we will be has not yet appeared. We know that when it does appear we will be like him, since we shall see him as he is* [1 Jn 3.2].

(4) You must not think that no one who serves as a soldier, using arms for warfare, can be acceptable to God. The holy David was one such, and the Lord offered a great a witness to him. Very many other just men of the same period were also soldiers. So was the centurion who spoke to the Lord as follows: *I am not worthy for you to enter under my roof; however, only say the word, and my boy will be healed. For I am a man placed under authority, and I have soldiers under me; I say to someone 'Go!' and he goes; and to someone else 'Come!' and he comes; I say to my servant, 'Do this' and he does it* [Mt 8.8–10; Lk 7.6–9]. The Lord said of him, *In truth I tell you: I have not found such faith in Israel.*

Cornelius was also a soldier. An angel was sent to him, who said, *Cornelius, your alms have been accepted and your prayers have been heard* [Acts 10.1–33]. The angel advised Cornelius to send for the blessed apostle Peter and to hear from him what he should do. And the man whom Cornelius sent to ask the apostle to come to him was also a devout soldier.

They were also soldiers, who came to be baptised by John, the holy forerunner of the Lord, and *the friend of the bridegroom* [Jn 3.29]. (Indeed, the Lord said of him, *Of those born of woman, none greater than John the Baptist has ever arisen*) [Mt 11.11]. They asked him what they should do; and he replied: *Do not intimidate anyone; do not bring false charges against anyone; and be satisfied with your wages* [Lk 3.14]. He certainly was not forbidding them to live under arms as soldiers when he instructed them to be satisfied with their pay.[4]

(5) It is true that those who abandon all such worldly activities and serve God also through the complete chastity of celibacy hold a higher place with him. However, as the apostle says, *Each one has his own gift from God, one in this way, another in that* [1 Cor 7.7]. So others are fighting invisible enemies on your behalf by praying, while you struggle against visible barbarians on their behalf by fighting. If only everyone shared a single faith, so that the struggle would be less and the devil and his angels more easily vanquished!

However, it is necessary in this age for the citizens of the kingdom of heaven, surrounded as they are by the lost and the impious, to be vexed by temptations, so that they can be trained and tested *like gold in a furnace* [Wisd 3.5–6]. We oughtn't therefore before the time is right to wish to live only with the holy and the just; then we might deserve to be granted that in its proper time.

(6) When you are arming yourself for battle, then, consider this first of all, that your courage, even your physical courage, is a gift from God. Then you won't think of using a gift from God to act against God. When one makes a promise, one must keep faith, even with an enemy against whom one is waging a war.[5] How much more so with a friend, for whose sake one is fighting! Peace ought to be what you want, war only what necessity demands. Then God may free you from necessity and preserve you in peace. For you don't seek peace in order to stir up war; no – war is waged in order to obtain peace.[6] Be a peacemaker, therefore, even in war, so that by conquering them you bring the benefit of peace even to those you defeat. For, says the Lord, *Blessed are the peacemakers, for they shall be called the sons of God* [Mt 5.9]. If, indeed, human peace is so delightful because of the temporary security that belongs to mortals, how much more delightful is divine peace, because of the everlasting security that belongs to the angels.[7] Therefore it ought to be necessity, and not your will, that destroys an enemy who is fighting you. And just as you use force against the rebel or opponent, so you ought now to use mercy towards the defeated or the captive, and particularly so when there is no fear that peace will be disturbed.

(7) Let your character be embellished by marital chastity, by sobriety and by simplicity of life. It is certainly shameful if someone who is undefeated by another human being is defeated by lust, or undefeated by iron, but overwhelmed by wine. If you are short of worldly wealth, don't seek it on earth by doing harm. If you possess it, preserve it in heaven by doing good. Wealth, when it turns up, oughtn't to swell a manly[8] and Christian spirit; when it goes away, it oughtn't to break it. Rather we should reflect on the words of the Lord: *Where your treasure is, there will your heart be also* [Mt 6.21; Lk 12.34]; and when we hear that, we should 'lift up our heart', and we should not be untruthful in making the response which you know that we make.[9]

(8) I know, moreover, that you are very zealous in such matters; I am delighted by your reputation and I congratulate you in the Lord. Consequently, this letter might serve you as a mirror in which you can see what you are like, rather than one from which you learn what you ought to be like. However, if you find in either this letter or in sacred scripture

anything you still lack for a life of goodness, then make urgent efforts in prayer and in action to acquire it. Give thanks also for what you do possess to God, as the source of the goodness you have, and in every good deed that you do, *give* him the *glory* [cf. Ps 115(113b).1], and yourself the humility. As it is written: *every excellent gift and every perfect present comes down from above from the father of lights* [Jas 1.17].

However much you advance, though, in the love of God or of your neighbour and in true piety, however long you are involved in this life, do not believe that you are sinless. *Surely human life on the earth is a time of testing* [Job 7.1]. Indeed, as long as you are in the body, it is continually necessary for you when you pray to say the words the Lord taught us, *Forgive us our debts, just as we ourselves forgive our debtors* [Mt 6.12; cf. Lk 11.4]. Remember to pardon quickly anyone who sins against you and begs mercy from you, so that you can pray truthfully, and are in a position to obtain mercy for your sins.

I have written this in haste to your dear self, as I was being pressed by our messenger, who is himself in a hurry. However, I give thanks to God that in some way at least I have not failed to satisfy your worthy desire. May the mercy of God ever preserve you, my distinguished, deservedly illustrious and honoured son.

Letter 220

428

Augustine greets the lord Boniface,[1] his son, whom he commends to the protection and guidance of the mercy of God for his present and his eternal security.

(1) I could never find a more trustworthy person, nor one who had easier access to your hearing when bringing my letters, than the man whom the Lord has now provided, the deacon Paul, the servant and minister of Christ, a man very dear to both of us. Consequently, I am able to speak to you, not to boost the power and honour that you wield in this unkind age, nor to safeguard your corruptible and mortal flesh – for that is ephemeral and it is always uncertain how long it will last. No, I address you rather on the subject of the security[2] that Christ has promised us, he who was dishonoured and crucified here precisely in order to teach us to disdain

rather than love the goods of this world, and to love and hope from him for the future that he revealed in his own resurrection. For *he rose from the dead, and now he does not die and death no longer governs him* [Rom 6.9].

(2) I know that there is no shortage of people who love you as far as the life of this world goes, and offer you advice by its lights, advice that is sometimes beneficial and sometimes not. After all, they are human, and they are wise as far as they can be with regard to the present, when they don't know what will happen the next day. However, as far as God is concerned, it's not easy for anyone to make it their care to prevent the loss of your soul. This is not because there's no one available who might do it; but rather because it's difficult to find a time when they can talk to you about such things. I've always longed to do this myself, but I've never found opportunity or time to discuss such matters with you. But I ought to discuss them with someone I love dearly in Christ.

Moreover, you know what state I was in when you saw me at Hippo, on the occasion on which you were good enough to visit me. I was so tired by my physical weakness that I could scarcely speak. So please listen to me, my son, now that I'm at least conversing with you by letter. I was never able to write to you when you were in a dangerous situation because I was thinking of the risk to the bearer, and also because I was wary of my letter falling into the hands of people I didn't want to have it. I beg your pardon, then, if you think I was more fearful than I should have been; still, I have said that I was afraid.

(3) Listen to me, then; or rather to the Lord our God, through the ministry of my own weak person. Remember what you were like when your first wife (of devoted memory) was still in her body, and when her death was still fresh: how the emptiness of this age made you shudder, and how you longed to be in the service of God! We know about, and we are witnesses to, the conversations you held with us at Tubuna on the soul and on your own intentions. My brother Alypius and I were alone with you.

In my view, indeed, the earthly concerns that fill you at present[3] cannot be powerful enough to blot that out utterly from your memory. Surely you actually desired to abandon all the public activities with which you were busy, and to give yourself instead to sacred leisure by living the life of the servants of God, that is of monks.

What was it that held you back from doing so, except this: you had in mind, and we were pointing out, the degree to which your activities were benefiting the churches of Christ?[4] If, that is, you were acting with the single intention of allowing them to lead a *quiet and peaceful life*, as the apostle says, protected from harassment from the barbarian invasions, *in all piety and chastity* [1 Tim 2.2]. Meanwhile, you yourself would have been looking for nothing from this world, except what you needed to support this present life of yours, and of those dear to you, girded as you would have been with a belt of chaste celibacy, and armed, in the midst of physical weapons, with the safer and stronger weapons of the spirit.

(4) While we were rejoicing that you had make this your purpose, you set sail, and then you married a wife.[5] The sailing you undertook out of the obedience that (according to the apostle) you owed to *higher authorities* [Rom 13.1]. However, you would not have taken a wife had you not been overcome by lust and abandoned the celibacy you had adopted.

I must admit that when I discovered this I was amazed and dumbstruck. My sorrow was eased to some extent by hearing that you wouldn't have been willing to marry her had she not become a Catholic. Despite this, though, the heresy of those who deny the true son of God had so much influence in your household that your own daughter was baptised by its adherents. But now, if the rumours that have reached us are not untrue (if only they were!), even maidservants of yours who were consecrated to God have been rebaptised by those heretics! This is a dreadful thing, and we ought to be weeping copious tears over it. People also say that even your wife was not enough for you, and that you defiled yourself by associating with some mistresses or other. Perhaps they are lying.

(5) What am I to say about the many dreadful activities which you pursued after your marriage, and which everybody knew about?[6] You are a Christian; you have a heart; you fear God. Reflect for yourself on the things I am unwilling to mention; and you will discover the number of misdeeds for which you ought to do penance. I believe that God is sparing you for precisely that purpose, and keeping you free of all danger so that you may perform penance as you ought, but on condition that you listen to the words of scripture: *Do not be slow to turn to the Lord, and do not delay from day to day* [Ecclus. 5.7].

You say that your cause is just; I am not judge of it, since I am unable to hear both sides. However, whatever your case is like, there is no need now to examine or debate it; surely you are not able to deny in the presence of God that you wouldn't have reached these straits, if you hadn't been so fond of the goods of this world?[7] Yet as a servant of God,[8] which was how we knew you before, you ought to have disdained them completely, and held them to be worthless. If any were offered you, you ought to have taken them for religious purposes. If any were denied you or merely entrusted to you, you oughtn't to have tried to get them in such a way that they led you to your present straits. For now, even though the things that attract you are valueless, dreadful things are being done, a few by you yourself, and a lot on your behalf. This, even though the things that you're fearing can only harm you for a short time, if at all; but what's being perpetrated can do you genuine harm, and for ever.

(6) If I may say one thing on the subject, it is this: many people associate closely with you in order to preserve your authority and security. Who cannot see that even if all of them are faithful and there is no need to fear treachery from any of them, still, surely, they desire to use you to get hold of goods which they too find attractive not in the light of God, but in the light of the world? As a result you are forced to gratify the desires of others, while you ought to be restraining and checking your own. To achieve this, you need to do a lot of things displeasing to God.[9] Even then, desires like this aren't fully gratified. They are easier to curtail in those who love God than in those who love the world, and sometimes they can be satisfied. That is why holy scripture says: *Do not love the world, nor the things that are in the world. If anyone does love the world, the father's love is not in him. For everything that is in the world is lust of the flesh, and lust of the eyes, and ostentation of this age, which does not come from the Father, but from the world. And this world and all its lust will pass away. But anyone who does the will of God remains for ever, just as God too remains for ever* [1 Jn 2.15–17].

Faced with so many armed men, whose desires must be fostered and whose ferocity must be feared, when, when, I ask, will you be able, if not to satisfy the lust of those who love this earth (for that can never be done), just to feed it a little, to prevent further destruction of everything? Only, perhaps, if you do things that God forbids and threatens punishment on those who do them. As you can see, the result has been so much damage that now almost nothing, however valueless, can be found to plunder.

(7) Next, what am I to say of the devastation wrought in Africa? The barbarians of Africa are succeeding here without meeting any resistance so long as you are in your present state, preoccupied with your own needs, and are organising nothing to prevent this disaster.[10] When Boniface was appointed in Africa to be *comes* of the Household and of Africa,[11] with high authority and a vast army, a man who as tribune[12] had pacified all the same tribes by attacking them and fighting them with only a few allied troops, would anyone have believed this? Would anyone have feared that by now

the barbarians would have become so bold, have advanced so far, have caused so much devastation, have plundered so widely, have made deserts of so many places that were full of people? Surely, anyone would have predicted that whenever you assumed your position as *comes*, the barbarians of Africa would be not only tamed, but even, eventually, tributary members of the Roman empire.[13] Now, though, you can see how human hopes have been turned upside down. I need not discuss this with you at greater length: you will have more thoughts on this topic than I have words.

(8) Perhaps, though, you will reply to this that the blame for such failures must be laid upon various people who have done you harm, and have repaid your dutiful virtues not with corresponding co-operation, but with the opposite.[14] I am not in a position to hear each side of this case or to judge it. Instead, you must look at your own case and examine it, and recognise that it is not between you and some other human beings, but between you and God. If you are living faithfully in Christ, you ought to be afraid of offending him.

My own attention, by contrast, is focused on cases of a higher nature; for people ought to be attributing the present sorry suffering of Africa to their own sins. Yet I don't want you to be numbered among the evil and wicked persons who are used by God as a scourge to inflict temporary punishments on whomever he wishes. For God keeps everlasting punishment in store for the wicked, unless they reform; yet he makes just use of their evil purposes to heap temporary troubles upon others.

You, though, attend to God; you, meditate on Christ, who has provided such great goods for us, though he himself endured great evils. All those who desire to reach his kingdom and live for ever in blessedness with him and under him, on top of this *love* their *enemies*, doing *good to those who hate* them and praying for those at whose hands they suffer harassment [Mt 5.44; Lk 6.27–8]; and even if for the sake of discipline they occasionally exercise an unpleasant severity, even in this they don't abandon their single-minded love.

Consequently, if the Roman empire provides you with good things, even if they are ephemeral and earthly (for it is an earthly, not a heavenly, institution and can only provide what is in its power); if then it has bestowed good things upon you, do not return evil for good. However, if it has inflicted evil on you, *do not return evil for evil* [Rom 12.17; 1 Thess. 5.15]. Neither do I wish to debate nor am competent to judge which of the two is the case. I am addressing a Christian: neither *return* evil for good, nor *evil for evil*.

(9) Perhaps you will reply to me: 'What do you want me to do when pressed by such necessity?' Are you asking me to give advice in the light of this world on how to safeguard this ephemeral security of yours, and on how to preserve the power and wealth that you now possess, or even increase it? If so, then I am unable to answer you. There is no secure advice to give for purposes that are so insecure. On the other hand, if you're asking my advice in the light of God, to keep your soul from death, and if you fear the words of Truth when he says, *What does it profit someone if he gains the whole world, but suffers the loss of his soul?* [Mt 16.26; Mk 8.36; Lk 9.25], then I certainly have an answer for you. I have some advice which you may hear from me. But what need is there for me to say anything different from that I quoted above?

> *Do not love the world, nor the things that are in the world. If anyone does love the world, the Father's love is not in him. For everything that is in the world is lust of the flesh and lust of the eyes and ostentation of this age, which does not come from the Father, but from the world. And this world and all its lust will pass away. But anyone who does the will of God remains for ever, just as God, too, remains for ever* [1 Jn 2.15–17].

Here is my advice. Seize it and act upon it. This will reveal whether you are a brave man. Conquer the passions that lead you to love the world; do penance for your past misdeeds, for the time when, under the sway of such passions, you were being dragged around by empty desires. If you embrace this advice, if you hold to it and keep it, you will attain those goods that are secure, and you will also move freely among those that are not secure, without putting your soul at risk.

(10) Perhaps, though, you will ask me a second question. How are you to achieve this when you are so tangled up in such great earthly needs? Pray with courage; speak to God the word you find in the psalm: *Rescue me from my state of need* [Ps 25(24).17]. These needs of yours will cease when those passions of yours are defeated. He listened to you, and to us on your behalf, when we prayed for your deliverance from the many great dangers of warfare, dangers visible and physical. But in such a case, one's present life alone is at risk (and that has to come to an end at some time); one's soul, however, will not perish unless it is held captive by harmful passions.

He himself will listen to you when you pray to overcome, invisibly and spiritually, your inner and invisible enemies, that is those passions themselves; to make use of this world as if you were not using it; to do good

with its good things, rather than to become bad. For they are in themselves good and are given to human beings only by God, who has power
over everything in heaven and on earth. They are given to the good
people, in case the things are thought to be evil; but they are also given to
the wicked, in case they are thought to be great goods, or the greatest of
goods.[15] Similarly, they are also taken away from the good, to test them,
and also from the wicked, to torment them.

(11) Who is unaware of this? Who is so stupid as not to see that both the
good and the wicked are granted good things on earth – the security of
their mortal bodies, strength in their limbs, which are destined to decay,
victory over human enemies, honour, temporal power and the rest – and
also that both the good and the wicked are deprived of them? On the other
hand, the security of the soul, together with the immortality of the body,
the strength of justice, victory over the hostile passions, glory, honour
and peace for eternity, these are given only to the good. It is these then
that you must love, these you must desire, these you must seek by any
means you can.

Give alms for the sake of winning and keeping these goods; pour out
your prayers, practise fasting as you are able without impairing your
physical health. But don't love the goods of this earth, however plenti-
fully you may possess them. Make use of them in this way: do much good
with them, but no evil for their sake. All such goods will perish, but good
works will not perish, even those achieved with goods that are perishable.

(12) If you did not have a wife, I would urge you to live in chaste celibacy, just as I did before at Tubuna. I should also add something that we
forbade you to do then: that now, in so far as you might without jeopardis-
ing peace in human affairs, you should withdraw from the affairs of war
and give yourself leisure for a life in the fellowship of the holy. Previously
you were longing to have leisure, which the soldiers of Christ use for
fighting in silence, not to kill people, but to conquer the *rulers and powers
and spirits of wickedness* [Eph 6.12], that is, the devil and his angels.

The holy inflict defeat on these enemies, though they cannot see them.
Despite this, they conquer the enemy they cannot see by conquering the
objects of their senses. Your wife inhibits me from urging you to this way
of life, as it is not right for you to live celibately without her agreement.
Even if you ought not to have married her after the words you spoke at
Tubuna, still she knew nothing of that and married you in innocence and
simplicity. Would that you might persuade her to embrace celibacy, so
that you could give yourself back to God without obstacle, as you ought to

do. However, if you cannot do that together with her, at least preserve decency within marriage; furthermore, ask God to deliver you from your needs, so that you will eventually be able to do what you are at present unable to do. On the other hand, your wife neither prevents you, nor ought to prevent you, from the following: from loving God and not loving the world; from keeping faith even in warfare (if it's still necessary for you to be involved in it) and from seeking peace; from performing good works with worldly goods and from avoiding evil works done for the sake of worldly goods.

It is love, my dearest son, that commands me to write like this to you, the love that makes you dear to me in the light of God, not of this world. For when I think of the words of scripture, *Correct the wise man and he will love you; correct the fool and he will hate you even more* [Prov 9.8], I certainly ought to consider you not a fool, but a wise man.

Letter 229

429/430

Augustine greets Darius,[1] his deservedly illustrious, most magnificent lord, and beloved son in Christ.

(1) I have heard from my holy brothers and fellow-bishops Urbanus and Novatus[2] of the type of man you are and of your stature. The former had the opportunity of your acquaintance near Carthage in the town of Hilari, and recently at Sicca, and the latter at Sitifis. They made it impossible for me to fail to know you! Moreover, just because my physical weakness and the double frost of winter and of old age do not allow me to speak with you face to face, it does not mean that I have not seen you. For they have revealed to me your face, not the face of your flesh, but that of your heart, Novatus in my presence when he was good enough to visit me, and Urbanus in a letter; consequently, I was granted a more delightful view of you in so far as it was more inward. This face of yours both you and I are able (by God's favour) to see with great joy in the holy gospel, as if in a mirror; there are written the words of Truth himself: *Blessed are the peacemakers, for they shall be called the sons of God* [Mt 5.9].

(2) Greatness and their own glory belong to warriors who are both very brave and very faithful (that is the source of the truer praise), to those

who struggle and face danger in order, with the help of God who gives protection and assistance, to bring defeat upon an untamed enemy and win respite for the empire by pacifying the provinces. However, greater glory still is merited by killing not men with swords, but war with words, and by acquiring or achieving peace not through war but through peace itself. For those who fight, if they are good men, are certainly aiming for peace, but still through bloodshed. By contrast, you were sent to avoid any blood being shed. [3] For others, then, the one is a necessity; for you, the other is a joy.

Therefore, my deservedly illustrious and most magnificent lord, and beloved son in Christ, rejoice that so great and true a good is yours and enjoy it in God, who has enabled you to be such a person and to undertake such an enterprise.

May God *confirm the achievement he has wrought through you for us* [Ps 68(67).28]. Accept this greeting of mine, and be so good as to repay me with your own. My brother Novatus told me in his letter that he has arranged for your eminent and learned self to become acquainted with me through my writings. If you have indeed read what he gave you, I too will have become familiar to your inner senses, without, I suspect, displeasing you, if, that is, your sympathy was readier than your severity as you read. It is a little to ask, but would be greatly appreciated, if you were to send just one letter to me, in return for both my letter and the other writings.

I greet also, with all due affection, that pledge of peace, whom you were so happy to receive through the help of the Lord our God. [4]

Biographical notes

ALARIC I (*c.* 370–410), a leader of one of the Visigothic clans settled in modern southern Bulgaria and northern Serbia. He was an Arian Christian. He is thought to have been disenchanted when the emperors Arcadius and Honorius neglected to accord him a high military post as compensation for his services. He first attacked Italian territory *c.* 400. He was defeated by Stilicho in the battle of Pollentia (402) and later at Verona (403). In September 408, he blockaded Rome, exacting a ransom payment from the senate. He repeated the blockade in 409. Finally, when efforts to reach an accord with the emperor once again proved fruitless, he attacked Rome a third time on 24 August 410 and sacked the city.

ALYPIUS, bishop of Thagaste, his and A.'s birthplace, disciple and close friend of A. Somewhat younger than A., he followed his lectures in rhetoric at Thagaste and Carthage. He preceded A. to Rome prior to 383 where he also took up reading the law in accord with his parents' wishes. There, he served as a judicial assessor to the *comes largitionum Italicianarum*, an official of the imperial treasury department with responsibility in Italy for oversight of mines and precious metals, for the levying of taxes, and for the payment of the army and the civil service (cf. *conf.* 6.10.16). He joined A. in embracing the Catholic faith at Milan in 387. He returned with A. to Africa to form a religious community at Thagaste, and was elected bishop of the town *c.* 394. His legal training equipped him for leadership among African bishops in a series of councils devoted to the Donatist controversy. He played a leading role in the conference of Carthage in

411. He was frequently despatched to Rome and to the imperial court at Ravenna to represent the causes of African Catholic bishops (cf. Letter 10*).

AMBROSE, bishop of Milan (373/4–97). Prior to accepting episcopal consecration at Milan, he studied rhetoric and law and served there in the imperial civil service. Later on he gained familiarity with scripture and the works of Greek Church Fathers and of philosophers such as Plato and Plotinus. His preaching was instrumental in the conversion of A. in 386. He baptised A. along with Alypius on 24–5 April 387. The Arian problem was at the centre of his pastoral and political preoccupations. He intervened regularly with Roman emperors whose courts were located at Milan during his episcopate. His most famous intervention occurred in 390 when he ordered the emperor Theodosius I to perform public penance to atone for a massacre at Thessalonika that same year.

ANULINUS, proconsul of Africa in 313. He despatched a letter to the emperor Constantine on 15 April 313 containing accusations against the bishop of Carthage, Caecilian (cf. Letter 88.2).

APOLLONIUS, a first-century wandering Neopythagorean holy man who was born at Tyana in Cappadocia, Asia Minor (modern Turkey). He was said to have been a miracle-worker and to have travelled extensively teaching and practising a religious form of the philosophy. A. took him to be a magician and was concerned about his being compared to Christ by anti-Christian pagans (cf. Letter 136.1).

APRINGIUS, proconsul of Africa in 411 and a Christian. As proconsul he governed the province of Africa Proconsularis with its capital at Carthage. He could appeal directly to the emperor, bypassing the vicar of Africa and the praetorian prefect. A. wrote to him asking him to practise moderation in punishing Donatists convicted of the murder of one of A.'s clergy, Restitutus, and the maiming of another, Innocent (cf. Letter 134). He was the brother of Marcellinus, who was tribune and notary for the Western empire in the same year. Both brothers were executed on 13 September 413 by Marinus for their alleged support of a plot against the emperor Honorius.

APULEIUS, second-century rhetorician and Platonic philosopher in north Africa, author of *Metamorphoses*. He was accused by Sicinius Aemilianus of having practised magic in order to win the love of Pudentilla, who was betrothed to Aemilianus' brother, Sicinius Clarus. He defended himself from the charge in his oration *Apologia* or *Pro se de magia* (cf. Letter 138.19). A. also knew him as the author of *De deo Socratis*, an exposition of Platonic demonology.

ARIUS, a Christian priest born in the third century in the region surrounding Alexandria in Egypt. He was condemned by his own bishop and by an Egyptian council of bishops for holding that the Son was created by the Father, and that he was not as fully divine as the Father, but radically subordinated to him. He found supporters for his position among eastern bishops. As a result of the ensuing controversy surrounding his views, he was condemned in 325 by a general council of bishops convened at Nicea in Asia Minor (modern Turkey) by the emperor Constantine.

AUXILIUS, commonly thought to be the Catholic bishop of Nurco in the north African province of Mauretania Caesariensis. However, if, as some would have it, the dossier of letters concerning Classicianus is dated to the later years of A.'s life (427–30), he may be another bishop about whom we know nothing other than the fact that he would have been young and recently consecrated at this time. He excommunicated the *comes* Classicianus, along with his entire household, on the charge of having violated church sanctuary by forcibly detaining a man who had sought legally sanctioned refuge there (cf. Letters 250 and 1*).

BONIFACE (1). He is first heard of fighting the Visigothic king Athaulf as a Roman soldier in a battle at Marseilles in 413. By 417 he was a military tribune stationed in Africa, but in 423 was named *comes* of Africa. His primary mission throughout this period was to defend Roman settlements in Africa from the advance of the Vandals. In 425 he was named *comes domesticorum et Africae*, a post which gave him command of a regiment of the army, the *domestici*, or Household Guard. He held the post until 427 when he fell into political and military intrigues centred upon rival generals Flavius Aetius and Flavius Constantius Felix, and upon the empress Galla Placidia. For two years he fought imperial troops sent from Italy to defeat him. Reconciled to the court and recalled to Italy in 432, he was made a military commander, and died in the same year after defeating Aetius near Rimini.

BONIFACE (2), bishop of Rome (418–22). He was a staunch supporter of A. in the campaign against Pelagius and his associates. He secured from the emperor Honorius an edict ordering all bishops to sign Zosimus' *Epistula tractoria* condemning the doctrines of Pelagius and Celestius as heresies. He passed on to A. two letters from Julian, bishop of Eclanum, disparaging A.'s position on the controversial issues. The letters occasioned the first book of A.'s *De nuptiis et concupiscentia*.

CAECILIAN (1). As archdeacon of Carthage he had been accused of neglecting the material needs of fifty imprisoned Christians from Abitina awaiting execution during the 'Great' Persecution under the emperor Diocletian during 303–5. He was elected bishop of Carthage *c.* 309/312 (the year of his election and consecration is disputed by scholars). His consecration was immediately contested because one of the consecrating bishops, Felix of Apthugni, was a suspected *traditor*. The matter was referred to the emperor by supporters of Maiorinus and, after his death, by supporters of Donatus. He was examined by the bishop of Rome, Miltiades, but was exonerated on 2 October 313. He was vindicated as well by the council of Arles on 1 August 314 and by the emperor Constantine himself on 10 November 316. He later attended the council of Nicea in 325.

CAECILIAN (2) served in an imperial office, perhaps as a provincial governor, prior to 396. He was vicar of Africa in 404 and possibly for a time during 405, but had probably been named proconsul of Africa when A. addressed Letter 86 to him (405). Hippo Regius fell under the jurisdiction of the proconsul of Africa who, unlike other north African provincial governors, was not subject to the vicar of Africa, and could take matters concerning his administration directly to the emperor, bypassing even the praetorian prefect. He was a legate of the senate at Rome in late 408 and early 409 during the initial siege of the city by Alaric, and led a delegation to the emperor Honorius at Ravenna. In 409 he was named praetorian prefect of Italy and

Illyricum with responsibilities as the emperor's chief-of-staff for judicial and administrative matters arising within those civil dioceses. While serving in March 414 on a mission to Africa, he received another letter from A. lamenting the executions of Marcellinus and Apringius.

CAECILIAN (3), ALFIUS, a *duumvir* at Apthugni (today Henchir Es-Souar, Tunisia) whose task it was during the Diocletian or 'Great' Persecution in 303 to seize the sacred books and vessels of the church. Eleven years afterwards he was the principal witness in the trial of Felix, bishop of Apthugni, who was accused of *traditio* during the Persecution (cf. Translator's note on Hand over). During a hearing before Aelian, the proconsul of Africa, which concluded at Carthage on 15 February 314, he acknowledged that Ingentius had put pressure on him to dictate a letter to Felix recounting the events that took place at Apthugni in 303. When shown the letter, he testified that he had not dictated the second part, which was the most incriminating against Felix because it implicated him directly in a plot to hand over the sacred books. As a result of this testimony, Ingentius was shown to have forged the postscript, and Felix was vindicated of the charge of *traditio*. Felix's acquittal enabled the council of Arles on 1 August 314 to re-affirm the episcopal consecration of Caecilian (1) as bishop of Carthage.

CELER, a wealthy imperial official with the high rank of *spectabilis*. He possessed a large estate near Hippo Regius. Although he inherited Donatist leanings from his family (cf. *ep.* 56.2), A. was able to draw him into the Catholic church *c.* 400.

CELESTINE, bishop of Rome (422–32). He intervened strongly in the affairs of the north African church. He acted decisively against certain clergy suspected of sympathising with the teachings of Pelagius and his associates. He styled himself the 'successor of St Peter', and arrogated to himself prerogatives which he believed pertained to the governance of the Western and Eastern Christian churches.

CELESTIUS, one of the principal associates of Pelagius. While at Carthage in 411, he was denounced for heterodox teachings concerning issues related to original sin and infant baptism. He taught that death was natural to human beings and not an inherited divine penalty for the sin of Adam. In addition, he argued that baptism bestowed forgiveness only for sins committed during one's lifetime; hence, it was unnecessary in the case of infants. He was condemned by a synod of the Carthaginian clergy during that year. In his essay *Definitiones*, published anonymously at this time, he argued for the possibility that human beings could live without ever committing sin. A. objected to this work in *De perfectione iustitiae hominis*. By 416 he was living at Ephesus in Asia Minor (modern Turkey). His controversial positions were condemned and he was excommunicated by the bishop of Rome, Innocent I, on 27 January 417.

CLASSICIANUS, referred to by A. as a *comes* (cf. Letter 250.1). He was a Catholic, excommunicated by bishop Auxilius for violating a legally sanctioned church sanctuary when he arrested a man perhaps accused of breaking an oath to repay a debt. He may have been the guarantor (*fideiussor*) of the debt; hence the man he arrested may have placed him in financial jeopardy. He was the recipient of A.'s Letter 1*.

CRISPIN, Donatist bishop of Calama (today Guelma, Algeria), at least between 394 and 411. Just prior to 399/400 he promised a debate with A. over the division of the church in Africa (cf. Letter 51). In Letter 66, A. accused him of having rebaptised about eighty people, consisting of tenant farmers and their families on an imperial estate which he had purchased at Mappala, outside of Calama (cf. *c. litt. Pet.* 2.83.184). He was condemned as a heretic and fined ten pounds of gold two years later when a Donatist priest of his diocese, also named Crispin, ambushed and assaulted Possidius, the Catholic bishop of the same town. Despite Possidius' successful appeal against imposition of the fine, he appealed against his conviction to the emperor Honorius (cf. Letter 88.7). The emperor re-imposed the sentence against him, but then yielded once again to the appeals of Catholic bishops against imposition of the fine.

CYPRIAN, bishop of Carthage (249–58). As a church leader and ecclesiastical writer, he was influenced by Tertullian and, in turn, influenced north African Christianity. He made a strong stand in favour of the rebaptism of those who had been baptised by heretics or schismatics, arguing that no valid baptism could take place outside the church. On this position he was opposed by Stephen, bishop of Rome (254–7). Both A. and the Donatists recognised him as a spiritual and theological authority. His emphasis on church unity against dissenters and schismatics fuelled A.'s own similar arguments against the Donatists. The Donatists identified with his position on rebaptism. He was martyred during the Decian persecution on 14 September 258.

DARIUS, a high-ranking imperial official (*vir illustris*) who was a Christian and friend of A. In 427/428 he was despatched to Africa from Italy to end the fighting between Boniface and imperial troops (cf. Letters 220 and 229). In this effort he was apparently successful. He and A. also exchanged *ep.* 230 and 231.

DONATUS (1) (*c.* 270–355), bishop of Carthage and eponymous hero of the Donatist cause in north Africa. He firmly opposed co-operation with imperial authorities during the Diocletian or 'Great' Persecution (303–5). After playing a key role in organising opposition to Caecilian's election as bishop of Carthage prior to 312, he was condemned on 3 October 313 by a synod of bishops convoked by Miltiades, bishop of Rome (acting under instructions from the emperor Constantine), for having rebaptised the *lapsi*, those Christians who had weakened under torture or its threat, and who had participated in the pagan cult during the persecution. He was undeterred by the emperor Constantine's later vindication of Caecilian (AD 316) and persecution of his opponents (cf. Letters 88.3 and 105.9). In 313 he succeeded Maiorinus as the rival bishop of Carthage to Caecilian. He used this office to promote his campaign against baptisms performed by ministers not in communion with himself. However, we lack any of his writings and we cannot specify his aims in this period with great precision. He outwitted an attempt by Gregory, the praetorian prefect for Africa, to depose him in 336, and in that same year convened a council of over 270 bishops at Carthage. An attempt in 346 to have the emperor Constans recognise him as sole bishop of Carthage failed when the emperor sent Paul and Macarius as legates to investigate the rival claims between himself and Caecilian's successor, Gratus. He was unable to persuade the legates to his point of view and is said to have complained,

'What has the emperor to do with the church?' During an ensuing period of violence, spurred on by the Circumcellions, and following Constans' decree of unity under Gratus, he was arrested and exiled, most probably to Gaul. He never returned to Africa.

DONATUS (2), proconsul of Africa in 408. He had been charged by the emperor Honorius with enforcing the severe laws against the Donatists promulgated along with the Edict of Unity (405) and in subsequent edicts (cf. *C. Th.* 16.5.44: 24 November 408). A. wrote imploring him not to impose the death penalty against the Donatists (cf. Letter 100). He was a devout Catholic and a property owner at Hippo Regius.

DONATUS (3), Donatist priest of Mutugenna, not far from Hippo Regius. Disappointed by the results of the conference of 411, he inflicted wounds upon himself and attempted suicide from which he was rescued by some Catholics (cf. Letter 173).

DONATUS (4), Catholic deacon, subsequently rebaptised when formally converted to Donatism. He was implicated in violent reprisals against Catholics following the conference of Carthage (1–8 June 411), and most probably took part in the attempt against the life of the Catholic priest Innocent (cf. Letters 139.2; 133; and 134).

DULCITIUS, tribune and notary at Carthage for the province of Africa Proconsularis (420–2). He was a Catholic, despatched by the emperor Honorius with instructions to suppress the Donatists. A. developed a friendship with him and wrote a treatise responding to eight questions posed by him, *De octo Dulcitii quaestionibus.*

ELEUSINUS, tribune serving at Timgad in Numidia (modern Algeria). He may have been commanding troops at an outpost near the town. He passed on to A. a request from the people of the town that he respond to two letters written by its Donatist bishop, Gaudentius (cf. Letter 204.9).

EMERITUS, Donatist bishop of Caesarea in Mauretania Caesariensis (Cherchel, Algeria), where he was born. He played an important role at the Donatist council of Bagai which, in April 394, condemned the Donatist bishop of Carthage, Maximian, along with his followers. He was the key representative of the Donatist bishops at the conference of Carthage in June 411, and distinguished himself both for his knowledge of Roman procedural law and for the deftness of his interventions. A. wrote *Ad Emeritum Donatistarum episcopum post conlationem* for him, a work no longer extant, some time prior to their chance encounter at Caesarea on 18 September 418. There, A. attempted again to convince him to make peace with the Catholic church, but he refused.

EVODIUS, bishop of Uzalis in Africa Proconsularis (modern Tunisia). A friend and companion of A. in their youth, he founded a monastery at Uzalis and became bishop there some time between 395/397 and 401. As an ally of A., he was zealous in opposing Donatism. On 16 June 404 he was despatched, along with Theasius, to represent the African Catholic bishops in a complaint to the emperor Honorius against Donatist and, in particular, Circumcellion aggression. Along with Theasius, he was instructed to appeal that the emperor apply to the Donatists the earlier legislation of the emperor Theodosius I against heretics, especially the edict fining those responsible for disturbing Catholics ten pounds of gold. At Rome, he and Theasius discovered that in the wake of the assault committed by Circumcellions against Maximian, the Catholic bishop of Bagai, the emperor Honorius had already promulgated the more radical Edict of Unity (12 February 405), in effect ordering the suppression of the Donatists. He was wounded in an attack by Donatists some time prior to 408 and was accused by Petilian, Donatist bishop of Constantine, of having persecuted Donatists. He died after 424.

FELIX, Catholic bishop of Apthugni (today Henchir Es-Souar, Tunisia). He was bishop during the Diocletian or 'Great' Persecution (303–5). Following the death of Mensurius *c.* 309/312, he was one of three bishops who consecrated Caecilian bishop of Carthage. He was accused by Caecilian's opponents of having been a *traditor* during the persecution (cf. Translator's note on Hand over). For this reason he was considered by the followers of Maiorinus and Donatus to have invalidated the episcopal consecration of Caecilian. They demanded that he be examined on the charge of *traditio*. In

313, he was cleared of the charge during a synod of bishops meeting at Rome under Miltiades, the bishop of Rome. He was also exonerated at Carthage on 15 February 314 by a tribunal conducted by Aelian, the proconsul of Africa. The tribunal determined that he was absent from Apthugni on the day of the *traditio*, and that he was not guilty of conspiring with Alfius Caecilian, the *duumvir* at Apthugni, to have the sacred books seized and burned in his absence.

FIRMUS, a Moorish prince, son of Nubel and brother of Gildo. Drawing on discontent over heavy Roman taxation, as chief of the Jubaleni he led a rebellion of the native people in the Roman province of Mauretania Caesariensis (in modern Algeria) *c.* 372–5. He succeeded in having himself recognised by various tribes as king. The revolt he led was violent; Roman cities were destroyed by his Berber forces. He supported the Donatist cause, and they supported his. He opposed the followers of Rogatus, a splinter-group of Donatists who referred to the latter as 'Firmians'. He was finally defeated by Flavius Theodosius and committed suicide.

GAUDENTIUS, Donatist bishop of Timgad in Numidia (in modern Algeria) (398–421). He was the successor of Optatus, and was one of the seven Donatist spokesmen at the conference of Carthage in 411. Some time around 420 the notary Dulcitius challenged him, ordering him to obey the edicts issued by the emperor Honorius in 412 including the handing over of church property to the Catholics. He refused and threatened to set himself on fire in his church. A. wrote *Contra Gaudentium* to him at Dulcitius' request (cf. *Letter* 204). It is not known whether he carried out his threat.

GILDO, son of Nubel, chieftain of an indigenous tribe in the Roman province of Mauretania Caesariensis. He opposed his brother Firmus' revolt *c.* 372–5 against the Roman occupation. In 386 he was rewarded with appointment by the emperor Theodosius to the high military and civil position of imperial commissioner (*comes*) of Africa. He openly broke with Theodosius during Eugenius' revolt (392–4), and began to back the Donatists against the Catholics in north Africa. His growing opposition to the Western empire led to an open revolt in 397 during which he received support from

Optatus, the Donatist bishop of Timgad. He was defeated and killed by his brother, Mascazel, in 398.

GRATUS, Catholic bishop of Carthage. He succeeded Caecilian as bishop when Donatus was the rival bishop. After the latter's forced exile in 347, he ruled without a Donatist rival for the remainder of his life. He convened a council of bishops in 348 to ban rebaptism and to seek to reform the clergy, whose habits provided a constant source of tension with Donatist sympathisers. He died before 359.

HONORIUS, FLAVIUS (384–423), son of the emperor Theodosius I and Roman emperor of the West (393–423). He was emperor during most of A.'s episcopacy. From the beginning of his reign until 402 he ruled from Milan; afterward the court transferred to Ravenna. He was weak with respect to his military leaders, in particular towards Stilicho, and was unable to halt the advance of the Gothic tribes or to prevent the sack of Rome in 410 by Alaric. After 421 he relied on assistance for governing from his co-regent, the emperor Constantius, and from his generals. In his religious policy, he showed considerable partiality to the Catholic church and conceded privileges to its clergy. In 405 he imposed the Edict of Unity against the Donatists, and in 418 and 419 he condemned members of the 'Pelagian' movement. He took a firm stance against the various pagan cults, and the effects of this policy were strongly felt in north Africa.

INGENTIUS, a witness in the trial for *traditio* of Felix, bishop of Apthugni. During the Diocletian or 'Great' Persecution in 303, he was a scribe in the imperial civil service at Apthugni. Eleven years later, he was a town councillor at Ziqua in Africa Proconsul (today Zaghorian, Tunisia). He put pressure on Alfius Caecilian, who had served as *duumvir* at Apthugni during the Persecution, to dictate a letter addressed to Felix concerning the events which had taken place there in 303. To this letter he forged a postscript falsely alleging that Felix had conspired with the *duumvir* in order to facilitate the handing over of sacred books. His forgery was discovered during a trial before Aelian, the proconsul of Africa, which concluded on 15 February 315. He confessed under the threat of torture. As a result of this and of Caecilian's testimony, Felix was vindicated (cf. Letter 88.4).

INNOCENT, a Catholic priest of Hippo Regius. Along with Restitutus, he was a victim of Circumcellion and Donatist violence at some time following the conference of Carthage in June 411, but prior to March 412. He suffered the gouging of one of his eyes and the severing of a finger. Cf. Letter 133.1; 134.2.

JANUARIUS, Donatist bishop of Casae Nigrae in Numidia (modern Algeria). He was one of the leading figures in the Donatist church from 394 to 411, and the primate of Donatist bishops during the conference of Carthage in 411.

JEROME (*c.* 347–419), influential church theologian, biblical expert and writer during A.'s lifetime. He pursued a career in the imperial service at Trier before abandoning it in favour of monasticism in 370, first at Aquileia, later in Syria where he was ordained a priest. He returned to Rome in 382 and was secretary to Damasus, the bishop of Rome. Following Damasus' death, he travelled to Bethlehem where he lived an ascetic life devoted to biblical study and theological controversy.

JULIAN (1), the Apostate (331–63), Roman emperor (361–3). Baptised and instructed as a Christian under bishop Eusebius of Nicomedia, he studied classical literature and philosophy, and entered the diaconate as a young man. Beginning in 351, he became familiar with Neoplatonism at Constantinople. While detained at Athens in 354 for suspicion of involvement in plots against the emperor Constantius, he deepened his knowledge of philosophy and rejected his Christianity. During his brief reign as emperor, he attempted social and fiscal reforms and restored imperial favour to the pagan cults, finally re-initiating a limited persecution of Christians. He banned all but classical authors from schools throughout the empire, and re-organised pagan worship. His edict revoking the banishment of bishops exiled by his predecessor, Constantius, resulted in the return to Africa of several Donatist bishops. He restored Donatist properties legally seized by Catholics in 347 and revoked the laws against rebaptism. He was celebrated for this by Numidian Donatists.

JULIAN (2) (380/386–*c.* 455), bishop of Eclanum (in southern Italy) (416–18). He dissented from Zosimus' *Epistula tractoria*, condemning the Pelagians, and was himself condemned and deposed from his see in 418. He subsequently wrote to Zosimus two letters asking for clarifications, and word of this reached A., who sent him Book 1 of *De nuptiis et concupiscentia*, an essay on the implications of original sin for marriage and sexuality. In response to A., he wrote four books dedicated to Turbantius, an Italian bishop who had sided with him against Zosimus (cf. Letter 10*.1). A. responded to the challenge initially with Book 2 of *De nuptiis* and with *Contra Iulianum*. The controversy grew heated but was limited by A.'s death in 430, which prevented completion of yet another work, called the *Contra Iulianum opus imperfectum*.

LUCIFER, bishop of Cagliari in Sardinia from at least 354 to 370/371. He was deposed from his see by the emperor Constantius for refusing to join the condemnation of Athanasius at the council of Milan (355). When the emperor Julian allowed exiled bishops to return to their sees, he travelled instead to Antioch where he became embroiled in a local church feud between rival factions in the Arian controversy. He ordained Paulinus, leader of one of the factions, as bishop of Antioch, thus fuelling the rivalry and contributing to a schism. A. complains that in taking such a radical step, he thwarted the attempt of more moderate bishops, such as Meletius, to reconcile extreme points of view between the two principal parties to the dispute (cf. Letter 185.47).

MACARIUS, one of two legates despatched to Africa some time between 343 and 345 in an effort to investigate the controversy between Catholics and Donatists, particularly at Carthage. Along with Paul, the other legate, he tended quickly to favour the position of bishop Gratus over that of Donatus. Thus, he developed a policy of encouraging unity between the two parties, a position which earned him further disapproval and opposition from the Donatists, especially from Circumcellions throughout Numidia. He reacted swiftly and severely, calling in troops, which resulted in many deaths among Donatists at Bagai including that of the bishop, also named Donatus. Following this incident, he proscribed Donatism and proclaimed unity between the two churches under Gratus. Attempts at conciliation by Donatist bishops were in vain. He arrested and flogged ten Donatist bishops. He had Marculus, the leader of the group, paraded throughout the province and executed on 29 November 347. He arrested Donatus and exiled him to Gaul.

MACEDONIUS, vicar of Africa (413–14), thus charged with the legal administration of the civil diocese of Africa. Macedonius was a Catholic Christian, devoted to A. as a spiritual son. Upon request, A. sent him the first three books of *City of God* (cf. Letters 152–5).

MACROBIUS, Donatist bishop of Hippo Regius (406–11). He was the recipient of A.'s *ep.* 106, complaining about his having rebaptised a Catholic subdeacon who joined the Donatists. Though initially critical of the activities of the Circumcellions, he later urged them to occupy Donatist churches in the face of the emperor Honorius' order (412) that they be forfeited to the Catholics (cf. Letter 139).

MAIORINUS, rival bishop of Carthage who opposed the election of Caecilian as successor to Mensurius *c.* 309/312. With the financial assistance of a wealthy Christian woman, Lucilla, and the support of Donatus, he allied himself with a large number of Carthaginians and Numidian clergy in opposition to the new bishop. Seventy bishops supported him in a local council presided over by the Numidian primate, Secundus of Tigisis. He was chosen by the dissident bishops as bishop of Carthage. With this action the schism which would later be called 'Donatist' was initiated (cf. Letter 88.1–2). He was also a party to the formal complaint which the council lodged with the emperor Constantine petitioning for Caecilian's removal. He ordained other bishops, but died shortly after taking office, probably some time in 313.

MARCELLINUS, FLAVIUS, a tribune (commander of a military regiment) and notary (a high-ranking official of the imperial chancery charged with various tasks concerning the maintenance of public order). He was a Catholic and a friend of A. who wrote him six letters and dedicated three works to him. He was appointed by the emperor Honorius to preside over the conference of Carthage, which was convened in June 411. Suspected of collusion in the revolt of the usurper Heraclian against Honorius, he and his brother Apringius were arrested and executed on 13 September 413 in spite of the intervention of African bishops led by A.

MARCIANUS, perhaps a Catholic priest at Urga, near Hippo Regius. As a Donatist priest he converted to the Catholic church prior to the Edict of Unity in 405. He was later attacked by Donatist clergy and by Circumcellions some time prior to June 410 (cf. Letter 105.3).

MARCUS, Catholic priest of Casphaliana, near Hippo Regius. He converted to the Catholic church from Donatism some time prior to the Edict of Unity in 405. He was later attacked by Donatist clergy and by Circumcellions some time prior to June 410 (cf. Letter 105.3).

MAXIMIAN (1), Donatist deacon at Carthage and eponym of a splinter-group of Donatists. He was excommunicated for reasons unknown to us by Primian, bishop of Carthage, in 391/392. Along with forty-three Donatist bishops, he protested against the action, but in vain. In 393 he was elected bishop of Carthage by more than a hundred Donatist bishops who deposed Primian in order to do so. He and his supporters were subsequently excommunicated by Primian and 310 bishops meeting at Bagai in 394. A schism was born which bore his name. It is not known when he died. A. described the movement as having opposed Donatist and Circumcellion violence (cf. *c. ep. Parm.* 2.3.7), and as a reform group within Donatism. It attracted a limited number of adherents. A partial reconciliation took place in 397 under the intervention of Gildo and the Circumcellions (cf. Letters 51.3–5; 87.6; 185.17).

MAXIMIAN (2), Catholic bishop of Bagai in Numidia (modern Algeria). About 401, he converted from Donatism to Catholicism and served for a year as Catholic bishop of Bagai. On 27 August 402 he resigned his see at the suggestion of bishops during a council meeting at Carthage, perhaps on the grounds that he had recently been a Donatist. For reasons unknown, it seems that he may once again have been in possession of the see in 404. He provoked Circumcellion aggression against himself when he had recourse to the judicial system in order to take possession of a Catholic chapel near the town. He was seized from the church, physically assaulted and left for dead. As he was borne away by Catholics singing psalms, he was seized a second time and thrown from a tower. He survived even this second attack. Rumours spread that he had been killed. He went to Ravenna to complain to the court of the emperor Honorius.

His direct intervention is thought to have moved the emperor to issue the Edict of Unity on 12 February 405.

MAXIMINUS, Catholic bishop of Sinitus in Numidia (modern Algeria). He was a convert to Catholicism from Donatism some time after January 406 and by 408 was bishop of Sinitus. At this time he and his people became the object of Donatist threats and abuse (cf. Letter 105.4)

MAXIMUS. In the proceedings concerning Felix, bishop of Apthugni, he was the spokesman of the party accusing the bishop of *traditio* during a preliminary hearing on 19 January 314. He further requested that testimony against Felix be taken by Alfius Caecilian, one of the *duumviri* present at Apthugni during the alleged *traditio* (cf. Translator's note on Hand over).

NECTARIUS, a pagan born in the town of Calama (today Guelma, Algeria), who rose to a high position in the imperial civil service. (Some scholars assume that he remained in Calama, but cf. Huisman, *Augustinus' Briefwisseling*, 9–20.) A. acknowledges that he is now 'nearing the end of his life' (Letter 91.6). He urges A. to beg for leniency toward non-Christian inhabitants of Calama, a number of whom were accused of committing acts of violence against the church there beginning on 1 June 408 and continuing eight days later (cf. Letter 90). The violence occurred when the town's Catholic clergy legally intervened against an unlawful pagan religious ceremony involving a dance which was carried out in front of the church. Once assured that A. would oppose any application of torture or the death penalty against those accused of violating the laws (cf. Letter 91), he wrote to A. a second time urging him to oppose even the confiscation of the goods of the accused, arguing that a life of poverty was worse than death (cf. Letter 103). His two letters to A. concerning the incidents (Letters 90 and 104) and the latter's responses (Letters 91 and 104) exhibit the clash between traditional Roman patriotism (love for one's home town or *patria*), rooted in civil theology, and Augustinian Christian civic ideals.

NICOMACHUS FLAVIANUS, VIRIUS (*c.* 335–94), a pagan and member of a senatorial family, who served in various posts in the civil administration. He was vicar of Africa in 376–7. In this role, he was governor of the Roman civil diocese of Africa, comprising seven provinces. He was deputy of the praetorian prefect and heard judicial appeals from the courts administered by the provincial governors of Africa (with the exception of Africa Proconsularis). On 17 October 377, the emperor Gratian despatched a constitution to him (*C. Th.* 16.6.2) prohibiting the Donatist practice of rebaptism and banning their meetings. In 389–90 he served as quaestor of the sacred palace, and in 390–2 and again from 393 to 394 as praetorian prefect for Italy, Illyricum and Africa. In this office, while supporting Eugenius in a civil war, he backed efforts to revive public, pagan cultic practices, hoping also to suppress Christianity. Eugenius appointed him consul for the year 394. He committed suicide following Eugenius' defeat.

OPTATUS (1), Catholic bishop of Milevis in Numidia (modern Algeria) during the fourth century. He was the author of six books against the Donatists, written between 364 and 367. The original title of the work is not known; however, it is a reply to an anti-Catholic essay by the Donatist bishop Parmenius, and influenced A's own theological writing against the Donatists.

OPTATUS (2), Donatist bishop of Timgad in southern Numidia (modern Algeria) (388–98). A notorious opponent of Catholicism, he is also known for his efforts to crush followers of Maximian in their attempt to reform Donatism, an effort which ended in schism. He seems to have been an unscrupulous supporter of the Circumcellions. He also supported Gildo in 397/398 during the latter's rebellion against the emperor Honorius. For this he was condemned and executed.

PAUL, with Macarius, one of the two legates despatched to Africa some time between 343 and 345 in an effort to investigate the controversy between Catholics and Donatists, particularly at Carthage. See the Biographical Note for MACARIUS.

PAULINUS OF NOLA (355–431). Born into a wealthy senatorial family at Bordeaux, he received a traditional Roman education stressing rhetoric, and by 378 was serving as a magistrate and possibly a governor in Campania in southern Italy. He returned to Gaul after 383 when his political fortunes soured under the emperor Valentinian II. He was baptised at Bordeaux in 389. While in Spain he and his wife, Therasia, a woman of a wealthy Spanish aristocratic family, embraced an ascetical lifestyle. He was 'elected' priest by popular acclaim at Barcelona in 394, later claiming that he had been 'dragged by force' into the priesthood (cf. Paulinus, *ep.* 1.10; 2.2; 3.4). In 395 he abandoned Spain for Nola in southern Italy where, with Therasia and some friends, he once again lived in ascetic retirement. At this time he described his wife to Jerome as 'my sister' (cf. Jerome, *ep.* 58.6). She died in 409. Coincidentally, the episcopal see of Nola became vacant and he accepted it. He was an ecclesiastical writer of letters and poetry focused upon Christian themes. He and A. engaged in a correspondence characterised by warmth.

PELAGIUS, eponym of a loosely constructed ascetical movement in the early fifth century. He fled Rome for Africa following the Gothic migrations in about 408–10. He did not remain long in Africa and by 413 he was settled in Palestine where, in 415, he had to defend himself against charges of heterodoxy before a council of bishops convened at Diospolis in Palestine. He was absolved on all counts. By this time A. was committed to opposing his theological views on human nature, original sin, free will and grace. On 27 January 417, Innocent I, bishop of Rome, condemned him along with Celestius for teaching heresy. In September of that year, Innocent's successor, Zosimus, rehabilitated the pair, but then reversed himself with the *Epistula tractoria* in June/July 418. The African bishops, led by A., pressed Rome firmly for the condemnation of the 'Pelagians', as this group was now called. The emperor Honorius also condemned their views definitively on 9 June 419.

PETILIAN, Donatist bishop of Constantine or Cirta in Numidia (today Constantine, Algeria) (*c.* 395–412). Baptised a Catholic in his youth, he was later converted to Donatism. Having been trained in classical rhetoric and law, he became a bishop during A.'s episcopacy and served as the chief spokesman of the Donatists. In 400/401 he wrote an *Epistula ad presbyteros*, a strong pamphlet outlining the Donatist case on historical and theological grounds. A. responded in 401 with Book 1 of *Contra litteras Petiliani*. He replied to A.'s work with *Ad*

Augustinum, and A. replied with Book 2 of *c. litt. Pet.* The two also sparred in 410 over Petilian's *De unico baptismo*, to which A. replied with *De unico baptismo contra Petilianum*. At the conference of Carthage in 411 he was for the last time the Donatists' principal representative. He was deposed from his see in 412, and is not heard of after 415.

POSSIDIUS, bishop of Calama (today Guelma in Algeria), disciple, close friend and first biographer of A. He lived with A. in the monastery at Hippo Regius from 391 until soon after 397 when he became bishop of Calama. He narrowly escaped an ambush following a council of bishops at Carthage on 25 August 403, during which he had challenged Crispin, his Donatist episcopal counterpart at Calama, to a public debate. Spurned by Crispin, he set out to visit Figula, an estate within his diocese. He learned that a Donatist ambush had been prepared for him, and retreated to another estate, Oliveta, where his attackers, led by Crispin, a Donatist priest with the same name as their bishop, caught up with him, threw stones at the house and set it on fire. He escaped death narrowly when Crispin prevented one of their party from splitting his head with a stone (cf. Letter 105.4). On 1 June 408, he intervened at Calama to impede certain rites connected with a pagan festival after they had been banned by the emperor Honorius on 24 November 407 (cf. *C. Th.* 16.10.9). A riot ensued and stones were hurled at his church. Eight days later, in accord with legal procedure, he formally complained to the city's officials and the church was attacked once again. On the following day when the church was stoned a third time and set ablaze, he narrowly escaped death by hiding from members of the mob, perhaps in his own house (cf. Letter 91.8). Shortly after this, he was delegated by other bishops to travel to the imperial court at Ravenna in order to beg the emperor for greater protection of the Catholic church in north Africa (cf. Letter 95.1). He was one of the seven Catholic spokesmen at the conference of Carthage in 411. He appealed with A. in 416 to Innocent, bishop of Rome, against Pelagius and Celestius. He took refuge with A. at Hippo Regius when the Vandals were moving eastward across north Africa from Spain (*c.* 428–30) and was present when A. died (28 August 430). He conducted a thorough inventory of A.'s works from the church's library at Hippo Regius. At some time after A.'s death, but before 437, he wrote a biography of A.

PRIMIAN, Donatist bishop of Carthage (*c.* 392–412). Shortly after his consecration as bishop he ran into opposition from a Carthaginian deacon, Maximian. He excommunicated the deacon, but incurred excommunication himself on 24 June 393 by a council of more than 100 bishops presided over by the Donatist episcopal primate of Byzacena. On 24 April 394 he was exonerated by a council of 310 bishops meeting at Bagai in Numidia. The same council condemned the followers of Maximian, ensuring a fully fledged schism within the Donatist church. He was a strong supporter of Optatus of Timgad, also in Numidia. In September 403, he rejected an invitation from the Catholics to discuss ways of ending the schism between the two churches. He led the Donatist delegation at the conference of Carthage in 411. Although he was certainly deposed in 412 as a consequence of the conference, nothing is known of him from this time.

REGULUS, MARCUS ATILIUS, Roman military commander. He was captured by the Carthaginians during the First Punic War, and was sent back to Rome to negotiate an exchange of prisoners, having vowed to return if he failed. He recommended to the Romans that they reject the terms offered and returned to Carthage, as he had promised, to face his death. About him, A. commented that 'among all their heroes, men worthy of honour and renowned for courage, the Romans have none greater to produce' (*civ.* 1.24).

RESTITUTUS (1), a Catholic priest of Hippo Regius. Soon after the conference of Carthage in June 411 (before 29 February 412), he was ambushed and killed by Circumcellions and members of the Donatist clergy. Another Catholic priest, Innocent, was severely beaten and maimed at the same time (cf. Letter 133.1; 134.2). A. asked for judicial clemency for the alleged assassins. Some historians identify him with Restitutus of Victoriana (cf. below, RESTITUTUS (2)). Others hold that the two priests are unrelated because A's accounts of Restitutus of Victoriana do not mention the assassination.

RESTITUTUS (2), Catholic priest of Victoriana who converted from Donatism to Catholicism prior to the Edict of Unity in 405. He was seized from his home, beaten and held captive for a number of days by Donatist clergy and Circumcellions some time prior to June 410, but was released by Proculianus, the Donatist bishop of Hippo at the time (cf. Letter 105.3).

ROGATUS, Donatist bishop of Cartenna in the province of Mauretania Caesariensis (Ténès, Algeria), and eponymous leader of a sect which broke away from mainline Donatists in 370 and which was largely concentrated in this western north African province. He held open the possibility that Catholics could be admitted to the Donatist ranks without rebaptism. The sect was also non-violent and thus opposed the Circumcellions. He was despised by the Donatist bishop Optatus of Timgad who mounted a vigorous campaign against him. Firmus also acted forcefully against him and members of his splinter group, *c.* 372–5.

SPONDEUS, a *procurator* responsible for the economic administration of Celer's estate near Hippo Regius. Following the conference of Carthage in 411, he acted forcefully to prevent Donatists under Macrobius, the Donatist bishop of Hippo Regius, from utilising the estate for clandestine meetings and worship. Following his departure for Carthage some time prior to 29 February 412, the Donatists used his own estate for such purposes (cf. Letter 139.2).

STILICHO, FLAVIUS (*c.* 365–408), half-Roman, half-Vandal, principal political and military leader in the Western empire from the time of the death of the emperor Theodosius (395) until his own death. He was *comes domesticorum*, commander of the imperial guard, in about 385, but by 393 Theodosius had named him *magister militum*, commander-in-chief of the army, a post he held for the remainder of his life. He conducted successful military campaigns as far west as Britain and as far east as Greece. In Italy, he directed the military campaign against Gildo during the latter's north African revolt against Theodosius in 397–8. In 400 he was named consul. He defended Milan, home of the emperor Honorius, from attack by Alaric and the Visigoths in 401. He defeated Alaric first at Pollentia in 402, then at Verona in 403, and was equally successful against the incursions of Radagaisus, an Ostrogothic chieftain, into northern Italy in 405–6. During the latter two years of his life he was accused of plotting treason against Honorius in favour of his own son, Eucherius. During a revolt against the emperor, he was executed at Ravenna by imperial troops on 23 August 408.

THEASIUS, Catholic bishop of Memblonatana, perhaps identified with Membressa (Medjez el Bab) or with Membrositanus (Sidi Ahmed bou Farès), in the province of Africa Proconsularis (modern Tunisia). Along with Evodius, he was despatched on 16 June 404 to represent Catholic bishops to the emperor Honorius in their complaint against Donatist and Circumcellion violence (cf. above, EVODIUS). At some time prior to October 408, he was wounded in an attack by Donatists. He was present at the conference of Carthage in 411, and was still bishop in 425. He died some time prior to 430.

THEODOSIUS I (*c.* 346–95). A military officer who in 379 was appointed emperor for the East by the emperor Gratian. In 387 he defeated Magnus Maximus, the usurper of the Western empire, who had killed Gratian and expelled Valentinian II from Italy. He installed his sons Arcadius and Honorius as emperors, respectively, for the Eastern and Western empires. He was renowned in Catholic circles as a pious, Christian emperor, largely because of his anti-heretical and anti-pagan legislation. For example, on 3 August 379 he proscribed all heretical sects and assemblies and banned rebaptism. In 380 he ordered all imperial subjects to profess the Catholic faith. In 381 he ordered all heretical churches to be confiscated. On 19 January 386 he ordered the death penalty to be applied to anyone who disturbed the practice of the Catholic faith. These measures had little effect upon Donatism in north Africa, as Donatism was not defined in legal terms as a heresy until 405.

TURBANTIUS, an Italian bishop during the second decade of the fifth century, who took the side of Julian, bishop of Eclanum, in his dispute with Zosimus, bishop of Rome, following the latter's publication of his *Epistula tractoria* in 418. He was the addressee of Julian's first of four books *Ad Turbantium*, written in response to A.'s *De nuptiis et concupiscentia*. He recanted his position and was reconciled to the church by 428 (cf. Letter 10*.1).

VALENTINUS, Catholic bishop of Baiana in Numidia (modern Algeria) and episcopal primate of Numidia. He may have been bishop of the town as early as 402. In January 406, he travelled to the imperial court at Ravenna as the head of an African Catholic delegation of bishops. A Donatist delegation of bishops arrived at the court and wished to debate with him in the presence of the praetorian prefects. Their request was denied on 30 January 406 (cf. Letter 88.10). He participated in numerous councils against the Donatists, including the conference of Carthage in 411. He also attended the council of Milevis in 416 when it took a strong stand against Pelagius and Celestius.

VINDICIANUS (HELVIUS), proconsul of the province of Africa (379–82). He was a well-known physician at Carthage, and in 382 awarded A. a prize in an oratorical contest, while also persuading him to abandon his belief in astrology (cf. *conf.* 4.3.5).

VOLUSIANUS, RUFIUS ANTONIUS AGRYPNIUS, proconsul of Africa, perhaps as late as 411 when he lived at Carthage and corresponded with A. (cf. Letters 138; 139). He left Carthage to return to Italy in 412. He was a pagan at the time, although his mother, whose name we do not know, was a Christian. His correspondence with A. concerned his own reasons for refusing baptism (cf. *ep.* 132; 135; 137). These included his difficulties in accepting the doctrine of the incarnation and his doubts that an empire guided by Christian political leaders would be capable of defending itself against its enemies, since Christ's teaching rejected the use of force (cf. Letter 138.9–16). He was a friend of Marcellinus with whom A. also corresponded about these objections (cf. Letters 136; 138). He served as prefect of the city of Rome in 417–18 at the time of the condemnation of Pelagius and Celestius by the bishop of Rome, Zosimus, and by the emperor Honorius. He later served as a praetorian prefect for Italy and Africa from 428 to 429 at the time of the revolt of Boniface. He died at Constantinople on 6 January 437, having been persuaded some time before by Melania the Younger to accept baptism.

ZOSIMUS, bishop of Rome (417–18). In September 417, he readmitted Pelagius and Celestius to full ecclesial communion after they had been excommunicated by his predecessor, Innocent, in January of that year. When the African bishops protested against this decision, he modified his stance in the *Epistula tractoria* of June/July 418. In this letter he condemned Pelagius and Celestius for heresy. The action provoked a schism among eighteen Italian bishops including Julian of Eclanum and Turbantius.

Notes to the text

Christianity and citizenship

Letter 90

1 Cf. Biographical note on Nectarius.
2 A commonplace sentiment in Roman antiquity. Devotion to the *patria*, to one's 'home-town', constituted the apex of the classical scheme of relig-ious and political virtues. Cf. Cicero, *De officiis* 1.57; *De partitione orator-iae* 25.8; *De re publica* 6.16. Acknowledging that he might be 'excused' from his 'duties' to his home-town on account of his advanced age, Nectarius clearly implies that, nevertheless, he has been officially requested to intercede with A., probably by Calama's municipal council (*curia*).
3 Calama, a small city 65 km southwest of Hippo Regius, was the scene of rioting beginning on 1 June 408, and continuing eight days later. Cf. Letter 91.8, pp. 5–6, for A.'s account of the events (cf. also Letter 104.5, pp. 13–14).
4 Bishops at A.'s time possessed ecclesiastical as well as a limited civil authority to hear cases and issue judgements which on occasion involved the application of penalties. The civil aspects of this judicial authority, known as the 'bishop's tribunal' (*audientia episcopalis, iudicivm episcopale*), derived from imperial constitutions issued by the emperor Constantine in AD 318 and 333 (*C.Th.* 1.27.1; *Sirm.* 1). Bishops looked to 1 Cor 6.1–6, where Paul warned Corinthian Christians not to litigate with each other before secular judges, but to be reconciled to one another within the Christian community (cf. *en. Ps.* 118.24.3). Among matters about which Augustine rendered judgements were claims involving property owner-ship, slavery, contracts and inheritances (*ep.* 33.5; 83; 8*; 20*; *en. Ps.* 25.2.13; 80.2.21; 118.24.3). Cf. Dodaro, 'Church and State'.

5 Nectarius distinguishes between civil damages (*damnum*) which could be set by a trial, and a range of possible criminal penalties (*supplicivm*). A. takes up the point at Letter 91.9 (pp. 6–7).

Letter 91

1 Cf. Biographical Note on Julian (1), the Apostate, and on Possidius.
2 Cf. Letter 90: Nectarius to A. (pp. 1–2 and n. 2).
3 The opposition which A. sets out between the earthly home-town of Nectarius and the other, 'much finer city' whose citizens are on pilgrimage (§ 1) adumbrates the central theme of the *City of God*. Cf. for example, *civ.* 1. preface; 1.35 (pilgrimage); 12.23 (everlasting peace); 15.18 (heavenly city).
4 Cf. Virgil, *Aeneid* 7.643–4. A. is punning here on *florere*: flourishing/flowering.
5 Cicero, *De re publica*. The exact location of this quotation is unknown; the extant text is fragmentary.
6 Cicero, *De re publica* 4.7.7 (*frag.*).
7 A. is thinking of those 'older Romans', the various speakers in Cicero's *De re publica*, such as P. Cornelius Scipio Aemilianus, C. Laelius Sapiens, Q. Aelius Tubero and Q. Mucivs Scaevola Augur. Cf. *civ.* 2.9; 2.14.
8 *Eunuchus* 3.5. A. makes a similar point with respect to the same text at *conf.* 1.16.26 and *civ.* 2.7; 2.12.
9 *De re publica* 4.10.11.
10 A. develops this specific argument at *civ.* 2.9–14. Similar criticisms of the theatrical content of Roman religion are found at *civ.* 6.7–9.
11 At *civ.* 6.8; 7.5; and 7.19, A. criticises attempts to interpret such rituals as symbolic explanations of natural phenomena.
12 Cf. *civ.* 6.10, where A. cites Seneca's *De superstitione* against the cult of Jupiter celebrated on the Capitoline hill at Rome.
13 The festival called the *ludi Florae* was traditionally celebrated from some time after 28 April until 3 May. Cf. *civ.* 2.27; 4.8.
14 A. appeals here to Nectarius' sense of morality and respect for law. Both Roman law and Christian ethics prohibited adultery. The Catholic church normally excommunicated those found guilty of it, a sanction which could only be removed upon completion of formal penance. Cf. Letter 153.9–11; 15 (pp. 76–7; 79–80); as well as the explanation given below, p. 267 n. 4.
15 The laws referred to were imperial 'edicts' or 'constitutions', decisions of the emperors on various matters which, when promulgated, had the force of law. On 15 November 407, Honorius published an edict in which pagan religious ceremonies were banned, Catholic bishops were given the right

to prohibit them, even using church personnel to do so, and magistrates and their staffs were obliged under pain of fines to enforce the regulations. See *C. Th.* 16.10.19 = *Sirm.* 12. A. does not identify the 'idolatrous ritual' celebrated at Calama.

16 Cf. above, n. 15, referring to *C. Th.* 16.10.19.

17 Formal notification to the authorities of an injury suffered by a party consisted in the complaint being recorded in public acts (*acta*), a mandatory step in preparation for judicial action by magistrates.

18 *hora ferme decima*: literally 'the tenth hour', near to 6.00 or 6.30 p.m., based on calculations of the position of the summer sun at Calama. Cf. Huisman, *Augustinus' Briefwisseling*, 114.

19 *primates*: a reference to the town's magistrates and councillors (*curiales*), who, A. suggests, might have been accomplices to, and even instigators of, the anti-Christian violence. See below, § 9.

20 Under Roman law from the fourth century, only those confessions secured by application of torture were considered valid. Cf. *C. Th.* 9.35.1 (AD 369); 9.35.2 (AD 376); 9.35.3 (AD 377). A. was unwilling to pursue inquiries by this means.

21 A. indicates to Nectarius that he will oppose application of the death penalty against pagan inhabitants of Calama convicted of playing any role in the criminal violence committed against Christians in this affair.

22 Late June or some time during July 408.

23 A. knew of an earlier case of anti-Christian violence committed by pagans distressed at recent imperial legislation banning their religious practices. In 399 rioting erupted at Sufes in the province of Byzacena (modern Tunisia) shortly after the publication by the emperor Honorius of a constitution, addressed to the proconsul of Africa, which ordered that statues of idols be removed from temples throughout the province (cf. *C. Th.* 16.10.18). Sixty Christians were killed after some of their number entered a temple and destroyed a statue of Hercules. A. accused members of the municipal council of complicity in the violence. Cf. *ep.* 50.

Letter 103

1 The reference is obscure: perhaps Nectarius is constructing a stock philosopher by conflating several literary elements. Some details recall Socrates, but the Academy was founded after him by his pupil Plato, and later became known for its sceptical criticisms of other philosophers' positions. The Lyceum was the name of a different school, founded by Aristotle. If the text is sound, Nectarius must mean by 'Lyceum' something like 'gymnasium' or 'philosophical school'. Alternatively, the text might be emended to 'in the Academy or Lyceum', or 'in the grove (*luco*) of the Academy'.

2 An ex-consul, born in 106 BC at Arpinum of a local aristocratic family. He entered public life and advanced relatively swiftly to a consulship in 63. His political fortunes were damaged when, following upon his conviction of Catiline and others for conspiracy, he helped persuade the senate to demand their executions without a trial. In the summer of 52, as an ex-consul, he reluctantly assumed the proconsulship of Cilicia, which kept him out of Rome for a year. Once he returned to Rome, he retired from political life though it was known that his sympathies were with Pompey during the civil war. Following a pardon from Caesar, he dedicated himself to philosophical leisure and writing. He died in 43 BC.

3 The *pallium* was a Greek cloak worn by philosophers.

4 Nectarius may be thinking of the Stoic community of the wise, or of the Cynic idea of being a 'citizen of the cosmos'.

5 Cf. Letter 91.1–2: Augustine to Nectarius (above, pp. 2–3).

6 Cf. Cicero, *De re publica* 6.28–9.

7 Cf. Letter 91.2 (above, pp. 2–3).

8 Cf. Plato, *Phaedo* 60bc.

9 Cf. Letter 104.3 (p. 12), where A. replies that he does not know of this sentiment in Roman literature. While the Epicureans believed that because death removes every kind of pain, it is not an evil, no philosophical school actually held that poverty causes misfortune. The theme can be found, for example, in Roman comedy. However, the suggestion that death is preferable to a life of poverty is made in Roman oratory (e.g. Cicero, *In Catilinam* 4.7–10; cf. also *De republica* 3, quoted at *civ.* 22.6). Nectarius appeals to commonplace literary sentiments, which Augustine rejects with an eye to philosophical writings.

10 That all vices are equal was a well-known Stoic position, defended by Chrysippus and Zeno. Cicero rejected this position.

11 Perhaps referring to a *confessio in iure*: a formal statement made before a judge in open court by the defendant, who admits responsibility and accepts liability for damages.

12 Cf. Letter 104.8–9 (p. 16). Nectarius is arguing here that pagans ought to be granted the same pardon which had been extended to those Christians who had confessed participation in the violence.

13 The Latin is extremely difficult. Huisman, *Augustinus' Briefwisseling*, 55 (cf. 126–7), translates to mean that the accused will be freed *from* being hated *by* the accusers, if the accusers admit defeat and drop legal proceedings. My translation depends on interpreting *accusatorum . . . invidia* as 'hatred against the accusers', and on taking *victi* ('once they had lost their case') with the following rather than the preceding clause. Nectarius

clearly fears a massive and indiscriminate retaliation against the town's inhabitants, one based in part upon A.'s assertion that it will be difficult to distinguish clearly between guilty and innocent parties. Cf. Letter 91.8–9 (pp. 5–7). Roman law provided for severe measures against formal accusations lodged without substantiation. Nectarius' remarks could be taken to imply a threat of legal counter-measures against such 'accusers'. Cf. *EDRL* 731, s.v. Tergiversatio.

Letter 104

1 A. refers to Letter 91 which he sent to Nectarius in July 408. Possidius (who may have delivered Nectarius' first letter to A.) was then visiting A. to discuss the disturbances at Calama (cf. Letter 91.8, pp. 5–6). It was then decided that Possidius would report the matter in person to the imperial court, and he departed Hippo Regius for Ravenna in August.

2 Letter 103 from Nectarius (pp. 8–10).

3 A. reiterates his opposition to the application of torture or the death penalty, and indicates that he would not wish for those convicted in this case to suffer confiscation of their goods to the point of depriving them altogether of the material means of survival. However, he insists that punishment is necessary.

4 Cf. Letter 91 (pp. 2–8).

5 Cf. Letter 103.3 (pp. 9–10).

6 Cf., for example, Sallust, *Bellum Catilinae* 1.3.

7 *C. Iul.* 4.15.76 is the only other Augustinian text which attributes this expression to Cicero. It is found in a fragment thought by some scholars to belong to his lost dialogue *Hortensius*, and is taken to refer to Socrates, Plato, and their disciples.

8 Or, possibly, 'to teach its basics'.

9 Cf. Letter 90 (pp. 1–2), and A.'s response, Letter 91.1 (p. 2).

10 Sallust, *Bellum Catilinae* 2.3.

11 Cf. Letter 91.9 (pp. 6–7).

12 Referring to Nectarius' remarks at Letter 103.3–4 (pp. 9–10).

13 Allusions to the material poverty voluntarily embraced by two Roman civic heroes, Lucivs Quinctius Cincinnatus and Gaius Fabricivs Luscinus. Cf. *civ.* 5.18.2. Most of the little known about Cincinnatus comes from poetry. He lived at Rome in the fifth century BC and distinguished himself as a hero when he rescued the consul Lucivs Minucivs from defeat by the Aequi in 458 BC. He then retired from public service to his tiny farm. On Fabricivs, cf. p. 256, n. 14.

14 Gaius Fabricivs Luscinus was a Roman war hero and consul in 282 and 278 BC, eulogised by Cicero as an example of frugality. He was said to be beyond bribery or political corruption of any sort. As censor in 275 (along with Q. Aemilius Papus), he expelled Publius Cornelius Rufinus from the senate for possessing ten pounds of silverware. The specific legal basis for this censure is unknown. However, a number of historical anecdotes attest that censors possessed the authority to act against public officials guilty of superfluous luxuries. From 217 to *c.* 18 BC, a series of laws (*leges sumptuariae*) attempted further prohibition of excessive luxuries. Cf. *EDRL* 724, s.v. Sumptus.
15 Referring to divine judgement after death.
16 The location of this saying in Cicero is unknown, but cf. *Pro Sestio* 24.
17 Cf. Cicero, *Pro Sulla* 8.25.
18 Cf. Letter 103.3 (pp. 9–10).
19 *Ibid.*
20 Cf. Nectarius' plea concerning this point at Letter 103.4 (p. 10 and p. 255 n. 12).
21 I.e. of charity.
22 Virgil, *Eclogues* 4.13–14.
23 Cf. Letter 103.3 (pp. 9–10).
24 Cf., for example, Seneca, *De clementia* 2.5; Cicero, *Tusculanae disputationes* 3.9.20. A. offers a fuller and more nuanced exposition of this argument at *civ.* 9.5 (AD 415/417). There, he points out that the Stoic philosopher Epictetus found room for mercy within the soul of the sage provided that it did not diminish his strength of determination to act on the basis of reason, and not sentiment.
25 *Pro Ligario* 12.37.
26 Cf. Letter 91.2 (pp. 2–3) and Nectarius' reply at Letter 103.2 (pp. 8–9).
27 A. is responding to Nectarius' argument at Letter 103.4 (p. 10) in favour of innocent bystanders. Cf. also below, n. 28.
28 Cf. Letter 91.8–9 (pp. 5–6).

Letter 95

1 Possidius was travelling to Ravenna to seek imperial protection following the riot at Calama (about which cf. Letters 90, 91, 103 and 104, pp. 1–22), and passed through Nola en route, carrying this letter with him. Cf. Biographical notes on Nectarius, Paulinus of Nola and Possidius.
2 Cf. *ep.* 94.4.
3 St Paul.
4 Goldbacher (*CSEL* 34/2) indicates a lacuna in the text at this point.
5 The last sentence is added in another hand.

Letter 136

1 Cf. Translator's note on Courtesy Titles, and Biographical notes on Volusianus, Apollonius, Apuleius and Marcellinus.
2 *Ep.* 132.
3 We do not know her name.
4 *Ep.* 135: Volusianus to Augustine. Marcellinus' conversation with Volusianus took place after the latter had already written to A., but before A.'s response had reached Volusianus. Cf. Letter 138.1 from A. to Marcellinus (p. 30), where A. acknowledges both receiving Volusianus' letter and responding to it (in *ep.* 137).
5 Cf. p. 274 n. 13.
6 Volusianus had voiced the conventional philosophical viewpoint of his time that divine law, reflecting the divine mind, must be supremely rational and hence incapable of logical inconsistencies. Divergences in proscriptions and laws between the Old and New Testaments (concerning, for example, forms of sacrifice, polygamy or divorce) suggest either two different 'gods' at work as lawgivers, or a fickle 'god' whose dignity is thus irreparably impugned.
7 *rei publicae moribus.*
8 This entire correspondence between A., Volusianus and Marcellinus was composed between September 411 and the end of February 412, just a year following the sack of Rome and at a time when Roman provinces in Europe along with the western extreme of Roman Africa were experiencing intense military and civil strife in connection with the migrations of Gothic and Vandal tribes.
9 The individual in question remains unidentified.
10 A. responds to Marcellinus' request in *ep.* 137 (to Volusianus) and Letter 138 (to Marcellinus, pp. 30–43), as well as in *civ.*, begun in 412 and dedicated to Marcellinus.

Letter 138

1 A. responds to Marcellinus (cf. Letter 136, pp. 28–30) over objections to Christianity which Volusianus had expressed both to A. (in *ep.* 135) and to Marcellinus. A. intends that this letter supplement his earlier reply to Volusianus (*ep.* 137). Cf. Biographical notes for Marcellinus, Volusianus, Vindicianus and Apuleius.
2 Cf. Letter 136.2 (p. 29).
3 *ratio.*
4 The question was whether Vindicianus was practising medicine or 'magic'. The distinction between them was not always clear in late ancient minds. See below, § 18.

5 Reading *a quibusdam postea*.

6 Terence, *Adelphoe* 824–5.

7 The beautiful, *pulchrum*, and the appropriate, *aptum*, were topics of ancient aesthetics and rhetoric about which A. wrote his first work, *De pulchro et apto* (*c.* AD 380), which is no longer extant. Cf. *conf.* 4.13.20.

8 Thus, something can be beautiful in itself, but inappropriately or ineptly placed with regard to a given situation. A joke might be humorous, but inappropriate when told during a sermon at a funeral service.

9 'Sacrament' (*sacramentum*), defined by A. as a 'sacred sign' (cf. *civ.* 10.5), symbolically bridges the human mind and eternal, divine reality by providing a model of the latter. Thus, Old Testament sacrifices are models for later, New Testament sacrifices (such as Christ's death or the eucharist), which in turn model the gift of oneself or of the church to God.

10 Cf. Letter 136.2 (p. 29).

11 Cf. Sallust, *Bellum Catilinae* 52.19.

12 *Ibid.*, 9.5 (cf. Augustine, *civ.* 1.6).

13 *Pro Ligario* 12.35.

14 Cicero, *De re publica* 1.39. The entire discussion of 'commonwealth' (*res publica*) in this paragraph is inspired by this text of Cicero, which serves also as the basis of A.'s discussion of Scipio–Cicero's arguments in *civ.* (especially at 2.21 and 19.21). Cf. Translator's note on Commonwealth.

15 I.e. they are from the scriptures.

16 A. reacts here against various explanations for moral evil such as evil demons, Fate, or the doctrine of the Manichaeans which held that an external, material principle of evil influenced human actions.

17 Reading *ut nihil aliud dicam*.

18 For a similar statement of this principle, cf. Sermon 302.10 (p. 113).

19 Cicero, *Pro Sulla* 8.25.

20 A.'s defence of Christian civic ethics at §§ 9–15 thus depends upon a method of interpreting scriptural passages concerning the justified use of violence in a manner consistent with his discussion of 'the appropriate' (*aptum*) at § 5 (cf. above, nn. 7–8). In response to Volusianus' objections that Christian political leaders would always be prohibited by the scriptures from resorting to violence, A. answers that no individual verse or group of verses ought to be understood literally or in isolation from other relevant scriptural texts, but ought to be interpreted as a part in relation to the whole.

21 The arguments in this section are expanded at *civ.* 3.29–31.

22 Sallust, *Jugurtha* 35.10.

23 Sallust, *Bellum Catilinae* 11.6.

24 Juvenal, *Satires* 6. ll. 287–95, translated by Stephen Robinson, in Juvenal, *Sixteen Satires upon the Ancient Harlot* (Manchester, 1983).

25 Cf. especially *civ.* 5.12–13.

26 A. replies to a point raised by Marcellinus. Cf. Letter 136.1 (pp. 28–9).

27 Although A. recognises the existence of good *daemones*, he normally employs the term to designate spiritual beings who are evil, for they fail to worship the true God. They are masters of deceit who pose as pagan gods, possess invisible cosmic powers and are able to collude with practitioners of magical arts through symbolic rites including sorcery. Cf. *civ.* 8.16–24; 9.6–9, 13, 19–23.

28 A. offers a considerable discussion of Apuleius in this context at *civ.* 8.14–19.

29 The *sacerdos provinciae* was the chief priest of a province, an elective post lasting one year, which combined civil and religious duties at the provincial level, including those of maintaining public games and presiding over the annual meeting of the provincial council.

30 Today near Tripoli in Libya.

31 The speech is not extant.

32 The charge against Apuleius was based on the *Lex Cornelia de sicariis et veneficis*, a law enacted in 81 BC under the dictatorship of Sulla. Cf. Paulus, *Sententiae* 5.23. The term *veneficus* (poisoner) could be indiscriminately applied to those who practised magic.

33 Following the *PL* text. The *CSEL* places a lacuna here.

Letter 10*

1 Cf. Biographical notes on Julian (2), Celestius, Alypius and Boniface (2).

2 Slave trade was legal, but regulated, throughout the Roman empire. It is, however, to be distinguished from the late ancient Roman practice by which parents could legally 'lease' their minor children into an indentured servitude for a fixed term of years. Cf. *C. Th.* 5.10.1 (AD 329) = *C.J.* 4.43.2. Children in this condition could be redeemed by payment at any time. In 391, the emperors Valentinian II and Theodosius determined that children thus 'leased' were to be unconditionally freed upon completion of their terms of service. Cf. *C. Th.* 3.3.1. By transporting the children 'to provinces overseas', the slave-traders sought to ensure that these children were unable later to find witnesses to testify to their freeborn status, and so they would be taken for slaves.

3 A.'s reference to twenty-five years is puzzling. He may have in mind an edict of Constantine which states that children who were sold or leased into slavery unaware of their freeborn status could be returned to that condition even after they reached twenty-five years of age. In A.'s time, it may have been inferred from the edict that at age twenty-five the indentured servant who is aware of his or her freeborn status may freely choose to accept the condition of slavery for life. Cf. *C. Th.* 4.8.6 (AD 325).

Parents who leased their newborn children sometimes sought assurances in the original terms of the contract that the children would not be required to serve more than twenty-five years, lest it be presumed that they had freely chosen to become slaves rather than to return to freedom. Cf. Humbert, 'Enfants' 200–1.

4 Hadrian was praetorian prefect of Italy and Africa from 401 to 405, and again from 413 to 414. The precise edict of Honorius to which A. refers is unknown. However, numerous Roman laws at the time targeted *plagium*, kidnapping people to sell into slavery. Cf., for example, *C.J.* 11.48.7 (AD 371) and *C.J.* 9.20 *ad legem Fabiam*. The violence against persons and property of the sort about which A. speaks in this section was treated in general Roman law. Cf., for example, *C.Th.* 9.10 *ad legem Juliam*.

5 Proscription involved the forfeiture of one's material goods and of one's civil personality: loss of the right of inheritance or legacies, of the right to initiate a judicial case. Cf. *EDRL* 658, s.v. Proscribere bona; Nicholas, *Introduction* 243–6.

6 Reading *vindicata*.

7 An edict promulgated by the emperor Valentinian III in 451 imposes a fine of six ounces of gold as the sole penalty for similar actions. Cf. *Nov. Val.* 33.

8 A. implies the collusion of coastal authorities and customs officials in this illegal traffic.

9 A. probably knows the identities of the officials responsible for enforcing the laws, but may omit mentioning them here because he believes them to be acting in collusion with the slave-traders. See the reference to 'patrons' below, § 8.

10 Speculation on this location is inconclusive, but A. mentions it at *serm.* 45.7, indicating that it was well known.

11 Possidius, *Vita Augustini* 24, states that A. used church funds, even ordering sacred vessels to be sold on occasion, so that slaves could be re-purchased and legally manumitted.

12 Cf. above, n. 9.

13 Something may be missing from the text here. The authority in question might be the proconsul for Proconsular Numidia or his delegate. On the other hand, some customs officials belonged to the military; in which case, the letter might have originated with the *comes* of Africa.

14 *pro eorum meritis.*

Letter 250

1 Cf. Translator's note on Courtesy titles and Biographical notes on Classicianus and Auxilius.

2 Classicianus' 'own security' was perhaps imperilled because he risked excommunication for violating the right of asylum. Or perhaps he was the guarantor of the debt (*fideiussor*) mentioned at Letter 1*.3, and was therefore liable for the debt owed by the accused. Guarantors of loans took on considerable financial risk by offering a surety on behalf of the principal debtor. On these possibilities, cf. Ducloux, *Ad ecclesiam* 198–200. On the legal background, see Buckland and Stein, *Text-Book* 445–55; Nicholas, *Introduction* 193–8; *EDRL* 350, s.v. Adpromissio. Cf. also Translator's note on Security.

3 The practice of granting asylum in Christian churches first emerged in a more or less *ad hoc* fashion from roughly the middle of the fourth century, in continuity with earlier Greek and Roman practices connected with the imperial cult of conceding asylum in sacred places. Imperial edicts issued in 392, 397 and 398 implicitly acknowledged the force of the Christian custom, but placed limits upon it. At the council of Carthage of 27 April 399, the bishops petitioned the emperor Honorius not to prohibit sanctuary in churches for any reason whatsoever. On 21 November 419, the emperors Honorius and Theodosius II issued an edict recognising the inviolable right of asylum in Christian churches (cf. *Sirm.* 13). For other Augustinian texts concerning asylum cf. Sermon 302.22 (pp. 118–19) as well as *ep.* 22*; 28*.5; 113–115; 151.11; 268.

4 A. employs the term *anathema* which, in fifth-century Africa, was interchangeable with *excommunicatio*. Both terms refer to the juridical act of a bishop or a council of bishops which separated an individual from communion with the church, meaning that one so condemned was no longer permitted access to the eucharist and was prohibited from holding any church office or ministry. In the African church of A.'s time, excommunication normally involved a bishop or council of bishops passing sentence on the accused and registering the action in the church's official acts, as A. indicates has happened to Classicianus (cf. also § 3). Excommunication was often used as a means to coerce a Christian accused of grave sin to accept the canonical penance imposed by the bishop (cf. *bapt.* 7.53.101; *serm.* 232.8). It is this satisfaction which A. urges on Classicianus as a way of appeasing the bishop. Cf. Letter 1*.4, p. 52. On canonical penance, cf. p. 267 n. 4.

5 Scripture offered examples of collective punishment: the Great Flood (Gen 7.21–3); the destruction of Sodom and Gomorrah (Gen 19.24–5); the killing of the first-born sons of the Egyptians (Exod 12.29); the extermination, on orders from Moses, of 23,000 idolaters by Levi's sons (Exod 32.28), of 250 followers of Core, Dathan, and Abiron guilty of treachery (Num 16.31–5); and of the idolaters at Settim (Num 25.5); Phineas'

slaying of 24,000 Israelite men along with Moabite women guilty of fornication (Num 25.6–9).

6 By 'washing of rebirth' A. understands baptism, by which original sin and all personal sins are forgiven. Elsewhere A. argues that a person (even an infant child) who dies without being baptised would not be saved. The collective excommunication imposed on Classicianus' household (*domus*) means that none of his future offspring, nor that of any of his slaves, could be baptised, even if the child stood in danger of dying.

7 By either of the two dating schemes of this letter, A. was involved at the time in a theological controversy over original sin and the importance of infant baptism. Rom 5.12 was a key verse in his armoury of scriptural texts against Celestius and Pelagius, and later Julian of Eclanum, each of whom held that baptism was not necessary for children who were yet incapable of committing sin. Cf. the Biographical notes. From this and other texts, A. argued instead that human beings inherited Adam's sin of disobedience along with his punishment. As a consequence, all human beings were condemned to eternal damnation. With rare exception, only baptism could remit original sin along with any sins which the baptised person had culpably committed.

8 Letter 1* (pp. 50–2) gives A.'s response to the letter from Classicianus, which is not extant.

Letter 1*

1 The letter is not extant.

2 Synesius, bishop of Cyrene and metropolitan of Ptolemais in Libya Superior, excommunicated Andronicus, governor (*praeses*) of Pentapolis, along with his entire household (πανέστιος), in 412, because he posted edicts on the door of the church denying the right of asylum to those who would seek it there. Cf. Synesius, *ep.* 42 (*Opere di Sinesio di Cirene. Epistole, operette, inni*, ed. A. Garzya (Turin, 1989)). Basil, a fourth-century bishop of Caesarea in Asia Minor, imposed a limited excommunication upon the entire families of a man and his accomplices accused of kidnapping a young girl. Cf. Basil, *ep.* 270 (*PG* 32.1004A).

3 See pp. 261–2 n. 5.

4 Cf. above, n. 6.

5 The penance referred to n. 4. Cf. also below, p. 267 n. 4.

6 A reference to the bishop of Rome. Elsewhere, A. acknowledges a certain primacy for the Apostolic See, but what this amounts to varies depending on the context. In many cases, A. expected the bishop of Rome simply to confirm the decisions taken by the African episcopal councils.

7 A. here reveals himself ready to intervene to restrict the right of asylum

for persons accused of breaking an oath. Upon reaching a conciliar consensus, African bishops normally despatched one or more bishops trained in the law (of whom there were many) to the emperor's court in search of an imperial rescript. There is no evidence that A. ever brought the matter before his fellow-bishops. However, integral accounts of the proceedings of these council meetings are not extant.

8 A. held that the consensus reflected in collegial decisions taken by episcopal councils expressed a greater theological and ecclesial authority than those reached by individual bishops. African church councils were heavily influenced both in their origins and procedures by practices common to bodies such as the Roman senate, municipal senates, and provincial assemblies or councils.

Sermon 335c

1 Otherwise known as *Sermo Lambot 2*. The date is undetermined.

2 In this context, the birthday (*dies natalis*) of a martyr refers to the day of martyrdom itself in which the martyr was born into eternal life. It is not known which martyr's feast day A. was commemorating in this sermon, nor the date or place where it was preached.

3 Usually A. uses different words for *love* interchangeably (cf. Translator's note on Love). Here, he quite self-consciously defines his terms (compare *doct. chr.* 3.10.16). I have followed him by translating in this sermon as strictly as possible 'charity' for *caritas;* 'love', 'lover', for *amor, amare, amator*, and *dilectio, diligere*; 'greed', 'be greedy for' for *cupiditas, concupiscere*.

4 At *civ.* 14.7, A. argues that even *concupiscere* is used in scripture in connection with a longing for good objects.

5 Cf. *serm.* 169.11.14–12.15. Love can prevent members of a band of thieves from informing against one another. But such love is rooted in greed for worldly goods. A. is setting up a distinction between true and false martyrs based upon the character of the love which motivates them.

6 The contrast between greedy people and martyrs is demonstrated by the motives for which they willingly suffer deprivations, and not by the distress suffered as considered in itself. A. here also anticipates the distinction between true and false martyrs that he will draw below at § 5. Cf. also *serm.* 107.7.8; 125.7.

7 There are textual problems here. C. Lambot, *Revue Bénédictine* 46 (1934) 398–406, comments: 'Some words about the tyranny of pleasures seem to have been lost.' Cf. *en. Ps.* 128.4.

8 Cf. *Io. ev. tr.* 26.4.1.

9 A slogan which A. adopted during his campaign against the Donatists.

Cf. *Cresc.* 3.47.51, where the phrase first occurs as such in A. His distinction between true and false martyrdoms can be traced to two concepts from Roman law: the penalty itself, and the ground or 'cause' for its imposition. Among its numerous other possible meanings, cause (*causa*), 'one of the vaguest terms of the Roman juristic language', can refer generally to the reason for a legal action being taken in a specific situation, as well as to the subjective motive, intention, or purpose of the accused. Cf. *EDRL* 382–3, s.v. Causa.

10 Parallel texts at *en. Ps.* 43.1.21; *serm.* 331.2.2; 331.6.5; 335.2; cf. also *serm.* 229F.5. A. employs texts from the Psalms and Romans to indicate that the martyrs' valid cause consists in confessing the name of Christ. Cf. below, § 11.

11 For parallel texts, cf. *serm.* 299F.5; 331.6.5; 335.2.2.

12 *caritas.*

13 *caritas.*

14 Thus the active confession of Christ despite the threat of persecution constitutes a political act on the part of the martyrs. This entire section finds a parallel, fuller development at *civ.* 5.14.

15 At *civ.* 5.12–13, A. contrasts the earthly glory which was the object of love for Roman heroes such as Marcus Atilius Regulus (cf. Biographical note on Regulus) with the martyrs' efforts to glorify God by their deaths.

16 Cf. *civ.* 5.14 where A. concludes, 'What else was there for [Roman heroes] to love except glory. For, through glory, they desired to have a kind of life after death on the lips of those who praised them.' This surrogate immortality provided Roman heroes with an additional motivation for facing death courageously.

17 'Fisherman' (*piscator*) is an allusion to the apostle Peter, who, according to tradition, was martyred at Rome.

18 A. condenses a number of points. All three condemned men (Christ and both thieves) suffer the same penalty, although Christ's 'cause' (*causa*), his legal situation, differs from that of the two thieves. A. adapts the Roman legal procedure of 'distinguishing/separating the cause' (*causam separare/discernere*) to the crucifixion scene depicted at Lk 23.39–43. By openly confessing his guilt and accepting the justice of his punishment, the 'good thief' hopes that Christ will determine that his legal situation now differs from that of the unrepentant thief, and will show him mercy. For illustrations of the general procedure in Roman law, cf. Justinian, *Digest* 16.3.1 (Ulpian); 41.4.2 (Paul); 49.4.1 (Ulpian). Cf. Lazewski, *La sentenza* 188–218.

19 Parallel texts at *serm.* 53A.13; 285.2; *Io. ev. tr.* 31.11.

20 *causam mutare:* a Roman juridical notion referring to the alteration of the

legal situation or standing of a party involved in a judicial matter. For examples, cf. Justinian, *Digest* 23.3.67 (Proculus); 28.6.10 (Ulpian); 41.2.3 (Paul). Cf. above, n. 18. By stating that the 'good thief' has 'changed his cause', A. means that he has ceased to be a thief, preferring instead an eternal reward to material wealth unlawfully acquired.

21 *causa.*

22 A reference to the resurrection of the body.

23 Lambot conjectures *creaturae*, 'his creation', for *creatoris*, 'the Creator'.

24 Cf. Translator's note on 'Just, justice'.

Bishops and civil authorities

Letter 133

1 Cf. Biographical notes on Marcellinus, Restitutus (1) and Apringius.

2 A. will have in mind the proscription against retaliatory violence at Mt. 5.38–9. Early Roman law recorded in the Twelve Tables (*c.* 450 BC) specified retaliation (*talio*) as the penalty for mutilation or amputation. The *Lex Cornelia de sicariis et veneficis* (81 BC) provided the normative legislation against murder through late antiquity. The law was modified by a number of *senatusconsulta* (decisions rendered by the senate in response to requests from magistrates) and later by imperial constitutions and edicts (about which cf. p. 252 n. 15). Penalties for murder were generally severe but dependent upon the legal status of the person killed, the circumstances of the killing and the social status of the accused.

3 A. petitions Marcellinus that the convicted Donatists be spared capital punishment or mutilation, or even condemnation to the mines with resulting loss of citizenship and certain death, but that they be sentenced instead to forced labour.

4 On torture as a means of securing confessions, cf. p. 253 n. 20. A. urges Marcellinus to opt for a less brutal means of coercion.

5 King Saul had attempted to kill David in the wilderness of Engedi.

6 I.e. Apringius, to whom A. writes Letter 134 (pp. 63–6).

Letter 134

1 Cf. Biographical notes on Apringius and Marcellinus.

2 Cf. p. 274 n. 13.

3 Cf. Letter 133 (pp. 61–3).

4 *securis*: cf. p. 269 n. 19.

5 Rom 13.1–7 was commonly cited by early church Fathers to legitimate the authority of civil rulers over Christians. Cf. Sermon 302.13 (pp. 114–15); Sermon 13 (pp. 119–26); Letter 100.1 (pp. 134–5) and Letter 220 (pp. 218–25). It also lies behind A.'s reasoning at Letter 153.19 (pp. 82–3).

6 *causas*: referring to legal cases and, by extension, to jurisdiction. Cf. above, p. 251 n. 4 on the 'bishop's tribunal'.

7 Apringius' brother Marcellinus (cf. Letters 133 and 136, pp. 61–3; 28–30) had presided over the Conference of Carthage (1–8 June 411) and ruled in favour of the Catholics. He ordered standing imperial edicts, which banned Donatist assemblies and confiscated their property, to be enforced anew. A. links this decision with renewed Donatist and Circumcellion violence against Catholic clergy.

8 Cf. Letter 153, in particular §§ 5–6 (pp. 73–4); 18–19 (pp. 81–3); Sermon 13.8 (pp. 124–5).

Letter 139

1 Referring to the court record of the interrogation and confession of those accused of murdering Restitutus and of maiming Innocent. Cf. Letters 133 and 134 (pp. 61–6). Cf. Biographical notes on Restitutus (1), Innocent, Spondeus, Macrobius, Celer and Donatus (4).

2 Reading *corpore confessi sive*. Goldbacher (*CSEL* 44.149) indicates a lacuna in the text.

3 A Donatist basilica in Carthage which would pass into Catholic hands as a result of the judgements rendered by Marcellinus following the Council of Carthage in 411. Cf. p. 128 and p. 266 n. 7.

4 For Boniface, cf. Letter 152.1 (p. 70 and p. 267 and n. 2). At the time of the writing of this letter, Peregrinus was a deacon of the church at Hippo Regius, frequently despatched as a messenger for A. Both the bishop and the deacon were in Carthage, in part, to ensure that Marcellinus carried out A.'s request for clemency toward the convicted assassins.

5 Marcellinus' brother Apringius, addressee of Letter 134 (pp. 63–6).

6 Letters 133 and 134 (pp. 61–6).

7 Or possibly, 'will make'.

8 A. informs Marcellinus and Apringius that he is prepared to appeal to the emperor Honorius at Ravenna against a death sentence in these cases.

9 Sissinius and Alexander were martyred in this southern Tyrol valley at Nonsberg near the Italian city of Trent in May 397, on the occasion of a pagan festival. Cf. Paulinus of Milan, *Vita Ambrosii* 52.2.

10 Referring to the first two books of *De peccatorum meritis et remissione et de baptismo parvulorum*.

11 *Breviculus conlationis cum Donatistis*, a work summarising the official acts of the Conference of Carthage (1–8 June 411). Cf. above, p. 266 n. 7 (Letter 134).

12 *Ad Donatistas post collationem.*

13 Cf. Letter 138 (pp. 30–43). A. addressed *ep.* 137 to Volusianus. For an explanation of the latter's rank, cf. the Translator's note on Courtesy titles and the Biographical note on Volusianus.

14 *Ep.* 140, also called *De gratia novi testamenti.*

15 Catholic bishop serving in the same territory as Fortunatus, bishop of Constantine in the Numidian interior. His mission to Carthage indicates the perceived gravity of the Donatist reaction in the Numidian country-side.

16 His identity is unknown, but he is thought by some to be Urbanus, later bishop of Sicca. Cf. Letter 229.1 (p. 225).

17 *principalis*: one of a small group of leaders who directed the municipal council of a given city.

Letter 152

1 Cf. Biographical note on Macedonius.

2 Boniface was bishop of Cataquas, a small town in Numidia near Hippo Regius. The term *antistes*, here translated 'representative' in relation to divine law, was used by Latin-speaking Christians in late antiquity to refer to bishops.

3 The letter from A. which Boniface carried to Macedonius is lost; its contents are unknown.

4 A reference to canonical penance, a practice through which Christians were permitted to atone for a major sin such as murder, heresy, and adultery only once during their lifetimes following baptism (cf. Tertullian, *De paenitentia* 7; Ambrose, *De paenitentia* 2.3.19). Not to be confused with excommunication, with which it may overlap (cf. p. 261 n. 4), the 'great penance', as A. called it, marked one for life, and required severe acts of penitence, e.g., fasting, for a long period. Penitents were barred from the eucharist for the stipulated duration of the penance. Canonical penance could not be repeated; reoffenders were permanently banned from the eucharist. Cf. Letter 153.7 (pp. 74–5).

5 The first three books of *civ.*

Letter 153

1 Cf. Biographical note on Macedonius.

2 Cf. Letter 152.2 (p. 70).

3 Cf. below, § 15; and Commentary on the gospel of John, 33.6 (p. 105).

4 Referring to the problem raised by Macedonius at Letter 152.2, concerning the unrepeatable character of canonical penance (cf. above, p. 267 n. 4). A. addresses this issue somewhat more directly below at § 7.

5 At the conclusion of a canonical penance, the bishop imposed hands on the penitent's head as a sign of reconciliation.

6 Where the commission by Christians of major crimes is concerned, A. seems to look for greater flexibility in the church's penitential practice than he currently finds. This impression grows stronger at § 21, where he states that he sometimes meets privately with offenders (cf. p. 84 and p. 269 n. 23). The closing lines of the letter express his awareness that others besides Macedonius will read it. Thus, the letter gives him an opportunity to express his views to other bishops as well as to civil officials.

7 Note the parallel treatment of Jn 8.3–11 in the Commentary on the gospel of John, 33, especially §§ 5–7, pp. 104–6.

8 *infirmitas communis*: a theme in A.'s ethics, based upon a commonplace Roman legal argument used in the defence of accused criminals. Cf. Cicero, *De inuentione* 2.33.101. As similarly employed by A., the argument denies any human being total immunity from sin and thus binds accuser and accused alike in a shared moral weakness. The object of the argument was to urge the judge to show mercy. Cf. also Ambrose, *De apologia prophetae Dauid* 16–19.

9 The general Platonic notion of 'participation', to which A. refers, allows a being to be good in so far as it shares in the form of the good. A. holds that God is Goodness itself, the highest order of good, and not good as a result of participation in another being. This identification of God with the highest good (*summum bonum*) is central to the logic of A.'s political thought: cf. *civ.* 8.8; 12.1–9; 19.4.

10 Cf. above, pp. 262 n. 6.

11 The 'common weakness' mentioned above, § 10.

12 Cf. Seneca, *De ira* 2.6–10; 3.26.3–21; 3.28.1; *De beneficiis* 4.26.2–3; 5.17.3; 7.27. Lucivs Annaeus Seneca was a prominent Roman statesman and writer during the first half of the first century AD. He resigned from political life in 62 to engage in literary pursuits. As a philosopher he was an eclectic Stoic. The correspondence allegedly exchanged between Seneca and St Paul is apocryphal. Jerome's *De viris illustribus* 12 is most likely the source of A.'s erroneous belief that the letters were still being widely read.

13 I.e. excommunication. Cf. p. 261 n. 4.

14 *cognitor*. Cf. below, p. 272 n. 6.

15 Cf. p. 289 n. 4 on *paterfamilias*.

16 The distinctions among types of killing which A. draws here correspond with those found in Roman law concerning homicide (cf. p. 265 n 2 (Letter 133)). See *EDRL* 487–8, s.v. Homicidium.

17 *fideiussor*. Cf. p. 261 n. 2.

18 Translating *pia verbera*.

19 Certain high-ranking imperial magistrates, when walking in public, were preceded by attendants called 'lictors' each of whom carried bundles of straight, wooden rods from which an executioner's axe (*securis*) projected. The axe symbolised both imperial authority and dominion in general, as well as the specific power of the magistrate to impose capital punishment.

20 Reading *fiat*.

21 Cf. Letter 152.2 (p. 70).

22 A. may be referring to the judicial powers granted by imperial edicts to bishops in certain cases (cf. p. 251 n. 4). He may also have in mind the ecclesiastical powers by which bishops threaten excommunication or canonical penance (on excommunication cf. p. 261 n. 4; on canonical penance, cf. p. 267 n. 4).

23 By indicating that, in order to avoid denouncing thieves in public, he sometimes confronts them privately, A. suggests that other means than the application of harsh penalties can be employed successfully to promote conversion.

24 Literally, 'and not to be aroused'.

25 Excommunication: cf. above, n. 22.

26 Cf. Letter 152.2 (p. 70).

27 *Ibid.*

28 Sallust, *Jugurtha* 1.5.

29 Translating *a quo admovetur et cui admovetur officivm*. Civil suits moved notoriously slowly through various tribunals. Court fees were high and had to be paid to a number of minor officials, including the *princeps officii*, the chief administrator of the magistrate's office, and the *exceptor*, the court stenographer who minuted trial proceedings and who provided litigating parties with copies of court records. In many cases the distinction between fees and bribes was unclear.

30 *patronus*, in this case a legal advocate or counsel. Cf. Cicero, *De officiis* 2.14.51; *De oratore* 2.69.280.

31 A decree of the emperor Valentinian set 12% per annum as the legal limit on interest in financial loans. Persons convicted of charging interest in excess of the legal rate were required to pay back the surcharge along with a penalty fee of 400% of the amount overpaid. Cf. *C. Th.* 2.33.2 (AD 386).

Letter 154

1 Possidius, *Vita Augustini* 20, reports that A. had written Macedonius a letter intervening on behalf of someone seeking a favour, probably judicial clemency.
2 Macedonius refers to the first three books of *civ.*, completed in 413. He had earlier complained that he had not yet received the promised books (cf. Letter 152.3, pp. 70–1).
3 The sacking of Rome by Alaric in August 410.
4 Macedonius anticipates the end of his appointment as vicar of Africa in 414.

Letter 155

1 *res publica*. Cf. Translator's note on Commonwealth.
2 Notorious tyrant of Acragas in Sicily during the sixth century BC who ordered a brazen bull constructed in which his opponents were roasted to death. Cf. Cicero, *Tusculanae disputationes* 5.26.75.
3 Cf. *civ.* 1.17–28.
4 5.38.110–11; 5.40.117.
5 *summum bonum*. Cf. p. 268 n. 9.
6 *Tusculanae disputationes* 1.31.75.
7 Terence, *Phormio* 318.
8 *virtus*, meaning strength or courage. In Roman thought, this was the defining characteristic of the male, *vir*. Cf. Cicero, *Tusculanae disputationes* 2.18.43.
9 *res publica*. Cf. Translator's note on Commonwealth.
10 A.'s argument depends on his version of the following section of text, which (like the Vulgate and Septuagint) mistranslates the Hebrew. In the original, the next section is a prayer for the well-being of the Psalmist's community.
11 A. makes a triple distinction: most people trust in material goods; the best philosophers trust in human virtue; the Christian trusts only in God.
12 Cf. *civ.* 2.21.2, citing Cicero, *De re publica* 1.25.39, a discussion which A. completes at *civ* 19.21–7.
13 *prudentia*.
14 The four virtues, which Ambrose was the first to call 'cardinal virtues' (cf. *Expositio evangelii secundum Lucam* 5.49.62). Though traditionally held throughout Roman culture, their elaboration here is derived largely from Stoic ethics. Cf. Cicero, *De inventione* 2.159–67. At *civ.* 5.20, A. suggests ways that the pursuit of human glory corrupts these virtues in rulers.
15 Cf. Sallust, *Bellum Catilinae* 6.

16 Cf. Letter 154.1, p. 88.

17 *finis boni*, 'the end of good'. Cicero wrote a book on the ethics of the Hellenistic philosophical schools entitled 'on the ends of goods and evils'. The basic question at issue was: what is the supreme good? A. gives the Christian answer here.

18 Terence, *Heautontimoroumenos* 75–7.

19 A. here objects to the commonplace Roman attitude toward reason (*ratio*), largely based in Stoic and Peripatetic psychology and ethics, both of which exalt the role of this mental faculty in eliminating altogether or at least in dominating all levels of fear. Stoic writers, in general, held that the mere possession of virtue by a civic hero guaranteed blessedness, even in the face of horrendous tortures and death. Cf., for example, Cicero, *Paradoxa Stoicorum* 16–19; *Tusculanae disputationes* 5.5.14. A. counters that, in time of trial, divine grace alone, and not virtue, ensures blessedness in the hope of an eternal reward. It is this grace, and not innate valour, which endows the human being with true piety, the subject of § 17. Cf. also *civ.* 5.20; 9.4–5; 14.9; 19.4.

20 Cf. Translator's note on Piety.

21 A reference to the *cingulum*, a waist band or belt, originally worn by all soldiers. In Roman late antiquity it was worn by judges as well as by many civil imperial officials as a symbol of their office and of its austere responsibilities.

22 *res publica*. Cf. Translator's note on Commonwealth.

Judicial authority

Commentary on the gospel of John, 33

1 Most biblical scholars hold that Jn 7.53–8.11, which includes the passage concerning the woman caught in adultery, is a non-Johannine interpolation to this gospel. Although it was found in Old Latin and Vulgate editions of John, it is not found either in the oldest or best Greek codices. A. was aware of textual questions surrounding the passage (cf. especially *adult. coniug.* 2.7.6), but believed that it was both authentically Johannine and canonical.

2 Literally, 'separated ones', they constituted a sect or party within Judaism at time of the writing of the New Testament. The Pharisees are portrayed in the gospels as fostering strict observance of the Law.

3 Nicodemus, a Jewish priest and member of the Pharisees (Jn 3.1) and of the Sanhedrin, the latter being the supreme Jewish religious council and court for Jews living (at the time of Christ) in Judaea. He visited Jesus secretly at night to talk with him about his mission and teachings. Before

the Sanhedrin, he defended Jesus' right to a fair hearing (Jn 7.50). He aided with the burial of Jesus (Jn 19.39).

4 In saying this, A. wishes to establish a legal basis in Roman as well as in the Mosaic law for charging them with calumny and collusion (cf. below, § 4). Cf. Deut 1.16 (LXX): 'And I charged your judges at that time, saying, Hear the causes between your brethren, and judge justly between every man and his brother, and the stranger that is with him.'

5 A. is referring to the doctrine of the virginal birth of Christ.

6 There are two ways to understand *cognitor*, which we have translated 'judge'. The other possibility is to translate *cognitor* 'defender'. By agreement of the parties involved in a litigation, a 'defender' could stand in for and speak on behalf of either party. Cf. Gaius, *Institutes* 4.83; *Rhetorica ad Herennium* 2.13.20, and *C. Th.* 2.1.1–7. Cf. also Buckland and Stein, *Text-Book* 708–10; Thomas, *Textbook* 103–12. Until the reign of the emperor Justinian (527–65), the *cognitor* also shared, in whole or in part, the legal jeopardy of the party he represented.

Against this interpretation, Christ is himself cast in the role of judge (*cognitor*) who investigates and 'brings justice' into the proceedings. Such an interpretation is suggested by the text of Is 4.2, alluded to in the statement following (cf. below, n. 7). Moreover, in late antiquity, *cognitor* was also used as a term for 'judge'. Cf. *C. Th.* 10.10.20 (8 April 392): *cognitores ordinarii*. A. occasionally uses the term when he clearly means 'judge' (cf. especially *conf.* 10.1.1; *ep.* 144.3; 153.16; *c. Iul. imp.* 2.10.34). The wider context of the commentary also supports this understanding; in the end it is Christ who, as judge, refuses to condemn the woman (cf. below, § 6).

7 Cf. Is 11.2–4: 'And the Spirit of the Lord shall rest upon him . . . and he shall judge the poor with justice . . .'

8 Cf. Lev 20.10; Deut 22.22–4.

9 Cf. Mt 5.17–18.

10 *praevaricator legis*. In Roman law, the charge of *praevaricatio* concerned a collusion to offer a counterfeit prosecution or defence.

11 *praevaricatores legis*: cf. above, n. 10.

12 Here, A. calls Christ the 'voice of justice' (*vox iustitiae*). The technique used to unmask and defeat his adversaries is rhetorical, and derives from Socratic dialectic. The question 'who is without sin' is tactical; it establishes a common ground for assent between the parties to the dispute and thus lays the ground for the defeat of Christ's opponents. On the technique in general, cf. Cicero, *De finibus* 1.6.18. On A.'s admiration for Socrates' verbal acumen, cf. *civ.* 8.3; 14.8. Cf. also Cicero, *De oratore* 3.16.60.

For A., legal and rhetorical defeat of the Pharisees and Scribes was not the sole end of Christ's use of dialectic. As Christ employed it, the art of dialectic drew out the implications of justice as yet uncovered from within the Mosaic Law. Christ therefore demonstrates that, in principle, justice thus holds truth and gentleness in perfect balance.

13 A. holds that Christ's unique condition of freedom from original sin and from all personal sin guarantees that he is the only completely just judge in history. Cf. Sermon 13.4–5 (pp. 121–3).

14 Cf. Letter 153.15 (pp. 79–80), where this same argument appears in relation to A.'s defence of bishops who appeal for clemency on behalf of criminals convicted of capital offences. Cf. also Sermon 13.8 (pp. 124–5).

15 I.e., Isaiah.

Sermon 302

1 Laurence was a Roman deacon martyred under the emperor Valerian, probably in 258. Deacons in the ancient Roman church also served as treasurers or bursars. A. preaches this sermon on his feast-day shortly after the mob killing at Hippo Regius of an unidentified imperial official, associated perhaps with enforcing the collection of customs duties (cf. p. 274 n. 15). The theme of Christian non-violence is thus skilfully interwoven into A.'s representation of Laurence as a martyr who resisted unjust civil authorities by verbal, rather than physical, means.

2 Reading *sanctae* with *lectiones*.

3 Probably Mt 5.1–12, commonly referred to as the Beatitudes, and frequently read in A.'s church during the eucharist when martyrs' feastdays were commemorated.

4 The sign of the cross was traced on the forehead of initiates (catechumens) at the onset of their formal introduction to the Christian religion. At this point they were said to belong to Christ (cf. *Io. ev. tr.* 3.2), and looked forward to a more formal preparation for baptism. Cf. *conf.* 1.11; *cat. rud.* 26.50; *serm.* 32.13; 97A.3; 301A.8.

5 On 'guarantor' (*fideiussor*), cf. p. 261 n. 2.

6 Or, 'Many evil people say, "So much evil!"'

7 Referring to the mob killing of an imperial official, the major concern of this sermon. Cf. §§ 15–21.

8 On the conditions which A. held as requisite for true martyrdom, cf. p. 264 nn. 9 and 10.

9 On the role of this corrupt official, cf. p. 274 n. 15. It is possible that the higher import tariffs fraudulently charged at the city's port caused a sharp rise in the prices of goods sold in the market at Hippo Regius. Exorbitant tariffs might therefore have led to more widespread financial hardship and even ruin.

10 Literally 'banditry'.

11 A court stenographer who minuted trial proceedings as the judge's secretary.

12 On A.'s knowledge of the laws concerning homicide, cf. above p. 269 n. 16 and p. 133 n. 2.

13 *rationem reddere,* to 'render an account'. The New Testament reminds Christians that they will have to 'render an account' to God (Mt 12.36; 1 Pet 4.5; Rom 14.12); church leaders will 'render an account' of their flock (Heb 13.17). The phrase was also used in secular life; for example, servants in a propertied household would render regular accounts to their masters. In philosophical terms, to 'render an account' meant to give a rational explanation. A. uses the phrase in connection both with his responsibility to God as a bishop for his flock, and with his intellectual defence and exposition of Christianity. Cf. Letters 134.1 (p. 63); 136.2 (p. 29).

14 Note the similar tone at Commentary on the gospel of John, 33.5 (pp. 104–5), where A. refers to these words of Christ as the 'weapon of justice' which acts like a 'wooden club'. Cf. the reference at § 2, regarding any threats sharp enough to 'pierce hearts that are hard and apathetic', referring to his auditors.

15 *miles,* a soldier. The term is also used in late antiquity to describe certain civil servants in the imperial bureaucracy (*militia officialis*). Citing Lk 3.12–14, A. implies an association between the official in question, and the 'soldiers' and 'publicans' (whom A. equates with 'tax-collectors', *telonearii*) addressed by John the Baptist. At § 16, he indicates that a merchant (*negotiator*) who conducts his trade by sea complained of having been defrauded by the official. For these reasons, the victim may have been a *custos litorum*, a soldier assigned to assist customs officials (*curiosi litorum*) with the assessment and collection of duties on goods entering the port of Hippo Regius. Cf. Delmaire, *Largesses sacrées* 287–8.

16 A. is punning in Latin: *'non . . . militia, sed malitia'.*

17 Cf. Letter 138.15 (pp. 38–9), where A. employs this text in rebutting the charge that the Christian religion proscribed recourse to physical force in all circumstances, even by legitimate civil authorities.

18 Or 'God doesn't belong just to them, and not to us.'

19 Note the parallel structure in A.'s questions to the implied question of Christ, 'If any of you is without sin . . .' (Jn 8.7). Cf. § 14.

20 That is, of being a bishop, with responsibility for his community.

21 A. indicates that he had interceded with the soldier in question, and asked him to stop oppressing merchants with exorbitant charges.

22 Cf. p. 289 n. 4, on *paterfamilias.*

23 Following the *PL* text. Lambot includes *'corporis'*, with several manu-

scripts, and explains this as a reference to corporal punishment. However, corporal punishment is too much taken for granted by A. to be described so solemnly. Secondly, the grammar is peculiar, suggesting the possibility that *corporis ipsius* is a later gloss. But the phrase remains obscure.

24 Cf. Letters 91 and 104 (pp. 2–8 and 11–12) concerning A's views on the collective civic responsibility to prevent unjust violence in the Calama affair.

25 Cf. p. 274 n. 13.

26 Cf. § 19, where A. also urges the head of the household to employ verbal persuasion against any resort to violence by family members. A.'s confidence in the power of language as a fundamental means for the promotion of justice is a consistent, major theme throughout the sermon. Cf. §§ 2; 3; 8; 14; 15; 16.

27 Some scholars have argued for the inclusion of this section, known as *Sermo Morin Guelferbytanus 25*, as the conclusion or peroration of Sermon 302; others have raised serious objections to its inclusion. A. may be speaking here of church asylum for those suspected of killing the imperial official. However, by this interpretation, it remains unclear why, in addition to civil authorities, a crowd would be threatening to storm the church. A second interpretation suggests that the murdered official had sought sanctuary in the church, and that A. is referring to the crowd which stormed the church, seized him and killed him. Cf. Ducloux, *Ad ecclesiam* 176–80. But this suggestion lacks any textual foundation.

28 On the legally sanctioned right of asylum in churches, cf. p. 261 n. 3. A. may also be thinking of a number of imperial edicts which granted protection to church buildings from acts of violence (cf., for example, *C. Th.* 16.2.31: 13 January 409).

29 Cf. Translator's note on Just.

Sermon 13

1 The sermon was preached at the basilica of St Cyprian at Carthage. A. was in the city attending a bishops' council.

2 St Paul.

3 Cf. Translator's note on Security.

4 I.e., as if to speak in a law-court.

5 Cf. p. 271 n. 2.

6 Cf. *Cresc.* 1.11.14–18.22, where A., in reference to this text, calls Christ a 'dialectician' (*dialecticus, disputator: Cresc.* 1.17.21). Christ's questioning and subsequent rebuke of the Pharisees and scribes over their efforts to corner him in a dilemma over the paying of taxes to Caesar conforms to

the same general Socratic pattern as that demonstrated in the parallel confrontation over the woman caught in adultery. Cf. p. 272, n. 12.

7 Note the parallel discussion at Sermon 302.12 (pp. 113–14). In that sermon (especially §§ 11–13), A. employs Rom 13.1 3 in order to urge his congregation not to rebel against public authorities. In this sermon, preached in the presence of civic and provincial authorities, A. employs the same text to urge authorities to practise justice toward those they govern.

8 Cyprian, bishop of Carthage, was put to death by Roman officials in 258. The basilica was built by the city walls at the site of his martyrdom.

9 An unsubtle allusion to the conventional payment of bribes to those responsible for recommending and handling the appointment of candidates to the judiciary.

10 Note the parallel structure of interior, forensic self-examination recommended by A. to the Pharisees and scribes when commenting on Christ's confrontation over the women caught in adultery: Commentary on the gospel of John, 33.5 (pp. 104–5).

11 Cf. Letter 153.15.

12 This is probably A.'s strongest statement against capital punishment in any of his writings.

13 A. has in mind the responsibilities legally associated with the role of *paterfamilias*, about which see, p. 289, n. 4.

14 Reading *impunitus*, with the *PL* text. *CCL* reads *imperitus*, 'inexperienced'.

The Donatist controversy

Letter 51

1 The letter lacks a salutation. Its addressee is Crispin, Donatist bishop of Calama (see Biographical note). Cf. also Biographical notes for Maximian (1) and Optatus (2).

2 The agreement concerned a follow-up meeting at Carthage to debate further the issues dividing them.

3 The Jews of the Old Testament.

4 Cf. Translator's notes on Hand over, and Pursue.

5 Neither Donatist nor civil officials were able to remove these two Donatist bishops from their sees, and the Donatists were later forced to reinstate them.

6 *gesta proconsularia*: official documents recording the charges against the two bishops and the decision of the proconsul Flavius Herodes deposing them from their sees. Cf. *Cresc.* 3.56.62.

7 A splinter-group in schism with the Donatists during 393–7, formed around Maximian, a Carthaginian deacon.

8 A. is speaking ironically.

9 Donatists held that baptism administered outside of their church was invalid. Catholic bishops, in particular, were unfit as ministers of baptism because their predecessors had been in communion with Caecilian. Consequently, Catholic converts to the Donatist church were habitually re-baptised, an action which outraged A., who argued that Christ, and not the bishop, was the actual minister of the sacrament. On rebaptism, cf. also pp. 127–8.

10 I.e., in the countryside and even in the town.

11 Christian communities in each of these cities were addressed in an epistle of St Paul. The foundation of A.'s case against the Donatists was the charge that they were not in communion with the universal church.

12 This example illustrates how inevitably disputes within the churches (in this case within the Donatist communion) led to the involvement of secular law in ecclesiastical matters. The property of the church belonged by law to the church legally recognised as orthodox. It was necessary, therefore, for each side to prove the other heretical.

Letter 66

1 The addressee is Crispin, Donatist bishop of Calama. By 'Mappalians', A. refers to tenant farmers and their families on an imperial estate at Mappala, outside of Calama, whom Crispin had rebaptised. Cf. Biographical note on Crispin. As at Letter 51.1 (p. 128), A. omits a courtesy salutation.

2 Referring to an edict of the emperor Theodosius I, dated 15 June 392, which stipulated the fine for all clerics of heretical sects. Cf. *C. Th.* 16.5.21. Cf. Letter 88.7 (pp. 148–9); *Cresc.* 3.47.51.

3 Reading *sac[c]ulo* with the *PL* text.

4 The language of one of the native peoples inhabiting north Africa at this time. A. did not speak it.

Letter 86

1 Cf. Biographical note on Caecilian (2).

2 Or 'renowned'.

3 A series of repressive edicts enacted by the emperor Honorius in 405 declaring the Donatists 'heretics', banning their religious assemblies and confiscating those private homes which were used for such meetings, threatening the Donatist clergy with exile and their accomplices with

harsh floggings. Donatists were also denied certain rights concerning contracts and inheritance. Cf. *C. Th.* 16.5.37, 16.5.38, 16.5.39, 16.6.3–5, 16.11.2.

Letter 100

1 Proconsul of Africa. Cf. Biographical note on Donatus (2).
2 On the use of Rom 13.1–7 in A.'s writings on political themes, cf. p. 266 n. 5 (Letter 134).
3 The proconsul Donatus had been directly charged in a rescript from the emperor Honorius to punish any persons who endangered the Catholic church. Cf. *C. Th.* 16.5.44 (24 November 408). A. urges Donatus against applying the death penalty in such cases.
4 Cf. pp. 277–8 n. 3 (Letter 86).

Letter 87

1 A. reviews much of the history of the Donatist controversy in this letter. Additional information on several points can be found in the Biographical notes for Emeritus, Optatus (2), Maximian (1), Nicomachus Flavianus, Rogatus, Firmus and Macarius.
2 The *artes* or *disciplinae liberales* were considered the basis of a general education in antiquity as well as in the Middle Ages. Writing toward the end of his life (AD 426/427), A. enumerated these disciplines as grammar, dialectic, rhetoric, arithmetic, music, geometry and philosophy (cf. *retr.* 1.6). See also *ord.* 2.12.35–16.44, where he includes poetry (2.14.39) and astronomy (2.15.42) among their number.
3 Thus 'catholic' (*catholicus*), a loan-word from the Greek *katholikos*, meaning 'universal'.
4 Reading *hominem malum*.
5 Referring to Optatus, Donatist bishop of Timgad.
6 Capital of the province of Mauretania Sitifensis, it is one of many Donatist bishoprics nearer to Timgad than was Caesarea.
7 Cf. p. 277 n. 11.
8 On the Maximianists, cf. p. 277 n. 7. A. alleges a lack of symmetry in the Donatists' dismissal of the arguments of this relatively smaller, splinter-group from their own ranks, while they likewise refuse to take account of their analogous position with respect to 'the nations that are Christ's inheritance', the Catholic church, from which they are dissenters.
9 The letter is otherwise unknown.
10 On the use of Rom 13.1–7 in A.'s writings on political themes, cf. p. 266 n. 5 (Letter 134).

11 A. comes close to insinuating that Nicomachus Flavianus was a Donatist. However, it is inconceivable that the emperor Gratian would have appointed a Donatist as vicar of Africa, and equally improbable that any Donatist would have accepted the appointment. Moreover, Flavianus was notorious as a pagan. Cf. Biographical note on Nicomachus Flavianus. A. uses the ambiguous phrases 'in communion' (*communicare*) and 'a member of your sect' (*uestrae partis homo*) with intentional irony. He is perhaps implying that, as a pagan governor, Flavianus at first showed lenience toward the Donatists, but that later, upon receiving Gratian's edict in October 377, he turned harshly against them.

12 A reference to the African Catholic delegation sent to the emperor Honorius at Ravenna in 404 to plead for legal assistance against the Donatists.

13 The 'Rogatists' were members of a splinter-group from the Donatists, led by Rogatus. Optatus directed a persecution against members of this sect. The non-violent Rogatists referred to the Donatists as 'Firmians' because of their close political alignment with Firmus. The Donatists referred to Catholics as 'Macarians', after Macarius, who oppressed the Donatists.

14 Some manuscripts read *Rucata*. It is a coastal city, today Skikda, Algeria. The identity of the Donatist bishop referred to is unknown.

Letter 88

1 Cf. Biographical notes on Januarius, Maiorinus, Anulinus, Felix of Apthugni, Maximus, Ingentius, Caecilian (3), Crispin, Theasius, Evodius, Maximian (1) and Maximian (2).

2 The initials in the address constitute a puzzle. The editors of *PL* argue that 'v.c.' must stand for *vir consularis*, 'a man of consular rank' rather than *vir clarissimus*, 'a man of the rank of renowned' (see Translator's note on Courtesy titles). Some editors have read 'now proconsul'. A.GGG.NNN. has been interpreted variously: perhaps *augustis nostris*, 'to our august emperors', gives the most likely meaning. Cf. Biographical note on Anulinus.

3 'Proceedings' (*acta*) refer in general to detailed, verbatim records of official proceedings including any executive or judicial decisions taken. Constantine issued the rescript to which Anulinus refers in AD 313. It relieved clerics (those loyal to Caecilian, not the proto-Donatists loyal to Maiorinus) of all public duties and tax burdens. Cf. Eusebius of Caesarea, *Historia ecclesiastica* 10.7.

4 Reading *debitae reverentiae*. The *CSEL* text is obscure here.

5 *pars*, elsewhere translated as 'sect'.

6 15 April 313. It is possible (following the *CSEL* text's punctuation) that this is the date of the unsealed enclosure rather than of Anulinus' own letter.

7 The council of Arles, 1 August 314.

8 In 317. The text of this edict is not extant. Cf. Letter 105.9 (p. 167); *c. litt. Pet.* 2.92.205.

9 *iudicivm publicum*, meaning that the case against Felix was conducted as a criminal trial with the proconsul presiding as judge.

10 I.e., vicar of Africa. As such, he was governor of the Roman civil diocese of Africa, comprising seven provinces.

11 Claudius Saturninus, as *curator civitatis*, was charged with carrying out the persecution of Christians, among other duties, at Apthugni in 303. Solus is referred to as a *servus publicus*, a slave in municipal service. The presence of military personnel guaranteed the application of force against those unwilling to surrender the sacred books.

12 *duumviri* were local magistrates chosen by the municipal council to govern the city. They presided over the council and exercised some judicial roles. As the name implies, they were normally assigned to work in pairs. Alfius Caecilian, the *duumvir*, is not to be confused with Caecilian, the bishop of Carthage, who was the subject of the judicial enquiry. On the forged letter, cf. the Biographical note on Ingentius.

13 Cf. p. 277 n. 3 (Letter 86).

14 Cf. Letter 105.3 (pp. 163–4), and the Biographical note on Restitutus (2).

15 Donatist bishop of Hippo Regius.

16 Reading *dissimulasset*.

17 Held at Carthage, 25 August 403.

18 Reading *Crispinus*.

19 For this edict cf. Letter 66.1 (pp. 132–3). The judgement against Crispin was rendered early in 404 at Carthage by the proconsul, whose name is unknown to us. Cf. Possidius, *Vita Augustini* 12.5–6.

20 Crispin travelled to Ravenna where the emperor Honorius re-imposed the sentence against him. Cf. *Cresc.* 3.47.51; Possidius, *Vita Augustini* 12.7–9.

21 The Catholic bishops met at Carthage probably between 14 and 29 June 404. The majority of bishops favoured an edict compelling unity, but A. and a minority of bishops prevailed upon them to adopt a less radical position. Bishops Theasius and Evodius were despatched to petition the emperor for more mildly repressive measures as well as military protection for the Catholic community. Cf. *ep.* 93.5.17.

22 Cf. Biographical note on Maximian (2).

23 Cf. p. 277 n. 3 (Letter 86).

24 I.e., bury them. On Circumcellions as martyrs, cf. p. 281 n. 6.

25 Cf. Sermon 335C (pp. 53–9).

26 The delegation travelled to Ravenna in January 406.

27 The Donatists wanted to debate with Valentinus before the praetorian prefects. The request was denied on 30 January 406.

28 The edict and *decreta* of 405, about which cf. pp. 277–8 n. 3 (Letter 86).

29 Reading *vostri* and *voluerunt* with the editors of the *PL* text.

30 Cf. Biographical note on Maximian (1).

Letter 173

1 Cf. Biographical notes on Donatus (3), Primian and Optatus (1).

2 Such coercion, according to written accounts, could range in degrees from verbal insistence to physical violence. A. himself calls the episcopacy a 'slavery' imposed upon him (*ep.* 122.1), and recounts his fear at being 'press-ganged' into accepting the office of bishop (cf. *serm.* 355.2; Possidius, *Vita Augustini* 4). Other examples are offered by Paulinus of Nola, Martin of Tours, Gregory Nazianzen, Gaudentius of Brescia, Porphyry of Gaza, Bassianus and Paulinianus, the younger brother of Jerome, to name a few. An imperial edict of 28 March 460 (*Novella* XI) forbade episcopal ordination through coercion. However, resistance to episcopal consecration constitutes a rhetorical commonplace in episcopal biography and hagiography.

3 Referring to Donatus' office as a priest.

4 In theory, the good or bad intention (*voluntas*) of the accused was weighed before judgements were rendered in Roman criminal proceedings.

5 I.e. baptism.

6 Optatus, Catholic bishop of Milevis (*De schismate Donatistarum* 3.4), and Tyconius, a Donatist dissident (*In Apocalypsin*, cited at Hahn, *Tyconius* 68), claim that in place of martyrdom many Circumcellions opted for suicide. Cf. Letter 185.11–15 (pp. 179–83). In defence of such actions, the Donatists reportedly cited scriptural examples such as that of the Jewish elder Razis (2 Macc 14.37–46). Cf. Letter 204.6 (p. 161). A. opposed their arguments by reasoning that suicide was murder and that it could not be equated with martyrdom. Cf. *c. Gaud.* 1.22.25; 1.27.30; 1.28.32; 1.31.36–9. Cf. also Letter 88.8 (p. 149), and Sermon 335C.5 with n. 9 (p. 264). He also disapproved of the suicides allegedly committed by Christian, consecrated virgins who were threatened with rape following the sacking of Rome in 410. Cf. *civ.* 1.17–27.

7 Frequently used by A. to designate monks, the term can also be extended to include Catholic lay persons.

8 The conference, involving Catholic and Donatist bishops, was held at Carthage in 411. Cf. p. 128.

9 Translating *praeiudicare*: here a juridical term meaning originally 'set a legal precedent'.

10 The Catholics at the conference reminded the Donatists that their predecessors had reversed an earlier condemnation of Primian. Cf. § 8. The Donatists adopted this position, thereby seeming to impugn the legal force of precedents. Cf. *brevic.* 3.16.28; *c. Don.* 2. A. implies that it would also bar them from condemning Catholic bishops on the basis of any earlier, alleged wrongdoings of Caecilian.

11 Referring to the seven Donatist bishops elected by their colleagues to represent them at the conference of 411. The Catholic bishops also had seven representatives.

12 I.e., the Catholic bishop of Carthage originally opposed by Maiorinus and Donatus.

13 An allusion to Exod 14.30. Donatists considered baptisms administered by Caecilian, his successors, and all Catholic bishops in communion with them, as invalid and therefore without salvific effects. At the Donatist council of Bagai in 394, Primian, along with 310 bishops, excommunicated Maximian, the bishops who had consecrated him, and their followers. Cf. *c. Gaud.* 1.54. On rebaptism, cf. pp. 127–8.

14 The Greek verb βαπτίζω originally signified 'washing' and only later, in Christian usage, 'baptism'. The true reading of the text is found in the Septuagint: 'He who washes himself after touching a dead body, if he touches it again, what good did his washing do him?' The crucial phrase 'if he touches it again' is thus missing in A's citation. In a later discussion of this passage, he claims that he was unaware that the text, which was frequently cited by the Donatists in defence of their rejection of Catholic baptism, was defective. He also points out that the phrase was omitted in numerous codices compiled even before the Donatist schism. Cf. *retr.* 1.21.3; *c. litt. Pet.* 2.7.14; and Cyprian, *ep.* 71.7.

15 The text (Jn 6.66) reads 'many' and not 'seventy'.

Letter 204

1 Cf. Biographical notes on Dulcitius and Gaudentius.

2 Timgad, a city in central Numidia (modern Algeria), was a known stronghold of Donatist resistance. In 419, Dulcitius decreed there the enforcement of standing imperial edicts suppressing the Donatists' cult and demanding that their properties be handed over to the Catholics. The town's formidable Donatist bishop, Gaudentius, barricaded himself and

volunteer members of his congregation inside the Donatist cathedral, and threatened to burn it, himself and the others, in the event of an attempt by imperial forces to seize it.

3 Absalom.

4 Elsewhere (*c. Gaud.* 1.1.1; *retr.* 2.59) A. refers to Dulcitius as an *exsecutor*, an imperial official charged with enforcing specific laws, in this case imperial edicts against the Donatists. A. may also be subtly reminding Dulcitius that he has no right, morally or legally, to put Donatist resisters to death.

5 Dulcitius wrote Gaudentius a letter urging him not to carry out his threat, and wrote to A. asking him to intervene with the Donatist bishop.

6 See p. 264 n. 9.

7 However, see Sermon 13 (pp. 119–26), in which A. interprets Psalm 2 as urging imperial officials to show clemency to those convicted of capital crimes.

8 In Augustine's Bible the books we know as 1 and 2 Samuel were part of the book of Kings.

9 In his response to Dulcitius' letter, Gaudentius raised the example of the Jewish leader Razis on account of the latter's suicide in the face of capture by Nicanor, a notoriously anti-Jewish army officer who served under Antiochus IV Epiphanes of the Greek kingdom of Syria during the Maccabean wars. Cf. p. 281 n. 6.

10 A. composed the work *c. Gaud.* in two books, dated to late 419 or 420, thus shortly after this letter.

Letter 105

1 For background historical information pertinent to this letter cf. Biographical notes on Caecilian (1), Marcus, Restitutus (2), Marcianus, Possidius, Maximinus, Crispin, Felix of Apthugni, Julian (1), Macarius and Theodosius I.

2 Cf. Translator's note on Hand over.

3 I.e., the bishop of Carthage, opposed by Maiorinus and Donatus.

4 Donatist bishop of Hippo Regius, contemporary with A.

5 Cf. Letters 51 (pp. 128–32), 66 (pp. 132–3), 88.7 (pp. 148–9).

6 A reference to the Edict of Unity promulgated by Honorius in 405. Cf. pp. 277–8 n. 3.

7 Cf. Letter 88.8 (p. 149).

8 On imperial edicts in general, cf. p. 252 n. 15. A. refers to the Donatists' petition for toleration presented in 361 to the emperor Julian. Cf. § 9. Their request was granted, and the edict's reception was celebrated throughout Donatist Africa. Cf. *c. litt. Pet.* 2.97.224. A.'s larger point is

that the Donatists are only prepared to demonstrate allegiance to imperial edicts when favourable to their cause. The 'sacred ceremony' may represent an allusion to the formal, political act, inaugurated during the early principate, by which the senate received and approved the emperor's edict. Cf. *EDRL* 410, s.v. Constitutiones principium.

9 Cf. Letter 88.1–3 (pp. 144–6) and Biographical note on Caecilian (1).

10 Cf. Letter 88.3–4 (pp. 145–6).

11 Cf. Letter 88.3 (pp. 145–6).

12 Paul and Macarius, despatched to Africa by the emperor Constans in 347, sided openly with the Catholics, thus provoking Donatus to exclaim 'The emperor has nothing to do with the church.' Macarius unleashed a persecution against Donatist leaders. In that same year, Constans issued an edict (now lost) uniting the two factions under Gratus, the Catholic bishop of Carthage.

13 Cf. above, n. 8. Rogatianus and Pontius were Donatist bishops who petitioned the emperor Julian in 362 to permit exiled Donatist bishops to return to their sees, to restore confiscated churches and to allow Donatist clergy to exercise their ministries.

14 On 20 February 373, Valentinian addressed an edict to Julianus, proconsul of Africa, banning the practice of rebaptism. Cf. *C. Th.* 16.6.1.

15 Gratian likewise prohibited rebaptism, but also ordered Donatist churches restored or turned over to the Catholics. He banned 'heretics' from assembling and confiscated their churches. Cf. *C. Th.* 16.5.4 and 16.6.2. In 378, he exiled Claudianus, a Donatist bishop, from Rome. Theodosius I was responsible for a long series of anti-heretical edicts, some of which concerned the Donatists. The most damaging of these was an edict of 15 June 392 imposing a fine of ten pounds of gold on clerics of all heretical sects. Cf. *C. Th.* 16.5.21. Cf. also Letter 66.1 (pp. 132–3).

16 On the anti-Donatist legislation of the emperor Honorius associated with the Edict of Unity (AD 405), cf. above, pp. 277–8 n. 3 (Letter 86).

17 The 'law' is probably a reference to *C. Th.* 16.6.4, a measure introduced by the emperor Honorius against the Donatists which accompanied the Edict of Unity in 405. On rebaptism, cf. pp. 127–8.

18 Jerusalem was to form the southern boundary of the land allotted by Joshua to the clans of the tribe of Judah.

19 Cf. Translator's note on Hand over.

Letter 185

1 A. refers to this letter retrospectively as a book entitled *De correctione Donatistarum*. Cf. *retr.* 2.48. Additional information concerning issues mentioned in this letter can be found in the Biographical notes on Arius,

Caecilian (1), Petilian, Maximian (1), Macarius, Maximian (2), Lucifer and Boniface (1).

2 Arian Christianity was an issue for Boniface also because it was the chief religion of the Gothic tribes whose migration throughout the empire was a cause of military and political concern. The same is true of the Vandals who crossed into north Africa in 429. Cf. Letter 220.3 (pp. 219–20).

3 Donatus is thought to have been sought out as a potential ally by Arian bishops at the time of the council of Serdica in 343. A. claims to know a work by Donatus (no longer extant) either on the Trinity or the Holy Spirit in which the Donatist leader expresses the position outlined here. Cf. *haer.* 69.2. Jerome, *De viris illustribus* 93, had claimed that Donatus' position was virtually Arian.

4 There is no evidence to support this suggestion of Donatist approaches to the Goths on the basis of a common Arian faith.

5 Cf. Letters 51.5 (pp. 131–2) and 87.1 (pp. 136–7).

6 For §§ 6–11, see Translator's note on Pursue. Caecilian was first exonerated by the Roman bishop Miltiades in 313, and then by the council of Arles in 314. Only after an additional Donatist appeal did Constantine adjudicate the matter himself. Cf. Letter 88.1–3 (pp. 144–6).

7 The conference of Carthage held in June, 411.

8 Cf. Translator's note on Security.

9 Cf. Sermon 335C.12 (pp. 53–9), especially n. 18 (p. 264) on the Roman legal procedure *causam distinguere.*

10 Cf. p. 264 n. 9.

11 The charge was lodged during the conference of Carthage by the Donatist bishop Petilian of Constantine. In response, A. observes that, whereas the Donatists lied at the conference when they claimed that the emperor Constantine had condemned Caecilian at Donatus' behest, by their own admission the Donatists concede that they, and not the Catholics, were the first to appeal to the emperor. Thus, they were the first 'persecutors' in the controversy. Cf. *c. Don.* 16.20.

12 In the Genesis account (16.1–16), Sarah, despondent that she might never bear Abraham a child, urged him to have one with Hagar, her servant. Once Hagar was pregnant, she scorned Sarah. Sarah complained of Hagar's contempt, and Abraham urged his wife to punish her servant woman. Paul, in Galatians (4.21–30), allegorises Sarah as a type for the new covenant and Hagar as a type for the old covenant. A. takes licence with Paul's allegory, aligning Sarah with the Catholic church and Hagar with the Donatists. Thus, Hagar's scorn of Sarah taken along with Sarah's punishment of Hagar parallels the Donatists' mistreatment of the Catholics and the Catholic disciplinary response.

285

13 A. recalls these earlier feats of the Circumcellions who, in the wake of the Macarian persecution, had sought out conflict with organised groups of armed pagan youths by profaning their religious festivals. Cf. p. 281 n. 6 and Lepelley, *Les Cités* 239–42.

14 Circumcellion violence erupted once again following the Donatist defeat at the conference of Carthage in 411.

15 For the edicts of earlier emperors, cf. p. 284 nn. 12, 14, 15. A. has in mind particularly the legislation promulgated by the emperor Honorius at the time of the Edict of Unity (AD 405). Cf. pp. 277–8 n. 3. On 30 January 412, Honorius, following the conference of Carthage in 411, ordered all Donatist clergy to be exiled, criminalised membership in the Donatist church, imposing on its members physical punishments and fines ranging from five to fifty pounds of gold, and ordered Donatist properties to be turned over to the Catholic church. He stopped short of prescribing the death penalty. Cf. *C. Th.* 16.5.52.

16 Omitting '*auctori*'. A possible emendation would be *eversoris ... auctoritatis*, 'rebel against authority'.

17 The 'deeds' (*tabulae*) mentioned here were account books or contracts recording the auctioning of slaves.

18 Cf. Biographical note on Maximian (1).

19 On the rebaptism controversy that divided Catholics and Donatists, cf. pp. 127–8.

20 Cf. above, p. 274 n. 13.

21 Terence, *Adelphoe* 57–8.

22 *Ibid.*, 69–75.

23 *indulgentia*: a pardon or amnesty usually granted by the emperor through an edict for a particular class of criminals.

24 *C. Th.* 16.5.21: p. 284 n. 15.

25 A petition that this Theodosian edict against 'heretics' be applied as well to Donatists was forwarded by the Catholic bishops meeting in Carthage to the emperor Honorius in 404. Honorius promulgated the Edict of Unity on 12 February 405.

26 A reference, in particular, to the edicts of the emperor Constans issued in conjunction with those of his delegate Macarius. Cf. pp. 284 n. 12. A. wanted specifically to avoid having the death penalty invoked. Cf. Letter 100.2 (pp. 135–6).

27 Cf. Biographical note on Maximian (2).

28 *iudex ordinarius*: 'ordinary judge' refers to the governor of a province in his capacity as judge. The governors were charged by the emperor Honorius with applying the laws against Donatists. Cf. *C. Th.* 16.6.4 (12 February 405).

29 The Conference of Carthage held in June, 411. See p. 128.

30 Cf. Letter 88.8 (p. 149).

31 A. is punning on two Latin verbs *perdere* (to lose) and *perire* (to perish).

32 Some read 'others who are not her sons' but this does not easily fit the context.

33 A. refers principally to the legislation of the emperor Honorius: an edict promulgated 15 November 407 (*C. Th.* 16.5.43), and in particular, one issued following the conference of Carthage in 411, intended to eradicate the Donatist religious presence in Africa. Cf. *C. Th.* 16.5.52 (30 January 412).

34 Referring to the petition of the Lord's Prayer, 'forgive us our debts, as we forgive our debtors'. Cf. Mt 6.12; Lk 11.4, and § 39. In early African Christianity, this prayer was repeated each day, as well as in the celebration of the eucharist.

35 A.'s point is that Catholics recognise the validity of a Christian baptism performed in the Donatist community. If a baptised Donatist 'returns' to the Catholic church, the baptism is therefore not repeated. However, in order for baptism to bear full spiritual fruit within the individual, the Christian life must be led within the Catholic church.

36 Some read 'giving away'. On 19 March 399, the emperor Honorius ordered Jovius, an imperial commissioner, and Gaudentius, *comes* of Africa, to destroy pagan temples and idols at Carthage. Cf. *civ.* 18.54.1. An edict issued on 20 August 399 by the emperors Arcadius and Honorius and addressed to the proconsul of Africa, Apollodorus, decreed the removal of idols from pagan temples. Cf. *C. Th.* 16.10.18.

37 Reading *abstulit*.

38 Cf. § 39, with reference to prayer for forgiveness of one's sins.

39 Cf. n. 35.

40 In the African church of this time, Catholic priests found guilty of serious charges were normally expelled from the clerical state. Writing in 382, Jerome denied the possibility of rehabilitating repentant clerical members of a schismatic movement. Cf. *Dialogus contra Luciferianos* 13, and the Biographical note on Lucifer. Cf. n. 42.

41 Cf. § 47 and n. 44 (p. 288). Just prior to the conference of Carthage in 411, the African bishops guaranteed Marcellinus that Donatist bishops would be permitted to retain their offices and functions following unity with the Catholics (cf. *ep.* 128.2–3; 142). There were precedents for this decision. According to a Latin translation of the eighth canon of the council of Nicea (AD 325), the clergy involved in the Novatianist schism were permitted to continue to function in their ministries provided that they had been reconciled to the local bishop. The council of Carthage in 345 permitted Donatist bishops who converted to retain their episcopal status and jurisdiction (cf. canon 12). A council held at Hippo

Regius in 393 and one held at Carthage in 397 decreed that, under certain circumstances, converted Donatist clergy could continue to minister to their converted congregations. Objections, however, from Athanasius, the bishop of Rome (399–401), led the council of Carthage in 401 to allow this privilege only when the local Catholic bishop gave prior consent.

42 The council of Elvira, convened near modern-day Granada, Spain (*c.* AD 300/303), barred from ordination those who had formerly undergone canonical penance (cf. canons 30 and 76). The same position was reaffirmed by the council of Toledo (canon 2) in AD 400. Two bishops of Rome, Siricivs (AD 384–99) and Innocent I (AD 401–17), also opposed the ordination of former penitents. Dismissal from the clerical state of those whose offences merited canonical penance dates back at least to the council of Nicea (AD 325). Canons from that council as well as from the council of Carthage in AD 345 mandated expulsion from the clergy as punishment for a number of disciplinary infractions. Later councils in Africa affirmed past decisions and extended the sanction to other categories of offences.

43 Referring to Pentecost. Cf. Acts 2.

44 Caecilian was first examined in 313 by the bishop of Rome, Miltiades, and by other bishops. Cf. Letter 88.3 (pp. 145–6). A. credits Miltiades with deciding to allow the Donatist bishops to retain their clerical status once reconciled to the church. Cf. *ep.* 43.16.

45 Catholics held that God did not give the gift of holy orders (diaconate, presbyterate, or episcopate) outside of the Catholic church. However, if an ordained Donatist cleric abandoned Donatism and was reconciled to the Catholic church, the divine character of his ordination would be recognised by the Catholic church without the requirement that he be ordained again.

46 Referring to the Donatist council of Bagai in 394. Cf. p. 282 n. 13.

47 '*If anyone has sinned*' looks like part of the quotation, but is not found in the Greek or Vulgate New Testament. These read '*if anyone has spoken against*', as Augustine writes in § 49.

48 By 'Arian', A. refers to a group of related Christian movements and teachings historically linked to Arius, who held that the Son and Holy Spirit had been created by the Father and thus were unequal to Him. Later, Eunomius taught a radical form of the same doctrine: the Son was 'unlike' the Father and the Holy Spirit was not divine. His followers refused to baptise in the name of the Trinity. Macedonius, who was deposed as bishop of Constantinople in 360, also denied the divinity of the Holy Spirit. Photinus was deposed as bishop of Sirmium (in modern Serbia) in 351 for heterodox views relative to the Trinity. It is thought

that he considered the Son to be a mere expression of the power of the Father.

49 On 'sacrament' cf. above, p. 258 n. 9 (Letter 138).

War and peace

Sermon: the sacking of the city of Rome

1 Dan 9:20–7. We do not know whether the liturgical calendar prescribed this text or whether A. selected it himself to conform to his intended theme. The second reading was probably Gen 18.17–32 (cf. §2).

2 The typology, based upon Ezek 14:14, is commonly found in the writings of both Greek and Latin Church Fathers. A. understands them specifically as types for those who live exemplary lives among three categories of Christians: the pastors of the church, religious ascetics, the married laity. Cf. *en. Ps.* 36.1.1; 99.13; 132.4–5; *qu. ev.* 1.12; 2.44; *ep.* 111.4; and *pecc. mer.* 2.10.12.

3 Translating *piae castigationis*.

4 A.'s choice of paternal discipline as a metaphor is guided by the ancient Roman institution of *paterfamilias* wherein the head of the household exercised full power (*potestas*) before the law over his direct descendants, slaves, and their direct descendants, and even over his wife and free servants in some cases. A.'s statement that God 'imposes discipline before he executes judgement' alludes to this right of the head of the household to sell his legal descendants into slavery, or even, when certain conditions were met, to have them put to death.

5 Gen 18.17–32: the patriarch Abraham's efforts to persuade God not to destroy Sodom.

6 This hero of the Old Testament book by the same name was the object of a wager between God and Satan as to whether he would maintain his exemplary virtue if sorely tried by loss of wealth and health. According to the narrative, he suffered extreme deprivations when God accepted the terms of the wager. His friends sought in vain to convince him that he must be a sinner to have merited such divine punishment. He steadfastly refused to accept their judgements or to blame God for his trials, in spite of his wife's urging that he do so. In recompense, God judged him favourably, restored his health and all his possessions two-fold. In the latter half of the fourth century AD, Christian writers and preachers cited him as the standard biblical model of the toleration of misfortune.

7 A. uses parallel arguments at *serm.* 15A.5–7; 81.2.

8 Similar arguments with application to the sacking of Rome are found at *serm.* 15A.3. At *ep.* 111.5, A. applies these biblical verses to explain the violence suffered both from the Circumcellions, and on account of Gothic migrations in Spain.

9 The story of Dives and Lazarus, briefly alluded to here and again at § 5, features in other of A.'s sermons concerning the sacking of Rome: see *serm.* 15A.2; 33A.4; 113A.2.

10 With O'Reilly, *De Excidio*. *CCL* reads 'it'.

11 *CCL* reads *gratis*. O'Reilly, *De Excidio*, omits.

12 A. offers parallel arguments at *serm.* 81.9.

13 This catastrophe was probably an earthquake which took place at Constantinople in 400. The 'fiery cloud' which was reported to have appeared in the night sky and the odour of sulphur are thought to be connected with a volcanic eruption which took place in conjunction with the earthquake. Cf. Cameron, 'Earthquake 400', and Cameron and Long, *Barbarians*, 91–102.

14 In the late fourth and fifth centuries, Constantinople was also a centre for Christian pilgrimages from and for trade with north Africa as well as other parts of the empire.

15 I.e. 'died'.

16 Cf. *civ.* 1.1.

17 A similar argument is found at *serm.* 81.9.

18 Both images, commonplace in A.'s writings as representations of divine judgement at the end of time, are employed at *serm.* 113A.11 with reference to the purification of Christians in the sacking of Rome.

19 A. argues in a similar way at *civ.* 1.8 that God uses the sufferings involved in the sacking of Rome as a way of strengthening the faith of pious Christians.

Letter 189

1 Cf. Biographical note on Boniface (1).

2 Probably Letter 185. Cf. pp. 173–203.

3 Cf. Translator's note on Security.

4 A. offers parallel scriptural arguments at Letter 138.9–15 (cf. pp. 34–9).

5 Cf. Cicero, *De officiis* 3.99–115, in particular 113.

6 Cf. *civ.* 15.4; 19.12.

7 A.'s point is that 'peace' within or between peoples suffers by comparison with eternal peace, which is the condition of the redeemed following death, and in which there will be no enmity or threat. Cf. *civ.* 15.4; 19.17.

8 *virilem*, the root of which is *vir*, man.

9 During the liturgy of the Eucharist, in response to the bishop's invitation 'lift up your heart', the congregation responded 'we have lifted it up to the Lord', symbolising their intention of transcending worldly goods and secular motivations for heavenly, eternal ones.

Letter 220

1 Cf. Biographical note on Boniface (1).

2 Cf. Translator's note on Security.

3 A. probably refers to Boniface's career ambitions which had progressed in conjunction with his decision to take a wealthy Arian woman, Pelagia, as his second wife, and to allow their daughter and servants to be baptised as Arian Christians (cf § 4). Arianism was the religion of the Goths, whose political and military fortunes in Italy, Gaul, and now also in Africa, were rapidly increasing.

4 A. and Alypius persuaded Boniface not to join a monastery, but to continue as a soldier defending Roman Africa from long-standing Berber, and from mounting Gothic, threats.

5 Cf. above, n. 3.

6 A. refers here to Boniface's open revolt against imperial forces loyal to empress Galla Placidia. Either Flavius Aetius or Flavius Constantius Felix, rival generals under the empress, is thought to have informed Boniface, falsely, that he had been ordered to return to Italy. Boniface seemed aware that a plot was being hatched against him, and defied the orders, subsequently defeating a series of regiments sent to Africa against him.

7 Whatever the truth of Boniface's version of events, A. locates the source of the spiralling intrigue and violence surrounding Boniface in the latter's personal ambitions.

8 *servus dei*, as at § 3, a reference to Boniface's desire to live as a monk.

9 The implication is that Boniface has had to tolerate acts of plunder and other civil disorder from his troops in order to retain their loyalty.

10 This threat seems to be A's major concern in writing Boniface.

11 He was appointed to this post in AD 425. It gave him command of a regiment of the army, the *domestici*, or Household Guard. The *comes* of Africa was field commander of the Roman army in the province of Africa Proconsularis, the capital city of which was Carthage.

12 *tribunus*, a military commander. A. has in mind a time ten years earlier (417) when Boniface commanded a small unit of troops and defeated tribes of nomadic Berbers who had overrun the southern frontier of the Roman province of Numidia.

13 A. refers here to the long-standing Roman policy of pacifying migrating

tribes of barbarians by offering them military, political and commercial alliances with the empire. Cf. Letter 229 to Darius (pp. 225–6).

14 Cf. p. 291, n. 6.

15 *summum bonum*: cf. above, p. 268 n. 9.

Letter 229

1 Cf. Biographical notes on Darius and Boniface (1).

2 Catholic bishops, respectively, of Sicca (today in Tunisia), and of Sitifis (today in Algeria).

3 Darius managed to make peace with Boniface and to conclude a treaty with the Gothic tribes pouring into Africa from Spain. Cf. Letter 220 (pp. 218–25). The treaty was short-lived. Boniface was forced to retreat with his army to Hippo Regius, which was besieged. Three months into the siege of the city, Augustine died, in August 430.

4 A. refers to Verimodus, Darius' son.

Index of proper names and places

Passing references are not included in the Index, and the endnotes are not exhaustively referenced.

Because of the need to subdivide the entries for 'Christ' and 'God', they are to be found in the Index of topics.

293

Index of topics

Passing references are not included in the Index, and the endnotes are not exhaustively referenced.

Cambridge Texts in the History of Political Thought

Titles published in the series thus far

Aristotle *The Politics and The Constitution of Athens* (edited by Stephen Everson)
0 521 48400 6 paperback

Arnold *Culture and Anarchy and other writings* (edited by Stefan Collini)
0 521 37796 X paperback

Astell *Political Writings* (edited by Patricia Springborg)
0 521 42845 9 paperback

Augustine *The City of God against the Pagans* (edited by R. W. Dyson)
0 521 46843 4 paperback

Austin *The Province of Jurisprudence Determined* (edited by Wilfrid E. Rumble)
0 521 44756 9 paperback

Bacon *The History of the Reign of King Henry VII* (edited by Brian Vickers)
0 521 58663 1 paperback

Bakunin *Statism and Anarchy* (edited by Marshall Shatz)
0 521 37973 8 paperback

Baxter *Holy Commonwealth* (edited by William Lamont)
0 521 40580 7 paperback

Bayle *Political Writings* (edited by Sally L. Jenkinson)
0 521 47677 1 paperback

Beccaria *On Crimes and Punishments and other writings* (edited by Richard Bellamy)
0 521 47982 7 paperback

Bentham *Fragment on Government* (introduction by Ross Harrison)
0 521 47982 7 paperback

Bernstein *The Preconditions of Socialism* (edited by Henry Tudor)
0 521 39808 8 paperback

Bodin *On Sovereignty* (edited by Julian H. Franklin)
0 521 34992 3 paperback

Bolingbroke *Political Writings* (edited by David Armitage)
0 521 58697 6 paperback

Bossuet *Politics Drawn from the Very Words of Holy Scripture* (edited by Patrick Riley)
0 521 36807 3 paperback

The British Idealists (edited by David Boucher)
0 521 45951 6 paperback
Burke *Pre-Revolutionary Writings* (edited by Ian Harris)
0 521 36800 6 paperback
Christine De Pizan *The Book of the Body Politic* (edited by Kate Langdon
Forhan)
0 521 42259 0 paperback
Cicero *On Duties* (edited by M. T. Griffin and E. M. Atkins)
0 521 34835 8 paperback
Cicero *On the Commonwealth and On the Laws* (edited by James E. G.
Zetzel)
0 521 45959 1 paperback
Comte *Early Political Writings* (edited by H. S. Jones)
0 521 46923 6 paperback
Conciliarism and Papalism (edited by J. H. Burns and Thomas M. Izbicki)
0 521 47674 7 paperback
Constant *Political Writings* (edited by Biancamaria Fontana)
0 521 31632 4 paperback
Dante *Monarchy* (edited by Prue Shaw)
0 521 56781 5 paperback
Diderot *Political Writings* (edited by John Hope Mason and Robert
Wokler)
0 521 36911 8 paperback
The Dutch Revolt (edited by Martin van Gelderen)
0 521 39809 6 paperback
Early Greek Political Thought from Homer to the Sophists (edited by
Michael Gagarin and Paul Woodruff)
0 521 43768 7 paperback
The Early Political Writings of the German Romantics (edited by Frederick
C. Beiser)
0 521 44951 0 paperback
The English Levellers (edited by Andrew Sharp)
0 521 62511 4 paperback
Erasmus *The Education of a Christian Prince* (edited by Lisa Jardine)
0 521 58811 1 paperback
Fenelon *Telemachus* (edited by Patrick Riley)
0 521 45662 2 paperback

Ferguson *An Essay on the History of Civil Society* (edited by Fania Oz-Salzberger)
0 521 44736 4 paperback
Filmer *Patriarcha and other writings* (edited by Johann P. Sommerville)
0 521 39903 3 paperback
Fletcher *Political Works* (edited by John Robertson)
0 521 43994 9 paperback
Sir John Fortescue *On the Laws and Governance of England* (edited by Shelley Lockwood)
0 521 58996 7 paperback
Fourier *The Theory of the Four Movements* (edited by Gareth Stedman Jones and Ian Patterson)
0 521 35693 8 paperback
Gramsci *Pre-Prison Writings* (edited by Richard Bellamy)
0 521 42307 4 paperback
Guicciardini *Dialogue on the Government of Florence* (edited by Alison Brown)
0 521 45623 1 paperback
Harrington *A Commonwealth of Oceana and A System of Politics* (edited by J. G. A. Pocock)
0 521 42329 5 paperback
Hegel *Elements of the Philosophy of Right* (edited by Allen W. Wood and H. B. Nisbet)
0 521 34888 9 paperback
Hegel *Political Writings* (edited by Laurence Dickey and H. B. Nisbet)
0 521 45979 3 paperback
Hobbes *On the Citizen* (edited by Michael Silverthorne and Richard Tuck)
0 521 43780 6 paperback
Hobbes *Leviathan* (edited by Richard Tuck)
0 521 56797 1 paperback
Hobhouse *Liberalism and other writings* (edited by James Meadowcroft)
0 521 43726 1 paperback
Hooker *Of the Laws of Ecclesiastical Polity* (edited by A. S. McGrade)
0 521 37908 3 paperback
Hume *Political Essays* (edited by Knud Haakonssen)
0 521 46639 3 paperback
King James VI and I *Political Writings* (edited by Johann P. Sommerville)
0 521 44729 1 paperback

Marx *Later Political Writings* (edited by Terrell Carver)
0 521 36739 5 paperback
James Mill *Political Writings* (edited by Terence Ball)
0 521 38748 5 paperback
J. S. Mill *On Liberty, with The Subjection of Women and Chapters on Socialism* (edited by Stefan Collini)
0 521 37917 2 paperback
Milton *Political Writings* (edited by Martin Dzelzainis)
0 521 34866 8 paperback
Montesquieu *The Spirit of the Laws* (edited by Anne M. Cohler, Basia Carolyn Miler and Harold Samuel Stone)
0 521 36974 6 paperback
More *Utopia* (edited by George M. Logan and Robert M. Adams)
0 521 40318 9 paperback
Morris *News from Nowhere* (edited by Krishan Kumar)
0 521 42233 7 paperback
Nicholas of Cusa *The Catholic Concordance* (edited by Paul E. Sigmund)
0 521 42233 7 paperback
Nietzsche *On the Genealogy of Morality* (edited by Keith Ansell-Pearson)
0 521 40610 2 paperback
Paine *Political Writings* (edited by Bruce Kuklick)
0 521 66799 2 paperback
Plato *The Republic* (edited by G. R. F. Ferrari and Tom Griffith)
0 521 48443 X paperback
Plato *Statesman* (edited by Julia Annas and Robin Waterfield)
0 521 44778 X paperback
Price *Political Writings* (edited by D. O. Thomas)
0 521 40969 1 paperback
Priestley *Political Writings* (edited by Peter Miller)
0 521 42561 1 paperback
Proudhon *What is Property?* (edited by Donald R. Kelley and Bonnie G. Smith)
0 521 40556 4 paperback
Pufendorf *On the Duty of Man and Citizen according to Natural Law* (edited by James Tully)
0 521 35980 5 paperback
The Radical Reformation (edited by Michael G. Baylor)
0 521 37948 2 paperback

Rousseau *The Discourses and other early political writings* (edited by Victor Gourevitch)
0 521 42445 3 paperback

Rousseau *The Social Contract and other later political writings* (edited by Victor Gourevitch)
0 521 42446 1 paperback

Seneca *Moral and Political Essays* (edited by John Cooper and John Procope)
0 521 34818 8 paperback

Sidney *Court Maxims* (edited by Hans W. Blom, Eco Haitsma Mulier and Ronald Janse)
0 521 46736 5 paperback

Sorel *Reflections on Violence* (edited by Jeremy Jennings)
0 521 55910 3 paperback

Spencer *The Man versus the State and The Proper Sphere of Government* (edited by John Offer)
0 521 43740 7 paperback

Stirner *The Ego and Its Own* (edited by David Leopold)
0 521 45647 9 paperback

Thoreau *Political Writings* (edited by Nancy Rosenblum)
0 521 47675 5 paperback

Utopias of the British Enlightenment (edited by Gregory Claeys)
0 521 45590 1 paperback

Vitoria *Political Writings* (edited by Anthony Pagden and Jeremy Lawrance)
0 521 36714 X paperback

Voltaire *Political Writings* (edited by David Williams)
0 521 43727 X paperback

Weber *Political Writings* (edited by Peter Lassman and Ronald Speirs)
0 521 39719 7 paperback

William of Ockham *A Short Discourse on Tyrannical Government* (edited by A. S. McGrade and John Kilcullen)
0 521 35803 5 paperback

William of Ockham *A Letter to the Friars Minor and other writings* (edited by A. S. McGrade and John Kilcullen)
0 521 35804 3 paperback

Wollstonecraft *A Vindication of the Rights of Men and A Vindication of the Rights of Woman* (edited by Sylvana Tomaselli)
0 521 43633 8 paperback